Routledge Revivals

The Rubber Industry

Originally published in 1948, this book remains one of the most comprehensive and detailed pictures of the rubber industry. It reviews the rise of the synthetic rubber industry and deals with the competition between natural rubber and synthetic rubber. The period between 1929 and 1942 is considered in greatest detail, but where necessary for an understanding of the problems of the industry, its early history and more recent developments are also covered. Within the field of natural rubber, special attention is given to the relative and competitive positions of estates and of small-holdings, and the treatment of smallholders under rubber restriction is discussed in some detail.

The work of the International Rubber Regulation Committee and the local administration of rubber restriction are analysed at length in the light of research into the records of the Committee and of various local administrative bodies, and into other official documents and Eastern newspapers.

The Rubber Industry

A Study in Competition and Monopoly

P.T. Bauer

Routledge
Taylor & Francis Group

First published in England in 1948 by Longmans Green & Co.

This edition first published in 2026 by Routledge
4 Park Square, Milton Park, Abingdon, Oxon, OX14 4RN
and by Routledge, 605 Third Avenue, New York, NY 10158.

Routledge is an imprint of the Taylor & Francis Group, an informa business

ISBN: 978-1-041-21339-0 (hbk)
ISBN: 978-1-003-72676-0 (ebk)
ISBN: 978-1-041-21342-0 (pbk)
Book DOI 10.4324/9781003726760

THE RUBBER INDUSTRY

A STUDY IN COMPETITION AND MONOPOLY

By

P. T. BAUER

Reader in Agricultural Economics,
University of London;
Fellow of Gonville and Caius
College, Cambridge

THE LONDON SCHOOL OF ECONOMICS
AND POLITICAL SCIENCE
(*University of London*)

LONGMANS, GREEN AND CO.
LONDON · NEW YORK · TORONTO

LONGMANS, GREEN AND CO. LTD.
6 & 7 CLIFFORD STREET, LONDON, W.1
NICOL ROAD, BOMBAY, 1
17 CHITTARANJAN AVENUE, CALCUTTA, 13
36A MOUNT ROAD, MADRAS, 2

LONGMANS, GREEN AND CO. INC.
55 FIFTH AVENUE, NEW YORK, 3

LONGMANS, GREEN AND CO.
215 VICTORIA STREET, TORONTO, 1

First published 1948

THIS BOOK IS PRODUCED
IN COMPLETE CONFORMITY WITH
THE AUTHORISED ECONOMY STANDARDS

Made and Printed in Great Britain by Butler & Tanner Ltd., Frome and London

PREFACE

MOST of the research for this study was pursued during my tenure in 1943–45 of the Leon Research Fellowship of the University of London, and I should accordingly like to thank the Leon Bequest Committee for enabling me to carry it out. The material was largely brought up-to-date towards the end of 1946 after an extensive tour of the rubber-producing districts of Malaya in the summer and early autumn of 1946. There are repeated references in this book to the report on that visit prepared for the Colonial Office; it is understood that this report will be published in the near future.

The British, Dutch and Indian authorities gave me free access to the papers of the International Rubber Regulation Committee, and this permission has been of great value. A similarly liberal attitude was adopted by Sir John Hay, who allowed me to make full use of his personal papers covering the discussions preceding the introduction of rubber restriction, as well as the actual operation of the regulation scheme. It gives me much pleasure to acknowledge the generous attitude adopted both by the authorities and by Sir John Hay. The selection of material, the manner of its presentation and the opinions expressed are, of course, entirely my own. I hope that neither the authorities nor my friends in the industry will resent the criticisms offered in this book, severe though they may appear to be. Some of these are directed against features which, in greater or smaller degree, seem to mark the operation of most commodity restriction schemes.

On many specific points of planting technique, labour legislation, the production and marketing of rubber and of the administration of regulation, I consulted associations, firms and individuals, especially retired officials, as well as planters and business men. It would be invidious to select individuals from a long list, and I hope they will all accept this general acknowledgment of much assistance readily given. Mr. W. G. G. Kellett has given valuable help in the collection and analysis of the statistics of the industry. His unique familiarity with these has been of particular value in the compilation of the Statistical Appendices, but he has assisted with many other calculations throughout the book. Dr. A. K.

Cairncross willingly provided assistance with an important and complex calculation.

My chief debt is, however, to Mr. S. R. Dennison, from whom I have received the greatest assistance throughout my work. But my obligation to him is far greater than could be adequately acknowledged in the few words of a preface.

LONDON, P. T. B.
October 1947

The books in this series are published by the London School of Economics and Political Science, but the authors alone are responsible for the views expressed in them.

CONTENTS

PART V

THE THREAT TO THE MONOPOLY OF NATURAL RUBBER

PART VI

THE PRESENT POSITION AND PROSPECTS OF THE INDUSTRY

APPENDICES

STATISTICAL APPENDICES

ABBREVIATIONS

S.S. . . .	Straits Settlements
F.M.S. . . .	Federated Malay States
U.M.S. . . .	Unfederated Malay States
N.E.I. . . .	Netherlands East Indies
R.R.I.M. . .	Rubber Research Institute of Malaya
R.G.A. . . .	Rubber Growers' Association
R.M.A. . . .	Rubber Manufacturers' Association of America
I.R.R.C. . .	International Rubber Regulation Committee
Indian Agent . .	Agent of the Government of India in Malaya and in Ceylon
M.A.J. . . .	*Malayan Agricultural Journal*; monthly publication of the Department of Agriculture
I.R.W. . . .	*India Rubber World*; American trade journal, monthly
I.R.J. . . .	*India-Rubber Journal*; British trade journal, weekly
N.E.I. Native Reports	*Reports on Native Rubber Cultivation in the N.E.I.*; issued periodically (between 1928 and 1941) by the Division of Agricultural Economics in the N.E.I. Department of Agriculture
Malayan Smallholding Reports	*Quarterly Reports on Conditions on Small Rubber Holdings in Malaya*; published in the *M.A.J.* by the Department of Agriculture
N.R.I.C. Reports .	*Reports of the Native Rubber Investigation Committee in the N.E.I.* (1925–27)

INTRODUCTION

THIS study is primarily concerned with the production of crude rubber (natural and synthetic); the activities of the rubber manufacturing industry are dealt with only in so far as they affect the fortunes of the rubber producing industry, or rubber industry for short. The discussion of natural rubber is confined almost entirely to the plantation industry (including smallholdings) which before the war supplied over 98 per cent. of the world's requirements; the small balance was represented by wild rubber, the produce of naturally occurring trees, and this will be referred to only incidentally.

Though the industry was young, by the 1930's rubber had become one of the world's leading raw materials. In international trade its place was comparable to such staple products as coal, wood and tobacco; measured by value, rubber was in 1937 the fifth or sixth most important raw material in international trade. Production figures are much less reliable, but it appears that measured by value of output rubber was among the seven or eight most important raw materials in the few years immediately preceding the Japanese war.

Rubber was by far the most valuable export from the British Colonial Empire; in the years after the great slump the value of rubber exports was about one-quarter to one-fifth of that of all domestic exports from the Colonies, and in 1940 and 1941 the proportion was probably much larger. A semi-official estimate of the value of rubber exports from the Colonies is as follows:

Domestic Exports of Rubber from the British Colonial Empire, 1937–41

(£ millions, to the nearest five million)

1937	1938	1939	1940	1941
50	30	40	65	65

Between one-third and two-fifths of these exports came from smallholders, and rubber was much the most important cash crop of any native population in the Colonial Empire. The economy of British Malaya, which was among the wealthiest colonial territories, was (and still is) largely dependent on rubber, which usually represented about three-quarters or more of the value of the agricultural output.[1]

[1] Rubber had also reached pre-eminence among exports from the Dutch Colonial Empire, and by 1939 considerably out-distanced the great traditional staples, such as petroleum products, sugar, tin and vegetable oils.

The quantitative significance of rubber as a direct source of dollar exchange to the British economy emerges from the following figures of the f.o.b. value of domestic rubber exports from the British Empire to the U.S.A. :

Approximate Value of British Rubber Exports to the U.S.A., 1937–41

(Million dollars, to the nearest five million)

1937	1938	1939	1940	1941
125	50	90	150	175

Before the war, domestic rubber exports from the British Empire to the U.S.A. were generally not far short of the total of all domestic U.K. exports to America ; in wartime conditions in 1940 and 1941 they far exceeded exports from this country to the U.S.A.

Rubber had become one of the most important U.S. imports ; its importance varied generally with the trade cycle, but was always high. The following figures summarise the position for the years 1937–41 :

Some Principal U.S. Imports, 1937–41

(Million dollars, in order of 1941 f.o.b. values)

	1937	1938	1939	1940	1941
Rubber	248	130	178	318	417
Wool	96	23	50	85	205
Coffee	151	138	140	127	177
Sugar	166	130	125	113	153
Tin	104	45	71	128	150

Except for 1938, when it was severely depressed, rubber occupied first place in this series ; in the exceptional years of 1940 and 1941 American rubber imports were more than twice those of any other commodity.

In the years before the outbreak of war in the Far East one-half of total world absorption (consumption) of rubber was by the U.S.A., where the automobile industry accounted for three-quarters of the total. The prosperity of the rubber industry thus largely depended on American economic activity and on the fortunes of the motor industry in particular. The U.S. motor industry (and thus the American demand for rubber) is liable to wide fluctuations ; thus, early in 1937 U.S. absorption of rubber was running at an annual rate of 650,000 tons ; a year later it had fallen to a rate of 300,000 tons, while by mid-1941 it was approaching a yearly rate of one million tons.

As well as presenting a general picture of the rubber industry, this study also discusses in detail the international rubber regulation scheme—perhaps the most powerful and certainly one of the most important raw material control schemes. It also reviews the rise of the synthetic rubber industry, chiefly in the U.S.A., and the principal aspects of future competition between natural and synthetic rubber.

The year 1929 has been taken as a starting-point for most of our survey. Some form of organised restriction of output was in force for at least part of every year between the end of the first World War (when the industry had only just been established) and the end of 1928, so that pre-1929 export and output figures are not only incomplete but also of little use for observing producers' reactions to price changes. Where they are necessary for an understanding of the problems of the industry, developments before 1929 are also reviewed.[1] As the years 1929–33 were the only period of free competition since the industry became of any importance, Part I is devoted to a detailed review of that period. While much of the subsequent argument and some of the conclusions are of necessity based on the experience of these years, the reader principally interested in the future of the industry and impatient of the detailed account can omit Part I, except perhaps Chapters 1 and 5.

[1] The Stevenson scheme (1922–28) has been discussed in detail by Mr. J. W. F. Rowe in *Special Memorandum* No. 34 of the London and Cambridge Economic Service (1931). Other pre-1929 events in the industry's brief history are fairly familiar, and many of these are also included in Mr. Rowe's *Special Memorandum*, or are available in other easily accessible publications.

PART I

THE INDUSTRY TO 1933

CHAPTER 1

THE STRUCTURE OF THE INDUSTRY

RUBBER is produced from the latex which occurs in the bark of the tree *Hevea brasiliensis*. The latex which issues when the bark is cut is collected, coagulated with an acid (generally formic or acetic acid) and the coagulum is washed and dried to produce crude rubber. All the processes are essentially simple. Tapping is the opening of the latex vessels in the tree by an incision in the bark. The flow of latex is generally affected less by the thickness of the cut than by its length, and satisfactory amounts can be obtained by a very thin cut. Some bark removal is, however, inevitable, and this naturally varies not only with the skill of the tapper but also with the frequency of tapping and with the tapping system adopted. If a tree is left untapped bark reserves will be greater, with the possibility of higher yields later; where bark removal exceeds bark renewal it will eventually be necessary to suspend or slow down tapping, or else to tap on imperfectly renewed bark. The drying of the coagulated latex consists of passing it through a series of rollers, and is conducted in a very simple plant known on the estate as the factory. On smallholdings the 'factory' is a shed housing one or two hand-mangles; the water is often eliminated simply by pressing with hands and feet. Final drying is done by placing the rubber in a hot chamber (usually termed smoke-house), or simply by exposing it to the sun.

Although there are certain differences in methods of cultivation and, of course, great differences of size, the basic processes (and the equipment) are essentially the same both on estates and smallholdings.

I

With the important exceptions of certain changes in acreage and in the cost of production (both of which are dealt with subsequently [1]), the structure of the industry altered very little between the late 1920's and the outbreak of the Pacific war. For simplicity of exposition this chapter describes the industry as it was in 1929.

The planted area at the end of 1929 was estimated by the late Dr. Whitford [2] at 7,635,000 acres in the East, and at 75,000 acres elsewhere. The total of 7,710,000 was made up as follows:

Table I

Areas Planted with Rubber at the end of 1929

(Thousand acres, to the nearest five thousand) [a]

	Mature	*Immature*	*Total*
Malaya	2,475	470	2,945
N.E.I.	2,125	1,030	3,155
Ceylon	490	50	540
Sarawak	85	175	260
India (including Burma)	130	40	170
British North Borneo	80	40	120
French Indo-China	100	195	295
Siam	35	115	150
Total	5,520	2,115	7,635
Other countries			75
Grand total			7,710

[a] As will be seen from the text, many of these figures are only approximations, and to indicate this, Dr. Whitford's estimates have been rounded off.

Though Dr. Whitford's figures were based on official estimates, most of them should be regarded only as approximations, while that of the N.E.I. native acreage (and consequently of the total N.E.I. area) was largely a guess. Dr. Whitford's estimates gained wide acceptance and were generally adopted by the Commercial Research Department of the Rubber Growers' Association (R.G.A.).[3] His figure of 2,115,000 acres for the immature acreage

[1] The latest acreage figures are shown in Table II of Statistical Appendix II; changes in the cost of production are reviewed in Chs. 3 and 16.

[2] A former manager of the Crude Rubber Department of the Rubber Manufacturers' Association of America. His five *Reports on Plantation Rubber*, issued between 1928 and 1934 by the Rubber Manufacturers' Association of America (R.M.A.), contain much valuable material. Tables I and II of this chapter are largely derived from Dr. Whitford's *Report on Plantation Rubber 1930*.

[3] Repeated revisions of his figures by Dr. Whitford between 1929 and 1934 will not be followed here, as no accurate figures were available until the advent of regulation, and even after 1934 some important gaps remained, notably of the planted area of the N.E.I. natives and of Siam.

Dr. Whitford's estimates of the acreage of India and Siam subsequently turned out to have been too low, which led to some complications in the early years of rubber regulation. At the end of 1929 the planted areas of India and Siam were each about 100,000 acres in excess of Dr. Whitford's figures.

was, however, below that of the R.G.A., whose statisticians estimated it at 2,700,000 acres. Dr. Whitford seems to have overestimated the mature N.E.I. native acreage in 1930 and correspondingly understated the immature acreage. In the light of subsequent information an estimate of 5,200,000 mature and 2,600,000 immature acres at the end of 1929, though probably conservative, seems as close as possible—always remembering the uncertainty of the native area in the N.E.I.

The comparatively small immature acreages in Malaya and Ceylon, which were accurately estimated, deserve some explanation. They reflect the policy pursued under the Stevenson restriction scheme (1922–28), when new planting was not prohibited but was officially discouraged, and with few exceptions no land was alienated for rubber planting. New planting was thus confined to owners of land to which a title had already been issued, but which was not yet under rubber. This was either land planted with other crops, or unplanted land held in reserve. Estates undertook some new planting on unplanted reserve land, which many of them had. Smallholders rarely have unplanted reserve land, and much of the planting they undertook was on land which had been under other products, chiefly coconuts or fruit trees; they thus had to sacrifice another source of income to plant rubber. This policy much restricted the scope of new planting in Malaya and Ceylon.

Dr. Whitford's division of the total acreage between estates and smallholdings was also largely based on official figures, but again with the important exception of the N.E.I. His figures are as follows:

Table II

Planted Area at the end of 1929 divided between Estates and Smallholdings

(Thousand acres, to the nearest five thousand)

	Estates	*Smallholdings*
Malaya	1,775	1,170
N.E.I.	1,355	1,800
Ceylon	370[a]	170[a]
Sarawak	10	250
India (including Burma)	115	55
British North Borneo	75	45
French Indo-China	295	—
Siam	—	150
	3,995	3,640

[a] The division of the Ceylon area is not Dr. Whitford's but is based on a 1930 R.G.A. estimate, which was broadly confirmed by subsequent information.

Thus in 1929, according to these figures 52 per cent. of the total area was cultivated by estates and 48 per cent. by smallholders. The smallholders were all Asiatics. Moreover, an appreciable proportion of the estate acreage in Malaya, Ceylon, British North Borneo and India also belonged to Asiatics, who thus, according to Dr. Whitford, had a clear majority (54 per cent.) of the total planted acreage. As it was later to be revealed that the Siamese and Indian acreages and the smallholdings area in Ceylon and the N.E.I. were all substantially under-estimated, it is certain that at the end of 1929 smallholders owned over one-half of the planted area, and that the Asiatic-owned acreage was over 60 per cent. of the total.

The distinction between estates and smallholdings has been of great importance since the earliest days of the industry. The estates are large or at least fair-sized units of several hundred or several thousand acres each, operated with substantial capital and employing large labour forces in receipt of a fixed daily wage. The majority of the smallholding acreage is in the hands of peasant proprietors, each with a holding of, say, two to five acres, who work with family labour, occasionally being assisted by outside workers paid on a share basis. In some of the producing territories much of the acreage officially classed as smallholdings is in larger holdings of 15–100 acres each, usually tapped with the help of outside labour, either on a share basis, or in receipt of piece-rates and paid according to the amount of rubber brought in. This type of property is sometimes known as a medium holding, and the greater part of the acreage is owned by absentees, non-resident businessmen, artisans and tradesmen, or Indian moneylenders. Even when the smallholdings or medium holdings rely on outside labour, their dependence is appreciably less than that of the estates and is generally confined to tapping only.

The estates, especially the European-owned estates, also differ from smallholdings and medium holdings by the adoption of an elaborate hierarchy for the production of rubber (to be reviewed subsequently). Putting it briefly, cultivation, tapping, manufacture and packing are carried out by outside labourers ; above the labourer there stands the foreman, over the foreman the conductor, who is supervised by the assistant manager, who in turn has a manager above him ; on European-owned estates the further stages in the hierarchy include visiting agents, engineers and accountants, the agency house, the secretarial firm, the board of directors and the shareholders. The list is not complete. On smallholdings and medium holdings the identical commodity is produced by the owner and his family, assisted perhaps by a few share tappers or contract tappers, possibly under a Chinese *kepala* (foreman).

The great bulk of the estate acreage is European-owned[1]; in Malaya about one-quarter of the estate area is in Asiatic, largely Chinese, ownership. The smallholdings and medium holdings are in Asiatic ownership; in the N.E.I. (where there are few medium holdings) the holdings are practically all in Indonesian hands; elsewhere a varying but generally appreciable proportion is in Chinese or Indian ownership. Apart from the N.E.I. it is, therefore, definitely inaccurate to refer to all smallholders as natives. There is a certain similarity between the larger medium holdings and the Asiatic-owned estates in methods of finance and technique of production; but on the whole the distinction between estates and smallholdings has always been clear.

Although the official line of division between estates and smallholdings has varied somewhat between different territories, it has generally been drawn at 100 acres.[2] From fragmentary data it would appear that in the late 1920's and in the 1930's, between one-third and one-half of the total acreage in Malaya officially classed as smallholdings consisted of holdings of between 15–20 and 100 acres each, and that about four-fifths or five-sixths of the acreage of medium holdings was Chinese-owned. In Malaya the great majority of Chinese and Indian owners of smallholdings are absentee owners of medium holdings. Very few of the Chinese and Indian estate labourers have had the opportunity of planting and developing rubber smallholdings, partly because of the ban on the alienation of land for rubber planting from 1922 to 1928 and again since 1930, and partly because of the reluctance of the authorities to alienate land to this type of owner; lack of capital for the acquisition of land and the development of the holding was also a factor, but one of subsidiary importance. In Ceylon, Sarawak and Siam the proportion of medium holdings within the general smallholdings acreage was probably of the same order as that in Malaya.[3] The

[1] In discussions of the rubber industry references to European estates usually include the comparatively small American- and Australian-owned acreage. Although the largest single unit in the rubber industry is American-owned, only about 5 per cent. of the estate acreage is in American hands.

[2] In the N.E.I. the official distinction was based on differences of land tenure and the local population held land on titles (where these were issued) of a different type from those issued to other owners. This lends further justification to the use of the term 'native' when referring to smallholders in the N.E.I.; it is also in accordance with official practice.

[3] This is suggested by occasional British and U.S. consular reports and by surveys conducted for the administration of rubber restriction.

ownership of a property of over 15 acres, or of several smallholdings totalling more than 15 acres, would generally lift the owner above the peasant class, and it is thus misleading to regard the official smallholdings acreage as entirely in the hands of this class.[1] In contrast, the bulk of N.E.I. native acreage is owned by peasant proprietors, each with a few acres.

It is often implied or suggested that the bulk of the smallholding area is to be found in the immediate vicinity of the villagers' houses. This is incorrect. There are often rubber trees, or patches of rubber trees, around the villagers' houses, frequently interplanted with fruit trees. Though the aggregate acreage of these patches is not inconsiderable, it is only a small part of the total area, which mostly consists of entire stretches of rubber, starting usually some little distance behind the Malay dwellings, and often separated from these by a belt of padi fields. The trees in the villages enjoy the advantages of a regular supply of fertiliser, but this seems more than offset by their greater age and by the effect of much worse tapping. The rubber in the extensive stretches some distance from the villages is generally much better than the patches in the villages. This applies quite clearly both to Malay and to Chinese holdings in most of the important rubber-producing districts of Malaya, and the difference is often very striking.

The difference in the condition of the holdings in or around the villages and the much larger stretches of smallholders' rubber in the interior is one reason, though not the only one, for the inadequacy of roadside observation (which was used for many purposes by the authorities, as well as by unofficial observers) as a source of information on smallholders' rubber. Reliance on data from holdings near the roads is likely to provide biased samples. Such holdings are often planted on land with a previous history of cultivation and were usually the first to be planted in the neighbourhood. Their trees, apart from being older than those further in the interior, usually suffered most from the bad tapping of the early days. Moreover, the holdings nearest to the roads are generally rested less than those in the interior, being last to go out of tapping during a slump or at low rates of release under restriction, because of the lower transport costs to the nearest dealer or larger

[1] In accordance with general official practice, in this study all properties of under 100 acres will be referred to as smallholdings ; where a distinction is necessary, however, the smaller holdings, owned by resident owners and generally operated without outside labour, will be referred to as peasant holdings and the larger smallholdings, generally employing some outside labour, as medium holdings. The peasant holdings of resident owners correspond more or less to the native holdings of popular parlance.

village. Again, in many districts Chinese smallholders followed the Malays, and the better Chinese holdings lie behind the Malay areas. Moreover, the rubber trees in and around the villages are often tapped by the wife and children of the smallholder, while the homogeneous holding in the interior is tapped by the owner or by a professional tapper. Similar considerations apply to the smallholdings near the principal rivers and thus to the value of riverside observation.

To conclude this brief preliminary discussion of the different classes of rubber producer with a comparison in terms of output, 49 per cent. of the 1929 production came from estates owned by European and American interests, 7·5 per cent. from Asiatic-owned estates, 40·5 per cent. from smallholdings, the remaining 3 per cent. being wild rubber.[1]

The limitations of the acreage figures already given, and of others to be given subsequently, should be clearly realised. Most rubber statistics have always been prepared for business men who have a deep mistrust of round figures, believing these to be evidence of careless work. Hence the pseudo-accuracy of many rubber statistics which sometimes becomes quite grotesque as, for instance, when in roundabout estimates of the approximate native rubber acreage of a N.E.I. residency the precise number of trees in that area is given to the nearest digit. The worst example of pseudo-accuracy occurred during the currency of regulation, when in 1934–36 a rather haphazard tree census in Sumatra and Borneo (whose rubber-growing residencies are several times the size of Great Britain) claimed to have found 582,365,725 trees, and from an estimate of the average density inferred that the area totalled 1,683,328 acres. Subsequent experience of the hazards of this kind of estimating has not led to any improvement. In 1939 a more detailed survey of these residencies was started; results so far, based on 46 per cent. of the area, show that the original estimates understated the actual area by about 1½ million acres, one-half of the total area. But the revised figure of acreage is given as 3,179,092 acres; the figure is probably subject to a margin of error of at least half-a-million acres or more.

All the main elements reviewed above are subject to some error. The estimate of the total acreage under rubber is hazardous, particularly because no really reliable figures of the N.E.I. native acreage or of the total planted area of Siam have ever been

[1] Dr. George Rae, in a paper read before the Midland Section of the Institution of the Rubber Industry, January 1931.

ascertained. Again, the age-distribution of the planted acreage and the proportion which had reached maturity by any given time are often conjectural. In the larger territories the planting season is between October and the end of January, and an area planted, say, in January 1925 but prepared for planting in the autumn of 1924 would often be classed as having been planted in the earlier year. Moreover, with the doubtful exception of the F.M.S. smallholdings since 1921, the estimates of the age-composition of smallholders' rubber throughout the East have always been precarious.

The figures which have been given are thus intended to convey only the general order of importance of the various classes of producer. With the exception of the planted area of the N.E.I. native producers they are adequate for this purpose.

II

Output figures are available only for Malayan estates and smallholdings, and for estates in the N.E.I.; for other territories exports are regarded as equivalent to production. The figures for 1929 are as follows:

TABLE III

Output of Rubber (Net Exports except for Malaya and N.E.I. Estates) in 1929

(long tons)

Malaya estates	246,000	
smallholdings	200,000	
		446,000
N.E.I. estates	152,000	
natives	107,000	
		259,000
Ceylon		80,300
Sarawak		11,200
India (including Burma)		13,400
British North Borneo		7,400
French Indo-China		9,500
Siam		4,300
		831,100

South America, Mexico, Africa and the Philippines exported some 26,000 tons, almost entirely wild rubber.

The total output came from a very large number of independent producers. The R.G.A., which was the most important association of producers, had a membership of some 600 companies, including a number of local companies as well as practically all sterling companies (enterprises domiciled in the U.K. and in a few instances in Eire). In 1930 the 600-odd companies produced 265,000 tons. The output of the largest was three-quarters of one per cent. of world production; four or five British companies each produced about one-half per cent. of world output. Two companies controlled by manufacturers and a few Dutch and Franco-Belgian companies were as large as, or even larger than, the biggest of the sterling companies, but none had an output exceeding 2 per cent. of world production.[1] Nor would the general picture be greatly modified if the secretarial or agency firms (and not the individual companies) were considered, as the five largest secretarial groups together accounted for only about 9 per cent. of the total 1929 output and for about 15 per cent. of total estate production.

The comparatively small size of individual units can also be shown by acreage figures. The arithmetic mean and median of the 1929 acreages of sterling companies whose reports and accounts are summarised in the 1931 issue of *Rubber Producing Companies* (the official year book of the Mincing Lane Rubber and Tea Share-brokers' Association) are given below:

TABLE IV

Planted Acreage of Sterling Rubber Companies Operating in Various Territories (financial years ending between 1st July 1929 and 30th June 1930)

Territory	*Arithmetic mean* [a] *of planted area (acres)*	*Median* [a] *of planted area (acres)*
Malaya	2,876	2,010
Sumatra	4,563	2,580
Java	3,775	2,159
Ceylon	1,546	1,016
Other territories	2,519	1,676
All territories	2,812	1,906

[a] The few very large companies (each with about one-half to three-quarters of one per cent. of world estate acreage), and in Ceylon the many very small companies, largely explain the divergence between the arithmetic mean and the median.

The figures refer to companies; the average size of estates was appreciably smaller as most sterling companies owned several, often widely scattered, properties. To facilitate comparison with other industries, it may be mentioned that the average capitalisation of rubber companies is of the order of £50 per planted acre, and the capitalisation of the bulk of sterling rubber companies was (and

[1] These figures still applied in 1941.

still is) about £100,000–200,000, and that of the few very large British rubber companies is only about £1,000,000–1,500,000. Speaking very broadly, the 1929 output of the 'average sterling company' (whether arithmetic mean, median or mode) was around 400-500 tons in Malaya and the N.E.I. and 250–300 tons elsewhere, against a total world estate rubber production of about 500,000 tons. A ton of rubber was worth about £90 c.i.f. consuming countries at the time, so that the annual output of the general run of sterling companies was worth about £30,000–40,000.[1]

The number of 'units of control' on the estate side of the industry ran into several thousands, while the smallholders interested in rubber numbered probably one million or more. These figures did not alter greatly between 1930 and 1941, except of course through the advent of regulation which superimposed a monopoly on a perfectly competitive system.

Although no rubber company owned more than about one per cent. of the total planted area around 1929–30, the range in size of individual units was nevertheless very wide. In 1929 sterling companies ranged from a few hundred to 31,500 planted acres.[2] The Dutch companies operating in Java were on the average even smaller than the sterling companies. At the end of 1929 the total rubber estate area in Java of 556,000 acres belonged to 546 company-owned estates. The very few large rubber producers in Java were sterling companies. The few big Dutch, Franco-Belgian and American companies (the largest with a planted area of about 90,000 acres) operated in Sumatra.

The large number of companies and their wide range of size has been much discussed since the 1920's, with particular reference to the responsibility of the secretarial and agency firms for the multiplicity of small companies. The multiplication of secretarial and directors' fees was not the original cause of the small size and large number of the rubber companies, which can be explained chiefly by the rapid growth of a hazardous industry. Eastern merchants and enterprising individuals developed the early estates

[1] The locally owned companies were even smaller; none of these had even one-quarter of one per cent. of the world acreage. Sixty-one locally domiciled public Malayan companies were analysed from various publications of Malayan stockbrokers. The arithmetic mean of their 1933 planted area was 1,190 acres and the median 1,285 acres. These were generally the larger and more important local companies.

Public companies and privately owned Chinese estates account for almost the entire Malayan estate acreage. The Chinese estates are individually much smaller than the great majority of properties owned by public companies.

[2] Dunlop Plantations was much larger (some 80,000 acres); most of its rubber was still immature at the time.

and subsequently floated these as companies. The pioneers were unable or unwilling to develop very large estates, as the future of the industry and the technique of cultivation were entirely conjectural. The investor, too, preferred to spread his risk by investing in a number of companies. Once established the system could not be easily unscrambled, with neighbouring properties in different ownership and interspersed with native or Chinese holdings. Moreover, the economies of large-scale production in rubber growing are of minor importance.

At the same time, there is no doubt that the maintenance of a large number of separate units has been to the advantage of the secretarial firms, which were therefore generally inclined to oppose amalgamation of small units, even where this would have been feasible. The interests of the secretarial firms were also reflected to a certain extent in the investment policy of the rubber companies. An examination of rubber company reports and accounts frequently reveals, under the heading ' other investments ', large holdings of other plantation company shares or investments in tin-mining companies. These are invariably in enterprises managed by the same secretarial or agency house. The liquid funds of one company in the secretarial group are used to facilitate the formation of another company, to ensure that the latter will be managed and its produce sold by the same secretarial and agency firm, and that its directors should be those of the secretarial firm or their nominees. In practice, several companies within a group would take up shares in another eastern enterprise, so that the latter would not be a subsidiary of any other company within the meaning of the Companies Acts. This use of their funds has hardly been in the best interests of the rubber companies. Tropical agriculture is a risky business, and to invest the surplus funds of a rubber company in other plantation ventures (usually rubber companies) seems difficult to justify, especially as they are generally all prosperous or depressed at the same time. If it be thought desirable to invest their surplus funds in rubber or other forms of tropical enterprise, then clearly the logical line of development would be simple expansion. These ' other investments ' have served to multiply directorships and secretarial and agency fees ; they have also given the secretarial firms an even more complete grip on some of the companies, since the companies holding shares in other enterprises would provide sufficient proxies to overcome all possible opposition. While several successful and prosperous enterprises have been assisted by this use of rubber company funds, it has undoubtedly led to abuses and has been a contributory cause of the financial stringency of some rubber companies. Before censuring the secretarial firms for this procedure, it should be remembered that it is far from unknown in other branches of modern industry.

III

During 1929 costs were appreciably reduced on estates in Malaya and Ceylon. Much higher yields than had been expected followed the withdrawal of the Stevenson scheme,[1] and by the end of 1929 it was evident that they could not be explained in terms of flush production, as was believed at the time. The real reason lay in the technical progress which had taken place between 1922 and 1928, and whose effects in Malaya and Ceylon were masked by restriction. Further substantial improvements in technique were introduced in 1929 and early in 1930 and, without as yet any reduction in salaries and wages, appreciable economies had been effected between the middle of 1928 and the beginning of 1930.

A fair amount of miscellaneous information is available on estate costs in 1929.[2] The returns to the Commercial Research Department of the R.G.A. are the most comprehensive and most consistently compiled data.[3] Around 1929–30 the returns were received from about 330–350 companies; the number varied slightly from year to year. In 1929 these returns covered about one million mature acres (some two-thirds of the mature area owned by sterling companies) with an annual output of about 160,000 tons,

[1] This was a compulsory restriction scheme in force in Malaya and Ceylon from 1922 to 1928. The Dutch remained outside the scheme, which collapsed after driving the price to inordinate levels. It had far-reaching repercussions. The famine prices of 1925–26 stimulated the enormous expansion of the N.E.I. native acreage, now believed to equal the entire planted area of Malaya. In America it engendered a hostility to British rubber producers which has not yet disappeared.

[2] The familiar difficulties of estimating costs of output are enhanced in rubber by various considerations. This subject is treated in 'Rubber Production Costs during the Great Depression', *Economic Journal*, Dec. 1943, and 'Notes on Cost', *Economica*, May 1945.

It will be seen when production during the depression is reviewed that the connection between money costs and supply price was tenuous. This section is concerned with the former; hence the discussion of estate costs only. Smallholders' rubber will be dealt with subsequently.

[3] In 1930 the R.G.A. started a cost enquiry in which the participating companies, representing the bulk of the total R.G.A. output, furnished (and have continued to do so since) returns of their monthly costs. These figures mostly exclude depreciation, amortisation and freight and selling charges, for which after 1934 standard figures were added. The returns are secret, but have always been made available to the International Rubber Regulation Committee, to whose records the present writer has been given access.

of which almost exactly 100,000 tons were produced in 1929 by companies with fiscal years ending in the last quarter of the year. The average (arithmetic mean) all-in costs for 1929 of these last-quarter companies was 5·93*d.* per lb., including 0·35*d.* for depreciation, but excluding freight and selling charges as well as amortisation. The costs of companies whose fiscal year ended during the first half of 1929 were about 0·5*d.*–0·6*d.* higher as these were still affected by restriction during the closing months of the Stevenson scheme.

The Economist of 10th May 1930 listed 103 rubber companies (virtually all larger units or members of the leading agency groups) which had shown their f.o.b. and/or all-in costs in their last published report. Many of these covered operations in 1928–29. The arithmetic mean of these f.o.b. costs was 6·15*d.* and the mean of the all-in costs 6·64*d.* The latter frequently, indeed almost generally, included freight and selling charges omitted from the R.G.A. figures.

From the 1930–34 volumes of *Rubber Producing Companies* it appears that 64 companies consistently disregarded a recommendation by the R.G.A. and continued to publish their costs throughout the slump. They were almost all small companies or companies outside the larger secretarial groups. There was an overlap of only two companies between these and the 103 companies whose costs were reviewed in *The Economist.* For fiscal years ending during 1929 the f.o.b. costs of the smaller companies averaged 6·15*d.* and their all-in costs 6·76*d.*, again including freight and selling charges. They were thus virtually identical with the average of the costs summarised in *The Economist.* If only companies with fiscal years ending in December had been chosen and freight and selling charges excluded consistently, the costs of the companies listed in *The Economist* and of those extracted from *Rubber Producing Companies* would have approximated very closely to those of the R.G.A. returns.

Thus all-in cash costs of sterling estate producers towards the end of 1929 were very generally around 6*d.*–7*d.* per lb., landed London. The figures are much in accordance with Mr. Rowe's estimate [1] of 6*d.* as the all-in cash cost per lb. of Malayan sterling companies at that time. The general run of f.o.b. costs was around 5*d.*–6*d.*, of which about half were direct costs and 50–60 per cent. labour costs (some indirect costs were also labour costs). Depreciation and amortisation charges may have required the equivalent of about

[1] London and Cambridge Economic Service, *Special Memorandum*, No. 34, p. 76.

1*d.*–1½*d.* per lb., suggesting all-in costs of about 8*d.*, or slightly less. The costs of Dutch companies were, on the whole, much the same as those of the sterling companies, though some important Dutch and American enterprises in Sumatra produced more cheaply, and by 1930 a few Dutch companies had remarkably low f.o.b. costs. Among sterling companies those operating in Malaya were the cheapest producers; many sterling companies in the N.E.I. had high costs, compared both to their Malayan rivals and to their Dutch and American competitors in the N.E.I. Costs in French Indo-China were still high owing to the comparative immaturity of the estates. Direct costs were relatively high in French Indo-China and India and low in Java.

There does not seem to be much relation between costs per lb. (on the 1929 figures) and size of company as measured by mature acreage. The 1930 and 1931 volumes of *Rubber Producing Companies* give sufficient information of the costs and the mature areas of 150 companies (providing 84 instances of all-in costs and 110 of f.o.b. costs) for the purposes of correlation analysis. No significant correlation could be found. Size and costs have also been compared for 45 Malayan dollar companies on the basis of data derived from a circular issued by a Singapore firm of stockbrokers. Here again there was no significant relation.[1]

On the other hand there was in both instances a significant negative correlation between costs and yield per acre, which is in accordance with expectations. This serves partly to explain the absence of any significant correlation between size and cost. The smaller companies were apparently no more likely to lose their soil through erosion, or to have selected poor land, than the larger units. The economies of large-scale production are not much in evidence on rubber plantations, and the savings to be achieved through greatly increased acreage supervised by each manager or assistant, and through centralisation of factory operations in one factory on each property, were not generally realised until the 1930's. The above comparisons are, of course, between companies and not between estates. The majority of the larger Malayan companies comprise a number of often widely-scattered estates or divisions, while several companies had estates both in Malaya and in the N.E.I. Such companies would still benefit by the spreading of London expenses and of other small items over a larger output but otherwise would derive little advantage from their size.

[1] The results of a correlation analysis based on more recent and comprehensive data will be found below, p. 272.

CHAPTER 2

THE IMPACT OF THE DEPRESSION ON MALAYA AND THE NETHERLANDS EAST INDIES

I

THE post-war boom for most primary producers, particularly in the East, was in the early twenties or mid-twenties. Government revenues, foreign trade figures, wage movements, profits earned and dividends declared, all point to the year 1929 as one of fairly stable conditions in the plantation rubber industry and the territories dependent on it. In spite of this, most of the Malayan administration reports referred to the year as one of difficulty, or even of depression for rubber and tin. The full onset of the depression was, however, not felt until the Wall Street crash.

With the data now available it is impossible to compile comprehensive figures of, say, national incomes. For Malaya, however, where the dependence on rubber was greatest, certain important elements of the national income can be reviewed.[1] The gross value of the 1929 output of Malayan agriculture (excluding the output of fisheries and of forest products) is estimated at 430 $\pm$ 20 million Straits dollars of which rubber accounted for 344 millions; for 1932 the estimate is 130 $\pm$ 15 millions, including 66 millions for rubber. The gross value of mining output in the two years was approximately 138 and 46 millions, including tin at about 122 and 40 millions.[2] These figures show both the importance of rubber and tin in agricultural and mining output, and the part their collapse played in the Malayan slump.

In the special conditions of the primary producing countries

[1] The calculations underlying these estimates are discussed in Appendix A.

[2] When no great accuracy is required the following 'ready reckoners' may be of use in converting the various currencies referred to in this study. One Straits cent is 0·28*d.*, and can be taken as ¼*d.* plus 10 per cent., while Straits dollars are converted into sterling (exactly) by dividing by 10 and adding one-sixth. Pence can be converted into Straits cents by multiplying by 3½. Until September 1931, 7 guilder cents almost exactly equalled 5 Straits cents, and subject to day-to-day fluctuations after September 1931, one Straits cent equalled approximately 0·9–1 guilder cent. One rupee cent equals two-thirds of one Straits cent. Until September 1931 one U.S. dollar cent was almost exactly one halfpenny, and one French franc 2*d.* From 1934 to 1939 one U.S. cent was worth about one halfpenny, while at the rate of exchange which has ruled since September 1939, 5 U.S. cents are worth 3*d.*

generally, and of Malaya in particular, foreign trade figures are useful indices of important aspects of the national economy. For Malaya, complications are introduced by the division into Straits Settlements, Federated Malay States and Unfederated Malay States. Net export and import figures are available for the F.M.S. and the most important U.M.S., but not for Malaya as a whole, since the authorities considered that the importance of the entrepôt trade of Singapore and Penang made it impossible to compile net figures. The trend of net export and import figures for Malaya as a whole did not, however, differ greatly from that of the F.M.S. The following table shows the decline in the value of net exports from the F.M.S. during the depression.

TABLE I

Net Exports of F.M.S. Produce, 1929–33

(Million Straits dollars)

	1929	1930	1931	1932	1933
Total	338	202	118	83	108
Rubber and latex	202	108	54	37	58
Tin and tin-ore	117	77	51	31	37

Net imports into the F.M.S. declined from 190 million dollars in 1929 to 63 millions in 1933. The F.M.S. (and Malaya as a whole) were among the most open systems in the world. They depended on imports not only for all manufactured goods, even the simplest, but for oil, petrol, sugar, coffee, tin, rice (two-thirds of the F.M.S. rice consumption was supplied by imports), tinned milk (the output of fresh milk was very small), edible oils and fats, most of their meat, many other foodstuffs and practically all their tobacco. Thus over a wide range net imports supply a reliable indication of consumption for the F.M.S. The figures of net imports in Table II all relate to commodities of which there was no, or only negligible, local production.

The severe reduction in consumption, affecting all classes and races, presents an instructive contrast with the experience of Britain, where real consumption was well maintained during the slump.

The sharp fall in export values shown in Table I was almost entirely due to the collapse of rubber and tin prices. The Singapore price [1] of rubber averaged 34½ cents per lb. in 1929 and only 7 cents in 1932, while tin fell from 104 dollars per *pikul* (133⅓ lb.) to an

[1] Unless otherwise specified, references to the price of rubber throughout this study are to the spot price of standard quality ribbed smoked sheet.

TABLE II

Sundry Net Imports into the F.M.S., 1929–32

	1929	1930	1931	1932
Tinned milk: thousand cases .	467	449	342	215
Tea: thousand lb.	4,408	3,801	2,969	1,852
Tobacco, cigars, cigarettes: thousand lb.	10,718	8,657	6,417	3,278
Matches: ten millions. . .	566	390	249	179
Beer and ale: thousand gallons .	298	234	148	115
Cotton piece goods: thousand yards	30,012	24,969	19,843	18,107
Kerosene oil: thousand tons .	31	21	16	14
Motor spirit: thousand tons .	47	48	33	23
Cycles: numbers	6,065	1,990	709	249
Motor-cars: numbers . . .	2,536	1,441	491	175

average of 60 dollars in 1931 when restriction was introduced and prices thereby raised. Import prices did not decline in proportion, and although there were sharp reductions in the prices of most imported foodstuffs, some raw materials and some classes of manufactures, especially those supplied by Japan, there was an appreciable worsening in the terms of trade of Malaya. A calculation based on the F.M.S. foreign trade figures shows that there was a fall of 62 per cent. in the unit value of F.M.S. net exports compared with one of only 22 per cent.[1] in the unit value of net imports between 1929 and 1932. For Malaya as a whole the deterioration in the terms of trade was very slightly less marked.

Although much of the deflation was borne by property owners and non-resident shareholders of rubber and tin companies, its

[1] The figures represent the arithmetic mean of the price decline of commodities (weighted by 1929 values) comprising 97 per cent. of the value of the 1929 net exports and 52 per cent. of net imports. A large proportion of F.M.S. imports were of the kind for which unit values cannot be calculated from information available in this country (mining machinery, railway material, 'other implements'). The result is thus more reliable for export than for import values, but the latter are unlikely to be seriously inaccurate. It will be seen below that the declines in the unit values of N.E.I. exports and imports were of much the same order as those of the F.M.S. when allowance is made for the depreciation of sterling.

Little assistance could be derived for these calculations from the official Malayan statistics. The Registrar-General, S.S. and F.M.S. used to issue an annual publication, *Malaya Average Prices*, and this contains tables of the price movements of 40 import and 19 export commodities, together with an index based on the 1924 export and import values. This, however, is worthless. First, though not stated explicitly, it is an unweighted arithmetic average. Secondly, the index of export values includes a number of re-exports. Thirdly, the import prices are all of commodities of which wholesale prices were regularly available, and consequently foodstuffs, raw materials and the simpler manufactured articles are heavily overweighted. The prices of these had fallen during the slump far more than those of the more complex manufactures, and so the index, which greatly understates the fall in the unit values of Malayan exports, considerably overstates the decline in the unit values of imports.

effect on the earnings of salary and wage-earners was spectacular. Between early 1930 and mid-1932 daily wages of Indian estate labour fell by about 50–60 per cent. and the fall in Chinese wages was even steeper. Earnings declined much more, as estate employment was approximately halved between the middle of 1930 and the spring of 1932. In many districts work (at wages 50 per cent. below the 1929 levels) was available only on four or five days a week, while workers' dependants became unemployed. Taken together, these factors suggest a decline in pay-rolls of about 80 per cent. While the cost of living of the Asiatic population also fell sharply, the decline was not in proportion to wages, let alone to earnings; it may be estimated reasonably accurately at around 40 per cent.[1]

Public finance figures are also of some use as an index, albeit only a partial one, of the deterioration in economic conditions. For fiscal purposes the S.S., the F.M.S., and the various U.M.S. are separate administrations. The figures for the F.M.S. are most suitable for the present purpose.

TABLE III

F.M.S. Government Revenue and Expenditure, 1929–33

(Million Straits dollars)

	1929	1930	1931	1932	1933
Revenue	82	66	52	44	47
(Estimated revenue)	(70)	(83)	(71)	(56)	(44)
Expenditure	84	82	62	54	50

The figures include federal, state and local expenditure and receipts. Gross receipts and expenditure of public utilities, and the net working results of the F.M.S. railways are also included. The figures are from the F.M.S. *Estimates*, the *Annual Reports* of the Auditor-General and the *Annual Reports* of the Chief Secretary to the Government.

Revenue estimates were violently upset. The 1932 F.M.S. revenue estimates were passed in November 1931 at 56 millions. Three months later an official circular revised this to 47 millions and in a few weeks this figure was again reduced to 42 millions. Two examples will show the order of magnitude of the decline in the sources of revenue. The number of gallons of liquor of every description (excluding toddy) imported into or manufactured in the F.M.S. fell from 1,668,000 in 1929 to 320,000 in 1932. The value of net rubber exports fell from 202 million dollars in 1929 to 37 millions in 1932, and the effect of this was magnified since the

[1] The official Asiatic cost of living in Singapore averaged 156 (1914 = 100) in 1929 and 99 in 1933, but it referred to a very much higher standard than that of the working or clerical classes.

rate of the export duty varied with the Singapore price (at 1929 prices it was around 3–4 per cent. *ad valorem*, while at slump prices it was one per cent.).

The substantial deficits caused much misgiving, and great efforts were made to improve the fiscal situation. The first steps were to raise indirect taxes and to extend their range. Before the depression the customs tariff of the F.M.S. was very short (petrol, tobacco and matches, liquors and spirits only). Between the end of 1930 and the end of 1932 the rates were raised several times, and taxation was extended to sugar, all edible oils and fats, tinned milk, coffee, tea, fruits and vegetables, kerosene oil and textiles (including eventually a specific import duty on the cheapest textiles at a rate not far short of 100 per cent. *ad valorem*), while many other manufactured articles also became liable to duty.

The general impoverishment and the mass repatriation of estate and mining labour affected the consumption of the taxed articles sufficiently to offset the increased taxation. A retrenchment commission, whose report was signed in October 1932,[1] observed that revenue had failed to respond to increases in indirect taxation. Though this did not prevent them from recommending its further extension, in the main the commissioners relied on drastic retrenchment to a maximum expenditure of 43·7 millions by 1933, or approximately one-half of the 1929 level. The Government was prepared to undertake drastic measures and actual expenditure in 1933 was just over 50 millions.[2]

II

Malaya thus presented a gloomy picture during the depression and it is not surprising to find officials, as well as unofficial public opinion, deploring her dependence on two industries. The large imports of foodstuffs, especially of rice, were deprecated, and various measures, including a temporary import duty on rice and padi,[3] were taken to encourage Malayan rice production, as well as the cultivation of other foodstuffs.

[1] The commission was appointed in March of the same year. Similar bodies had been formed a few months earlier in the S.S., as well as the N.E.I. The findings of the last were the gloomiest and even envisaged a complete administrative collapse as a result of the fiscal deficit.

[2] Further aspects of the depression, including its reflection in Malayan bankruptcy and criminal statistics, are reviewed in 'Some Aspects of the Malayan Rubber Slump', *Economica*, Nov. 1944.

[3] Padi is the unhusked grain of the rice plant.

Yet Malaya's specialisation in rubber and tin had real advantages. It was agreed by all observers that in the late 1920's the standard of living of all classes in Malaya was far higher than in India, Ceylon or the rice-producing countries of South-east Asia. Money and real wages were substantially higher in Malaya than in India or China ; real wages exceeded those of South India by at least 75 per cent., and probably by more. To quote one authority, Mr. C. A. Vlieland in his *Report on the 1931 Malayan Census* refers to the material benefits which the varied races living in Malay derived from the commercial prosperity of the country. Economically, Malaya was a veritable Eldorado (Vlieland's expression) to the poorest masses of South and South-east Asia. 'So it comes about that there is a continuous stream of immigrants from China, India, Java . . . coming to seek their fortunes in Malaya . . . they no less than the Europeans hope to amass in Malaya, if not a fortune, at least a competence with which to return to their country and live at a standard they could not hope to attain by remaining there.' [1] The benefits derived by the Malays were reflected in housing and health standards and in material possessions, including occasionally a motor-car.[2] This high standard was achieved in the face of poor soil conditions,[3] and resulted largely from commercial prosperity. A policy of self-sufficiency or even of large-scale diversification might well have resulted in an appreciable reduction in the standard of living.

This dependence on two main export products rendered the Malayan economy very vulnerable to changes in external conditions. But the various Malayan administrations could have met a depression by embarking on public works and/or distributing food at nominal cost, or even free, to unemployed or under-employed workers. The case for public works was strengthened by the

[1] *Report*, p. 6.

[2] Information relevant to these matters can also be found in an interesting but apparently little-known series of reports on economic conditions in certain rural (padi and coconut growing) districts of Ceylon. The reports, published between 1937 and 1944 as *Bulletins* 5 to 13 of the Ceylon Bureau of Industry and Commerce, summarise the results of enquiries organised by the Ceylon Ministry of Labour, Industry and Commerce. The statistical technique and presentation compare favourably with most enquiries of this type. The poverty disclosed was appalling, and contrasted vividly with the conditions of the Malayan rubber-growing smallholder, or the Indian estate labourers. The reports may be read with advantage by those who deprecate the Malayan smallholder's preference for rubber, or Malaya's dependence on rubber and tin.

[3] 'The basic factor controlling Malayan agriculture is the general poverty of the soil . . . Cultivation of rapidly growing crops or annual food crops soon demonstrates the rapidity with which fertility falls when the land has been cleared.' Sir F. Stockdale, *Report on a Visit to Malaya, Java, Sumatra and Ceylon in 1938*, p. 9.

absence of some of the most important practical difficulties. The country's balance of payments was still favourable and there was no foreign indebtedness. Again, the labour force which consisted almost entirely of immigrant labourers was exceptionally mobile, both geographically and occupationally. Moreover, the alternatives were employing the workers or leaving them unemployed, often in a semi-starved condition, until they had to be repatriated at the expense of the Government; and the repatriated workers were likely soon to be required again. Retrenchment was, however, the order of the day; in fact it appears that the decision to suspend public works was taken just when the need became most urgent. According to the *Annual Report* for 1931 of the Commissioner of Police, F.M.S.: 'By the middle of the year the programme of useful and economic works had been almost exhausted. At the same time it was decided to restrict the output of tin' (with a resulting sharp rise in unemployment among mining coolies).

The reason for the official refusal to pursue a policy of public works financed by loans was stated by the Chief Secretary to the F.M.S. Government in the Federal Council in June 1930. Replying to an unofficial member who suggested the flotation of an internal loan the proceeds of which were to have been spent on public works, the Chief Secretary stated that bad as was the fiscal situation the Government was far from bankrupt and there was no justification for the suggestion. In fairness to the Malayan administrators it must be remembered that the views expressed by the Chief Secretary were at that time widely held in this country too.[1]

III

Critics of the reliance of Malaya and Ceylon on two or three major products were wont to refer to the Netherlands East Indies and their diversified economy as examples to be followed. While manufacturing activity in the N.E.I. was still only on a very small

[1] The experience of Ceylon during the depression largely resembled that of Malaya and a review of the principal statistics would be little more than needless repetition. For those wishing to pursue the matter further it may be pointed out that the economy of Ceylon is—and was even more in 1929–33—a predominantly open system, and net imports thus serve as a consumption index for many essential commodities. There were only three exports of any consequence: tea, rubber and coconut products. Two sessional papers printed with the 1933 *Proceedings* of the Ceylon State Council throw interesting light on some features of Ceylon's internal economy: the *Report of the Coconut Commission* and a memorandum by the Chief Veterinary Surgeon, Ceylon, on the principal branches of the country's animal husbandry. The fall in consumption during the depression is particularly well reflected in the *Annual Reports* of the Excise Commissioner, Ceylon.

scale, and these territories also imported various foodstuffs, they produced substantial quantities of practically every important product of tropical agriculture and had export surpluses of most. Yet during the slump their plight was quite as bad as that of Malaya and Ceylon, as rubber, tin, coffee, sugar, tobacco, copra, cinchona, and tea, were all overtaken by the depression.

Some of the data are incomplete but there is no dearth of information to illustrate the trend of events. Foreign trade figures may again be taken first.

TABLE IV

N.E.I. Net Exports and Imports, 1929–33

(Million guilders)

	1929	1930	1931	1932	1933
Exports	1,484	1,186	749	544	470
Imports	1,152	919	593	384	329

The contraction of consumption and of economic activity generally is reflected in the following import figures of certain commodities with small or negligible domestic production.

TABLE V

Sundry Imports into the N.E.I., 1929–33

(Thousand metric tons)

	1929	1930	1931	1932	1933
Cigars and cigarettes .	5·0	4·3	3·3	1·5	0·5
Biscuits	8·2	6·9	4·7	3·0	3·1
Brandy	2·6	1·8	1·1	0·6	0·4
Gin	2·9	2·7	2·2	1·6	1·4
Matches . . .	11·8	10·3	8·2	5·0	3·2
Sulphate of ammonia .	130·5	123·5	123·0	79·0	33·2

Figures from the official *Economisch Weekblad*

There was also a notable deterioration in the terms of trade. According to the official figures published periodically in the *Economisch Weekblad*, in 1932 the index of the unit value of exports (1928 = 100) averaged 29 and that of imports about 60. The index of rubber export prices fell furthest, to an average of 15 in 1932 and nine in June of that year.

The fiscal system was more broadly based than in Malaya; it included income and company taxes and a variety of government monopolies, as well as a wide range of customs and excise duties and land and poll taxes on the native population. The Government also operated many commercial enterprises, such as the famous Banka tin mines, as well as rubber estates and other plantations. When the effects of the depression began to be reflected in government revenues strenuous efforts were made to increase these and thus to reduce the mounting deficits. Virtually every tax was raised repeatedly, and customs and excise duties were increased sharply at yearly or even shorter intervals and their scope extended. In 1932 a number of special 'crisis taxes' were introduced. Salaries, wages and allowances were cut, government enterprises from which no immediate revenue could be expected were closed, and virtually all capital expenditure by the Government was suspended. All these efforts remained fruitless in the face of the rapid contraction of incomes. The following table shows the deterioration of the fiscal position during the slump :

TABLE VI

N.E.I. Government Ordinary Revenue and Expenditure, 1929–33

(Million guilders)

	1929	1930	1931	1932	1933
Revenue	524	441	378	284	242
Expenditure	515	524	481	421	393
Surplus or deficit	9	– 83	– 103	– 137	– 151

The figures exclude the receipts and outgoings of the commercial enterprises of the N.E.I. Government, chiefly tin and coal mines, tea, rubber, and cinchona estates and forests. The working results of these showed surpluses totalling annually some 60–70 million guilders in the late 1920's and less than one million guilders in 1932.

The adverse fiscal situation had a bearing on subsequent events in the rubber industry. The necessity of finding new sources of revenue was the chief consideration influencing the Colijn Government to reverse earlier Dutch decisions against rubber restriction. It was expected, and rightly as it turned out subsequently, that rubber restriction would result in important fiscal benefits to the N.E.I. The value of rubber exports had fallen calamitously during the slump from 281 million guilders in 1928 to 34 millions in 1932.

Wages in Java fell to very low levels as a result of the slump both in rubber and sugar. The overcrowded labour market was further depressed by the thousands of Javanese workers who lost their employment in the Outer Provinces and returned to Java.

In 1929 daily wages were 50–60 cents or more. By 1932, according to a British consular report, native workers in the poorer districts of Central and East Java accepted work for a ten-hour day at a daily wage of 10 guilder cents or less, even if this involved walking five miles to and from work. Such rates may have been exceptional; in the principal rubber-growing districts from 15 to 20 cents was more usual.

Incomplete as are these various figures, they suggest that during the slump the N.E.I. fared no better than Malaya. It may have been that the sustained and stubborn deflationary policy pursued in the N.E.I. offset such influence as the diversity of their economy may have had in mitigating the effects of the depression.

The producing territories were brought to the verge of an economic collapse by the slump in a few commodities—in Malaya only two. The effects were all-pervasive and it was seriously believed that unless conditions improved a complete administrative collapse would result. In such circumstances it was hardly surprising that any measure for improving matters, so long as it was administratively feasible and not obviously inequitable, would be welcomed by the authorities without too much enquiry into its long-term effects. The most important of these measures was rubber restriction.

CHAPTER 3

GENERAL REVIEW OF THE RUBBER SLUMP

EXCEPT for the years 1929–33 some form of organised restriction was in force almost continuously ever since the rubber trees planted during and after the boom of 1910 reached maturity, so that it is only in these years that producers' reactions to price changes can be observed. The disproportionate effects of comparatively slight maladjustments also emerge from a study of the depression. Moreover, no doubt because of its exceptional severity, the great slump seems to have left a particularly marked and lasting effect on the outlook of the leaders of the industry.

I

Its youthfulness and rapidity of growth are remarkable features of the industry. The total area under rubber in 1905 was estimated at about 65,000 acres ; by 1930 it was about eight million acres. Over 90 per cent. of the acreage had been planted since 1910, and none of this had been replanted by 1930. A rubber tree comes into bearing five or six years after planting and will, unless ruined by maltreatment, yield satisfactorily for 25 or more years. As a result of the very rapid growth of the industry and the longevity of the trees, in 1930 virtually none of the fixed capital had been renewed since it was first invested. Even by 1940 the original tree population accounted for almost the whole of the planted area. The organised restriction which has been a feature of most of the short life of the rubber industry was thus applied in conditions of particular immaturity. No other branch of agriculture has ever developed so rapidly, and it is unlikely that there is any other industry of comparable importance which has not renewed the fixed capital which was first invested.

Although 1929 was a year of comparative stability in the industry, and even the prices ruling at the end of the year were not so bad as was claimed at the time, the industry was undoubtedly highly vulnerable. On the demand side rubber was very largely dependent on the United States and on the motor industry. In 1928–29 some 75–80 per cent. of the world rubber absorption was by the motor industry, and the U.S.A., which at that time had four-fifths, and produced seven-eighths, of the world's motor cars, accounted for about three-fifths of world absorption. The cost of rubber in tyres is a very small percentage of the cost of buying or running a car,[1] and as the possibility of substitution between reclaimed and crude rubber is limited, the short-period demand for rubber is very inelastic.[2]

The main facts about the American motor industry during the slump are familiar and need not be repeated in detail. In 1929 the output of automobiles reached 5,358,000 units; in 1932 it was 1,371,000 units, the lowest since 1915 (with the exception of the war year of 1918). The seasonally-adjusted monthly index of motor car production fell from 153 in June 1929 (1923–25 = 100) to 16 in October 1932. The automobile slump affected not only tyre sales for original equipment but also replacement sales, which were further depressed by rapid technical change. In 1921 the rubber slump had been accentuated by the displacement of the fabric tyre by the cord tyre; in the great slump there was a supersession of the cord by the balloon tyre. Balloon tyres contain more rubber than cords, but last much longer, and their introduction therefore diminished over a period of a few years the amount of rubber required for replacement. American output of tyres fell from about 77 millions in 1928 to about 40 millions in 1932.

Apart from the slump in demand, the big American tyre manufacturers had to face other difficulties, some of which had repercussions on the rubber market. Although they had one of the world's most highly organised commodity markets at their disposal, the large manufacturers frequently regarded hedging as a gamble, though they were not averse to 'taking a view' (without covering) when they considered prices to be unduly low. In the conditions of 1929–32 they suffered very large inventory losses, which ran into many millions of dollars. Heavy losses were also incurred as a result of the recurrent price wars between the leading manufacturers. These had been frequent since the late 1920's and were particularly violent during the slump. The fact that the industry was working much below capacity greatly strengthened the position of buyers generally and in particular of the two great mail-order

[1] The cost of crude rubber was not a dominant item even in the cost of tyres. According to the Rubber Manufacturers' Association of America, crude rubber represented 22 per cent. of the selling value of the average tyre in 1929 and 6 per cent. in 1932; in Great Britain in 1932 the proportion was about 4 per cent. of the retail price of tyres.

[2] The influence of the advent of synthetic rubber is discussed in Chapters 17 and 19, below.

houses. These took full advantage and played off one manufacturer against another. The result was, in the words of one trade paper, 'price cuts deep enough to draw blood'.[1] The outcome was an unwillingness and/or an inability to hold stocks, and the continued large supplies could find a market only at very low prices.

Absorption of reclaimed rubber remained substantial even during the period of extremely low crude rubber prices. This was yet another of the troubles bequeathed to the industry by the Stevenson scheme, since the use of reclaim was popularised by the famine prices of 1925–26, and once the manufacturers discovered some of its real advantages, such as uniformity, economy in power and filling material, it came to stay as a compounding material of rubber manufacturing. Its increased popularity with manufacturers emerges from a simple comparison. In 1923 the price of crude rubber in New York averaged 29·6 cents and that of reclaim 10·4 cents; in 1932 crude rubber averaged 3·4 and reclaim 3·8 cents; yet the ratio of absorption of reclaim to crude rubber was slightly higher in 1932.

Outside the U.S.A., rubber consumption was well maintained, the secular rise in demand almost exactly offsetting the effects of the slump. This can be seen from Table I.

TABLE I

Absorption of Rubber in Importing Countries, 1929–33

(Thousand tons)

	Absorption outside the U.S.A.	*Absorption in the U.S.A.*	*Total absorption*
1929	337	467	804
1930	333	376	709
1931	325	355	680
1932	352	337	689
1933	409	412	821

[1] In an effort to improve sales, one of the big U.S. rubber manufacturers produced a rubber hot-water bottle which, so it was stated, was a most successful imitation of a beautiful Greek vase. The intensity of the slump was apparently responsible for the lack of success of the experiment, for the bottle failed to enjoy the large sales which *a priori* reasoning and market research had led the makers to expect.

A more ambitious plan, designed to solve the banking crisis, cure unemployment and rescue the rubber industry, was put forward in the winter of 1932–33, when the widespread hoarding of notes endangered the stability of the American banking system. Four years before the publicity given to the Gesell plan by Lord Keynes, an American chemist suggested that U.S. banknotes should be made of latex-treated paper of poor ageing quality, which would discourage saving and hoarding and induce spending.

These figures show that the fall in American absorption accounted for almost the entire decline between 1929 and 1931, and for more than the total between 1929 and 1932 ; absorption in other countries was actually higher in 1932 than it had been in 1929. Within the U.S.A., tyres and tubes were entirely responsible for the decrease in absorption ; there was a slight increase in other uses.

II

The vulnerable position of the industry was accentuated by the low elasticity of supply of important groups of producer. Direct costs of the majority of estates were around one-third or two-fifths of total cost, and these producers could be expected to maintain production at a fairly constant rate (at which bark renewal approximately equalled bark consumption), until the price declined below direct costs.[1] With the exception of Java, the most important producing territories relied on immigrant labour, and this enhanced the bias towards low elasticity of supply. Many smallholders had virtually no cash costs and could thus be expected to continue production even when prices were very low. Indeed, it was widely held that they would produce more at lower prices, but this turned out to have been unfounded.

As in the slump of 1921–22, the effects of the fall in demand were greatly accentuated by an increase in capacity, or more precisely, in the area reaching maturity.[2] Table II shows the increase in the mature area in the various territories after 1929. Although all territories showed an increase in mature area, the most striking rise was in the N.E.I. native acreage. This increase—subsequently found to have been far greater than indicated by the figures in this table—was the principal legacy of the Stevenson scheme.

The simplest way of showing producers' reactions to the decline in price is by following the output per mature acre,[3] which indicates

[1] Economists might ask how direct costs of 3*d*.–4*d*. were compatible with a market price of 10*d*. under conditions of perfect competition, especially as the annual output can be varied with the intensity of tapping. Some of the theoretical and practical issues involved are discussed in 'Notes on Cost', *Economica*, May 1945.

[2] Capacity is an elusive and in many ways unsatisfactory term, especially where labour rather than land is the principal scarce factor. For the sake of simplicity it may be defined as the output which can be produced from a given area when the entire acreage is being tapped at a rate at which bark renewal approximately equals bark consumption.

[3] Tables showing actual outputs and estimated capacity, as well as variations in the output of different classes of producer and of all producing territories, will be found in Appendix B.

Table II

Mature Acreage in Various Producing Territories, 1929–33

(Thousand acres, to the nearest five thousand)

	1929	1930	1931	1932	1933
Malaya	2,360	2,435	2,585	2,685	2,760
N.E.I. estates	920	975	1,040	1,135	1,235
N.E.I. natives	550	800	1,125	1,350	1,550
Ceylon	490	500	520	535	540
Sarawak	60	90	140	200	250
India (including Burma)	120	130	140	150	165
British North Borneo	65	70	80	90	95
French Indo-China	80	100	125	185	260
Siam	35	55	80	115	145
Total	4,680	5,155	5,835	6,445	7,000

There are minor discrepancies (negligible compared to the inaccuracy of the acreage figures) between the acreages in this table and those in Ch. 1. These result chiefly from certain revisions by Dr. Whitford, as the above figures have been taken from his later reports; and from certain minor corrections made possible by information which has become available since his investigations.

broadly the extent to which producers are working below capacity. A fall in the yield per mature acre generally indicates the postponement of tapping of areas which had come into bearing.[1] The yield figures, necessarily approximate, are given in the following table.

Table III

Estimated Output per Mature Acre, 1929–33

(lb. per acre, to the nearest five lb.)

	1929	1930	1931	1932	1933
Average London Price (pence per lb.)	*10·3*	*5·9*	*3·1*	*2·3*	*3·2*
Malaya—estates	410	380	375	365	355
Malaya—smallholdings	480	460	445	385	465
Malaya—total	440	415	405	375	400
N.E.I. estates—Outer Provinces	375	365	390	360	360
N.E.I. estates—Java	390	385	400	325	380
N.E.I. estates—total	380	375	395	345	365
N.E.I. natives	430	245	170	105	165
Ceylon	360	350	260	210	275
Sarawak	420	225	170	85	105
British North Borneo	225	200	155	120	170
India (including Burma)	240	205	155	65	85
French Indo-China	215	175	135	120	150
Siam	275	190	100	60	110

[1] Variations in the yield per surface unit reflect not only changes in the intensity of tapping but may be due to changes in soil condition or in the age composition of the mature area. These considerations do not apply to such large variations as are shown in the table.

These figures, though they are only estimates, show well how differently the various classes of producer reacted to the steep decline in the price. The supply of rubber from the estates in the Outer Provinces of the N.E.I. was least elastic; these estates produced at an almost constant rate throughout the slump. The rate of production of Malayan estates was also fairly stable. At the other end of the scale the N.E.I. smallholders produced in 1932 only about one-quarter as much rubber per mature acre as in 1929; several of the smaller producing territories reacted in the same way. The supply of smallholders' rubber was more elastic than that of estate output, principally because of the ability of the smallholders to turn to alternative sources of earnings.[1] It will also be noted that in 1929 the yields from smallholdings were appreciably in excess of those from estates both in Malaya and in the N.E.I.; the planted area of Sarawak, which showed the third highest yields per mature acre in 1929, was also almost entirely in the hands of smallholders. As could be expected, producers working most below capacity in 1932 responded most readily to the slightly better prices of 1933. Though on balance the supply of rubber was inelastic, it was not quite so inelastic as has sometimes been suggested, and important groups of producers were working much below capacity.[2]

The increase in capacity indicated by the changes in the mature acreages shown in Table II above, naturally accentuated the effects of the fall in demand; after 1931 it became the dominating factor. Chronologically, the fall in consumption was responsible for starting the price on its steep decline. Absorption began to fall in the autumn of 1929; stocks had been rising since 1928, but only with the decline in absorption did they begin to exert a really depressing effect on price. The following table summarises prices and stocks over this period.

[1] Mr. P. Lamartine Yates, *Commodity Control* (1943), which includes a chapter purporting to be a serious analysis of rubber regulation, comments as follows on smallholders' production: 'The native, like peasants everywhere, tends to produce more rather than less when the price begins to fall. . . . in general the reaction to a price fall is quite insignificant; indeed, there is no experience to show how low price would have to fall before native output was seriously curtailed.'

[2] The experience of these years suggests that the expression of the elasticity of supply as a small proportionate change in output in response to a small proportionate change in price can be misleading when capacity changes substantially. Such a change would normally be regarded as 'other things not being equal', but for certain purposes it seems preferable to express the elasticity of supply in terms of capacity working, as a small proportionate change in the rate of capacity working divided by a small proportionate change in price, even though this procedure also entails some difficulties.

TABLE IV

Principal World Stocks at the end of each Quarter and Quarterly Averages of London and New York Prices, 1929–33

	Stocks: 1,000 tons	Stocks: Months' absorption at current calendar yearly rate	Price: Pence per lb.	Price: Cents per lb.
1929 1st quarter	305	4·6	11·3	22·8
2nd "	300	4·5	10·6	21·0
3rd "	320	4·8	10·5	20·7
4th "	385	5·7	8·6	17·4
1930 1st "	425	7·2	7·7	15·4
2nd "	430	7·3	6·8	13·8
3rd "	480	8·1	4·9	9·8
4th "	505	8·5	4·4	8·7
1931 1st "	545	9·6	3·9	7·8
2nd "	545	9·6	3·0	6·4
3rd "	570	10·1	2·3	5·5
4th "	605	11·4	3·0	4·7
1932 1st "	645	11·2	2·6	3·9
2nd "	600	10·5	1·9	2·9
3rd "	610	10·6	2·4	3·5
4th "	640	11·2	2·5	3·4
1933 1st "	650	9·5	2·2	3·0
2nd "	620	9·1	2·9	4·9
3rd "	635	9·3	3·8	7·4
4th "	665	9·7	4·1	8·3

The figures include Malayan stocks (Singapore, Penang and up-country) and those at Para and Manaos, in London and Liverpool, in the U.S.A. and stocks afloat. The 'surplus' stocks were much smaller than would appear from the table, as necessary working stocks were equal to about 5–6 months' absorption.

The lowest price was actually reached in June 1932 with a London price of 1·7*d.* and a New York price of 2½ cents; these prices included freight, landing and delivery charges.

At times the rate of decline was very rapid, with the price falling by 15 per cent. or more within a week. The general downward trend from the end of 1929 was occasionally checked or reversed by news of restriction discussions.[1] As well as increases in price founded on actual negotiations there were several fairly sharp but ephemeral spurts, when rumours spread of agreement in negotiations which were actually taking place, or of negotiations which were of no importance at all or the existence of

[1] A rally in the London price in October 1931 reflected the depreciation of sterling. There was also a local rise in American prices in May 1932 when an import duty on crude rubber was recommended as a revenue measure by the Finance Committee of the Senate. According to the trade press the measure was dropped on 'lobbying by shorts'.

which was pure conjecture. Some of the *canards* sprung on a very credulous market had every appearance of having been put into circulation by interested parties, but it was not until well into 1932 that the market began to receive them with any degree of scepticism. Generally speaking, prices were falling so steeply and swiftly as to render any but the most short-period decision and calculation quite valueless. This was well brought out by a sulphur-dusting experiment of the Ceylon Rubber Research Scheme in 1931. The experiment was designed to ascertain the improvement in yield due to combating *Oidium heveae* (the cause of secondary leaf fall) by sulphur-dusting. On the results, sulphur-dusting could be recommended as an economic proposition, assuming the market price at the time the experiment was concluded. But by the time the *Tropical Agriculturist* (the monthly magazine of the Ceylon Department of Agriculture) with the results of the experiment had reached the planters, the Colombo price had fallen so steeply that the economics of the recommendation were reversed.

When in September 1930 the London price fell below 4*d.* calculations were made of a type which became increasingly frequent over the next few years. These aimed at estimating the chances of survival and the life-expectation of the various companies, on the basis of assumed prices in conjunction with the costs as given in or calculated from the last published reports and the available liquid funds of individual companies. Some of these calculations were interesting, but the estimates based on them were invariably upset, partly because prices fell below the most pessimistic expectations, but even more because of the unexpected plasticity of costs.[1] Between the end of 1929 and the middle of 1932 sterling companies generally reduced their costs by about 60 per cent., and locally registered Malayan companies by about 65 per cent. ; the cost reduction of the Dutch companies was of the same order.[2] By 1932 f.o.b. costs of $1\frac{1}{2}$–$1\frac{3}{4}$*d.* and all-in-costs of 2–$2\frac{1}{2}$*d.* were frequent among sterling companies ; company chairmen repeatedly stated in 1932 and 1933 that with a London price of 3*d.* it would be possible to make a reasonable profit. This reduction in costs which resulted from increased efficiency, as well

[1] A careful calculation covering 364 sterling companies with a mature area of about one million acres was published in November 1930. It was found that on the basis of costs and liquid assets given in their last reports, companies owning some three-quarters of the mature acreage reviewed could last only two years with rubber at or below 3*d.* per lb., and some nine-tenths of the area would succumb within three years, whether in production or on a care-and-maintenance basis.

[2] Details are shown in Appendix E.

as from reductions in wages and salaries, was an important element in the maintenance of estate output in face of the steep fall in the price.

Profits and dividends disappeared. *The Economist*'s survey of rubber company profits and dividends gives the following picture :

TABLE V

Rubber Company Earnings and Payments, 1928–33

(Years to 30th June)

	Earned for ordinary shares (per cent.)	*Paid on ordinary shares (per cent.)*
1928–29	8·4	6·2
1929–30	8·0	5·8
1930–31	1·4	1·2
1931–32	− 1·6 (loss)	0·1
1932–33	− 1·3 (loss)	0·1

This was the most unfavourable experience of any industrial group whose profits were analysed by *The Economist.* Very few rubber companies had debenture charges to meet and hardly any had issued preference capital, and the absence of dividends cannot be attributed to the absorption of profits by prior charges.

The plight of the companies was reflected in share values. On the London Stock Exchange the *Investors' Chronicle* index of rubber share values (31st December 1923 = 100) which averaged 123 in 1929, with a peak of 147, declined to 19 in June 1932, with an average of 31 for the year. In Batavia the index of rubber shares (1928 = 100) touched eight in June 1932. The market capitalisation of many sound rubber companies with issued capital around £50 an acre fell to around £3 per acre by mid-1932. Some estates changed hands in Malaya for a few pounds per acre ; poor-yielding areas were virtually unsaleable. New investment in rubber ceased. Total capital issues of rubber companies on the London Stock Exchange were £90,000 in 1932 and just over £200,000 in 1933, against several millions annually in the 1920's. The depreciation allowances of companies were also very small.

III

The output of smallholders' rubber during these years far exceeded expectations and confuted all estimates. It is now proposed to review the comments of experts and officials on the actual rate of production of smallholders' rubber and of the output to be expected from year to year. Only officials and leaders of the industry of undoubted integrity will be quoted. The survey is of considerable practical interest; the comments, and the views underlying them, greatly influenced the assessments of various classes of producer under the international rubber regulation scheme, with results to be shown later. It may also serve some secondary purposes; for instance, to reveal from another angle the immaturity of the industry, or to throw light on the expert knowledge which professional participants in organised produce markets supposedly possess.

The great surprise of 1929 was the high rate of output from Malayan smallholdings. Addressing the shareholders of a large British rubber company in February 1929, a recognised leader of the industry (who was chairman of the N.E.I. Committee and of the Statistics Committee of the R.G.A., as well as a past chairman of the R.G.A.) estimated Malayan smallholders' output for 1929 at 120,000 tons; they actually produced 200,000 tons. At first the explanation was sought in flush production following the enforced resting under the Stevenson scheme, and when this could no longer be maintained it was thought that the smallholders were dissipating their capital by excessive bark consumption. As the output per mature acre of the smallholders in 1929 appreciably exceeded that of estates (about 480 lb. against 410 lb.), while under the Stevenson scheme the estates had been assessed about 100 per cent. higher than smallholdings, this somewhat striking reversal was universally attributed to overtapping by smallholders, and an early fall in their output was freely predicted. Thus at the next annual meeting (February 1930) of that company, the same chairman said: 'It is perfectly clear from the very high yields of Malayan native rubber in 1929 that the benefits which accrued from enforced resting during the years of restricted exports in the improvement of bark reserves were even greater than the advocates of restriction claimed these would be. It is likewise evident that the native smallholdings are again squandering their bark reserves at a very rapid rate and that when they come to the end of their tappable bark on the lower panels of their trees there must be a pronounced falling off in the production from these areas. I cannot say just when the contraction in output from the native smallholdings now being overtapped will come, but it must be imminent before we are through 1930.'

After reaching 200,000 tons in 1929, Malayan smallholders'

output fell only very slightly to 197,000 tons in 1930, remained at that figure in 1931, fell further to 177,000 tons in 1932 (under the stress of very low prices), but rose again rapidly to 220,000 tons in 1933, and to 253,000 tons during the twelve months to May 1934, when restriction was introduced. The last figure was over double the capacity estimated by the chairman just quoted.

This unofficial leader of the industry was in very good company. The Deputy Registrar-General of Statistics, S.S. and F.M.S., in an article in the *Malayan Agricultural Journal* (*M.A.J.*) in February 1930,[1] dealt in some detail with the surprisingly high output of the smallholders : 'During 1929 beyond doubt, and to a lesser extent during the period July–December 1928, the smaller holdings were overtapped . . . and . . . it must be accepted as almost certain that after the wintering season in 1930 (February–March) though the average yield per acre on smallholdings will continue at a far higher rate than was generally thought possible, the rate of production is certain to fall appreciably below that of 1929 output.' This forecast proved entirely incorrect. Next year the same officer made another attempt :[2] 'Throughout 1930 the production per acre on smallholdings was maintained at a higher rate than that of the larger holdings. On the former economic necessity has caused the heaviest possible tapping to be adopted. There are many conflicting opinions as to how long this can be continued before it so affects the smallholders' bark position as to reduce their output seriously. In the writer's opinion—*formed after close inspection of smallholdings all over the country*[3]—the output per acre on large estates will exceed that on smallholdings within a year or 18 months from the date of writing.' It will be seen subsequently that until the advent of restriction, output per mature acre on smallholdings appreciably exceeded that on estates, and that in the second half of 1933 and the early part of 1934 the excess was around 35–40 per cent. and was increasing.

It will be noted that the remarks quoted (and the list could be extended almost at will), were not so much forecasts or estimates, but rather comments on what was believed to be happening on the

[1] 'A Review of F.M.S. Rubber Statistics, 1929', *M.A.J.*, Feb. 1930.

[2] 'A Review of F.M.S. Rubber Statistics, 1930', *M.A.J.*, May 1931.

[3] My italics. This officer, as well as being Deputy Registrar-General of Statistics, was also in special charge of rubber statistics. In the article just quoted he stated : 'It is well known that of holdings of under 100 acres each, more than ninety-nine per cent. are smallholdings of which the average area is about $2\frac{1}{2}$ acres each.' It is now known that at least one-half of the smallholdings area is in holdings of over 3 acres each, and this was easily ascertainable in 1931.

properties of Malayan smallholders. These were easily accessible, individually-surveyed holdings, mostly in the western (highly developed) part of Malaya. In the N.E.I. the position is radically different, and the native rubber holdings, or rather forests, are in vast, sparsely populated areas of Sumatra and Borneo where there is no land registration. Yet a systematic investigation of conditions of Malayan smallholdings was not begun until the middle of 1931. Until then there were only casual observations by passers-by or by harassed administrators. The first investigation, begun in the summer of 1931, was prompted by the obvious necessity of reconsidering the established ideas on Malayan smallholders' rubber. According to an editorial note in the *Malayan Agricultural Journal*, August 1931 : ' It has to be admitted that reliable information as regards the capabilities of rubber under smallholding conditions is almost entirely lacking. Statistics clearly indicate that the general ideas on the yield of smallholdings that obtained in pre-restriction days were very far removed from actual facts. It is no less possible that common present-day views on the question of bark consumption and renewal and bark reserves on smallholdings may be just as far removed from the truth. It is hoped that the scheme decided upon will, after a course of 12 months, place at our disposal sufficient information to provide a basis for calculation, instead of the matter being one largely of pure conjecture as it has been in the past.' This was indeed devastating comment on the confident statements of experts and officials, and on the ' close inspection ' of smallholdings by the Deputy Registrar-General of Statistics.

The official smallholdings enquiry of 1931–33, the results of which will be reviewed in detail later, found that bark reserves on the holdings inspected were equivalent on the average to seven-years-and-five-months' bark consumption at the smallholders' rate of bark removal. Thus even if their bark had completely ceased to renew, the smallholders would have been able to continue tapping at the same rate as before for an average of almost seven and a half years, ranging on individual holdings from just under three to sixteen years. *Not one single tree was found on which tapping had to be suspended owing to lack of bark ; moreover, it appeared that bark consumption was below the rate of bark renewal.*

The progress of this enquiry was curiously reflected in the *Annual Reports* of the Director of Agriculture. Proposals for the enquiry were put forward in 1930 ; it was begun in 1931 and concluded in 1933. According to the 1930 *Annual Report :* ' Preliminary observations appear to indicate that in the effort to obtain as large a yield as possible the rate of bark consumption on smallholdings may be considerably outstripping the rate of renewal.' The 1931 *Report* was less confident: 'Tapping was continuous and bark removal excessive on holdings the owners of which had no other sources of livelihood . . . it was found, however, that bark consumption was considerably less than had been anticipated.' The 1932 *Report* does not lend itself to quotation, as its views on the subject reveal a studied vagueness. In the introduction (signed in 1933) to the report of the enquiry, the Director stated that previous views on bark consumption and reserves on smallholdings had been proved to be totally wrong. Nevertheless, up to the outbreak of the Japanese war the alleged overtapping and excessive bark consumption (even at times of severe restriction) on smallholdings was a recurring theme of official Malayan publications. Even had there not been the specific evidence of the smallholdings enquiry, certain general considerations, allied to easily ascertainable facts, should have suggested the need for caution; these are discussed in a note appended to this chapter.

The experts were no more successful in their comments on N.E.I. native rubber. Here, caution was particularly advisable, as the native holdings covered enormous unsurveyed areas. The experience of the Stevenson scheme should also have served as a warning. Even during 1929–31, discussions of the supply price of substantial amounts of N.E.I. native rubber were in terms of London prices of between 1*s.* and 1*s.* 6*d.* per lb. The authors of the well-known *Report to the Rubber Growers' Association on Native Rubber in the N.E.I.* (1929) were generally fairly cautious, but they too greatly over-estimated the supply price of native rubber. They thought that exports from Palembang (one of the principal native rubber-growing residencies) would remain below 15,000 tons a year unless the London price rose above 10½*d.* In 1933, exports from Palembang reached that figure with an average London price of 3¼*d.* in depreciated sterling.

A member of the Council of the R.G.A., who had for eighteen years been editor of the *Straits Times*, argued in June 1930 in the *Investors' Chronicle* that for years to come a London price of one shilling would be required to call forth an annual output of 100,000 tons of N.E.I. native rubber. A few months later the late Dr. Rae argued in a paper read to the Midland Section of the Institution of the Rubber Industry, that with a London price of 4*d.* N.E.I. native rubber would disappear. All these estimates were in undepreciated sterling. In 1933 an average price of 3¼*d.* (depreciated sterling with the N.E.I. guilder still on gold at an unchanged parity, which meant a reduction of between one-quarter and one-third in the guilder receipts of the natives) resulted in an output of 114,000 tons. During the last quarter of that year, with a London price of 4*d.*, production was at a yearly rate of 160,000 tons, and was rising rapidly. In the spring of 1934 N.E.I. native exports were running at an annual rate of 300,000 tons with a London price of 5½*d.*–6*d.*, all in depreciated sterling.

Perhaps the most interesting among the mistaken estimates was that emanating from the highest authority. The Division of Agricultural Economics in the N.E.I. Department of Agriculture used to publish periodic official *Reports on Native Rubber Cultivation in the Netherlands East Indies.* These contained much the best analysis of this subject. Yet in September 1930 the *Fifth Report* concluded that the supply of native rubber would vanish should the Batavia price fall to 12 guilder cents per half-kilo. In 1932 the price averaged 8 cents per half-kilo, and for long periods it fell below 6 cents, yet substantial amounts were still forthcoming, while in 1933 when the price averaged just over 10 guilder cents the native output at 114,000 tons exceeded all previous figures.

The substantial N.E.I. native exports during the slump years, when the London price was below 3*d.* for two years and averaged 3¼*d.* or less in depreciated sterling for three successive calendar years, were a useful corrective to the various estimates. Thus an official *N.E.I. Native Report* issued in August 1932 suggested that in Djambi (a large residency) many holdings would be tapped at full capacity if the local price were to rise to 10 cents per kilo, and that in a few districts this would happen even with 7 cents per kilo. These prices corresponded to 7–8 cents per half-kilo in Batavia. Thus in important districts full tapping would be ensured by prices 35–40 per cent. below the level at which, according to an official report issued less than two years previously, all tapping would cease.

Even more striking illustrations of the worthlessness of these estimates can be found in the experience of the years 1934–36. Between June 1934 and December 1936 N.E.I. native exports under rubber regulation were kept in check by means of a special export tax designed to depress local prices sufficiently to keep native exports within the permissible level. In 1935 the average Batavia price less the average rate of tax was around 9¼ guilder cents per half-kilo (2¼*d.* per lb.) of dry rubber; native exports were 142,000 tons. In 1936 on the average over five-sixths of the Batavia price had to be taxed away to keep native exports within the permissible limits. Though the native producer was left with only about 1*d.* per lb. of dry rubber at ports of shipment, native rubber exports still totalled 149,000 tons.

The estimates and views so far quoted were largely those of disinterested persons. The same cannot be said of the market reports published regularly by Mincing Lane firms and purporting to be analyses of the principal aspects of the rubber situation. Anyone not bemused by the market jargon so freely used cannot help asking whether the 'analyses' reflect ignorance only, or whether they are intentionally misleading.

In May 1930 the Belgian associate of a leading Mincing Lane firm circulated its 'analysis' which of course culminated in a bullish forecast. The writer(s) failed to refer to smallholders' output, estate costs, wage rates, U.S. consumption, or indeed to hardly any relevant factors. He (or they) summed up: 'Ayant *minutieusement examiné* les différents facteurs de la situation actuelle du caoutchouc, nous devons bien en conclure *sans le moindre parti pris* (my italics) que l'amélioration doit être franchement escomptée. Cette amélioration sera justifiée dans le courant de mois de juin où l'on se rendra compte que les arrivages réduits par la restriction de mai necessiteront de forts prélèvements sur les stocks.'

An important Mincing Lane firm estimated that for 1933, unless the London price *averaged* over 3¾*d.* (note the pseudo-accuracy) total supplies would be 633,000 tons, of which 435,000 tons would come from Malaya, 150,000 tons from the N.E.I. and 48,000 tons from all other sources. For that year the price averaged 3¼*d.*, while exports totalled 853,000 tons, of which 407,000 tons came from outside Malaya. Early in 1933 another leading firm in its *Annual Review of the Rubber Market*, stated that no great increase in N.E.I. native output over the 1932 level was to be expected unless the London price rose above 6*d.* In 1933 (with an average price of 3¼*d.*) the output was 80 per cent. over that of 1932, and subsequent events made it clear that at 6*d.* it would have increased four- or five-fold.[1]

Most of these market reports were of little value. Yet they were produced regularly by brokers and dealers for the benefit of speculators. The authors and readers were supposed to represent expert opinion which is to act as a stabilising factor in the

[1] A further market report by a leading firm, which reveals very doubtful business ethics, is discussed below, p. 130.

commodity markets. It is probable that the worthlessness of rubber market opinion, together with the large American participation in the rubber markets, were contributory causes to the exceptionally violent price fluctuations in rubber, even though the primary cause was the inelasticity of both demand and supply.

NOTE ON BARK CONSUMPTION ON SMALLHOLDINGS

Throughout the 1930's and until the outbreak of the Japanese war the alleged over-tapping of the trees and the excessive bark consumption on smallholdings was a recurring theme of official Malayan publications, the *Annual Reports* of the Rubber Research Institute of Malaya and the addresses of rubber company chairmen. Yet there were present in Malaya certain general considerations which should have suggested the need for a more cautious and critical attitude than was usually adopted towards these repeated assertions.

After 1934 there was the obvious point that under rubber regulation the yields per mature acre were reduced to about 200–300 lb. per acre, particularly in years of low releases. Such yields could certainly be obtained with very little strain on the trees. Even when yields on smallholdings had been of the order of 500 lb. per acre, or even higher, no overtapping was found by impartial experts such as Dr. Whitford, Major Bridges, Mr. Meads and various Dutch investigators.

The large proportion of the Malayan smallholdings acreage owned by non-Malays was another consideration which was generally overlooked. About one-half of the smallholdings area is in Chinese or Indian ownership (very largely Chinese), and none of this rubber would ever be overtapped except accidentally. Moreover, a large proportion of the nominally Malay holdings belong to Javanese who are well known to be good tappers. According to the 1931 Malayan census 'other Malaysians' actually exceeded the number of Malays in Johore, while in Selangor the numbers were almost equal. These 'other Malaysians' are comparatively recent immigrants from the chief islands of the Netherlands East Indies, mostly Javanese, Banjarese and Menangkabaus, the majority being Javanese. Most of these 'other Malaysians', particularly the Javanese, are careful and good tappers. It is doubtful whether the smallholdings area owned by Malays proper, as distinct from other Malaysians, has in recent years been more than two-fifths of the total Malayan smallholdings acreage; the proportion may be even less. Moreover, the Malays themselves are Asiatic peasants, not primitive tribesmen. Not many peasants of any race or nationality are likely wilfully to ruin their property, least of all a holding which is so difficult to ruin, as well as to replace, as a rubber smallholding.

There are also certain technical complications to be remembered. One of these is the need to allow for the effects of selective tapping. Many mature trees are generally left untapped on smallholdings. The smallholder taps trees here and there, and practises a rough and ready rotational system of tapping by resting individual trees and not entire areas as do the estates. In normal times something like one-quarter of all trees may be left untapped on the smaller holdings. This presents an obvious difficulty for estimates of bark consumption. If the trees left untapped were as good as those in tapping, then in calculating overall bark removal the bark consumption on the trees actually tapped should be deflated in the same proportion as the number of trees in tapping bears to the total number of trees on the holding. If, at the other extreme, all the untapped trees were dead, obviously these would not have to be allowed for at all. In actual fact the untapped trees are usually of smaller girth and of poorer yield than those in tapping, but very few are dead. In estimating bark consumption the right course seems to be to allow for those trees which will be tappable by the standards of the smallholder by the time the bark on the existing trees is likely to be exhausted, or the yield of these trees reduced sufficiently to necessitate the tapping of other trees. In practice this theoretically ideal solution is likely to be very difficult or impossible to adopt, and the better course is to allow fully for all tappable trees in estimating bark consumption. This course was adopted by the official Malayan smallholdings enquiry of 1931–33.

Again, assertions on excessive tapping are meaningless without reference to the rate of bark renewal and the period of the tapping cycle. On European estates in Malaya the standard tapping cycle is approximately eight years, so that bark excised is not tapped again for another eight years; these estates, moreover, prefer not to tap higher up the tree than 36 inches from the ground. They accordingly work to a bark consumption limited to three-quarters of an inch on half-circumference every month, so that in a full cycle of eight years only 36 inches of bark are consumed on a full circumference. It is of interest to note that the Sumatran and Malayan estates of the United States Rubber Company work to a tapping cycle of six years and accordingly permit and indeed encourage a bark consumption one-third in excess of that on most European estates in Malaya. The American practice is based on the view that the increase in the number of latex vessels secured through increased thickness of bark by tapping eight-year instead of six-year renewed bark is too small to justify a restriction of bark consumption which is likely to result in loss of rubber. This suggests that the standard practice may not be unchallengeable. On smallholdings the tapping cycle is likely to be even shorter, as the lower ground temperature, the higher humidity and better soil conditions would all conduce to a quicker rate of renewal than could safely be expected on estates. Moreover, smallholders who do not rely on outside labour with substantial cash wages, find it economic to tap trees and panels which would be uneconomic by estate standards where yields per tree need be higher than smallholdings; this point, which is very widely overlooked, is elaborated in Appendix D, below.

Lastly, opinions on smallholders' rubber were often based on roadside observation which, for reasons suggested in Chapter I, above, usually results in biased samples. More often than not they were also the views of interested parties.

These various considerations suggest that assertions on excessive bark consumption on smallholdings would need to be examined critically. The failure of first-hand observers to find evidence of overtapping on smallholdings is thus not surprising.

CHAPTER 4

PRODUCTION DURING THE SLUMP

THE general course of the slump was reviewed in the previous chapter. It is now proposed to consider in more detail the course of production in each of the different territories. The emphasis will be largely on the position of the estates ; the conditions of smallholdings will be treated in the next chapter.

I

The following table shows Malayan production during 1929–33 [1] :

TABLE I

Production of Rubber by Malayan Estates and Smallholdings and Average Price of Rubber, 1929–33

	Production (thousand tons)		*Average price (pence and Straits cents per lb.)*	
	Estates	*Smallholdings*	*London*	*Singapore*
1929	246·0	200·0	10·3	34·5
1930	236·9	197·3	5·9	19·3
1931	239·8	197·0	3·1	10·0
1932	240·1	177·0	2·3	7·0
1933	240·8	219·8	3·2	10·2

Estate production in 1930 was affected by the 'tapping holiday', the complete cessation of tapping during May recommended by the British and Dutch producers' associations. When this factor is allowed for, total estate output was virtually constant for five successive years. The sustained rate of production in the face of a

[1] The statistics of output, price and yields per acre for these years are presented in considerable detail in Statistical Appendix I ; the salient points only are given in the text.

The monthly and quarterly figures in the text are seasonally corrected ; in the Appendix both the corrected and the actual figures are shown. Seasonal variations should clearly be eliminated from production figures wherever possible. The only comprehensive calculations available are those of the U.S. Department of Commerce published as *Trade Information Bulletin* No. 804 (July 1932). Data on seasonal variations of the N.E.I. estate output were also published early in 1933 in the *Economisch Weekblad.* Throughout this study seasonal variations are eliminated on the basis of the American calculations.

steep decline in price (the range of price was from a maximum of 1*s.* $1\frac{1}{2}$*d.* in February 1929 to a minimum of $1\frac{11}{16}$*d.* in June 1932) was much commented on at the time, and over-complex explanations were often put forward. The main reason was simple; though prices had fallen sharply they were still above direct costs which were also being reduced rapidly, and the majority of estates maintained production as long as the price remained above direct costs and the rate of bark removal did not exceed the rate of bark renewal. In a few instances, companies increased their output to provide for the payment of fixed costs, but such a course was not unreasonable; it was often based on a favourable opinion of the recuperative powers of the trees, or on the view that future prices might be even lower than those ruling at the time.

The tapping holiday, inconclusive Anglo-Dutch conversations in June 1930, the strong opposition to restriction by an important group of N.E.I. estates manifested at a meeting of Dutch producers in July, and the announcement early in September that the N.E.I. Government would not apply compulsory restriction to the native producers, were the milestones along the road of rubber prices from 8*d.* in April to $3\frac{7}{8}$*d.* in September. No more than a few estates could make ends meet at 4*d.* or 5*d.*, and there was an almost ceaseless clamour for some form of restriction. In view of the refusal of the N.E.I. authorities to participate, statutory restriction of output or exports was ruled out; the Malayan authorities did however adopt a measure, pressed for by the European estates, which amounted to partial restriction. The ban on the alienation of land for rubber planting which had been in force during the Stevenson scheme, was reimposed in August 1930, less than two years after the termination of that scheme.[1]

In July 1930 a 20 per cent. reduction in minimum wages was decreed with effect from October.[2] In August–September planters' salaries were generally reduced and large-scale dismissals of salaried employees and wage-earners began. Between August 1st and December 31st some 60,000–70,000 Indian estate labourers, about one-fifth to one-quarter of the employed Indian estate population, were dismissed.

[1] This was a unilateral decision of the Malayan authorities which was not followed in the N.E.I. With a small exception in 1939–40, the ban on the alienation of land has never since been lifted in Malaya; from 1934 onwards it was coupled with prohibition of new planting.

[2] Suggestions were also advanced at this time and put into practice early in 1931, that tappers who worked in the forenoon only should be paid only three-quarters of the minimum rates; cf. pp. 226–27, below.

The trend of smallholders' output was also contrary to expectations; both in 1930 and in 1931 it was less than 2 per cent. below the level of 1929 at 197,000 against 200,000 tons. During the last quarter of 1930 smallholders' production was running at an annual rate of 188,000 tons. The fact that this decline was slight and still left the yield per acre on smallholdings at a much higher level than that on estates, led to a renewed crop of comments and forecasts about the substantial decline very soon to be expected in smallholders' output. This, however, still refused to decline in 1931 when it again totalled 197,000 tons. There had been a slight reduction during the summer, when the London price fell to below $2\frac{1}{2}d.$ (seasonally adjusted output declined from 51,000 tons in the first quarter to 45,000 tons in the third), but with slightly higher prices following the departure from the gold standard it rose to 53,000 tons in the fourth quarter.

Every fall in price, in conjunction with the sustained high rate of production, elicited renewed demands for restriction; these were more insistent in Malaya than in London and the good old days of the Stevenson scheme were frequently recalled.[1] During the closing weeks of 1931, news spread again in Malaya of a renewal of Anglo-Dutch restriction talks, and this maintained the price around 3*d.* in London and 10 cents in Singapore throughout most of December and January. This time the rumours had some foundation, as since the beginning of December discussions had been in progress between British and Dutch producers in consultation with the British Colonial Office. The talks failed again, as the N.E.I. Government refused to apply compulsion to their native producers, while the Dutch Government in turn refused to press the N.E.I. authorities. From February 1932 the market anticipated the decision, and the price gradually declined from about 3*d.* in January to $1\frac{13}{16}d.$ by the end of March.

In view of the Anglo-Dutch negotiations and of the temporary

[1] According to a leading supporter of restriction (who was a member of the R.G.A. Council), writing in the *Straits Times* in January 1931: 'The Stevenson Scheme never failed, but was wilfully destroyed by the Baldwin Government for undisclosed reasons.' This was one of many similar statements. The share of Malaya and Ceylon (where the scheme operated) in world exports had fallen to 55 per cent. and their acreage was less than one-half of the world acreage when restriction was brought to an end.

A market report by a well-known Mincing Lane firm of brokers proposed 'to disregard ethics and confine itself to facts'; immediately before the Stevenson scheme the price had been $6\frac{3}{4}d.$ and all estates were losing money; during its currency the price averaged over 1*s.* 7*d.* and all estates made profits, while after its abandonment prices crashed again. The intended inference was obvious. The responsibility of the Stevenson scheme for the state of affairs in 1931–32 was not discussed among the facts.

price stability, dismissals and wage-cuts had been suspended in Malaya since about November 1931. After March the process was resumed with redoubled force and the wave of cuts and dismissals in the spring of 1932 singled out April–June 1932 as the acutest phase of the slump. The Singapore price fluctuated around 5 cents throughout the spring and declined to $4\frac{3}{4}$ cents early in June. Managers were instructed frequently to work to an f.o.b. cost of not more than 4 cents (1*d.*) per lb., no easy task even with the wage-rates of 1932. By mid-1932 estate wages were less than half the 1929 rates. The wage-reduction coupled with strenuous efforts towards greater economy and efficiency brought costs down to very low levels. By the second half of 1932 all-in costs of under 2*d.* per lb. were not unusual. Important economies were achieved through improvements in both estate and factory practice. In estate factories physical output per man generally more than doubled in the two years after mid-1930. In the field, cultivation work was largely suspended and selective tapping widely adopted, so that the maintenance of total output when estate employment was almost exactly halved between mid-1930 and mid-1932, was less surprising than would at first appear.

Prices remained near their lowest level throughout June. Early in July there was a sudden improvement which gained ground until it developed into a minor boom, carrying the London price to $3\frac{1}{8}$*d.* by September. There was some slight basis for this change. Exports and absorption at last reached equilibrium by the summer and stocks ceased to rise for the first time for years. At the end of June it was discovered that through a statistical error Singapore stocks had been overstated by approximately 18,000 tons for some years past, and that actual stocks there at the end of June were 16,000 tons instead of 34,000 tons as previously estimated. After September there was a renewed decline in the price and the year closed with rubber at $2\frac{3}{8}$*d.* in London. The average price of this year was lower than ever before or since, at $2\frac{5}{16}$*d.* in London and 7·01 cents in Singapore. The short-lived price rise had an immediate effect on wages, at any rate in certain districts. Estates found that their labour was drifting to smallholders who were either taking on wage-earners where they had previously tapped themselves, or were reopening holdings previously out of tapping. There was as yet no general rise in wages.

The mature estate area out of tapping began to be recorded during 1931; fairly complete figures are available for 1932. For Malaya as a whole the mature estate area out of tapping rose steadily from 274,000 acres at the end of January 1932 (19 per cent. of the tappable area) to 339,000 acres at the end of August (24 per cent.). On Penang Island the proportion reached 70 per cent. After August the trend was reversed and by the end of the year the area out of tapping had fallen slightly to 315,000 acres (22 per cent.). The reversal was primarily due to the rise in prices in July–August. A contributory cause was the announcement in July of a reduction in quit rents. The maximum rent (payable by about three-quarters of the estates in the F.M.S. and the S.S.) was reduced from four to two dollars per acre, a saving of about one-half cent per lb. This reduction often turned the scales in favour of a decision to carry on rather than close down and hand back some marginal areas to the government.

At last, in 1932, Malayan smallholders' output declined slightly by about 10 per cent. from the level of 1931. This was the result of the very low prices during the first half of the year and not of shortage of tappable bark. Monthly production had fallen to 12,500 tons in June and during the second quarter output was at the rate of 162,000 tons a year. There was a noticeable reaction to the price rise of July and August. By October seasonally-adjusted output had risen to 17,300 tons and remained fairly high throughout the remainder of the year. Production in 1932, as indeed throughout the slump, revealed quite clearly that Malayan smallholders' output, though not highly sensitive to changes in price, varied directly and not inversely with prices.[1]

The reduction in output during the first half of 1932 was the result of the suspension of tapping on poorly-yielding holdings mainly in the Straits Settlements, or on holdings more distant from the principal markets, for instance in parts of Pahang and Upper Perak. In 1932 the Malayan Department of Agriculture began to collect some scanty data (based on roadside observations) on the acreage of smallholdings out of tapping. In December of that year it was estimated that some 15–16 per cent. of the tappable smallholdings area in the F.M.S. was untapped. Many of the smallholdings out of tapping were Chettiar or Chinese holdings which had been worked with hired labour. Some Malay owners, who had previously employed tappers (usually share-tappers) and had to dispense with these workers, also suspended tapping during padi planting and harvesting. There was thus some transfer of labour, but not of land, from rubber to food production.

The opening months of 1933 saw a weakening of the market,

[1] Detailed production figures will be found in Statistical Appendix I.

the result partly of the high level of smallholders' exports and of a further deterioration in economic conditions in America. By February and March the low prices of the spring and summer of 1932 were almost reached again; the price declined to 2*d.* in London and to below 6 cents in Singapore. The closure of the American banks in March threw the markets into confusion. With the resumption of trading an improvement in conditions soon developed and continued throughout the year with only minor setbacks. The considerable increase in absorption, mainly in America, coupled with more substantial belief in the approach of restriction, were responsible for the change. The price touched 4*d.* in July and averaged slightly over 4*d.* during the last quarter.

The smallholders reacted promptly to the better prices. After March 1933 the area out of tapping decreased every month and output rose steadily. The estimates of the Department of Agriculture, though extremely rough, serve to illustrate the general trend. In March the smallholdings area out of tapping was estimated at 27 per cent. of the tappable area, in June at 13 per cent. and in September at 9 per cent. During the last quarter of the year smallholders' output was running at an annual rate of 256,000 tons, which was in excess of the rate of estate production, though the smallholdings area was much smaller than the estate area.

II

Much of what has already been said about the experience of the Malayan rubber industry during the slump applies equally to the N.E.I. The price movements were of course similar, though the N.E.I. producers did not enjoy the advantage conferred on the Malayan producers by the depreciation of sterling. In the N.E.I. there was a clear distinction between the estates in Java and those of the Outer Possessions, especially the East Coast of Sumatra.[1] At the end of 1929, of a total estate area of 1,353,000 acres, Java comprised 556,000 acres, the East Coast of Sumatra 563,000 acres and the rest of Sumatra 195,000 acres. Over two-thirds of the Java rubber estates combined rubber growing with the cultivation of another crop, usually coffee, sometimes tea. There is virtually

[1] East Coast of Sumatra is an administrative rather than a geographical term. It refers to an important residency, the leading centre of rubber, tobacco and palm-oil estates in the Outer Provinces of the N.E.I. (Outer Provinces or Possessions: all the islands of the N.E.I. except Java and Madoera).

no Asiatic estate rubber in the N.E.I.; with negligible exceptions the estate area is in European and American ownership.

The labour situation in Java differed considerably from that in the Outer Possessions or in Malaya, the estates having access to virtually unlimited supplies of labour from the native villages of this densely populated island; labour costs were generally the lowest of any of the large producing territories, though they fluctuated with the prosperity of the various agricultural industries, especially sugar. The proximity of native villages enabled the estates to increase or decrease their labour force at very short notice. The estates in the Outer Possessions relied largely on immigrant labour from Java and a substantial proportion of their labour force was still indentured in 1930. The estates had always been aware of the advantages of indentured labour but the reverse side of the picture became obvious during the depression, when wage reductions in other territories began in earnest and the Sumatran estates could not follow suit. The substantial repatriation expenses also acted as a heavy burden.

In 1929 it was widely believed that the estates in the N.E.I. would be in a better position to face a period of low prices than their Malayan competitors. The view that Malayan costs were excessive was given wide currency by Mr. Ormsby Gore's report,[1] which had, however, been written before the termination of the Stevenson scheme. Although the withdrawal of the scheme was followed by an increase in yields and fall in costs which largely eliminated the difference between estate costs in Malaya and the N.E.I., the outcry in Malaya about the disastrous prices at the end of 1929 confirmed the views of the competitive weakness of that territory. Moreover, the earlier start of the N.E.I. estates in bud-grafting was likely in the long run to enhance any advantage they already enjoyed.

Rubber production in the N.E.I. during the depression is summarised in Table II.

The price of rubber during the second half of 1929 was already considered too low by many estate producers in the N.E.I. The Anglo-Dutch recommendation for a tapping holiday in May 1930 was widely supported; it was observed by the N.E.I. Government's own estates. The Government was, however, emphatic in its refusal to support compulsory restriction. Statutory regulation was also opposed by a numerically small but powerful group of interests, mainly companies with large estates in Sumatra.

[1] *Report on a Visit to Malaya, Java and Ceylon during the Year 1928*, Cmd. 3235.

TABLE II

Production of Rubber in the N.E.I. and Price of Rubber, 1929–33

(Production figures in thousand long tons; prices in guilder cents per half-kilo)

	Estate Production			*Native production* [a]	*Total production*	*Batavia price of standard sheet*	*Singapore price of medium blankets*
	Java	*Outer Provinces*	*Total*				
1929	65·4	85·8	151·2	106·9	258·1	50·4	45·1
1930	65·4	85·5	150·9	89·0	239·9	30·5	26·1
1931	70·2	93·4	163·6	88·4	252·0	14·5	13·2
1932	58·7	89·9	148·6	61·5	210·1	7·8	6·8
1933	73·5	96·0	169·5	114·0	283·5	10·5	7·9

[a] For native rubber, exports have been taken as equivalent to output.
Detailed figures of output and price will be found in Statistical Appendix I.

With the exception of the tapping holiday, production was maintained at an even level throughout 1930 both in Java and the Outer Possessions, and only very few estates had ceased production by the end of the year. The reflux of labour from the Outer Possessions to Java had, however, already begun in June and it was to continue at varying rates for about three years. In 1931 output actually increased, reflecting the maturity of the areas planted during the Stevenson boom. The acreage out of production increased, and by the end of the year 11 per cent. of the mature estate area in Java and 8 per cent. in the Outer Possessions was out of tapping. In the summer some of the opponents of restriction began to waver when the London price fell below 3*d.* and eventually below 2½*d.* Yet the leading opponents of restriction stood firm as late as August when the London price had already fallen to 2¼*d.* All cost estimates, whether by interested parties or outside observers, show that many of the N.E.I. estates were now losing money heavily. Thus even when allowance is made for the low costs and favourable forward sales of these producers their tenacious opposition was surprising, especially as an uncompromising speech by the R.G.A. chairman in May 1931 made it clear that the chances of unilateral restriction by the British were very slender.

During 1932 estate output was much less regular than it had been in the previous year. It rose slightly in the early months, but after the further price fall in the spring of 1932 the acreage out of tapping increased rapidly and output declined. The area out of tapping in Java rose from 12 per cent. of the tappable acreage at the end of January to 44 per cent. by the end of August;

it declined again to 22 per cent. by the end of December as a result of the July–August improvement in prices. In the Outer Provinces the acreage out of tapping also increased, though less rapidly; from 9 per cent. at the end of January it rose to 21 per cent. by the end of August and fell only very slightly to 20 per cent. by the end of the year. The number of estates which had closed down rose from 169 at the end of January to 460 by the end of August. The smaller estates were generally the first to suspend operations.[1]

Labour forces were substantially reduced, though less readily in the Outer Possessions than in Java. In the former, estates hesitated to discharge their labourers because of the heavy repatriation expenses and the even heavier costs of recruitment. In June 1932 the cost of repatriating a Javanese man from the East Coast of Sumatra was the equivalent of about £4 and the cost of recruitment about £13. Many Sumatran estates had substantial reserve land, and the labourers were offered allotments for the cultivation of foodstuffs on condition that they would accept lower pay and work for half or three-quarters of the day on the estate. There were, nevertheless, large-scale dismissals, especially after the British departure from the gold standard. Estate employment in the Outer Possessions declined by about one-half between mid-1930 and the end of 1932. On the East Coast of Sumatra employed estate workers (on all plantations, not only on rubber estates) numbered 336,000 at the end of May 1930, whereas by the end of 1932 the number had declined to 176,000, the lowest figure since 1911. Estate wages in Sumatra were reduced by about 30–35 per cent. between the spring of 1930 and the end of 1932. This is only intended to indicate the order of magnitude; the actual changes were rather complex. In Java the estates could afford more easily to discharge their workers, and wages there declined by some 70–80 per cent. within a period of three years, which seems to have been the steepest fall which occurred in any of the rubber-producing territories.

In 1933 there was a substantial improvement. The trend of prices and output was steadily rising, while by the end of the year the area out of tapping had fallen to 11 per cent. of the mature estate acreage in Java and to 16 per cent. in the Outer Possessions. Throughout the early months of 1933 there was much agitation in

[1] The official N.E.I. figures suggest that the average size of estates on which tapping was suspended was very small, no doubt because the rubber acreage on the mixed rubber and coffee estates was smaller than that of the purely rubber-growing estates, and the mixed estates were the first to cease tapping.

favour of restriction; by the autumn its early advent was confidently expected.

III

The remaining producing territories can be dealt with more briefly. Their quantitative importance has always been much smaller and the factors influencing production and exports were on the whole similar to those in Malaya and the N.E.I. Mature acreage and export figures for all the territories reviewed are shown in Chapter 3, Table II, and Appendix B, Table I.

In Ceylon the general range of estate costs in 1929 was of much the same order as in Malaya; a lower level of wages reflected a lower productivity of labour. But Ceylon was in a weaker position than either Malaya or the N.E.I. to face competitive conditions and years of slump prices. A large proportion of the area had been planted in the earliest days of the industry. Forty per cent. of the 1930 acreage had been planted before 1911, compared with 14 per cent. for all territories. The estates were generally small, mainly because of the early development of the industry, and their fixed costs were heavy. Moreover, the effects of mistakes in plantation technique were particularly noticeable. The majority of the planters had gained their experience in tea and applied to rubber the methods of tea planting, notably clean weeding. The ensuing loss of top-soil was particularly marked in the hilly areas of Ceylon and much, often irreparable, harm was done. An appreciable proportion of the Ceylon rubber acreage, especially on the mixed rubber and tea estates, had been planted at too high altitudes, 1,500 feet and over; while the price remained high and the *status quo* was largely maintained by restriction, these estates could continue production but they were hardly fit for a competitive struggle. Tapping is also costly on hilly estates, as much of the tapper's time is taken up by walking from tree to tree.

There are no official figures of the output of estates or smallholdings, but from the production figures of a large number of Ceylon companies published in the *India-Rubber Journal* until the beginning of 1932, it appears that the proportionate fall between 1929 and 1931 in the output of these companies was greater than the decline in Ceylon exports, so that it seems probable that estate output was curtailed more than smallholders' production.

Some three-quarters or four-fifths of the 540,000-odd Indian estate labourers in 1929 were on tea estates; perhaps one-fifth were on rubber estates and a few thousand on coconut plantations.[1] Rubber estate wages were thus primarily dependent on conditions in the tea industry. In 1929 statutory minimum daily wages for Indian estate workers (men) were 54, 52 and 50 rupee cents on up-country, mid-country and low-country estates respectively. Reasonably efficient tappers normally earned appreciably more than the minimum rates. The procedure for changing the minima was more rigid than in Malaya. This fact, together with the less acute depression in tea, explains why estate wages in Ceylon fell less sharply than in Malaya, the reduction being about 35 per cent. between 1929 and 1933. Attempts were also made to pay only three-quarters of the minima for morning work. This practice was challenged in the courts by the official Agent of the Indian Government. In what was widely regarded as a test case final judgment was given against the estate, and the payment of three-quarters of the minimum rate for morning work was declared illegal. This judgment because of its effects on prime costs led to the closure of a number of estates and undoubtedly affected the volume of exports.

By 1930 there were frequent references in official documents to the plight of the industry and to the suspension of tapping on many estates. There are no exact figures of the area out of tapping, but according to the Director of Agriculture some 200,000 acres of mature rubber (about 40 per cent. of the tappable area) were untapped in Ceylon in 1932. It was officially estimated that the number of Indian estate labourers on rubber plantations declined by about one-half between the end of 1929 and the end of 1932. Production declined by about 40 per cent ; it was not possible to maintain output while halving the labour force as was done in Malaya and Sumatra.

In view of its several unique features and subsequent importance, the French Indo-China rubber industry, though of minor significance during the slump, deserves some detailed treatment. Rubber in French Indo-China has always been grown almost entirely by Europeans. As well as some very large units (similar to the leading Dutch and American estates on the East Coast of Sumatra), there were many comparatively small estates belonging to French civil servants and merchants and employees of industrial and commercial enterprises, but whether large or small they were financed

[1] No exact figures are available and the estimates are taken from one of the *Annual Reports* of the Controller of Indian Immigrant Labour, Ceylon.

by European capital and cultivated according to European methods. Some two-thirds or three-quarters of the planted area was still immature around 1929–30. Approximately one-third of the planted acreage was bud-grafted and most of this was immature.

The rubber is grown on two distinct types of soil, grey (*terres grises*) and red (*terres rouges*) ; around 1930 most of the mature rubber was on the former and almost the entire immature acreage on the latter. The yield per acre on grey soils averaged around 240–250 lb., against 350–360 lb. on red soils. Great hopes were attached to the future yields on red soils, especially from budded stock. These expectations were well-founded, as the late development of the industry enabled the French planters to avoid many technical mistakes the consequences of which were much in evidence in Malaya and in the N.E.I. This applied particularly to the layout of the estates, to the selection of planting material and to the methods of soil conservation.

At the onset of the slump, costs were still high and the reduction during the slump was less than in the other territories. The comparative immaturity of the tappable trees and the poor yields on the grey soils were the governing factors.[1] In April 1931 an average cost of 6·50 francs per kilo (5·9*d.* per lb. at the then rate of exchange) was assumed for the purpose of calculating the subsidy to the French Indo-China rubber industry designed to bridge the gap between slump prices and costs. This was reduced to 5 francs per kilo from April 1932 and to 4 francs from October 1932. At 2·7*d.* to one franc (to allow for the depreciation of sterling) these figures equalled 6·12 and 4·90 pence per lb. The French planters claimed that even on the best estates costs were higher than these figures. It was stated that on the best high-yielding estates, costs, including an allowance for depreciation but not for amortisation, were around 5 francs per kilo in 1932.

By the spring of 1930 the planters were agitating both for control

[1] Wage reductions, though substantial (of the order of 20–25 per cent. between 1929 and 1932), were not as severe as in Malaya or Java, as wages of indentured workers could not be reduced until the expiry of their contracts, and then only with official consent. Moreover, in view of the subsidy the inducements for cutting costs were not so great. M. Yves Henri, Inspector-General of Agriculture, French Indo-China, writing in 1932 in the official *l'Économie Agricole de l'Indo-Chine*, discussed costs in French Indo-China late in 1931. Converting his figures at the pre-September 1931 rate of exchange, they worked out at about 18 Straits cents per lb. for f.o.b. costs, half of which were direct costs. These were some 60 to 75 per cent. higher than Malayan costs at the time. All-in costs were stated to have been 25 Straits cents per lb., almost double that of most sterling companies. If the figures had been converted at the exchange rates ruling after September 1931 the difference would have been even greater.

measures and for direct government assistance. The position of French Indo-China differed from that of all other important producing territories in that on balance the French Empire was a substantial net importer of rubber, and thus the French Indo-Chinese product could be effectively assisted by protective measures. After months of intensive lobbying and competitive press propaganda by the colonial and the consuming interests, the original plan for a straight tariff was dropped and the industry assisted by a subsidy at rates varying with the market price of rubber. The subsidy was designed to bridge the gap between the market price and a calculated average cost subject to periodic revision. The maximum rate of subsidy was 3 francs per kilo on all rubber exported ; this was the rate during most of the slump and it was about two or three times the market price of rubber. As the subsidy was financed by an import duty on all rubber imported into France it was an instance of the ' levy subsidies ' familiar in British agriculture in the 1930's. Its advocates claimed that it had saved the industry from collapse, and it is undoubtedly true that without government assistance, the rubber industry of French Indo-China would have had to face great difficulties since, as well as having high costs, the estates were short of cash and were much in debt to the banks.[1] The heavy subsidy and the rapid increase in productive capacity explained the rise in exports during the slump.

In spite of the high costs a bright future for the industry was visualised by planters and officials alike. M. Henri estimated that by 1940 French Indo-China would export 60,000 tons of rubber, and this turned out to be an accurate forecast.

The other territories can be dealt with more summarily. In both Sarawak and Siam rubber was grown almost entirely by smallholders. In the incidence of processing charges and transport costs, as well as in the easy access of smallholders to food crops (especially in Siam), there was a resemblance to the larger N.E.I. native rubber-growing residencies, though unlike in the N.E.I., an appreciable proportion of the smallholdings area of Siam and Sarawak was in Chinese hands. A large proportion of the planted area was very young ; around 1930 almost three-quarters of the estimated planted acreage was immature and most of the mature area was also young. Under the impact of slump prices the industry operated much below capacity, but exports increased rapidly

[1] As well as the subsidy, loans on specially easy terms were granted to planters with young rubber, to enable them to bring their properties to maturity.

during the second half of 1933 in response to the slightly better prices.

In India (which at that time included Burma), though wages were much lower than in other rubber-producing countries except Java, the yields per acre were so low that producers were unable to compete at slump prices and were on the verge of being squeezed out. In 1931 production in Burma (where the industry was comparatively young and therefore had somewhat better ultimate competitive potentialities) was adversely affected by the revolt of that year.

The organisation of the rubber industry of British North Borneo, the relative importance of estates and smallholdings, the size of the estates and of the smallholdings, were closely similar to those of Malaya. The differences were the absence of Indian labour, the fairly heavy transport costs and the lower estate yields; the industry in British North Borneo was also younger than in Malaya.

CHAPTER 5

THE POSITION OF THE SMALLHOLDINGS

IT has already been shown that there was widespread misunderstanding of the conditions of production on smallholdings and that this resulted in complete failure to estimate the response of output to changes in price ; it was also to have significant results in the administration of rubber restriction. We shall now review some of the main elements in smallholders' production, chiefly during the slump, first in Malaya and then in the N.E.I., the two territories whose smallholdings industries are by far the most important.

I

The report of the enquiry into bark reserves, consumption and renewal on Malayan smallholdings which had been instituted in 1931, was published in January 1934.[1] The results were remarkable, though they aroused far less interest than they deserved. In a sense they were comparable to the discovery in the late 1920's of the enormous native rubber areas in the N.E.I.

The investigation was on a comparatively small scale. Ninety smallholdings [2] were examined and 100 trees measured and recorded on each. The Department of Agriculture was responsible for the investigation, and close liaison was maintained with the Rubber Research Institute of Malaya (R.R.I.M.) on technical matters. The report claims that the holdings investigated were thoroughly representative of the mainland of Malaya. Most of the averages of the report are arithmetic means ; where the mode and median are given in subsequent paragraphs they have been calculated from the data in the appendix to the report.

The average age of the trees was 16 years (arithmetic mean, mode and median were the same). The density of the stand was much greater than on estates of similar age ; the arithmetic mean was 211, the median and the mode were 193 trees per acre, against some 80–100 on estates.[3]

[1] *Bark Consumption and Bark Reserves on Small Rubber Holdings in Malaya*, Department of Agriculture, S.S. and F.M.S., Economic Series, No. 4, 1934.

[2] One hundred had been scheduled for investigation but ten had to be rejected after the work had progressed some way, and these were not replaced.

[3] The economics of the differing planting densities on estates and smallholdings are discussed in Appendix D.

The major surprises were provided by the figures of bark reserves and bark consumption, and by the proportion of diseased trees. Bark reserves were expressed in vertical inches on a quarter-circumference. It was found that they averaged 146 vertical inches on a quarter-circumference, or roughly half the bark below 6 ft. from the ground, which is generally taken as the limit of economic tapping on smallholdings. At the average rate of bark consumption on the holdings these reserves were sufficient for seven years and five months, even in the absence of any bark renewal. The lowest reserve was one of 2 years and 11 months, whilst the highest exceeded 16 years. The average for Johore was slightly higher than the general average; this was again interesting, in view of the fairly continuous tapping there throughout the Stevenson scheme. The rate of bark consumption was far lower than had generally been believed. This was partly due to the large percentage of the trees left untapped, even on holdings in production. On all holdings investigated 22 per cent. of all trees had been left untapped for twelve consecutive months, 9 per cent. for three to four months, 7 per cent. for five to six months, while the trees in production were tapped on the average only 20 days a month. On trees in tapping, bark consumption averaged 2·05 vertical *quarter* inches per month (median 1·91) and, allowing for the trees untapped, the overall average was 1·64 vertical *quarter* inches per month (median 1·56), and the *annual* rate of bark consumption thus averaged 4·92 inches (1·64 × 12÷4).[1] The rate of bark renewal appeared satisfactory, and frequently the bark was tappable again three years after removal. Whilst not enough was known of the history of the holdings to say with absolute certainty that the rate of bark consumption in the past had not exceeded bark renewal, it appeared that the forecasts of an early decline in output had been based on 'more or less casual observation, and holdings tapped on the systems which have been studied are not likely to suffer from an excess of bark consumption over bark renewal'.[2]

[1] As late as November 1931 the *M.A.J.* still wrote: 'Judging from returns so far in hand in connection with the bark consumption investigation, three *inches* is a usual width of bark removal during a *month*, although cases of two *inches* occur, as well as several cases of four and five *inches*, and a few of six *inches*.' My italics.

[2] *Bark Consumption and Bark Reserves on Small Rubber Holdings*, p. 42.

The 1932 *Annual Report* of the Chief Secretary to the F.M.S. Government, referring to the preliminary results of the enquiry, went as far as to say: 'Data so far collected justify the statement that the rate of bark renewal on the average smallholding in Malaya considerably exceeds the rate of excision.' The *Annual Report* of the Colonial Secretary, S.S., covering the same year, still maintained the contrary, though without referring to any evidence.

In view of the substantial reserves of tappable bark and the high current rate of renewal, this appeared to be a very conservative statement. There was no prospect of an exhaustion of bark reserves and no likelihood of a decline in output at any foreseeable time, except of course a reduction in response to very low prices. Not one single tree was found untapped owing to shortage of bark. Only eight out of 9,000 trees examined were found dead; they were killed by root diseases. The deadly root diseases which had taken such heavy toll on estates were almost entirely absent, though it had been taken for granted that they would be rampant on smallholdings.[1]

Output per acre averaged 477 lb. (median 468 lb.), ranging from 192 lb. to 889 lb. The investigation covered smallholdings owned by Chinese, Javanese and Indians, as well as by Malays. For Malay-owned smallholdings only the average was 481 lb. and the range from 241 lb. to 778 lb. The high minima are noteworthy.

These findings are eloquent comments on the statements about native methods which were being made with such assurance by the leaders of the industry, and it is perhaps not surprising that while the establishment of the smallholdings enquiry had been fully reported in the *Bulletin* of the R.G.A., as well as in its 1931 *Annual Report*, no reference to the results can be found in these publications.

Smallholdings were tapped perhaps somewhat more severely than estates in good times and bad (though the difference was not very great when allowance is made for the many untapped trees on smallholdings, where the resting of individual trees corresponds to the rotational resting of areas on estates), and observers believed that the rate of tapping would prove too heavy to be maintained. The analogy with estate conditions was, however, imperfect. Declining yields on estates had been largely due to soil deterioration, especially erosion resulting from clean weeding, excessive silt pitting and other mistaken methods of cultivation, and from the depletion of the stand, chiefly through root diseases, particularly *Fomes lignosus*. The smallholdings which are rarely clean weeded had kept their top soil which on estates had often been washed away by heavy rain; the dense cover, moreover, as well as supplying vegetable débris and improving the water-retaining capacity of

[1] The *India Rubber World*, May 1931, in a leading article, contrasted the disease-ridden smallholdings with the healthy, carefully-cultivated estates. It was argued that the danger of a widespread blight was ever present on smallholdings which, therefore, constituted an unreliable source of rubber. That the reverse was, in fact, true, was shown not only by the Malayan smallholdings enquiry, but also by similar later investigations in the N.E.I. and in Sarawak.

the soil, also helped to maintain a low temperature combined with high humidity near the ground and thus gave ideal conditions for bark renewal. Moreover, several years of research by the Pathological Division of the R.R.I.M. had by 1933 overthrown the accepted views on root disease, and had revealed that clean weeding actually contributed to the spread of *Fomes lignosus*. Altogether there was no difficulty in explaining the high level of bark reserves on smallholdings.

The smallholders prepared their rubber well, and the largest areas were not far from the most important markets, while by the 1930's communications in western Malaya were generally very good. These factors explain the comparatively small margins both between the Singapore quotations of standard quality ribbed smoked sheet and those of Chinese smoked sheet (Malayan smallholders' rubber smoked by Chinese dealers), and between the Singapore quotations and the up-country price received by the smallholder. While quotations in given districts often showed such wide ranges that it is difficult to speak of an average price, it appears that around 1930–32 the bulk of smallholders' rubber in Malayan up-country districts fetched only 1½–2½ cents per lb. less than the Singapore price for ribbed smoked sheet—a margin of usually five to ten per cent. In 1932 when Singapore prices were very low, the margin was only about one cent. Cash costs of production were very small; the Kuala Lumpur correspondent of the *Straits Times*, in an account of conditions in an extensive rubber-growing district in Selangor, reported that in the summer of 1932 the smallholders produced good dry rubber at a cost (excluding rent) of about one-half cent per lb. or less.

It is thus easy to see why the great majority of the smallholders found it worthwhile to tap their trees throughout the slump. According to the smallholdings enquiry, tapping tasks (the daily work of the tapper) on smallholdings averaged 390 trees, and these would be tapped in about 3½ hours. This light work for a short working day secured the owner adequate cash for his needs even in bad times, and sufficient money to owner and share-tapper when prices were better. During the worst period of the slump the smallholdings were often tapped by the dependants of the owner, who himself went out fishing or woodcutting. The holdings were thus tapped in most districts at all times except at the bottom of the slump, but this was not identical with overtapping as had been believed.

II

The sustained high rate of smallholders' production was also relevant to another much-debated question in Malaya: the country's dependence on imported food, principally on heavy rice imports. A Rice Cultivation Committee was set up in 1930 to investigate the main features of the rice situation in Malaya, as well as the possibilities of increasing the output of Malayan-grown rice. This investigation, too, brought to light some unexpected aspects of the Malayan economy. Though on the average Malaya imported some 60–70 per cent. of her rice requirements, it was found that the Malays were much less dependent on imported rice than had been believed; the indigenous population grew some 75–80 per cent. of its rice requirements. The Chinese and Indian population, who between then outnumbered the Malays, were entirely dependent on imports. The Rice Cultivation Committee, and in particular its chairman, the then Director of Agriculture, were very anxious to see Malaya more nearly self-sufficient. The various measures proposed to this end included the extension of Government irrigation schemes and the refusal to alienate land suitable for padi for other purposes. A tariff on imported rice was rejected, though it was introduced subsequently. During the slump there was an increase in Malayan rice production, but this was not fully maintained after 1932.

There were two major stumbling-blocks in the way of a substantial extension of rice cultivation. The Malay rulers definitely opposed the alienation of suitable padi-growing land to Chinese and to Indians. The relations between Chinese, Indians and Malays were satisfactory, but on this point the Malay rulers used to be adamant, and the British administrators did not press the matter until about 1940.

The other obstacle was the rational economic attitude of the rubber-growing smallholders, who appreciated that rubber was still the most profitable crop among the available alternatives, except for those producers who were furthest from the principal markets, or whose holdings were particularly poor-yielding. The price of rice and padi also fell sharply after 1929, and throughout the depression the great majority of the rubber-growing smallholders could obtain more rice with the proceeds of rubber than by growing it direct. This is suggested by the data summarised in the following tables, in which rubber and padi are compared first (Table I) as means of securing a given quantity of rice, and secondly (Table II) as cash crops.[1]

Table I

Comparison between Rubber and Padi as Means of Securing a Given Quantity of Rice, 1929–33

	Average yield of smallholders' rubber (lb. per mature acre) (1)	*Singapore price of ribbed smoked sheet (cents per lb.)* (2)	*Assumed average price received by smallholders (cents per lb.)* (3)	*Estimated gross proceeds per acre (dollars)* (4)	*Assumed expenses per acre (dollars)* (5)	*Estimated net proceeds per acre (dollars)* (6)
1929	485	34·5	30·5	150	8	142
1930	460	19·3	16·8	77	8	69
1931	445	10·0	8·0	36	4	32
1932	385	7·0	6·0	23	4	19
1933	465	10·2	8·7	40	4	36

	Average retail price of No. 1 Rangoon rice in Malacca (cents per gantang; 1 gantang rice = 8 lb.) (7)	Gantangs *rice obtainable with proceeds of rubber (6)÷(7)* (8)	*Average yield of cleaned rice* (gantangs *per acre*) (9)	*Rice equivalent of expenses* (gantangs) (10)	*Net yield of rice (9)–(10)* (11)	*Balance in favour of rubber in* gantangs *of rice (8)–(11)* (12)
1929	52	273	83	30	53	220
1930	46	150	73	30	43	107
1931	28	114	101	30	71	43
1932	22	86	110	30	80	6
1933	23	156	106	30	76	80

On the assumptions of these tables Malayan smallholders not too distant from the principal rubber markets could, even in 1932, obtain more rice indirectly by purchasing it with the proceeds of rubber growing than by producing it direct, and this in the worst year of the acutest rubber slump. In 1932 these producers could obtain about 690 lb. (86 *gantangs*) of cleaned rice with the proceeds of the yield of an acre of rubber against about 640 lb. (80 *gantangs*) of rice when grown direct. According to a Chinese spokesman in the F.M.S. Federal Council in 1933, the advantage in favour of rubber was even greater, rarely less than 100 lb. of rice per acre. The relationship was probably reversed in the spring of 1932 when

[1] The sources, assumptions and calculations underlying the data are reviewed in Appendix C.

the price of rubber was around 5 cents in Singapore. The figures are rough averages and conditions differed in various parts of the country, but the conclusions are valid for most of western and southern Malaya where smallholders were particularly dependent on rubber.

TABLE II

Comparison between Rubber and Padi as Cash Crops, 1929–33

	Average yield of padi per acre (gantangs) (1)	*Price per* gantang (*cents*) (2)	*Gross proceeds from padi* (*dollars per acre*) (3)	*Cash equivalent of cost of padi production* (*dollars*) (4)	*Assumed net proceeds from padi* (*dollars*) (5)	*Estimated net proceeds of rubber as Table II Col. 6* (6)	*Difference in favour of rubber* (*dollars*) (7)
1929	202	14·0	28	14	14	142	128
1930	180	13·0	23	13	10	69	59
1931	248	8·0	20	7	13	32	19
1932	272	7·5	20	6	14	19	5
1933	260	6·7	17	6	11	36	25

Much the greater part of the Malayan rice output is consumed by the growers, and padi is not usually marketed; the comparison attempted in Table I is thus of greater significance and also less hazardous than that of Table II.

The decline in the yield of rubber per mature acre after 1929 reflects, of course, the fall in total output divided by the mature area which actually increased during the slump; it does not mean that the poorest-yielding holdings continued in production.

The comparisons and calculations summarised in the foregoing tables refer to Malay-owned holdings only; there was no padi growing by other races in Malaya.

There were some other advantages in favour of rubber. The various items of expenditure in rice cultivation were so many causes of the indebtedness of the smallholder. The purchase of a plough, of a draught animal, or of manures, the maintenance of the family of the cultivator until the harvest, were all likely to send him to the moneylender-shopkeeper. The rubber-growing smallholder (though he may be in debt for other, irrelevant, reasons) does not require seasonal credit and only very rarely medium-term credit. Moreover, the weather risks which are negligible in rubber are substantial in padi growing. Again, even during the spring of 1932, rubber was always easily saleable, and the ubiquitous Chinese dealers seem to have been sufficiently numerous in all rubber-growing districts to ensure a fairly lively competition among buyers, which was by no means generally true for padi. Finally, rubber growing entails much less hard work than padi culture. Instead of toiling in the mud of a wet padi field sometimes for days on end, the Malay rubber-grower rarely had to work more than three or four hours a day, and could take a day or a week off whenever he wished. Padi growing is more seasonal than rubber cultivation and leaves the cultivator free for longer periods; over most of western and southern Malaya this advantage is more than offset by the poor yields of padi and by the much harder work required by padi cultivation. Rubber tapping is among the least exacting forms of work in tropical agriculture, especially where great care is not demanded.

Thus there were solid grounds for the smallholders' preference for rubber in western and southern Malaya, where padi yields are particularly poor, and with the improvement in the rubber market rice production lost much of the increase achieved during the slump. In October 1933 a small import duty on rice was imposed in the Malay States (not in the S.S.); the authorities preferred to call it a cess for the encouragement of local rice production. The measure was introduced against strong opposition by representatives of the Chinese and Indian communities, who pointed out that even though the rate of duty was comparatively small it would affect the cost of living of the poorer sections of the community, especially of the large Chinese families.[1] The effect on local rice production was negligible. The authorities subsequently admitted that the measure had been a mistake and it was withdrawn in 1935.

It is quite feasible that a rubber slump should coincide with a rice shortage, which would have a highly unfavourable effect on the terms of trade of Malaya. This actually happened in 1921–22, and the experience of those years was frequently cited in support of the rice tariff in 1933. It seems that a much better policy would have been the maintenance by the Malayan governments of a large revolving stock of rice. With an unfavourable rubber/rice price ratio the cultivation of rice (both as wet and dry padi) could be expanded sufficiently to render the Malay population self-sufficient within perhaps two years. Should the deterioration in the price ratio be permanent, and a reflection of a long-period decline of the rubber industry, a large-scale repatriation of Indian and Chinese labour would have to be accompanied by an expansion of food production by, and for, those who remain.

[1] To prevent smuggling from the S.S. into the Malay States, the import of rice into the latter was confined to a number of specific ports. The effect of this was to increase substantially the burden of the duty in certain districts. Rubber estates and rice dealers in the important rubber-growing districts of southern Negri Sembilan used to import their rice through Malacca; under the regulations following the imposition of the duty they had to import through Port Dickson, and the additional cost of transport exceeded the duty.

When the present writer visited Malaya in 1946 many smallholders were asked how they had managed to make a living during the great depression of the early thirties when the Singapore price of rubber at one time declined below 5 Straits cents (1½*d.*) per lb. The answer was generally that as the cost of living, especially the price of rice, had been very low at that time, it had been possible to make ends meet, though in some instances it had been necessary to rely to a greater extent than before on other activities such as fishing or hawking, or the production of *rattan* to supplement the income from rubber. But among smallholders, as distinct from unemployed or under-employed labourers, there was apparently little hardship even in 1931–32. The smallholders were unanimous in saying that they were glad to possess a rubber holding, and that in spite of its violent price fluctuations, rubber had proved a very satisfactory crop, highly suitable to their requirements.

The benefits of rubber growing for smallholders are also well understood by Malayan administrators familiar with conditions on smallholdings. They were emphasised to the present writer in Malaya by Mr. R. Boyd, who is at present Director of Co-operation, Malayan Union, and who has had over thirty years' experience in the country and whose knowledge of rural Malaya is impressive ; as well as by other administrators with decades of residence in rural Malaya. These administrators also pointed out that with the pre-war technique (in the absence of mechanisation) padi growing was a most thankless pursuit over most of central and southern Malaya. Yet since the early 1920's rubber production by smallholders has been strongly discouraged by the authorities in many different ways, and official pressure was always exercised in favour of food production and against rubber growing. Even when there was no ban on the alienation of land for rubber planting, the official policy was to discourage land alienation to smallholders for this purpose.

This policy was said to be justified by the excessive dependence of the country on the rubber industry and by the heavy reliance on imported food. While the concern of the authorities with the country's dependence on rubber is understandable (though it ought not to be overlooked that this dependence has been the source of Malayan prosperity and of the country's high administrative standards), it is questionable whether enforced food cultivation by smallholders was a desirable policy. Much of this enforced food cultivation was on entirely unsuitable soil which yielded a negligible contribution to the food resources of the country. In the course of a visit to Malaya in 1946 it was found that in some areas land had been alienated to smallholders on condition that it would be brought under padi, and this restriction has been maintained for many years, even though the yields were negligible or indeed purely nominal. It appeared that the authorities were more concerned with the acreage under padi than with the amount of food actually produced. In assessing the merits of such a policy it must also be remembered that the smallholders are much less dependent on purchased foodstuffs than are the hundreds of thousands of estate labourers. The Malay population is about four-fifths self-sufficient in rice; the urban population and the Indian and Chinese estate labourers have always been almost wholly dependent on purchased food, mostly on imported supplies. Enforced cultivation of foodstuffs might have been regarded as an insurance premium, but it is incongruous that this premium should be levied on the smallholders who have always grown a much larger proportion of their requirements than the estate labourers or the urban population. In short, insurance premia are levied on one section of the community as a partial safeguard against risks arising largely from the activities of the other sections. The ban on the alienation of land for rubber planting from 1922 to 1928 and again from 1930 to 1934 also pressed hardest on smallholders, who rarely have unplanted reserve land, while, as will be seen later, the planting provisions of rubber regulation threatened their very livelihood; all these were policies supported by or initiated by the Malayan authorities. At the same time the authorities were inclined to encourage estate production, which is based on large labour forces who grow virtually no food, and certainly less than the proprietors or tappers of smallholdings.

III

The native producers in the N.E.I. were much in the limelight in the late 1920's, chiefly as a result of the part they played in the failure of the Stevenson scheme. Even though some market circles tried at the time to minimise the importance of the rapid rise in the N.E.I. native exports after 1922, and what was perhaps more significant, the enormous areas planted by the natives since the mid-1920's, these matters clearly could not be concealed. The position of these producers merits some consideration, as it is clear from the latest acreage figures, as well as from other evidence, that they are likely to exercise a very considerable influence on the future of the industry.

Between 1924 and 1930 several investigations took place into the extent and conditions of the native rubber areas of Sumatra and Borneo which produce 99 per cent. of N.E.I. native rubber. Mr. T. J. Cumming's *Report on a Visit to Djambi* (1924), the *Reports of the N.E.I. Rubber Investigation Committee* [1] (1925–27), the Tayler-Stevens *Report to the R.G.A. on Native Rubber in the N.E.I.* (1929), Dr. Whitford's five *Reports on Plantation Rubber* (1928–34), all reviewed the conditions in the native rubber-growing areas. From 1928 till the outbreak of the Japanese war the Division of Agricultural Economics in the N.E.I. Department of Agriculture issued periodic *Reports on Native Rubber Cultivation in the Netherlands East Indies*. These reports and Dr. Whitford's observations were perhaps the most valuable. In addition to these more or less systematic investigations, a number of planters, business men and casual visitors recorded their impressions in papers like the *Straits Times* or the *Deli Courant*. While some of these reports embodied the results of much and often careful work and served to give a fairly good general picture of the native rubber situation, they were of very limited value for estimating either the planted area or future supplies. The area was still unsurveyed, and it was plainly impossible for one or two men to estimate the rubber acreage in a residency like the Western Division of Borneo, which is larger than England and Wales.[2] The investigators had to estimate the planted area in indirect and devious ways, on the basis of exports, assumed yields per acre, proportion of the area untapped, and the ratio of mature to total acreage. Such estimates were bound to be extremely hazardous.

As well as sheer physical distance, the planting technique of the natives (discussed below, pp. 67–68) enhanced the difficulties of observers. The immature trees were barely distinguishable from the surrounding jungle.[3] Most of the area was planted

[1] This was a mixed committee of British and Dutch planters and N.E.I. officials, who carried out a series of investigations in the N.E.I. native rubber-growing districts.

[2] The large rubber-growing residency of South and East Borneo is several times bigger but there the rubber is more concentrated, while in Western Borneo it is widely scattered.

[3] This was explicitly stated in the *N.R.I.C. Report on Djambi*. 'Rubber only a few years old is barely recognisable, because the land after the padi harvest is simply abandoned. *Lalang* occurs sporadically only, so that the young rubber develops among secondary forest growth, so-called *blukar*, and one may even pass a young rubber field without noticing it. Anyone who has spent a day in such environment is cured of any intention to have the young fields surveyed, or the trees counted. The young trees are

after 1924, so that the investigators during the late 1920's had a particularly difficult task in estimating the acreage of young rubber. The estimates of the proportion of the mature area tappable by local labour in any given residency were also highly conjectural. These were based on assumptions of the total mature area or of the number of trees, the daily task of tappers, the number of labourers (generally estimated by dividing by 4½ the number of inhabitants according to the last population census), and of the number of tapping days on an area in production. Even on the last point views diverged widely; estimates by investigators of the Native Rubber Investigation Committee ranged between 180 and 270 days a year.

While views on the extent of the planted area at the close of the 1920's ranged from about one to two-and-a-quarter million acres, there was greater agreement on potential capacity. The N.E.I. authorities estimated that it would be about 350,000 tons by 1934, while Dr. Whitford put it at 375,000 tons for that year. Tayler and Stevens thought that it would reach 300,000 tons by the mid-1930's. Subsequent events revealed all these to have been substantial understatements. All were agreed that very large areas would reach maturity by the mid-1930's.[1]

A large though uncertain proportion of the N.E.I. native rubber was planted as a by-product of rice cultivation. For centuries past the natives of Sumatra and Borneo had cleared plots of land year by year from virgin or secondary jungle, and after taking off one or two rice crops allowed the clearing (*ladang*) to revert to secondary jungle, which in turn might be cleared again a few years later. This system was retained after the advent of rubber except that the latter was frequently planted together with the padi. After the second rice crop was harvested the rubber was left alone until it became tappable. The cost of adding rubber to the existing system of cultivation was negligible in terms of cash or effort. In some areas, of which the most important was the Oeloe

left alone for five to eight years; the age at which tapping is started depends on the market price of rubber and on the question whether or not older fields are available for tapping.'

Lalang (*Imperata arundinacea*) is a dangerous spear-grass, common in the secondary jungles of Malaysia. *Blukar* is any kind of secondary jungle.

[1] 'All' still excluded some of the most influential R.G.A. leaders, one of whom said in an important address in February 1929 that he was very sceptical of the grandiose figures of the N.E.I. native rubber which had become current. Subsequent events revealed that the 'grandiose figures' current in the late 1920's substantially understated the N.E.I. native potential output, and greatly over estimated the supply price of native rubber.

Soengei district of South and East Borneo, rubber was planted on its own and not on rice clearings. The Native Rubber Investigation Committee estimated that in the mid-1920's it cost about £5–£6 to bring to maturity with hired labour an acre of native rubber in the Outer Possessions. This was a notable contrast with the capital costs of the estates which at that time were about £60–£80 per acre.

Planting was generally very dense, with initial stands of 300–500 trees an acre against 120–180 on European estates, which were, moreover, subsequently greatly thinned out. The dense stand, apart from ensuring high yields per surface unit, also entailed favourable conditions for cultivation by smallholders: lower ground temperature, humid atmosphere, ample supply of vegetable débris and maintenance of soil fertility. These were indicated by the Malayan smallholdings enquiry; in the N.E.I. the stands were even denser than those on Malayan smallholdings. The dense stand also resulted in heavy shade two or three years after planting; the rubber tree is shade-resisting while most of its competitors and enemies are not, so that the dense planting helped to give the rubber a good start.[1]

There was at the time much ill-informed comment on the ravages of disease in native holdings in Sumatra and Borneo, very similar to that about the conditions on Malayan smallholdings. 'Rampant root diseases' were referred to particularly freely. The available evidence was by no means conclusive. The findings of the Native Rubber Investigation Committee on conditions in the different residencies around 1925–26 were conflicting. According to the *Report on Tapanoeli* over 75 per cent. of the trees were diseased; the investigators of the neighbouring residency of the West Coast of Sumatra thought that the figure was around 10–15 per cent. The views expressed in the interesting *Report on the Western Division (Pontianak) of Borneo* are worth quoting. It will be noted that they were at variance with the opinions then current

[1] Mr. Rowe (*op. cit.*, p. 65) thought that the very dense stand of native rubber might, and indeed was likely to, shorten the productive life of the smallholdings as compared with estates. This seems doubtful, especially when the heavy casualties on the estates from root diseases and loss through wind damage are allowed for. As yet there is little evidence on the relative life expectations of estates and smallholdings; what there is, in Malaya at any rate, shows that the survival rate of smallholdings is as good, if not better, than that of the estates; and even if the reverse were true it would not follow that this was due to the density of the native stands.

It appears that the economics of planting density, which are different for estates and smallholdings, have not always been fully understood. The matter is discussed in Appendix D.

but were much in accordance with the subsequent findings of the Malayan smallholdings enquiry: 'A curious difference between fields planted and maintained on principles of European management and fields planted and kept in the native way is clearly visible. The European method is one of wide planting, often made wider still by subsequent thinning-out and formerly also combined with clean weeding. The result has been rapid and thorough decomposition of the organic matter in the soil, resulting in its subsidence, leaving the old lateral main roots bare often up to 2 feet over the new soil surface, and the final result of course is a great number of trees standing aslant or tumbling down. The native as a rule plants 10 by 10 feet and leaves the undergrowth under the rubber undisturbed. *Lalang* does not occur on this soil, and so the undergrowth consists of harmless weeds and *Hevea* seedlings. The effects of this method may be seen in 20-year-old native fields where practically no gaps occur and the trees stand upright.'

In view of the findings of the Malayan smallholdings enquiry and of the subsequent performance of N.E.I. native producers it can be safely said that some of the early investigators much over-estimated the ravages of disease on the N.E.I. native holdings, while possibly they also under-estimated the great recuperative powers of the *Hevea*, which is believed to be the hardiest domesticated tree.

It was, however, generally agreed that much of the new planting of the 1920's should be regarded as replacement planting. According to the *N.R.I.C. Report on the East Coast of Sumatra*, '... there is already a surplus of trees there, but new fields are still being planted, either as reserves or substitutes for the old fields, or in the hope of selling them later on. Considering the enormous bark consumption, the planting of new fields as reserves is a wise policy and necessary for permanent maintenance of native rubber growing in this district.'

So far native holdings have survived much longer than had been expected, but replacement will eventually become necessary, for reasons of technical progress, if for no other. In judging the merits of new planting as a form of replacement it should be noted that not only is almost unlimited land available in most districts of Sumatra and Borneo, but also that rubber takes virtually nothing out of the soil, and probably nothing at all which under native conditions would not be put back through decomposed leaves, branches and twigs. In the words of the *N.R.I.C. Report on Western Borneo*: 'There can be no objection against the planting of rubber on abandoned *ladangs*, either in the coastal plain or in the hilly country. Even if rubber cultivation would no longer pay it would be better to have the land under *Hevea* than under *lalang*. In the coastal plain on neglected land the *Hevea* is simply absorbed as a forest tree in the quickly-growing forest vegetation, so that after a couple of years it is sometimes hard to rediscover the *Hevea*.'

This important feature of rubber cultivation (which raises important issues of planting policy, as we shall see in our discussion of restriction) should be clearly borne in mind in considering the merits of rubber as a native crop, or of the extensive cultivation methods in Sumatra and Borneo. The leading technical experts are unanimous in emphasising the very small demands of the rubber tree on plant food. As Dr. W. B. Haines, formerly Head of the Soils Division of the R.R.I.M., put it: 'Our knowledge of the effects of fertilisers has been mainly built up from experience with seasonal crops. These usually end in the removal of a large amount of plant food from the soil in the harvested crop. The case of a rubber plantation offers a very striking contrast. The crop is not seasonal, nor does it remove permanently any very appreciable quantity of plant foods. The natural cycle of changes is that of a forest in which a considerable proportion of the available food passes round in a continuous cycle from the soil to the tree and from the tree back again to the soil in the form of leaf-fall. The necessity of manuring arises, therefore, not so much from the necessity to renew losses taken away by the crop, as from the needs caused by a break in the natural forest cycle.' [1]

With few exceptions the rubber-growing districts of the Outer Possessions are sparsely populated and labour has generally been regarded as the limiting factor on output. During the 1920's some of the native districts depended on labour from Java or from other parts of the Outer Possessions, and it was estimated that by 1932, when the 1925–26 plantings came into bearing, local labour would be insufficient to tap the mature area in all the important districts with the exception of Oeloe Soengei in Borneo. It was thought that the substantial deficit of labour in the Outer Possessions as a whole could be bridged only by heavy immigration from Java. These estimates did not prove altogether reliable, and in many important districts a large proportion of the mature area, and possibly the entire acreage, could, in fact, have been tapped by local labour in 1933 or 1934. In a few districts the migrant labour of the 1920's had settled. The number of owner-tappers had also

[1] *M.A.J.*, May 1930. This is only one of many similar authentic statements.

increased considerably through the acquisition by local labourers of holdings of their own. Again, in certain areas, notably Tapanoeli and the West Coast of Sumatra, the younger generation of the local population gradually took to tapping. The great reduction in government expenditure on public works also released labour for tapping. The experience of the depression years, which was confirmed by the trend of exports in 1934–36, in 1941 and again in 1946, suggests strongly that the dependence on outside labour was greatly overstated.

Over-estimates of the supply price of labour were partly responsible for the discomfiture of the forecasts of the supply price of N.E.I. native rubber, reviewed in Chapter 3. The Native Rubber Investigation Committee thought in terms of daily earnings of 50 guilder cents to one guilder as necessary to secure hired tappers in the most important native rubber-growing residencies.[1] In 1931–33 earnings of 10–15 cents by hired tappers were frequent and instances of earnings of 6–10 cents were noted in the official *Reports on Native Rubber Cultivation.* Admittedly most of the early estimates assumed that the Javanese worker could earn 60 cents or more in Java, where by 1932 earnings had fallen to 15 cents or less; but even allowing for this factor, it appears that the earnings needed to ensure a supply of tappers (including owner-tappers) had been greatly overstated. This resulted partly from under-estimates of local labour supplies, and also from the failure to allow for the relative attractiveness of rubber tapping as against other forms of agricultural work; the short hours, compared with a much longer working day in picking pepper or collecting jungle produce, were an important attraction.

The supply price of labour was not the only uncertain factor in the supply price of N.E.I. native rubber. There was also much variety in the payment received by the native for his rubber, and in

[1] The Tayler-Stevens report, published in November 1929, expressed this view about the labour position in Djambi: 'It seems doubtful if this residency has ever produced the maximum possible quantity of rubber, because of lack of sufficient labour . . . From all the information we were able to collect it appears very improbable that sufficient immigrant labour would be attracted unless the price of rubber rose at least to 2*s.* per lb.' An official *N.E.I. Native Report* which reviewed the situation in Djambi early in 1932 estimated that tapping would start on a large scale at a price equivalent to 3*d.* to 3½*d.*, landed London (depreciated sterling), while by the middle of the year the figure was reduced still further. Even in the autumn of 1930 experts thought in terms of a London price of 1*s.* or over as the minimum necessary to ensure large supplies of labour in the native districts. By October 1931 the Registrar-General of Statistics, S.S. and F.M.S., returning to Singapore from a visit to Palembang, stated that a London price of 4*d.*–6*d.* would draw enough labour to Palembang to ensure the full tapping of the mature area of that residency, the largest native rubber-growing area in Sumatra.

the spread between the Singapore price and that paid in the interior of Sumatra and Borneo. Barter trade was still widespread in the early 1930's, the Chinese dealers paying for the rubber with imported goods. Thus although the trader frequently paid more than the nominal market price for the rubber, payment was in imported commodities on which he made a large profit. Yet again, the dealer might make an advance to the smallholder, usually in textiles or other imported goods, and charge very high interest in terms of rubber.

The view taken by the natives about the maintenance of a given price also influenced short-period supplies considerably. A London price of 7*d.* in the autumn of 1922 called forth heavy exports from Borneo after the price had been hovering around that figure for several months. In 1926 a price of over 2*s.* in the early spring resulted in a sharp contraction of exports as it followed a period of prices of 3*s.* and 4*s.*, and the native producers had not yet readjusted their ideas to the lower levels and were expecting a return of the higher prices.

The quality of N.E.I. native rubber had greatly improved since the mid-1920's, but it was still sold in slabs or lumps which had to be re-milled before shipment to consuming centres, and these processing charges introduced another variable. Again, most of the rubber came from inland districts and had to bear some transport costs and middlemen's charges. These cost items fluctuated considerably both with general economic conditions and with the cost of imported commodities, while competition between local steamship companies and other transport enterprises often had important repercussions. In 1924–25 a competitive freight war between two lines on the Pontianak-Singapore run brought about within a year a fall in freight rates equivalent to over one Straits cent per lb. of dry rubber, equal to one-half or one-third of the freight from Singapore to London.

In 1929 Dr. Whitford estimated at 7–8 dollar cents per lb. the spread between the New York price of re-milled native rubber and that paid in the principal native districts of Borneo and Sumatra. With the average New York price of 1932 (3·4 cents) even one-half of the 1929 margin would have resulted in a negative value for rubber in the interior of Sumatra and Borneo. By that year, however, the spread had been reduced to 2½ dollar cents (2 cents by the second half of the year), a remarkably low figure as it included transport costs from the interior of Borneo and of Sumatra to New York via Singapore, as well as re-milling costs in Singapore and landing charges there and in New York. Middlemen accepted much-reduced remuneration and gave nearly full weight for rubber. Transport and re-milling costs declined sharply. In the barter trade the price of imported textiles in particular had fallen greatly, enabling the Chinese dealers to offer goods to the native producers on terms which made it worth the latter's while to continue to produce rubber. The competition of Chinese dealers in the Outer Possessions and of re-millers in Singapore struggling to keep open their mills also served to reduce the margins between the Singapore and the local prices. Moreover, a gradual narrowing in the margin between ribbed smoked sheet and re-milled blankets also helped to maintain native shipments.

The sharp reduction in the remuneration accepted by the owner, tapper and middleman, and the general narrowing of the spread between the world price and the local prices, were analogous to the sharp fall in costs which enabled so many estates to continue production throughout the slump ; it was another aspect of the income deflation which occurred throughout the rubber-producing territories. At the same time many of the pre-1930 items in the costs of transport, distribution and processing had been unduly high, and even with a return to prosperity through the N.E.I. these could not be expected to be re-established ; they had been on a temporary and unstable basis before 1930.

To summarise the position, little was known of the planted acreage or its age distribution, or about labour supplies, while the plasticity of costs and the very sharp fall in alternative earnings and in the cost of living were not allowed for. There is thus no difficulty in explaining the failure of the estimates of N.E.I. native rubber production, especially as in many instances wishful thinking was a weakness additional to the insufficiency of the data.

PART II

THE ESTABLISHMENT OF INTERNATIONAL REGULATION

CHAPTER 6

RESTRICTION NEGOTIATIONS AND THE INTERNATIONAL AGREEMENT OF 1934

I

IN 1928 Mr. Ormsby Gore (now Lord Harlech), then Parliamentary Under-Secretary of State for the Colonies, noted and deprecated a widespread tendency in the rubber industry to look to restriction for a solution of all difficulties, and to shelter behind output control as a substitute for competitive reduction of costs.[1] His remarks evoked much protest in Malaya but they were confirmed by the widespread demands for a re-imposition of restriction almost immediately after the end of the Stevenson scheme in November 1928 and well before the onset of the slump.

The first move came in 1929 from a group of Dutch producers, and early in 1930 an Anglo-Dutch Liaison Committee was formed by the British and Dutch producers' associations to consider ways and means of meeting the situation. The tapping holiday recommended for May 1930 was widely accepted and observed, even by opponents of compulsory restriction. The smallholders tapped as before. The tapping holiday was generally recognised to have been a failure. It was not until the summer of 1933 that the discussions which were to lead to the international regulation agreement were started. In the intervening period there were frequent discussions, both official and unofficial, but these always proved abortive, chiefly on account of the unwillingness of the N.E.I. authorities to apply a statutory restriction scheme. Some Dutch estate producers no doubt hoped that the British would again adopt

[1] 'The rubber industry is not yet on a stable basis of costs but is faced with revolutionary discoveries that may treble the output and halve the cost per lb. If this possibility is realised many of the older and less progressive estates will be doomed to extinction . . . There is an attitude of mind unfortunately too prevalent on the directing boards of some companies which makes light of this possibility, ignores scientific research and looks to Government for assistance in fixing prices on what the least efficient estates consider a reasonable level.' *Report on a Visit to Malaya, Java and Ceylon during the Year 1928*, p. 148.

an independent restriction scheme, as they had done in the Stevenson scheme; although this hope was not without some foundation, British official opinion, as well as that of the more far-sighted producers, was clearly against such a course. The decisive factor was that the N.E.I. authorities repeatedly stated that as there was no land registration, restriction of native production was impossible, while control by means of a special tax on native exports would be inequitable and was therefore unacceptable. They also emphasised categorically that control of new planting by native producers was impossible. A communiqué in March 1932 announcing the breakdown of discussions which had been in progress for four months appeared to mark the final failure of restriction negotiations.

In 1933 a change in the official Dutch attitude became apparent. There were various statements, from the Prime Minister, the Governor-General of the N.E.I., and others, to the effect that the N.E.I. administration had revised its views and would favour a practicable regulation scheme. Tentative Anglo-Dutch discussions were accordingly resumed in the summer of 1933, after the Dutch producers' association (the International Association for Rubber and Other Products) had appointed a strong Rubber Restriction Committee. The British producers were somewhat cautious and it was only during the autumn, after the R.G.A. had also constituted a Rubber Regulation Committee, that discussions entered a more serious phase. While it was agreed at the outset that the adherence of all producing territories of actual or potential importance was necessary and the smaller producing countries were approached at an early stage, the actual decisions on the principal features of rubber regulation were taken at a few meetings of two British and two Dutch representatives of the largest plantation enterprises.

In certain directions the range of the discussions was narrowly circumscribed. The British insisted on prohibition of new planting. For administrative and political reasons the Dutch would consider only a quota scheme and were in favour of some new planting. As a compromise, permission for a substantial amount of replanting (uprooting of existing plantations and their subsequent replanting) was coupled with the prohibition of new planting (planting on land not carrying rubber at the inception of the scheme). It was agreed to permit the replanting of a total of 20 per cent. of the existing acreage, with a maximum of 10 per cent. in any one year during the currency of the proposed scheme, which was expected to be five years. An assumed average of 4 per cent. of the planted area was thus the limit of replanting each year; this was thought to be the approximate equivalent of the rate of depreciation of the planted acreage. The latter was estimated at over eight million acres and the limit of replanting set at 1·6 million acres. As we shall see, this decision was to be of crucial importance, and in spite of its superficial equity it was soon to become apparent that it endangered the very existence of the smallholding industry.

The basis of the settlement of territorial quotas required early decision. Potential capacity was too uncertain and vague, while acreage figures were insufficient, and it was decided to turn to past performance as a starting-point. The choice was largely confined to one or more of the years 1929–32, since before 1929 the Stevenson scheme was still in operation, while export figures for the whole of 1933 were not available when the discussions began. Some argued for 1929 exports, as in that year the industry was supposed to be working near capacity; 1932 exports were proposed by others, as that was the year of lowest prices and exports would thus indicate the competitive strength of the various territories. This latter suggestion was unacceptable to several producing territories whose exports had almost vanished in 1932, but were rising again in 1933. The average of the annual exports of the years 1929–32 was finally adopted, and this became known as the 'permanent basis' of each territory.

Provision had also to be made for very large areas planted after 1925 (tôtalling about 40 per cent. of the planted acreage in 1933) which were still immature in 1929–32. It was agreed that quotas should be the aggregate of the permanent basis and of agreed allowances for known immature areas. The following table shows the scale of yields adopted for acreage immature in the basic years:

TABLE I

Assumed Yield of Areas Immature in 1929–32 for the Calculation of Immature Allowances under the Regulation Scheme

(lb. per acre)

	Seedling	*Budded*
5-year-old rubber . . .	60	400
6 " " " . . .	180	600
7 " " " . . .	400	1,000
8 years old (fully mature) . .	500	1,200

As an average of several years had been adopted as the permanent basis, the determination of the point from which allowances for immaturity on these scales were to be calculated was a matter of agreement. A table of allowances was adopted which would have been applicable if 1932 exports had been chosen as the permanent basis instead of the average of 1929–32; thus areas planted before 1925 received no allowances, being regarded as fully mature for the purposes of this calculation, while 1926 and 1927 plantings (five and six years old in 1932) were assumed to have produced appreciable yields during the years included in the permanent basis. This particular method of calculation had certain obvious drawbacks. It assumed that young rubber was included in the permanent basis to the following extent:

Seedling:	1925 plantings	400 lb. per acre
	1926 ,,	180 ,, ,, ,,
	1927 ,,	60 ,, ,, ,,
Budded:	1925 ,,	1,000 ,, ,, ,,
	1926 ,,	600 ,, ,, ,,
	1927 ,,	400 ,, ,, ,,

Young rubber might have given these yields in 1932 but obviously could not have given them on the average throughout the period 1929–32, as 1927 rubber, for instance, was only two years old in 1929. Thus any territory with an exceptionally large percentage of 1925–27 rubber would be penalised. Again, in certain territories notably India and Burma, rubber matures more slowly and 1923 and 1924 plantings, which were not yet fully mature in 1929–32, received no immature allowances, though they made little contribution to the permanent basis of these territories.

The outstanding difficulty in computing quotas was that of the N.E.I. native area, for which no acreage figures were available, let alone data of age composition. The same applied to Sarawak and Siam, which were, however, less important. It was realised that the N.E.I. Government would reject a scheme which did not give some recognition to the productive capacity of the native areas planted after 1925. Although their actual extent was not known, all observers agreed that they were enormous, and that about three-quarters of the total area had been planted since 1924. The method of calculating the quota by reference to the permanent basis and immature allowances was discarded in this instance; instead, it was decided that throughout the period of restriction the N.E.I. native quota should bear the same ratio to the N.E.I. estate quota as did native to estate exports in 1929, when the ratio was 71½ per cent. Native exports would thus be a constant proportion $\frac{71\frac{1}{2}}{171\frac{1}{2}}$ of total N.E.I. exports. This was more favourable to the native producers than any other of the years 1929–32.

At first sight this appeared to be generous treatment of the N.E.I. natives whose output had contracted after 1929. The reverse was in fact true. Some three-quarters of the N.E.I. native area had been immature in 1929, as against one-quarter of the estate area, so that quotas based on the 1929 output ratio were quite inadequate. Native exports were rising very rapidly in 1933 with London prices around 3½*d.*, and it was evident that the prices visualised under restriction would draw out practically the entire potential native output. The quota was less than one-half of the potential native output as estimated by Dr. Whitford, by Tayler and Stevens and by the N.E.I. Department of Agriculture; the basic quotas of all other major producers approximated to their potential capacity, even though they had not been computed on that basis. The Dutch negotiators (representatives of the two largest Dutch plantation companies) agreed, however, that the British acceptance of an N.E.I. native quota of 71½ per cent. of the estate quota was a concession, and in return they consented to a small *ex gratia* allowance to be added to the Ceylon quota. This was to compensate that territory for the adoption of a permanent basis disliked there, and also to placate a difficult State Council. They also accepted a re-calculation of Malayan exports for 1929–32 which, in practice, resulted in an *ex gratia* allowance, rising from slightly under 5,000 tons in 1934 to over 11,000 tons in 1938; this was to provide for additional allowances to Malayan smallholders.

Agreement on the essential principles of the scheme was reached by the British and Dutch representatives in October 1933, and the draft proposals were forwarded to the N.E.I. Government. On the British side the Colonial Office was kept informed of the progress of the negotiations. The consent of most of the local estate producers' associations was secured within a few weeks. The Sarawak Government was also approached at an early date and its adherence secured; a quota calculated roughly on the same basis as for other territories was offered and accepted, though in the absence of reliable acreage statistics its calculation was necessarily approximate.

The inclusion of French Indo-China was regarded as essential by the British and Dutch administrators and by responsible unofficial opinion in London and Amsterdam.[1] The French Empire was still on balance a substantial net importer of rubber, and a regulation

[1] Sir Cecil Clementi, Governor of the Straits Settlements, addressing the Legislative Council in October 1933, stated that the adherence of French Indo-China was a necessary prerequisite of regulation. This was freely challenged in the press (among others by a prominent representative of local planting interests) on the grounds that the climate

scheme, while beneficial to the planters and to the French treasury, would worsen the French balance of payments. Special provision had to be made to secure French participation, and the terms agreed with the French planters and their government provided for virtually unrestricted exports from French Indo-China in exchange for acceptance of the prohibition of new planting. This was to guard against uncontrolled expansion of the planted area such as had destroyed the Stevenson scheme.

The participation of Siam was also deemed necessary. Her exports were still comparatively small but the possibility of heavy new planting was an obvious danger ; moreover, the non-adherence of any rubber-producing territory would have put a substantial premium on the illicit export of rubber from the participating countries. The Siamese Government was approached soon after the beginning of the negotiations with an offer of a quota calculated on the standard method,[1] guaranteed minimum exports and alone among the participating territories a limited amount of new planting. The Siamese authorities eventually accepted these terms in April 1934, subject to ratification by the People's Assembly.

II

The British authorities had made it clear to the producers that they would not consent to the proposed scheme without definite assurances from the N.E.I. Government that its provisions could be fully implemented. These assurances were slow in forthcoming. Although the main proposals had been transmitted to the N.E.I. Government in October 1933, by March of the following year the British representatives were still not informed of the methods by which the N.E.I. Government proposed to control native exports and planting.

The slow progress of the negotiations with Siam and the delay of the N.E.I. authorities protracted the negotiations beyond expectation. The anticipation of restriction, together with the improvement in absorption, gradually raised the London price from 3½*d.* per lb. in mid-1933 to 5*d.* by March 1934. The better prices resulted in a rapid increase in the exports of certain producers, of

of French Indo-China was unsuitable for rubber growing on any scale and that the territory would never become an important rubber producer. Seven years later French Indo-China exported some 65,000 tons a year at lower costs than those of the estates in Malaya or the N.E.I., and possessed huge areas for expansion.

[1] In the absence of official acreage statistics immature allowances were calculated from acreage figures based substantially on Dr. Whitford's estimates.

whom the N.E.I. natives were the most important. Their exports had been rising throughout most of 1933 and in March 1934 were 20,000 tons against 4,000 tons in March 1933; by April–May they were running at an annual rate of over 300,000 tons. The Malayan smallholders also increased their output rapidly. Their 1933 production had exceeded all previous figures at 220,000 tons; during the last quarter of that year, with a London price of just over 4*d*., their output was at the annual rate of 260,000 tons, and in the few months preceding the introduction of restriction it rose to 300,000 tons. This was substantially in excess of estate production, though the mature area of the smallholders was only about two-thirds of that of the estates. During the twelve months up to the end of May 1934 Malayan smallholders' output was the equivalent of about 520–530 lb. per mature acre, the highest yield of any substantial class of producer ever recorded.

The following table summarises the output of the four largest classes of producer during the months preceding the introduction of restriction.

TABLE II

Output [a] of Certain Classes of Producer, January–May 1934

(Seasonally adjusted figures; long tons)

	Malaya		*N.E.I.*		*London price (pence per lb.)*
	Estates	*Smallholdings*	*Estates*	*Natives*	
January . .	19,800	17,400	13,100	15,300	4·4
February . .	23,600	18,800	15,800	17,600	4·9
March . . .	22,100	24,000	17,600	21,300	5·2
April . . .	22,200	23,500	17,000	24,400	5·9
May . . .	22,000	26,800	16,400	29,400	6·4

[a] Exports for N.E.I. natives.

Exports from the smaller producing territories, notably Siam, Sarawak and India, also rose rapidly, but their quantitative importance was comparatively small. From March 1933 to March 1934, Sarawak rubber exports rose from 600 to 1,400 tons, Siamese exports from 300 to 1,300 tons, and Indian exports from 400 to 1,400 tons.

The high rate of smallholders' production was significant for several reasons. It should have disposed finally of the idea that smallholders would produce less as the price rose, or that bark reserves on smallholdings were nearing exhaustion. The inadequacy of the N.E.I. native quota of about 145,000 tons in 1934 was also strikingly confirmed. The N.E.I. native output in the spring of 1934 at a yearly rate of 300,000 tons was achieved without assistance from migrant labour.[1] The export figures revealed that while smallholders' production had fallen sharply under the impact of the extremely low prices of 1932, large quantities were forthcoming at prices unprofitable to the majority of the estates; the long-period supply price of the bulk of smallholders' rubber was substantially below that of most of the estate rubber.[2]

The rapidly rising exports greatly enhanced the impatience over the slow progress of the negotiations. It was widely suspected, particularly in the East, that the N.E.I. natives were again the cause of the difficulty. The *Straits Times*, which had been critical of restriction proposals, re-stated its opposition, and pointed to the repeated statements of leading N.E.I. administrators to the effect that new planting in Sumatra and Borneo could not be controlled. These doubts were shared by several leading administrators in Malaya, including Sir Cecil Clementi who scarcely concealed his scepticism of the practicability of controlling new planting in the Outer Provinces. As late as the autumn of 1933 the Resident of the East Coast of Sumatra had told Sir Cecil Clementi in the course of an official visit that effective control over new planting by the local population in Sumatra was impracticable.

Meanwhile the British negotiators continued to press the Dutch for the required assurances. In March 1934 the chairman of the Dutch producers' association informed the chairman of the R.G.A. that the required assurances had been received from the N.E.I. Government, which undertook to impose a specific export tax which would reduce the price received by the native producers to a level sufficient to keep exports within the required limits. Nothing was said of the control of native planting, nor was sufficient information provided about the rate of tax visualised by the N.E.I. administration. Naturally the British authorities were not satis-

[1] This was explicitly stated in one of the official *N.E.I. Native Reports*.

[2] The rapid increase in smallholders' output called forth an unusually candid paragraph in one of the Mincing Lane market reports, reviewing the year 1933: 'We think that the experience of 1933 has convinced most of those who thought that they could, by means of scientific cultivation, beat the native producer and win through without any help, of the error of their ways.'

A well-known rubber company chairman had made a substantially similar point at an annual general meeting earlier in 1933: 'So long as the potential supply at 4*d.* exceeds consumption, the deplorable conditions now ruling cannot be rectified unless shipments are regulated.'

fied with this inadequate Dutch statement, though the majority of the R.G.A.'s Rubber Regulation Committee was. To clarify matters, in April 1934 an emissary was sent by the Colonial Office to The Hague to obtain the required assurances, failing which the discussions were to be broken off.

The Dutch representative who conferred with the British emissary, and who spoke on behalf of both the Dutch and the N.E.I. Governments, dealt with the control of exports and of planting. He emphasised the administrative difficulties but stated that the N.E.I. Government could definitely keep native exports within the permissible limits as long as the London price was not much above the equivalent of 4*d.* gold [1] (the Dutch equivalent of 4*d.* at the rate of exchange ruling before September 1931). The latter condition was strenuously and successfully opposed by the British representative. He emphasised that it had been agreed that the price must be 'reasonably remunerative to the average efficient producer', and that the actual level could not be foreseen. Though he added that he visualised a London price of 7*d.*–8*d.* with exportable releases of 70–75 per cent., he would not agree to any particular pivotal price. After much discussion the Dutch representative gave the assurance that native exports would be effectively controlled at the levels fixed under the scheme, but not below 70,000–80,000 tons annually, which would have been a most unlikely occurrence. This was to be achieved by a special export tax, the proceeds of which would be spent specifically for the benefit of the native rubber-growing districts. The N.E.I. Government envisaged a tax of 10 guilder cents per half-kilo with a Batavia price of 16 cents per half-kilo; the expenses from the interior to the ports were estimated to average some 2½ cents, leaving the native a net return of 3½ cents per half-kilo, which was a sufficiently low price to enable exports to be effectively controlled.[2]

The N.E.I. authorities also gave a large measure of assurance on the control of new planting. Supervision was said to be close

[1] As between September 1931 and September 1936 sterling was already depreciated in terms of gold, while the guilder was still on the gold standard at an unchanged parity, there was some point in referring to the gold equivalent of a given London price of rubber. There was, however, no justification for persisting with this habit until 1940, and to say, as rubber producers were wont to do, that the shilling rubber of 1940 was really only 6*d.*, after allowing for the rise in the price of gold.

[2] According to the Dutch representatives at the discussions in the autumn of 1933, it was unthinkable that the N.E.I. Government would consent to a tax of 8 cents per half-kilo on native rubber, while two years previously an official spokesman had stated that the Government would not agree to a special export tax at any level. The tax was eventually to rise to 29½ cents per half-kilo.

in the more densely populated districts, while in the sparsely populated areas there was insufficient labour for substantial new planting. An ordinance prohibiting new planting would be introduced, and evasion could be expected to be on a very small scale, while any illicitly planted trees would be eradicated. The Dutch Government, therefore, felt that it could sign an agreement which prohibited new planting. This was a complete reversal of the position taken up as recently as 1932.

These assurances were regarded as satisfactory by the British authorities. Very shortly afterwards the Siamese Government also accepted the terms offered. The successful conclusion of the negotiations and the signature of the agreement were announced on 28th April 1934. This agreement was between the producers' organisations, as had been the Tea Control Agreement of 1932. At the last moment it was decided to turn the scheme (with insignificant alterations) into an intergovernmental agreement, embodied in an international treaty.[1] This was signed on 7th May by the United Kingdom (on behalf of the Straits Settlements and the Malay States, Ceylon, British North Borneo, Sarawak), India, the Netherlands, France and Siam. The Indian and Siamese signatures were subject to ratification by the Indian States and the People's Assembly respectively; this qualification was to prove important. The signatory governments controlled some 98 per cent. of the world's rubber.

III

According to the preamble of the international agreement, which was to be operative from 1st June 1934, it was signed 'with the object of reducing world stocks to a normal figure and adjusting in an orderly manner supply to demand and maintaining a fair and equitable price level which will be reasonably remunerative to efficient producers'. The intention, as well as the wording, will be familiar to students of the economic policies of the 1930's, as identical aims, framed in very much the same language, were expressed in the tin, tea and sugar control schemes, as well as in the British agricultural marketing schemes, to mention but a few examples.

The object was to be attained by regulating exports from the participating territories, by prohibiting new planting, and by pro-

[1] Cmd. 4583 of 1934. The 1938 agreement which renewed the scheme for 1939–43 is reproduced as Appendix I to the *History of Rubber Regulation*, the account by the International Rubber Regulation Committee of its work, published in 1944.

hibiting the export of planting material. Basic quotas were allotted to each of the participating territories (except French Indo-China),[1] and exports limited according to percentage releases fixed from time to time by the International Rubber Regulation Committee (I.R.R.C). The basic (or territorial) quotas were as follows :—

TABLE III

Basic Quotas under the International Rubber Regulation Scheme, 1934–38

(long tons)

	1934	1935	1936	1937	1938
	$\frac{7}{12}$ of [a]				
Malaya	504,000	538,000	569,000	589,000	602,000
N.E.I.	352,000	400,000	443,000	467,000	485,000
(revised 1936) . .			500,000	520,000	540,000
Ceylon	77,500	79,000	80,000	81,000	82,000
India	6,850	8,250	9,000	9,000	9,250
(revised 1935) . .		12,500	12,500	12,500	13,000
Burma	5,150	6,750	8,000	9,000	9,250
(revised 1935) . .		8,000	8,500		
British North Borneo .	12,000	13,000	14,000	15,500	16,500
Sarawak	24,000	28,000	30,000	31,500	32,000
Siam [b].	15,000	15,000	15,000	15,000	15,000
(revised 1935) . .		40,000	40,000	40,000	40,000

[a] Seven months of control in 1934.

[b] Siam was guaranteed minimum exports of 50 per cent. of her basic quota for 1934, 75 per cent. for 1935, 85 per cent. for 1936, 90 per cent. for 1937 and 100 per cent. for 1938.

New planting was forbidden : 'prohibited absolutely under penalties that shall be effectively deterrent, such penalties including the compulsory eradication and destruction at the expense of the owner of the plants so planted'. Siam was allowed the planting of 31,000 acres, and all territories were permitted to plant very small areas for experimental purposes only. In accordance with the agreement reached in the Anglo-Dutch negotiations, replanting by individual producers was allowed up to 20 per cent. of their holdings during the currency of regulation, with a maximum of 10 per cent. in any one year. Owners would have to notify the territorial administrations of their intention to replant and provide such particulars as were desired by the authorities. It should be noted that the 10 per cent. and 20 per cent. referred to each owner's planted area, as well as to the total of each country.

[1] No quota was fixed for French Indo-China. Exports up to 30,000 tons were allowed without restriction ; exports in excess of this figure carried a liability to deliver a percentage of the excess to the I.R.R.C.

Minor features of the agreement included permission to carry forward deficiencies from any one year to the next, up to 12 per cent. of the permissible exportable amount. Excess exports up to 5 per cent. of the permissible amount were tolerated, and the excess was to be debited against the following year's exports. Individual owners were prohibited from holding stocks at any given time in excess of 20 per cent. of their shipments during the preceding twelve months, or alternatively twice their permitted monthly exports.[1] Aggregate dealers' stocks in any territory were limited to 12½ per cent. of the permissible exportable amount in each control area. These provisions did not apply to Singapore and Penang, nor to the smaller territories where stocks were to be limited to 'normal proportions having regard to the amount of rubber internally consumed'. The purpose of limiting stocks was twofold: first, to ensure an even flow of rubber in accordance with the decisions of the I.R.R.C., and secondly, to prevent a large accumulation of stocks before the termination of regulation, as had occurred during the closing months of the Stevenson scheme.

International regulation was to be administered by the International Rubber Regulation Committee, consisting of delegations from the participating countries with voting powers proportionate to the territorial quotas, French Indo-China being assigned a quota for this purpose. The most important function of the Committee was the fixing of the rates of release; after 1938 it also had powers to fix permissible percentages of new planting and replanting. On major issues, including the fixing of rates of release, a three-quarters majority was required, which meant that no decision could be reached unless the Malayan and N.E.I. delegations were in agreement. Each delegation was to vote as a unit, one of its members acting as voting member.

The I.R.R.C. was to invite three representatives of rubber manufacturers to form an Advisory Panel of Manufacturers to advise the Committee on matters affecting manufacturers' interests, notably on rates of release.

The agreement was well received, and even the American reaction was not unfavourable. The *Rubber Age* and the *India Rubber World* (the two leading U.S. trade journals) were both sympathetic, stating that so long as the Committee's ideas were moderate and the price reasonably stable and not greatly above the

[1] The limitation of producers' stocks and the planting provisions referred to individual owners, while the rest of the agreement dealt with territories, leaving the control of individual producers to the local administrations.

level then ruling (6*d.*–7*d.* in London), the manufacturers would not object. The Rubber Division of the Department of Commerce in its *Rubber News Letter* was also friendly. The Committee was reminded, however, that in aiming at a reasonably remunerative price the great reduction in costs over the preceding few years should not be overlooked ; 1933 costs were 60 per cent. below those of 1929, and 75 per cent. below those of 1927. Comment in the East was enthusiastic ; even the *Straits Times* was impressed by the comprehensiveness of the scheme and by the categorical obligations imposed on all participants, including the N.E.I. The paper urged the Committee to pursue a moderate policy ; a London price of 6*d.* should be reasonable, even allowing for increased wages and salaries. In the House of Commons the Secretary of State for the Colonies declared that those best informed considered the scheme administratively practicable. He also stated explicitly that in Malaya the smallholders would be treated in exactly the same way as the estates.

The R.G.A. view on restriction was summarised in some notes for the press and in the chairman's speech at the annual meeting held in May. The gist of the notes was the necessity of a regulation scheme in view of the excess capacity with which the industry was saddled ; regulation would benefit all concerned, including the manufacturers, to whom a moderate price policy was promised. The R.G.A. chairman also emphasised the equity of the scheme : ' It is inevitable in any scheme involving the general application of definite principles to a group that there should be inequalities, but they need not be more than trivial.' The unanimous support of producers was also stressed, perhaps overstressed, in the notes for the press, in which it was claimed that ' the rubber growers of the East had agreed unanimously to a system of restriction '. While it is very probable that the majority of the smallholders would have supported a scheme which promised to raise and maintain the price of rubber, they were never consulted, and the unanimity of the more efficient half of the industry was, therefore, hypothetical.

CHAPTER 7

THE ESTABLISHMENT OF REGULATION

THE account now to be given of the establishment of regulation in the various producing territories is but the barest summary of the most important provisions of the mass of local legislation which introduced restriction. Enactments, ordinances, and decrees, running into hundreds of pages for the larger territories, were an inevitable feature of a vast scheme controlling estates, smallholders and dealers whose numbers reached six figures in Malaya and possibly seven in the N.E.I. The *History of Rubber Regulation* mentions, with something not unlike pride, that in Ceylon the *Rubber Control Handbook* comprised some 376 pages. This complexity proved a considerable hardship to smallholders and small estate owners, most of whom were illiterate and certainly unable to grasp lengthy documents in involved legal language, the interpretation of which was further complicated by the practice of the inclusion of powers which the authorities did not propose to exercise except in certain contingencies. Efforts to explain to the smallholders the gist of the local legislation were generally insufficient, and there is copious evidence of the smallholders' failure to understand important provisions of the regulation, and of the financial losses they suffered as a result.[1]

I

As soon as the regulation plan began to take shape, the administrative application of the scheme to Malaya was examined by the Malaya Territorial Sub-Committee of the Rubber Regulation Committee of the R.G.A. While the Sub-Committee realised that the actual machinery of local control had to be framed by the local governments, attention was drawn to certain points which appeared both equitable and expedient. It was suggested that the principles underlying individual assessments should, as far as possible, follow those on which the Malayan territorial quota was calculated, and wherever possible they should be based on the average 1929–32 outputs together with immature allowances on the international

[1] For explicit admissions that the smallholders were quite unfamiliar with the provisions affecting them, see *Malayan Agricultural Journal*, March 1939, p. 113, and May 1939, p. 193.

scale. Additional allowances to producers with an abnormally large proportion of 1925-27 rubber were also proposed, as owing to the method of calculating immature allowances such producers might suffer hardship; additional allowances were also to be considered for mature acreage rested during 1929–32.

The Sub-Committee's remarks on the division of the Malayan quota are of interest: 'Your Sub-Committee appreciates that the application of the methods indicated in the foregoing paragraphs will be difficult, if not impossible, to smallholdings since there are no reliable records of outputs from these. It seems therefore that the determination of assessments for smallholdings must be a matter for the judgment of the authorities, your Sub-Committee being confident that their endeavour will be to do justice to all sections, and that assessments will be determined on the basis of capacity and such statistics as are available, rather than by political considerations.' The Sub-Committee then referred to the high exports from Malayan smallholdings during 1929–32, equivalent to about 448 lb. per mature acre, and recommended a division of the permanent basis between estates and smallholdings in proportion to their outputs in the basic years, adding that the immature allowances to smallholdings should be at the international rate. It was also pointed out that the Malayan quota included an allowance ranging from 4,700 tons in 1934 to 11,300 tons in 1938, given specifically to smooth over any difficulties that might arise over the assessment of smallholdings.

The Sub-Committee's report (unpublished) was submitted for examination to the Malayan authorities, as well as to an influential local *ad hoc* body known as the Rubber Regulation Committee (Malaya). The latter was of the kind invariably described in Malaya as 'thoroughly representative of all interests'; it comprised 26 or 27 estate representatives and one, possibly two, representatives of smallholders.[1] The actual work was done entirely by a sub-committee of nine, all of whom were estate representatives. Their report (also unpublished) followed closely that of the R.G.A. Sub-Committee, though it omitted to refer to the extra allowance included in the Malayan quota and especially assigned to smallholdings. The following extract from the report of the Committee is representative of its proposals: 'As far as is known, the average exports from native holdings over the basic period were equivalent

[1] Several members of this Committee (as of other similar bodies) each represented no more than about 30,000 acres of high-cost producers, as against the 1,300,000 acres of low-cost or no-cost smallholdings.

to 448 lb. per acre. It is, therefore, recommended that the permanent basis for smallholdings should be 450 lb. per acre. The internationally agreed scale of allowances for rubber planted in 1925 and onwards applies equally to smallholdings.'

The necessary legislation had been prepared in advance and was rushed through on the announcement of the international agreement. The export ledger system evolved during the Stevenson scheme was again used in Malaya (and in Ceylon). Under this system the right to export rubber was confined to registered exporters, in practice estate producers and rubber dealers ; the smallholder does not export his rubber direct, but sells it to a dealer who is the actual exporter. Export ledgers were kept at all ports of shipment, with accounts for registered exporters using that port. Producer-exporters were credited with the rights issued to them in the normal course of administering the scheme, and dealer-exporters with rights they bought, or with coupons they paid in, while all exporters were debited with the rubber they exported. Estate producers were not issued with separate documents for their exportable allowance but were simply credited in the customs ledgers ; smallholders were issued with coupons. Export credits were freely transferable between estate producers within the same administration, the S.S., the F.M.S. and each of the U.M.S. being separate administrations ; for transfers between administrations the consent of the Controller of Rubber was necessary, and this was generally, but not invariably, given. Coupons were not transferable between different administrations. There was thus one price for export rights (estate producers' export rights) throughout Malaya, but different local prices for smallholders' coupons.[1]

Regulation was administered by the Controller of Rubber, Malaya, a senior civil servant stationed in Kuala Lumpur. The Controller was assisted by the General Advisory Committee appointed in May 1934, chiefly to discuss the allocation of the Malayan quota between the various administrations. Its membership was eight : the Controller of Rubber as chairman, four representatives of European estates (one each for the S.S., the F.M.S., Johore and Kedah), one representative of Chinese estates, one Malay member to represent the smallholders, and an official

[1] Producers' and dealers' stocks were regulated in accordance with the provisions of the international agreement. A detailed discussion of the different treatments of export rights in producers' and dealers' hands would be lengthy. Most of the provisions are set out in the *Annual Reports on the Working of Rubber Regulation in Malaya*, especially for 1934, 1935 and 1937. These reports will be referred to as *Annual Reports* of the Controller of Rubber.

to act as liaison officer for the smaller administrations (Trengganu, Kelantan, Perlis and Brunei). According to the 1934 *Annual Report* of the Controller of Rubber : 'The immediate object for which this Committee was formed was to advise the Controller on the apportionment of the quota, but insensibly it became a General Advisory Committee and most questions affecting Malaya as a whole were referred to it. Although not a statutory body, the Committee owing to its representative and pan-Malayan character was able to render very valuable service, and its advice carried great weight.' It was rather ingenuous to term ' representative ' a committee which consisted of two officials (one of whom was not usually concerned with rubber), five estate members and a solitary representative of smallholders. This was yet another instance of the identification of the industry with the estates, an attitude understandable on the part of the estate producers but less easy to excuse when assumed by the Controller of Rubber.

The importance of a fair internal division of the territorial quota was widely realised. The inequities and the corruption under the Stevenson scheme were still well remembered in Malaya. The Malay spokesman, addressing the F.M.S. Federal Council in May 1934, welcomed the Rubber Regulation Bill but anxiously pleaded for a fair treatment of the smallholders, to which the Rubber Controller-designate replied that substantial justice would be ensured to all.

Estates were assessed by assessment committees, which sent questionnaires to all estates to obtain figures of their acreages and of their 1929–32 outputs. When sufficient information was forthcoming the estate was assessed without inspection ; otherwise the property was inspected. This favoured the larger, European-owned, estates, which were rarely inspected. The standard production of estates was based on their average 1929–32 outputs, together with allowances for rubber not fully mature, as well as for rubber mature but untapped during that period. It had first been planned to refuse allowances for mature rubber untapped during the slump since no such allowances were included in the basic quotas under the scheme. This decision was subsequently reversed, with the result that estates able to claim allowances for mature rubber untapped during the basic years were assessed on the basis of yield per tapped acre, instead of yield per mature acre. It was soon realised that the basic quota was generous, and estates claiming that their 1929–32 production did not represent their capacity were often given additional allowances. Many estate producers were, in fact, though not formally, assessed on what they claimed as their capacity.

The scale allowances for rubber immature during the basic years were calculated on lines roughly similar to those in the computation of the territorial quotas ; seedling rubber was allowed a maximum of 500 lb. per acre and budded rubber a maximum of 1,200 lb. The maximum scale allowances were conditional on a certain minimum average girth per tree and a minimum stand per acre ; the more densely planted Asiatic estates sometimes failed to reach the minimum girth. Scale allowances at the budgrafted rate were given to approved clones [1] only, but there were very many (about 130) of these. The maximum allowances were almost invariably given to producers who claimed them, as long as the trees reached the standard girth and were left untapped on reaching maturity. When they were tapped and yielded less than the scale allowances these were not reduced until 1937. On the other hand —again until 1937—rubber assessed according to scale and not according to average output during 1929–32 could not usually obtain higher assessments than the maximum scale allowances, even if better yields could be proved. The scale allowances for budded rubber were extremely generous and were very often granted to young trees of a girth and age which would not be tapped in normal commercial estate practice. Assessments were not generally revised until 1937. There were annual increases as young rubber approached full maturity, but these were based on records and with few exceptions were automatic. There were occasional inspections to supplement deficient or check doubtful returns, or in response to requests from planters claiming that they had been under-assessed.

The estates, especially the larger producers, were on the whole satisfied with their assessments. There was some dissatisfaction by owners of seedling rubber immature in 1929–32 whose assessments were limited to 500 lb. per acre, though such rubber was often capable of higher yields, and also by many Asiatic owners whose records were inadequate, and whose more densely planted trees had a lower average girth than those of the larger properties, though their acreage yields were no less. The system generally favoured the European estates, which owned practically the entire budgrafted area, and whose trees, often planted too

[1] Clone is a collective noun and refers to the vegetatively-propagated offspring of one mother tree. All such vegetatively-propagated offspring of a given mother tree are of identical genetical constitution.

widely, had a high average girth; they also had better records, were rarely inspected, and their owners and managers understood the working of the scale allowances better than did their smaller competitors. After 1935, the 'replanting bonus' (the maintenance of assessments on areas cut out for replanting) further enhanced the favoured treatment of the larger, European-owned properties. By 1935–36 it was an open secret in Malaya that the European estates were preferentially treated, though the inequity was less pronounced than it had been under the Stevenson scheme.

Smallholdings had perforce to be assessed on different lines in view of their very large number and the complete absence of individual records. They were formally assessed by the district officers on reports of inspectors who were either unemployed planters or estate managers inspecting in their spare time. For administrative reasons the assessments of smallholdings were expressed in units and not in lb. per acre. A unit was the assumed yield per acre of standard smallholders' rubber; it actually represented a share in the total quota allotted to smallholders. The lb. per acre value of a unit could not be exactly told beforehand; it emerged only after the total number of units was known and set against the quota for smallholders.

In their work inspectors were to be guided by certain official directives issued by the Survey Department and reproduced in the 1934 *Annual Report* of the Controller of Rubber. These reveal that the Malayan authorities still held the views on the productivity of the smallholdings which were generally current in the late 1920's, and that the lessons of the smallholdings enquiry and of the high yields of 1929–33 were ignored. The official directives were an open invitation to inspectors to under-assess the smallholders. The suggestions for assessment were broadly as follows. First-class rubber capable of yielding over 400 lb. was to be termed class A and was to be assessed at four units, with fewer units to be granted to smallholdings in categories B, C and D. An A′ class, capable of yielding 500 lb. was recognised but was also to receive four units only; though a subsequent increase might be possible, for the time being 500 lb. was to be regarded as the maximum theoretical yield for smallholders' rubber. In practice this ceiling was never lifted, and was reached only in a handful of exceptional instances. It will be recalled that less than a year earlier the smallholdings enquiry found an average yield of 477 lb. with a maximum of 889 lb. Thus a smallholding yielding 400 lb. was far from first-class rubber.[1] It was pointed out that in the absence of production figures assessments were bound to be arbitrary, but inspectors were specifically reminded to discount yields based on too drastic tapping systems which could not be maintained. This was indeed a superfluous warning in view of the attitude of the planting community towards smallholders' rubber. Each holding was to be assessed in an integral number of units ; should a fraction result from the inspector's valuation of individual acres this was to be rounded off to a higher integer only if the fraction was three-quarters or over ; thus 9·8 units to be taken as ten, but 9·7 as nine units. There were to be no allowances for untapped trees corresponding to the allowances given to estates for areas out of tapping.

Most remarkable of all was the instruction that areas under *blukar* (secondary jungle) need not be inspected and were only to be reported as overgrown rubber. It had been established by several first-hand enquiries in Malaya, as well as in the N.E.I., that smallholders' rubber under *blukar* yielded satisfactorily, especially after being cleaned, which the smallholders were certain to do under the stimulus of better prices. This disregard of smallholdings under *blukar* vitiated the Malayan acreage statistics for several years ; the planted area of smallholdings at the end of 1935 was thus reduced by more than 100,000 acres below the 1934 figure. These areas were gradually reinstated, and by 1938 the area was almost back to the 1934 figure. The smallholdings quota, when expressed in lb. per acre, was thus somewhat inflated during 1935–37 by the incorrect reduction in the divisor.

There were twenty inspectors for the smallholdings area of about one-and-a-quarter million acres, and the work of inspection, which was concluded within a few months, was frequently very cursory. Owners of densely planted holdings and those with heavy undergrowth amidst their rubber fared worst, partly because of the planter's chronic scepticism of the yielding capacity of such areas (which was reinforced by the official instructions), and also because such holdings were more trouble to inspect carefully and were often omitted altogether. Smallholders' assessments were fixed for

[1] In March 1934, just at the time when the application of regulation to Malaya was being discussed, the results of the smallholdings enquiry were reviewed in the *M.A.J.* The article stated : ' After reviewing the evidence presented by the author, supplemented by our own knowledge of the statistical position and observation over some 20 years in Malaya, we can but agree with the conclusions that neither by reason of previous neglect nor present practice can it be expected that the production of smallholdings will decline either in the near future or during the next decade.' This opinion, however, carried no weight with the restriction authorities.

each year until the end of 1938, as all the rubber which would be assessable in those years was already planted. Such forward assessments were bound to be hazardous, especially with such cursory inspection.[1]

The Rubber Controller-designate stated in the Federal Council in May 1934 that the basic quota would be divided at the outset into separate shares for estates and smallholdings, which would be kept apart, so that changes in the principles of assessment, or a revision of individual standard productions, would only affect others within the class, and any over-assessment of individual estates would be at the expense of other estates and not of smallholdings. This contention would have been acceptable if the division was to be equitable and the respective shares of estates and of smallholdings determined in accordance with the computation of the basic quota of Malaya, as had been suggested by the R.G.A. Sub-Committee. If, however, the initial division between estates and smallholdings were inequitable, the over-assessment of individual estates *could* affect the smallholder, for the fact that the total of the individual assessments in each class did not differ greatly from its share in the Malayan territorial quota could be used as a spurious justification for the division.

This appears in fact to have happened. An extensive search[2] has failed to trace any public statement on the basis of the division of the Malayan territorial quota between estates and smallholdings. The Controller of Rubber published the division each year without stating how it had been determined. The confidential minutes of the General Advisory Committee which assisted the Controller of Rubber contain the only information which could be traced. These seem to suggest that after the estates were assessed the sum total of their assessments was deducted from the Malayan basic quota, and the smallholdings were given the residue.

[1] 'As there are many large tracts of smallholdings of fairly uniform yielding capacity it will not be necessary to visit each holding in such tracts.' *Minutes* of the second meeting of the General Advisory Committee on Rubber Regulation. The statement just quoted was even less true for smallholdings than it would have been for estates.

[2] It covered the complete files from 1934 to 1940 of the following official documents: the *Annual Reports* of the Controller of Rubber, of the Chief Secretary to the F.M.S. Government, of the Director of Agriculture, of each of the Residents in the F.M.S., of each of the Advisers to the U.M.S., of the Rubber Research Institute of Malaya, as well as the *Proceedings* of the Federal and Legislative Councils, together with the complete files for these years of the *Malayan Agricultural Journal*, *The Planter*, the *Straits Budget* (the weekly edition of the *Straits Times*), the *R.G.A. Bulletin*, the *India-Rubber Journal*, the *India Rubber World*, the (New York) *Rubber Age* and the *Rubber News Letter* of the U.S. Department of Commerce. Nor could the information be found in the official minutes or the correspondence of the I.R.R.C., nor among the many private papers of the leaders of the industry to which the writer has had access.

Whatever the basis of the division, the outcome was certainly remarkable. This can be shown in a series of five simple tables. The first two tables are purely formal summaries of the division of the quota for the years 1934–40; the exact figure for the quota division for 1941 is not available, but it is known that the division was virtually the same as in 1940.

Table I

Internal Distribution of the Malayan Territorial Quota,[a] 1934–40

	Estates		Smallholdings	
	Thousand tons	*Per cent. of Malayan quota*	*Thousand tons*	*Per cent. of Malayan quota*
1934	312·5	61·1	199·1	38·9
1935	334·6	62·5	200·4	37·5
1936	352·6[b]	61·7	219·4	38·3
1937	373·2	61·8	230·9	38·2
1938	377·4	61·7	234·5	38·3
1939	395·9	61·9	244·0	38·1
1940	407·4	62·3	246·4	37·7

[a] The total of these quotas slightly exceeded the Malayan territorial quota, and this necessitated the eventual introduction of internal cuts (reductions in rates of release below the internationally agreed rate).

[b] For administrative reasons, some properties owned by Indian moneylenders were transferred in 1936 from the estate to the smallholdings quota. Their assessments totalled some 6,000 tons, and to this extent all the tables slightly overstate the true smallholdings quota from 1936 onwards.

Table II

Quotas of Malayan Estates and Smallholdings expressed in lb. per acre, 1934–40

(To the nearest 5 lb.)

	Estates		Smallholdings	
	Per acre	*Per mature acre*	*Per acre*	*Per mature acre*
1934	350	385	340	365
1935	375	405	340	355
1936	395	420	375	385
1937	415	440	395	400
1938	425	450	400	405
1939	430	470	405	420
1940	435	500	405	425

The figures in this table are based on the records of the I.R.R.C. Allowance has been made for the areas replanted after 1934 and newly planted after 1938. As all calculations based on acreage statistics, these figures are liable to a margin of error which is, however, certain to be small and not in excess of 2–3 per cent.

The results of the quota division emerge from Tables III–V.

TABLE III

Annual Output of Rubber per Mature Acre of Malayan Estates and Smallholdings, 1929–40

(Lb., to the nearest 5 lb.)

	Estates	*Smallholdings*	*Smallholdings as per cent. of estates*
1929	410	485	118
1930	380	460	121
1931	375	445	119
1932	365	385	106
1933	355	465	131
1934	Regulation introduced during the year.		
1935	295	240	81
1936	275	230	84
1937	375	330	88
1938	290	200	69
1939	290	200	69
1940	410	370	90

These figures have been calculated by dividing the actual output by the mature area, i.e. by the acreage five or more years' old. The sharp fluctuations in the last column in 1932–33 reflect the smallholders' reaction to the very low prices of 1932 and to the recovery of 1933.

TABLE IV

Shares of Estates and Smallholdings in Malayan Rubber Production, 1929–40

	Estates		*Smallholdings*	
	Tons	*As per cent. of total Malayan production*	*Tons*	*As per cent. of total Malayan production*
1929	246,000	55·2	200,000	44·8
1930	236,000	54·6	197,000	45·4
1931	240,000	55·1	197,000	44·9
1932	240,000	57·6	177,000	42·4
1933	240,000	52·2	221,000	47·8
June–Dec. 1933	149,000	50·9	144,000	49·1
June 1933–May 1934	251,000	49·7	253,000	50·3
Jan.–May 1934	102,000	48·3	107,000	51·7
		Regulation introduced		
June–Dec. 1934	160,000	59·7	108,000	40·3
1935	243,000	64·0	137,000	36·0
1936	233,000	63·9	132,000	36·1
1937	314,000	62·4	189,000	37·6
1938	246,000	68·1	115,000	31·9
1939	245,000	67·7	117,000	32·3
1940	334,000	60·8	215,000	39·2

TABLE V

Comparison of Previous Output [a] *of Malayan Estates and Smallholdings with their 1934 Quotas*

(Tons, to the nearest 5,000 tons)

	Estates	*Small-holdings*	*London price, pence per lb.*
(*a*) Output for calendar year 1933 . .	240,000	220,000	3·2
(*b*) Output for twelve months ending May 1934	250,000	250,000	4·5
(*c*) Annual rate of production based on seasonally corrected output, March–May 1934	265,000	300,000	5·8
(*d*) 1934 quotas	310,000	200,000	—
(*e*) (*d*) as per cent. of (*a*)	129	91	—
(*b*)	124	80	—
(*c*) [b]	117	67	—

[a] These are production figures; stock changes are allowed for.
[b] In the spring of 1934 the price was nearer to the price visualised under restriction than it had been in 1933. The quotas of different classes of producer may be considered fair if their ratio is roughly proportionate to approximate unrestricted outputs at the prices envisaged under restriction. This lends special interest to the comparison of (*c*) with (*d*).

The tables amply show where the burden of restriction fell. To forestall possible objections it must be stated at once that sales of rights from smallholders to estates, whether directly or indirectly (*via* dealers who buy coupons first and uncouponed rubber subsequently) were of negligible importance, except in 1938 and 1939 when such sales took place to a minor extent—only about 5 per cent. of the total quota in each year. In 1940 net sales were in a reverse direction, and the estates sold rights to smallholders *via* the dealers. The position is evident from a comparison of the shares of estates and of smallholdings in Malayan production (Table IV) with their shares in the quota (Table I). The different trends of the outputs of estates and of smallholdings reflect the enforced curtailment of the latter.

The average output of smallholdings during 1929–32 was 193,000 tons and this, of course, was their permanent basis for restriction purposes. Their 1934 quota of 199,000 tons almost exactly equalled their permanent basis, together with a special allowance of around 5,000 tons included in the Malayan quota to smooth over any difficulty of the assessment of smallholdings. Thus they received no immature allowances whatever. When the assessments of the Chettiar-owned estates included for administrative reasons in the smallholders' quota are also deducted, it appears that the smallholders hardly received any immature allowances in 1934–38 though they had planted almost a quarter-of-a-million acres between 1925 and 1929, and these allowances were, of course, to have applied to rubber planted during these years.

Thus, contrary to specific official assurances, the smallholders were again, as under the Stevenson scheme, greatly under-assessed. It is possible to estimate very roughly the loss inflicted on smallholders by their under-assessment. If the shares of estates and smallholdings in the quota had been proportionate to their probable unrestricted outputs at prices visualised under restriction, the quota would have been divided about equally. If the estate and smallholdings quotas had been calculated on the same basis as had been adopted internationally for the computation of the total Malayan quota the division would have been about 55 per cent. for estates and 45 per cent. for smallholdings. These estimates are subject to a margin of error, but on any reasonable basis of division the share of smallholdings should not have been less than 45 per cent., and possibly about 48 per cent., especially as it is explicitly claimed in the *History of Rubber Regulation* (p. 47) that official instructions were issued in 1934 that the smallholders were to be given the benefit of any doubt in the division of the quota. On the basis of a 48 per cent. share in the territorial quota, smallholders' quotas over the years 1934–40 should have totalled approximately 400,000 tons more than they actually did, and some two-thirds of this amount, say 270,000 tons, would have been exportable under the restriction scheme. Taking a conservative over-all value of export rights at an average of 4*d.* per lb. up-country throughout this period, the loss to smallholders may be estimated at about £10 millions, or 85 million Straits dollars. As this came about through under-assessment of land which remained under rubber, there was little or no transfer of resources to other uses to be set against the loss.[1]

[1] This calculation is, of course, intended to indicate orders of magnitude only. If assessments had been equal, the price of export rights or the price of rubber or the volume of exports, would probably have differed from the actual levels, and in strict logic this should be allowed for in computing the loss to smallholders through under-assessment. It is plainly impossible to estimate this quantitatively.

This calculation was first published in an article ' The Working of Rubber Regulation in the *Economic Journal*, Sept. 1946. It was there erroneously stated in one place (p. 396) that the calculation referred to the years 1934–41. Actually it referred to 1934–40 only, as is clear from the tables in that article, as well as from the context. If the year 1941 had also been included (for which the data are not so complete), the calculated loss would have been about £2 millions (17 million Straits dollars) higher.

TABLE VI

Comparison of Previous Outputs of N.E.I. Estates and Natives with their 1934 Quotas

(Long tons)

	Estates	*Natives* [a]	*London price, pence per lb.*
(*a*) Output for calendar year 1933	170,000	115,000	3·2
(*b*) Output for twelve months ending May 1934	180,000	185,000	4·5
(*c*) Annual rate of production based on seasonally corrected output, March–May 1934	220,000	300,000	5·8
(*d*) 1934 quotas	205,000	145,000	—
(*e*) (*d*) as per cent. of (*a*)	121	126	—
(*b*)	114	78	—
(*c*) [b]	93	48	—

[a] For the natives exports have been taken as output. The export figures for March–May probably include some reduction in stocks and thus slightly overstate the actual output. The amount involved is, however, certain to be very small. The natives kept no stocks and dealers' stocks were also comparatively small: moreover, the exports were fully in accordance with the rising trend since mid-1933.

[b] The considerations summarised in the second note to Table V also apply to these figures. Moreover, in the N.E.I. very large native areas were reaching maturity in about 1933–34 for which little or no allowance was made in the 1934–35 quotas. It should also be noted that the supply of N.E.I. native rubber was definitely elastic, and the 1933 production was at a rate of only about one-third of the officially and very conservatively estimated capacity.

than would have been justified by their average dry weight. Moreover, to avoid losses to re-millers and other processors of native rubber, the frequent—and generally upward—changes in the export tax applied to wet rubber within a day or two of the announcement but to dry rubber only after some four or five weeks, and this stimulated the export of dry rubber in the intervening period. Thus an incidental result of the special export tax was the sharp rise in the proportion of native rubber exported dry, from 15 per cent. for the first quarter of 1934 to almost 100 per cent. by the end of 1936. These were, however, secondary effects beside the very heavy burden of the tax, and to simplify the discussion all subsequent references will be to the dry rate which applied most widely.

There were widespread doubts of the effectiveness of the prohibition of new planting. The difficulties were well illustrated in a consular report of the U.S. Trade Commissioner in Batavia. The Commissioner had in the autumn of 1934 visited Palembang in south Sumatra, where an American oil company was just extending its operations. A road had been cut across the jungle in the midst of which, many miles from the nearest native village, a large area of rubber was unexpectedly found. From time to time the natives trekked across the jungle, established temporary huts and camps, tapped the trees and thereafter returned to their villages. The Trade Commissioner doubted the practicability of the control of new planting.

Self-sown seedlings presented a special difficulty which applied throughout the East, but was greatest in the N.E.I. In extensive areas under rubber many self-sown *Hevea* trees grow up some of which become tappable by native standards, while others serve as a cover crop. On a strict interpretation of the regulation agreement and the locally issued decrees many of these self-sown trees were to be eradicated, but this was plainly impossible in the Outer Provinces of the N.E.I.

III

(*a*) *Ceylon*

In Ceylon estates and smallholdings alike were assessed on inspection. The assessment of producers with reliable records was based on the highest output of the years 1929–32. Other producers were assessed on estimated capacity at normal rates of bark consumption, after taking into consideration the type of soil, the age of the trees, planting density and other factors deemed relevant. Smallholders were generally assessed according to the average proved yield of smallholders' rubber in a given area. The scale allowances were at lower rates than in Malaya or the N.E.I.

These principles of assessment were divorced from the basis on which Ceylon's territorial quota had been determined. The total of individual assessments greatly exceeded the basic quota, and heavy internal cuts were a feature of rubber regulation in Ceylon until 1939. In 1935 many estate producers were reassessed on the basis of their average 1929–32 outputs instead of the highest production in any single year; as, however, some producers continued to be assessed on the basis of potential capacity, assessments still exceeded the basic quota. It was also found that the immature areas, especially those planted between 1926 and 1928, were larger than had been assumed in computing the basic quota, and this again contributed to the discrepancy.

Producers could appeal against the assessments, and there was a non-European majority on the assessment committees and on the appeal tribunal, while the Rubber Controller was a Singhalese. It is thus somewhat unexpected to find that the estate quota expressed in lb. per acre was much in excess of that of smallholdings.

In 1934 the average figure for large estates (over 100 acres) was 330 lb. per planted acre, against 265 lb. for small estates (10–100 acres) and 195 lb. for smallholdings (under 10 acres).[1] Substantially the same ratios prevailed throughout the operation of regulation, and were of the same order for the planted and for the mature acreage. In contrast with Malaya, much of the rubber of Ceylon smallholdings is not only on poor land but is also interplanted with other crops which in Ceylon adversely affect yields. The difference is nevertheless surprisingly large, especially as the estates had no budded rubber.

(*b*) *British North Borneo*

In British North Borneo the transfer of rights was forbidden. The Controller of Rubber in his *Annual Reports*[2] referred to this as a cardinal feature of the machinery of regulation and as an essential condition of its success. No reasons were given for this repeated statement. Smuggling of rubber from Sarawak might have caused inconvenience but would hardly have destroyed the regulation machinery, and it is not easy to understand the grounds for the Controller's insistence on the non-transferability of rights.

After a short initial period during which estates were assessed in accordance with their average 1929–32 outputs, potential productivity was accepted as the basis, which was interpreted as the average yield on alternate daily tapping. Where the ABC system of tapping was practised, yields could be raised by 33 per cent. in computing the standard production. A unique feature of assessments was the appreciable allowances given to estates which had used fertilisers during the previous six months. These allowances were granted without proof of additional yields so derived.

[1] These figures differ from those in the annual *Administration Reports* of the Rubber Controller, Ceylon, where, for some reason, the figures are calculated by dividing the aggregate standard production of each group by the mature acreage plus one-half the immature acreage. Moreover, up to 1939 the aggregate standard production much exceeded Ceylon's territorial quota; the Controller's figures refer to the average standard production per acre, while those given in the text have been corrected, to give a picture nearer the actual state of affairs, by reducing them in the same proportion in each class, and the result shows the average quotas of the three classes of producer. The ratios between the figures agree closely with those given by the Controller.

[2] These *Annual Reports* of the Controller of Rubber, or more precisely *Confidential Reports on the Operation of Rubber Regulation in the State of North Borneo*, have not been published, but copies are available among the papers of the I.R.R.C. They are unsatisfactory documents; the information supplied is inadequate, and the general tenor of the reports throws considerable doubt both on the equity of the local regulation machinery and on the competence of some of its administrators. It is remarkable that the reports should have been kept confidential though they cover issues which materially affected the welfare of thousands of producers.

The basis of smallholders' assessments varied considerably. At first they were based on the estimated district average exports per acre in 1929–32. Subsequently standard assessments given on individual inspection were introduced, though on unorthodox lines. 'The basis of assessment of smallholdings is the same as for estates. Before restriction was enforced, smallholders almost without exception tapped far too heavily, the favourite system being a half-cut tapped every day. Bark consumption had therefore to be reduced by two-thirds,[1] and production by 50 per cent., as yield in relation to bark consumption tends to follow the law of diminishing returns. A cut of 50 per cent. in production was in the interests of the smallholders themselves as it was just sufficient to stop them from living on their capital, but a severer cut would impose on them too large a share of the burden of restriction and they are therefore allowed to export the full amount of their assessments.'[2]

It is difficult to understand how this method was to have operated at varying rates of release, for if a 50 per cent. cut in output would have fitted one international rate of release, it could not possibly have been suitable with a different rate. Actually a 50 per cent. reduction in production below the output before regulation was extremely severe and far in excess of the cut imposed on estate producers. While it is not clear how it was possible to fix assessments on this system as smallholders had no past production figures, it is obvious from the trend of exports that their output had fallen heavily during the slump, and that a 50 per cent. cut below the production of say 1931–33 was even more severe than would appear at first. Even without any reduction being applied to the smallholders' assessments these would have been grossly unfair compared to those of the estates; it seems, moreover, that further reductions, varying with the international rate of release, were subsequently applied to the meagre assessments of the smallholders. The Controller's remarks on the over-tapping of native rubber have a familiar ring and are unlikely to have been more reliable than the many similar statements about the smallholders in Malaya. According to one of the Controller's subsequent *Annual Reports*: 'assessments continue to be revised annually on productive capacity and in the case of smallholdings on girth measurement, bark consumption and other factors reported at periodical inspections.'[3] These factors were, however, apparently defined solely

[1] To reduce it to the same rate as on estates tapping on the ABC system.
[2] *Annual Report* of the Controller of Rubber for 1934.
[3] *Annual Report* of the Controller of Rubber for 1938.

in terms of estate technique. According to the official rubber restriction rules: 'Normal production means the amount of dry rubber that can be produced by tapping ripe bark on mature trees in such a manner that the rate of bark consumption does not exceed the rate of renewal. A tree shall not be deemed mature if its circumference at three feet above ground level is less than 18 inches.' This definition of maturity may apply to estates but is most misleading for smallholdings where, owing to the dense planting, trees are of much smaller girth and are readily tapped when their circumference is appreciably below 18 inches.

The average assessment of smallholdings was far below that of estates throughout the regulation period. The figures did not become available until 1939, when the average estate assessment was about 505 lb. per acre (510 lb. per mature acre) against 215 lb. per acre (the same per mature acre) on smallholdings. Incomplete but reliable information makes it clear that roughly the same ratio prevailed throughout the restriction period. The figures clearly refute the Controller's contention that estates and smallholdings were assessed on the same basis. As will be seen shortly, in Sarawak, just across the frontier from British North Borneo, smallholders' rubber was found in 1937 to give an average yield of 490 lb. per acre. The estate assessments on the other hand were absurdly high; neither in Malaya nor in the N.E.I. had estate yields ever averaged 500 lb. per acre and estate yields in British North Borneo are known to be below those in Malaya and the N.E.I. It appears that in British North Borneo the smallholders were treated worse than in any other producing territory. The opening passage of the Controller's first (1934) *Annual Report* suggests how this may have come about: 'Before bringing restriction into force the Government called a conference at which representatives of the European, Chinese and Japanese producers were invited to express their views on the manner in which the scheme should be carried out. The legislation enacted was based on the recommendations of this conference.' There is no mention of smallholders or of their representatives.

According to the Controller's *Annual Report* for 1935, the smallholders were complaining that they were unable to make a living with their low assessments. This was not surprising; more unexpected is the following statement: 'Large producers complained that too big a share of the burden of restriction was being placed on their shoulders.'—this at a time when their per acre assessments exceeded those of smallholdings by about 100 per cent. on rubber which was almost certainly of poorer yielding capacity.

The total of standard assessments much exceeded the territorial quota, which was itself unfavourable, reflecting the sharp fall in exports after 1929. The heavy internal cuts pressed hardest on the under-assessed smallholders. The standard assessments of estates (based on assumed potential productivity, and divorced from 1929–32 outputs) were irrelevant to the fairness of the basic quota. Estate interests were wont to argue that the heavy internal cuts were evidence of the poor treatment of North Borneo under the scheme. The planters apparently succeeded in converting the Controller to this view, who consented to a general increase in assessments to serve as a bargaining counter in negotiations for a better quota on the renewal of regulation.[1]

(*c*) *Sarawak*

The inadequacy of the administrative machinery did not permit the introduction of individual restriction in Sarawak before 1938. Until then exports were kept within the permissible limit by several over-all measures. Local labour in Sarawak was insufficient for the tapping of the entire mature area, and the control of immigration restricted the number of tappers and the quantity of rubber produced. The collection, manufacture, storage and export of lower grade rubber (scrap and lump) were also prohibited from time to time. For a few months in 1934–35 no tree was to be tapped more than once a day on a quarter-circumference, or every other day on one-half circumference, but this prohibition was subsequently removed. These measures proved insufficient and

[1] This can be seen from a circular issued in June 1937 by the North Borneo Planters' Association, quoting a letter from the Controller which suggested that all assessments should be increased to yields equivalent to 'ABC plus one half' to justify claims for a substantially higher quota after 1938. This would have raised the average estate assessment to some 570 lb. per acre and that of smallholdings to about 300 lb. Circulating this letter, the chairman of the Planters' Association commented : 'I think we may take it for granted that there will be a certain amount of jockeying for position on the part of all producing countries during the next eighteen months, and it would certainly be folly to adopt a formula of assessment less favourable than that adopted elsewhere. But when it is proposed to put forward a claim, based on the assumption that the average estate production in North Borneo under alternate daily tapping is properly estimated at 570 lb. per acre per annum, then I feel bound to suggest that such optimism cannot be justified by performance, past, present or future. I find it difficult to believe that any good can come from a claim resting on such exaggeration, and do not see how I can conscientiously lend my support to it.' Thus the planters were more moderate than the public servant. This kind of bargaining technique, while it influenced the fixing of territorial quotas only indirectly, if at all, nevertheless furnishes a small but perhaps not uninteresting example of the arbitrariness of quota schemes.

tapping holidays, the total prohibition of tapping for four-weekly periods, were soon introduced.

The compulsory tapping holidays, though an administratively simple method of control, had certain drawbacks, such as the hardship which was inflicted on districts whose crop was adversely affected by unfavourable weather before or after a tapping holiday. Individual restriction was therefore introduced in 1938. The smallholdings, which accounted for over 90 per cent. of the planted area, were surveyed and assessed with assistance from the Malayan Survey Department. The planted area was found to be 228,000 acres, against the previous official estimate of 213,000 acres, and Dr. Whitford's figure of 260,000 acres.

In conjunction with the survey a series of tapping tests were made under the supervision of a senior officer of the Survey Department. One hundred plots totalling 375 acres and stated to have been representative were examined. The annual yields ranged from 169 lb. to 944 lb. per acre, with an average of 489 lb. The planting density varied from 60 to 680 trees per acre, with an average of 239 trees. The yields were very close to those found by the Malayan smallholdings enquiry of 1931–33, as were most of the findings of the survey. As in Malaya and in the N.E.I., the yield per acre was found to increase with the number of trees. This is shown in the following table.

TABLE VII

Planting Density and Yield per Acre on Smallholdings in Sarawak

Stand per acre	*No. of plots*	*Average stand*	*Average yield per acre (lb. per annum)*
1–100	10	80	320
101–150	8	126	451
151–200	28	185	470
201–300	28	228	507
301–400	16	348	564
Over 400	10	494	630

Forestalling the argument that the yields were due to overtapping, the Superintendent of the survey commented in the report[1]: 'If a close estimate of the potential production of Sarawak

[1] *Report on Rubber Regulation in Sarawak* (1937). This document has apparently not been printed (though its contents were made public in the East); a mimeographed copy is available among the papers of the I.R.R.C. The results of the subsequent survey for assessment purposes are embodied in the published *Report on the Rubber Survey and Assessment of Sarawak* (1938).

is to be made, it is the yields actually obtained by normal Asiatic methods, and not those which would be obtained by European methods, which must be known. And drastic as the former may appear, there is little doubt that they can be maintained year after year.' In spite of this, when the survey figures were put before the I.R.R.C. some delegates again referred to the rough-and-ready methods of the smallholders and to their excessive bark consumption.[1]

Although there were various administrative difficulties, the regulation machinery in Sarawak worked fairly well, especially after the introduction of individual restriction. The prohibition of new planting was also successfully enforced, though this was not easy as the bulk of the area was unsurveyed until 1937. There was considerable discontent over the prohibition of new planting, especially the eradication of self-sown seedlings.

(*d*) *Siam*

Rubber restriction was not introduced in Siam until July 1935, as a new quota had to be negotiated following the rejection of the original agreement by the People's Assembly. A rudimentary system of assessments was established, with the standard productions fixed by government officials in the rubber-growing districts. Individual assessments were subject to certain maxima per tree and surface unit. A generous quota and the guaranteed minimum exports enabled Siamese exports to be kept within the permissible limits without an efficient machinery of control. It appears that the restriction of new planting was not enforced. Occasional returns furnished by the Siamese authorities to the I.R.R.C. purporting to show the planted area varied greatly and generally showed large increases over previous estimates.

(*e*) *Burma*

In Burma the administration of regulation and the assessment of holdings were in the hands of the Burma Rubber Licensing Committee.[2] Estates with records were assessed on the largest output in any one year between 1928–33. In the absence of crop

[1] The Sarawak authorities claimed that the true average yield was actually understated owing to the accidental omission of two of the best yielding districts. Before this survey, Sarawak rubber, when discussed at all, was referred to with the contempt with which smallholders' rubber was generally treated. The survey ascertained that it yielded well in excess of estate rubber in Malaya and the N.E.I.

[2] The administration of regulation in India was very similar to that in Burma and will not be discussed here.

records, holdings were assessed at 150 lb. per acre when ten years old or older, at 125 lb. when nine years, and at 100 lb. when eight years old. These low rates reflected not only the late maturity and low yields of rubber in Burma, but also the poor permanent basis of the territory and the generous treatment of estates with past production records, whose assessment at the maximum output over 1928–33 necessitated more severe treatment of others. The basic quota of Burma was raised in 1935 and assessments were revised. Estates with past production figures were treated as before. Others were grouped into three classes: well-managed, fair and poor estates. The first were assessed at 300 lb. on full maturity (ten years or over), the second at 240 lb. and the third at 180 lb. Eight- and nine-year-old rubber received lower assessments.

Some of the estates and many of the smallholdings were in remote parts of Burma and often had no postal address. To minimise the risk of loss, the coupons had to be fetched by the owners or their authorised agents from district headquarters; this often involved long journeys and considerable individual hardship. To reduce expense and inconvenience export rights were issued only once a year. When the international release for the first quarter was announced, the Burma Licensing Committee took a view on the probable average rate of release for the whole year and licences were issued accordingly. Though the estimates were intended to be conservative, on two occasions they substantially exceeded the releases for the year and there were heavy over-exports which had to be corrected subsequently.

(*f*) *French Indo-China*

No regulation machinery was established in French Indo-China as exports from that territory were not restricted. The obligation to deliver certain quantities of rubber to the I.R.R.C. was commuted into a money payment at the average London price of rubber, financed by a small export tax. The money was distributed among the British, Dutch and French rubber research institutes. New planting was effectively prohibited.

PART III

RUBBER REGULATION IN PEACE AND WAR

CHAPTER 8

EARLY DIFFICULTIES, 1934–35

I

THE first meeting of the I.R.R.C. was held within a week of the signing of the international agreement and rates of release were fixed for June–December 1934. These were 100 per cent. for June–July, 90 per cent. for August–September, 80 per cent. for October–November, and 70 per cent. for December. There was no obligation to keep exports within these rates during each month or quarter and the decision was in fact for an $87\frac{1}{7}$ per cent. release for 1934. The comparatively generous rates of release were intended to ease the task of the local administrations by introducing restriction gradually. Following this decision the London price declined somewhat, from over *7d.* to around $6\frac{1}{2}$*d.* For the rest of the year it fluctuated between *6d.* and $7\frac{1}{2}$*d.*

Shortly after this meeting a number of difficulties ensued which almost destroyed the scheme. The first was the failure of the Siamese Assembly and of the Indian States to ratify the agreement, unless their territorial quotas were substantially raised.

On the acreage figures assumed for its calculations the Siamese quota appeared generous. The Siamese contended, however, that the planted area had been under-estimated, and the rising export figures confirmed the argument. Their demands rose rapidly; at first, 25,000 tons was thought rather high by the I.R.R.C., and when 35,000 tons was mentioned this was considered exorbitant, but the claim was soon advanced to 40,000 tons. Various methods of coercing Siam were considered, but she obtained her demands, was granted a quota of 40,000 tons for each year from 1935 to 1938, and joined the scheme with effect from 1st July 1935.

When the Indian quota was negotiated towards the end of 1933 between the R.G.A. and the South Indian Association in London, the computations were based on the 1929–32 exports and on the acreage figures. The quota so calculated was agreed without consultation with the Indian States which produce 98 per cent. of Indian rubber outside Burma. These claimed that the quota calculation was vitiated by serious omissions, and accordingly refused to ratify the agreement. The official acreage figure was based on voluntary returns by planters who had replied to a questionnaire sent to them some years before. The questionnaire was in appearance not unlike a tax paper, and many producers, chiefly proprietors of small estates and of smallholdings, had not replied. Moreover, the exports from the Travancore port of Aleppey had also been omitted from the permanent basis, as they were not included in the Indian trade returns. These contentions were unchallengeable, and as the Indian signature of the agreement was conditional on ratification by the States, the Indian quota was raised. A small addition had also to be made to the quota of Burma, where again exports had been inadequately recorded.

The quota increases had to be embodied in a protocol signed by all parties to the 1934 agreement. This procedure entailed considerable publicity and created much dissatisfaction in some territories, notably Ceylon and British North Borneo, which also considered themselves harshly treated ; formal requests for increases in their quotas were received in 1935.

The most serious difficulty, however, was a sharp difference of opinion which arose between the British and the Dutch soon after the inception of the scheme. The special export tax on N.E.I. native rubber was raised from 10 cents per kilo in June to 20 cents in July ; it was reduced to 16 cents in September to compensate for a fall in the world price. The N.E.I. authorities considered these rates already very high, and insisted that British ideas of a substantially higher level of prices—and therefore of higher rates of tax—could not be entertained.

The N.E.I. delegation to the I.R.R.C. expressed the same view, and a deadlock ensued at the October meeting at which the release for the early months of 1935 had to be fixed ; the Dutch pressed for 80 per cent. and the British for 70 per cent. The British representatives reminded the N.E.I. delegation that at the decisive Hague meeting the pivotal price of 4*d.* gold (about 6½*d.*) had been abandoned and the Dutch had accepted the scheme and its obligations without reference to any fixed price. The British members proposed formally to communicate to all signatory governments the Dutch opinion that the price could not be allowed to rise above 6½*d.*, as this was said to involve a new principle contrary to the original basis of the scheme. The meeting adjourned without a decision ; at the adjourned meeting a compromise of

75 per cent. was reached for the first half of 1935. The London price fell from 6¾*d.* to 6¼*d.* on the announcement of this decision.

There was much dissatisfaction within and outside the Committee with the Dutch attitude. The British argument at that meeting is summarised in the *History of Rubber Regulation* (p. 99) : 'It was evident, however, that regulation on this basis was in the long run unworkable ; it in fact meant that exports were regulated not by reference to the fair and equitable price level reasonably remunerative to efficient producers, but by the level at which the Dutch could control their native exports. There was no reason *prima facie* why the price level at which an export tax on native rubber in the Netherlands East Indies could be successfully operated, which was determined by one set of circumstances, should coincide with the equitable price level for the efficient producer, which was determined by an entirely different set of circumstances.' In other words, a fraction of the price 'reasonably remunerative to the efficient producer' would elicit such quantities of native rubber as to endanger regulation.

The order of magnitude of the burden of the tax in 1934 can be illustrated by a few figures. From September onwards the rate of the tax was 16 cents per kilo, slightly under one-half the price of Java standard sheet in Batavia, and about one-half of the Singapore price of medium blankets, the grade into which most of the N.E.I. native rubber was processed. At the ruling prices in the most important interior markets the native producer was left with about 4 cents per half-kilo of dry rubber, after bearing the special tax at 8 cents per half-kilo. This ratio between the tax and the net return was eventually to rise to the remarkable figure of 20 to 1.[1] The net return was generally below that of 1932, the year of the lowest rubber prices ever recorded. In October 1934 in important districts of Palembang it was estimated at 2–2½ cents per kilo of wet rubber, equivalent to about ¼*d.* per lb. and tapping fell off considerably, but it was expected that at 5 cents per kilo (½*d.* per lb.) large-scale family tapping would be resumed. Local interests in Sumatra and Borneo pressed strongly for higher releases. Just before the October meeting of the I.R.R.C.,

[1] Throughout the operation of the special export tax, the ordinary 5 per cent. *ad valorem* revenue export duty continued to be levied on the f.o.b. value of native exports after payment of the special tax. By the end of 1934 this *ad valorem* rate amounted to between 30 and 40 per cent. of the average price in the interior, and was soon to exceed 50 per cent.

A detailed review of the operation of the special tax will be found in Tables V and VI of Statistical Appendix II.

the Palembang Chamber of Commerce sent a telegram to the Netherlands Minister for Colonies which concluded: 'An increase in the world price by tightening restriction is unnecessary and undesirable, as the natives can produce at a reasonable return at half the present world price.' Thus what appeared to the I.R.R.C. as an internal administrative difficulty in the N.E.I. was a reflection partly of the inadequate N.E.I. native quota, but principally of the very different ideas on efficient production. In various guises this problem returned throughout the currency of rubber regulation.

II

When the I.R.R.C. reviewed the position early in 1935 it was found that although world absorption in 1934 at 920,000 tons had been a record, stocks at the end of the year were almost exactly what they had been at the outset of the scheme.[1] The price had averaged 6¾*d.* per lb. during the seven restriction months and was just over 6¼*d.* at the end of the year. These prices were considered inadequate and the Committee proposed to take energetic steps to reduce stocks and to improve the price. In the spring of 1935 there was a temporary fall in the price to 5½*d.* This was thought to be much below 'the minimum necessary to secure a reasonable return to efficient growers'.[2] The Committee, therefore, reduced the rate of release for the second quarter to 70 per cent. from the 75 per cent. decreed in October 1934, and fixed a rate of 65 per cent. for the second half of the year. But for the greater part of 1935 the situation both in London and in the East was dominated not so much by the 'efficient producer' with costs around 4*d.*–5*d.*, but by the N.E.I. natives who, satisfied with a price of 1*d.*–1½*d.*, came near to destroying rubber restriction. The history of regulation in 1935 is largely that of discussions and of measures to deal with this danger.

During the autumn of 1934 a tree census was started in the native areas of the Outer Provinces to obtain data for a system of individual assessment and restriction. This system was actually introduced experimentally in 1935 in a few districts which were

[1] Absorption and stock figures from 1934 to 1941 are given in Statistical Appendix II, Tables XI and XII.

[2] *History of Rubber Regulation*, p. 100. The *Straits Times* stated at the time that the price of 20 cents in Singapore (about 6*d.* in London) should be regarded as thoroughly satisfactory, as it yielded a profit of about 8 cents per lb. The U.S. Trade Commissioner in Singapore estimated the all-in cash costs of Malayan rubber companies in 1935 at around 11 cents (3*d.* per lb.) delivered Singapore.

comparatively small and relatively easily accessible and controllable. In the principal residencies the special export tax continued to apply, though it showed signs of strain. As a general yardstick the N.E.I. authorities aimed at keeping the difference between the Batavia price and the special tax at the approximate level of the very low Batavia prices of 1932–33. To minimise dislocation the authorities wished to avoid too frequent changes, and a slight improvement in the margin, resulting from a small increase in the Batavia price early in 1935, was not offset by a rise in the tax. From February onwards large excess exports developed in spite of an appreciable reduction in the net return to the natives, resulting at first from a fall in the price without a reduction in the rate of tax, and subsequently from successive increases in the tax.

By the end of June over-exports of native rubber totalled 25,000 tons, some 40 per cent. of the permissible exports. According to the twenty-second *N.E.I. Native Report* (covering the first quarter of 1935) the pressure to export came largely from the thousands of smaller holdings planted after 1925 whose productivity had increased with growing maturity; these producers were said to have virtually no costs, and to be prepared to tap at very low prices. The difference between the Batavia price and the duty was reduced by changes in the tax to 8 cents per half-kilo in August, 7 cents in September, 6 cents in November and 5 cents in December. The Batavia price referred to the highest grade of rubber, and 5 cents per half-kilo (1½*d.* per lb.) f.o.b. port of shipment was appreciably above the value of the bulk of native rubber exports. By the autumn the price in the interior had fallen to about 2–3 cents per half-kilo of *dry* rubber; by December, it was often as low as 2 cents per kilo (¼*d.* per lb.) in the most important districts. Yet there was still some tapping. The tax was then 26 cents per kilo, thirteen times the price in the interior. The year closed with native exports totalling 142,000 tons, 30,000 tons over the permissible amount and much in excess of the worst fears of the I.R.R.C. and of the N.E.I. authorities.[1]

Further problems were raised by the very large proceeds of the tax. When it was introduced, ideas of the annual yield did not exceed 10 million guilders. In 1935 the yield was 25 millions, and the authorities were uncertain how to dispose of the money

[1] This was with a native quota of about 170,000 tons. The British Consul-General in Batavia reported in a despatch to London early in 1935 that he had been informed by the highest official authority on native rubber that the total capacity was around 700,000 tons, and not 350,000 as had been assumed.

in the sparsely populated native districts, where the civil service had been severely retrenched during the depression. A fraction only of the proceeds was spent by the end of 1935. An American consular report, reproduced in part in the *Rubber News Letter*, stated in the spring of 1936 : 'Consideration is being given to a revision of the provision pertaining to use of these funds, so that the money may eventually be used for the general good, instead of only for native rubber-producing districts.' [1]

By the spring of 1935 it became clear that regulation was in serious danger. The N.E.I. authorities advised the Netherlands Ministry of Colonies that unless the native quota was substantially raised a complete breakdown would be inevitable. A request was accordingly put forward to the I.R.R.C. for a large increase in the N.E.I. quota, to be allocated wholly to the natives. Ceylon and British North Borneo also submitted formal requests for quota increases, and all three claims were referred to a small Sub-Committee of the I.R.R.C. for investigation and report to the main Committee. The I.R.R.C. had no power directly to raise a quota embodied in the international agreement ; it could only recommend such a step to the signatory governments, and if this was accepted a protocol would be signed embodying the alteration.

The N.E.I. argument that, failing a revision of the quota, regulation would collapse could be simply supported by reference to the trend of exports. The return to the native producer was depressed to below the 1932 level by the spring of 1935, but exports were running at a rate almost treble that of 1932. The low cost of living, the fall in the prices of other products, and the vast and increasing mature area were held responsible for this development. It was stated that the N.E.I. Government was faced with an economic impossibility in attempting to work regulation with the existing quota. It was added that further reductions in the net return to the native producers might lead to open rebellion. Annual native exports of at least 170,000–180,000 tons were required ; the N.E.I. Government estimated that there were some 600,000 rubber-growing smallholders, and an annual exportable minimum of 300 kilos had to be allowed for each.

The Dutch proposed an increase of 85,000 tons in the N.E.I.

[1] Some eighteen months before, the official nineteenth *N.E.I. Native Report* had stated : 'The principle that the proceeds shall be spent for the benefit of the inhabitants of the rubber-producing areas is *inseparably* bound up with this particular system of restriction. A proportion of the proceeds is withheld from the exporter, and this is defensible only if the amounts so withheld are spent *at once* for the benefit of the districts from which the money is derived.' (My italics.)

quota from 1936 onwards, all to be added to the native quota which would be raised to 270,000 tons for 1936. It was also requested that excess exports at the end of 1935 should be cancelled to enable the N.E.I. Government to make a fresh start. The Dutch emphasised that once the N.E.I. quota was increased, the N.E.I. Government and the N.E.I. delegation to the I.R.R.C. would withdraw their opposition to higher prices; thus not only would the scheme be saved, but it would be a better scheme than before.

The Sub-Committee declared these proposals to be unacceptable. A large increase in the basic quota was sure to result in renewed demands for quota increases from other territories. The Sub-Committee might be prepared to recommend an increase in the N.E.I. quota, but a sacrifice would have to be made by the N.E.I. estates as evidence of good faith. Accordingly, while the native quota should be raised by 85,000 tons, the N.E.I. quota as a whole would be increased by 57,000 tons only, the balance to be found by transfer from the estate quota which would thereby be reduced by about 12 per cent. Such a gesture would impress the signatory governments with the seriousness of the situation, their consent would be more easily obtained, and demands from the other territories could also be warded off.

By raising to 270,000 tons the native share in the N.E.I. quota for 1936 of 500,000 tons this proposal involved a reversal of the relative shares of estates and natives. It did not please the N.E.I. delegates; the personal interests of at least one member were considerably involved, and for economic and political reasons the proposal was certain to be highly unpopular with the European community in the N.E.I. and with important interests in Holland. Various counter-proposals were rejected by the Sub-Committee, whose final recommendation to the main Committee (and of the latter to the governments) was for an increase in the N.E.I. quota of 57,000 tons for 1936 and 55,000 tons for subsequent years, on the understanding that the estates would surrender 28,000 tons for the benefit of the natives. This latter stipulation, though part of the Sub-Committee's report, was not to be included (allegedly for unspecified political reasons) in the formal protocol, which was to deal only with the increase in the territorial quota. Moreover, it appears from the records of the discussions between the Sub-Committee and members of the N.E.I. delegation that the latter were told that nobody would ask any questions if the N.E.I. Government found it possible to control native exports without the internal transfer. After much protest and argument all the signatory governments agreed to the Sub-Committee's proposal, and the revised N.E.I. quota was embodied in a protocol signed in 1936.

Excess native exports had risen to 38,000 tons by November 1935. The N.E.I. Government then purchased and cancelled estate rights totalling 20,000 tons ; over-exports were reduced by about 6,000 tons in December and the remaining excess was cancelled by the Committee.[1] The export rights cost six million guilders, paid from the proceeds of the special tax. This use of the money was scarcely in accordance with the official promises to employ the funds solely in the interest of the rubber growing districts. The natives had admittedly exceeded their permissible exports, but these were based on a totally inadequate quota, calculated on principles different from those underlying the other basic quotas. Moreover, the difference between the Batavia price and the special tax during 1935 ranged from about 11½ cents per half-kilo of dry rubber in January to 5¼ cents in December ; this was the maximum the native producer could obtain for his rubber at port of shipment, whereas the price of the estate export rights bought by the Government with the proceeds of the tax was 14½ cents per half-kilo.

It remains to be recorded that not one ton was ever transferred from the estate to the native quota. During 1936 the N.E.I. authorities succeeded in keeping native exports within the permissible levels by raising the special tax until it reached 59 cents per kilo, and in the interior the proportion of the proceeds taxed away exceeded 95 per cent. In 1937 individual restriction was universally introduced and the control of native exports was simplified.[2] The failure to transfer part of the estate quota was never raised by the British delegates, some of whom had important estate interests in the N.E.I.

The formal claims of Ceylon and British North Borneo for

[1] The cancellation of the excess exports was not included in the protocol (though it had been recommended by the Sub-Committee) and was effected by resolution of the Committee. This was contrary to the international agreement, which prohibited excess exports over 5 per cent. and stipulated the deduction of all excess exports from the permissible amount of the following year.

[2] The leader of the N.E.I. delegation stated in a memorandum submitted in 1937 to another Sub-Committee of the I.R.R.C. : 'In the course of 1936 the native export duty was raised to such a level that an equilibrium was found at which exports could be controlled. There was thus no need to reduce the estate quota ; the internal adjustment would only have become necessary if the exports could not have been kept within the permissible amounts.'—*I.R.R.C. Minutes*, pp. 1889–90. The rate of tax required to reach equilibrium is not mentioned in the memorandum.

quota increases were examined along with the N.E.I. request. These claims were based partly on the discovery of additional areas planted after 1925 and also on alleged substantial discrepancies between potential capacity and basic quotas. The claims of both territories were rejected, since the additional acreages were comparatively small and revisions of that magnitude were general, while potential capacity did not enter into the calculation of quotas. The adverse decision aroused much protest in Ceylon, where a withdrawal from the scheme was seriously proposed. The improvement in prices in 1936 and the promise of better quotas during the second period of restriction gradually appeased the discontent.

III

Although much of the Committee's time was taken up by the quota revision claims, by 1935 the regulation machinery was gradually getting into its stride. Before fixing rates of release the I.R.R.C. usually examined, with the Advisory Panel of Manufacturers, various estimates of prospective absorption, and considered, in the light of the price and of the cost returns furnished by the producers' associations, whether stocks should be increased or decreased. The guiding factor was whether the market price was 'remunerative to efficient producers', and the actual level of stocks a secondary consideration; or rather an unremunerative price was taken as evidence of excessive stocks. There was often a fair measure of agreement between the Committee and the Panel, but in case of disagreement the former naturally prevailed. The manufacturers had accepted the scheme, which stipulated a 'fair and equitable price reasonably remunerative to efficient producers' (which in practice meant estate producers), and once this was admitted most of the Committee's decisions (though by no means all) could be defended. The manufacturers were also hoping for some price stability under regulation, as a relief after the heavy inventory losses of the slump years. The consent of the Panel was also more easily obtainable as its members realised that dissent would serve little purpose. A feature of the discussions at the I.R.R.C. meetings of 1934–35 was the frequent reproaches administered by members of the Committee to manufacturers for holding large stocks, which suggested a distrust of the Committee. The manufacturers were advised to reduce these stocks and to rely on the Committee for current supplies; such a policy was said to be conducive to greater stability. Soon the manufacturers would be blamed for having reduced their stocks, thereby creating a shortage of supplies and being thus responsible for the runaway market of 1936–37.

The release for the third quarter of 1935 had at first been fixed at 70 per cent. and subsequently reduced to 65 per cent., while for the fourth quarter the rate was first announced as 65 per cent. and subsequently reduced to 60 per cent. Substantial inroads were made into stocks, which were reduced by 100,000 tons over the year in spite of the over-exports from the N.E.I. The market was slow to respond to the tightening of restriction and the price failed to rise to levels considered satisfactory by the Committee. During the spring and early summer it fluctuated around 5½*d*., and though there was a subsequent rise, the average for the year was 6*d*. and this was regarded as definitely unremunerative to 'efficient producers'.

Since the beginning of the year the Committee had received regular returns from the British and Dutch producers' associations of the average costs of production of estate producers. For 1935 the costs of the Malayan producers as given in the returns averaged 6·25*d*. per lb. and those of the N.E.I. producers 6·66*d*. per lb. It thus appeared paradoxical that the majority of estate producers paid dividends for a year during which the average price was below the cost of production. The explanation generally given was the failure of producers to provide adequately for depreciation and amortisation; dividends were thus supposedly being paid out of capital. This explanation was received with considerable scepticism by manufacturing interests.

IV

A feature of considerable significance in the internal administration of regulation throughout the currency of the scheme was apparent by the autumn of 1934, when a brisk trade developed in export rights [1] in the major producing countries. There was much unreasonable agitation against the free transfer of rights separately from physical rubber. The 'organised traffic' in rights and coupons and the 'gambling in rights' were condemned on

[1] In official Malayan terminology rights referred to estate export rights as distinct from smallholders' coupons. In the next few pages 'rights', 'coupons', and 'licences' are used indiscriminately, in accordance with the convenient, though not strictly accurate, unofficial practice.

semi-moral grounds in the press. The responsibility for the substantial areas out of tapping and the resulting unemployment, especially in the villages, was also laid at the door of the transfer of rights.

This last point, which was a recurrent theme in the newspapers of Malaya and Ceylon and can also be found in many official reports, rests on a palpable fallacy. The rural unemployment and the areas out of tapping reflected the level of output determined by the releases under regulation and had nothing to do with the traffic in rights. When coupons were issued (usually quarterly) the smallholders promptly sold them to dealers; having thus disposed of their export rights, the rubber they produced was unlicensed, and was bought by the dealers to marry with their rights.[1]

The extraordinary misunderstanding about the effect of low releases and high coupon prices on the area out of tapping is well brought out in the official *Economic Survey of the Colonial Empire*, issued in 1935 by the Colonial Office. Referring to the large increase in the untapped area on Malayan smallholdings between the end of 1934 and the end of 1935, it states: 'There are several contributory causes to this large increase (to an estimated 38 per cent. of the mature area), the most important being the high price which can be obtained for coupons.' In fact, the area out of tapping simply reflected the rate of release which, at the end of 1935, was 60 per cent. The official quarterly *Malayan Smallholdings Reports* repeated regularly that the high coupon prices were responsible for the suspension of tapping and for the resulting rural unemployment. To take a series of quotations for 1938–39: 'The practice of selling coupons without rubber is directly responsible for the majority of untapped holdings' (*Malayan Agricultural Journal*, August 1938). 'In Kedah the sale of coupons by smallholders is giving rise to serious unemployment' (*M.A.J.*, January 1939). 'In the Kuala Muda district of Kedah 300 tappers have been thrown out of work as a result of widespread sales of coupons' (*M.A.J.*, February 1939). The simple fact was that during the second half of 1938 and the first half of 1939 the international rates of release were reduced to 45 and 50 per cent., and naturally

[1] The smallholders were, occasionally and to a minor extent, sellers of rights to estates *via* dealers who bought unlicensed estate rubber to match with the rights bought from smallholders. In Malaya, as we have seen (above, p. 98), these net sales never exceeded a few thousand tons. In Ceylon there is no evidence of substantial net sales of rights from one group to another. In the N.E.I. rights were not transferable between estates and smallholders.

there was a sharp fall in output as producers were not allowed to export in excess of their permissible amounts and the trees had perforce to be left untapped. This consideration seems to have escaped the authorities. Yet it is hard to think of a more obvious point, unless it is the fact that when one producer sells coupons someone else must buy them and there can thus be no reduction in output on this score.

The price of rights would vary with the degree of restriction, with the market price of rubber and with the supply price of unlicensed rubber. It could be expected to settle at a level equal to the difference between the market price of rubber over the period of the validity of the rights or the period over which the dealers are prepared to hold them, and the supply price required to draw out enough unlicensed rubber to provide the exportable quantity over the same period.[1] There were usually substantial fluctuations around this equilibrium price, partly because export rights and coupons were issued at the beginning of each quarter while unlicensed rubber was often bought near the end. Their purchase was a highly speculative business, as dealers had to estimate the market price of rubber and the short-period supply price of unlicensed rubber some months forward. In the better organised markets competition was usually sufficiently keen to deprive dealers of monopoly profits which would have absorbed losses due to incorrect market forecasts. Early in 1937, for example, the prices offered by dealers for N.E.I. native coupons turned out to have been too high and the dealers suffered appreciable losses.

The price of unlicensed rubber cannot be regarded as the supply price of a given quantity of rubber, since the revenue derived from the sale of export rights is obtained by the owner for possessing an assessable rubber holding, and many sellers of unlicensed rubber could not have continued production solely on the proceeds from that rubber; thus some Java estates regularly sold rubber without rights, and often for as little as 4–5 guilder cents per half-kilo (about 1*d.* per lb.) which, though it may have been their marginal prime cost, was certainly far below the supply price of larger quantities of estate rubber. The price of uncouponed smallholders' rubber reflects more nearly the supply price of such rubber over the period of the currency of the coupons and possibly even the long-period supply price, where rubber cultivation was

[1] The prices of export rights and coupons in Malaya, the N.E.I. and Ceylon throughout the restriction period are reviewed in Table VII of Statistical Appendix II.

not the sole or main source of the smallholders' livelihood. If he could obtain 5–7 cents per half-kilo for rubber while still finding time to cultivate his *ladang*, the smallholder in Sumatra and Borneo would continue to do so even without the additional revenue derived from the sale of licences. Malayan smallholders were apparently prepared to produce substantial quantities of rubber as long as the price was around 4–5 Straits cents per lb. up-country; this had emerged from the experience of the slump and was confirmed by the readiness with which unlicensed rubber was produced with the price at or above that level; there was a notable contraction of supplies when the price declined below these values.[1] It seems that the price paid for unlicensed smallholders' rubber, while not a true long-period supply price in view of the income derived from the sale of coupons, would usually elicit, over a prolonged period, a quantity of rubber comparable to that produced under restriction. This is probably a reasonable guess for most of the smallholding rubber in Malaya and the N.E.I.

The operation of the special export tax provided, however, an unequivocal indication of the supply price of N.E.I. native rubber during 1934–36, since the proceeds of the tax were not returned to individual smallholders, and the net return which elicited the rubber produced was a genuine supply price.

[1] Both in Malaya and in the N.E.I. the supply price of unlicensed rubber from smallholdings was often higher than from estates at times of low releases, as the former could and the latter could not turn to rice, coconuts or other products. This explains why Malayan smallholders were, at times, to a small extent sellers of rights to estates. This is no indication of relative long-period supply prices.

CHAPTER 9

THE SCHEME IN PROSPERITY AND RECESSION, 1936–39

I

THROUGHOUT the second half of 1935 stocks were falling steadily. For 1936 the I.R.R.C. planned a further stock reduction of at least 100,000 tons. The exportable release was fixed at 60 per cent. for the first half of the year. The price rose only slightly, and fluctuated around 7¼*d.*–7½*d.* throughout the early months of the year. Absorption was rising satisfactorily and observers were disappointed by the absence of market response to the favourable and improving statistical position.

There were various reasons for the hesitant attitude of the market. The administrative difficulties in the N.E.I. were reflected in repeated increases in the special tax which by February had reached 33 cents per kilo, and it was feared that should the guilder be devalued the resulting rise in the guilder price of rubber would create insurmountable difficulties. Some observers also thought that the ruling price was not far removed from the level aimed at by the Committee. This was not so; the I.R.R.C. had concluded that 7½*d.* was not satisfactory; the cost returns indicated average costs around 6*d.*–6½*d.*, and a price of 8½*d.*–9*d.* was thought necessary to secure a reasonable return to the 'average efficient producer'. It will be noted that the profit alone (2½*d.*) necessary for the efficient producers was several times the net return left to the N.E.I. natives after the payment of the special tax.

The policy of stock reduction was accordingly continued. The rate of release for the second half of 1936 was raised to 65 per cent. but exports were expected to remain below absorption which was rising at an accelerated rate. By the autumn manufacturers were anxious about supplies; the Committee insisted that the policy of stock reduction must continue as the price was still unremunerative; the manufacturers began to emphasise that the price had risen from 3*d.* in 1933 to over 7*d.* in 1936.[1]

The much-feared Dutch devaluation occurred in September, but N.E.I. native exports were effectively controlled by further

[1] According to the *History of Rubber Regulation* (p. 104), the Advisory Panel admitted that 7½*d.* was not 'generally remunerative'; an interesting shift of emphasis from the efficient producer.

steep rises in the special tax; the early introduction of individual restriction was also announced. By October stocks had been reduced to about 5–5½ months' absorption and the Advisory Panel pressed for a release which would prevent their further diminution. At the end of October the Committee decided on a 70 per cent. release for the first half of 1937, which on all reasonable assumptions was certain to result in a further reduction in stocks. The market realised this and also appreciated the fact that there would probably be a shortage of spot rubber. The decision also revealed that the Committee was aiming at higher prices than those ruling. The price rose from 7¾*d.* to over 8¼*d.* within a few days.

These prices exceeded the cash costs of reasonably managed estates by 100 per cent. or more, and a rubber share boom now developed. The commodity boom and the share boom reinforced each other, since profits made in one market could be re-invested in the other. By mid-December the price reached 9½*d.* and an acute shortage of spot rubber emerged. Stocks at 460,000 tons (including stocks afloat) showed a reduction of about 180,000 tons over the year and were equivalent to about 5½ months' absorption only at the average 1936 rate, and consumption was still rising. The demand for spot rubber was increasing with the rapidly developing speculation and the continued improvement in absorption.

At the urgent request of the Advisory Panel the Committee met again in December. The Panel asked for an increase of the release to at least 80 per cent. for the first quarter of 1937. The Committee considered that such a sharp increase would result in dislocation and raised the release to 75 per cent. only for the first quarter and to 80 per cent. for the second quarter. The market had feared higher rates. The price rose to over 11*d.* by the end of the month; it would have risen much further but for the withdrawal of some of the large manufacturers from the market.

During most of January the price was around 10½*d.*–11*d.* with spot and near rubber still very scarce, and it was clear that without additional supplies further increases would be inevitable when manufacturers re-entered the market. After some preliminary sounding the American Government addressed a formal *démarche* to the British and Dutch Governments protesting against the excessive rise in the price of rubber and requesting the release of larger supplies. The French Government was also anxious about the inadequate stocks, and through the French representative on the Committee pressed for higher exports.

The Committee met again in January, chiefly to consider these requests. The American member of the Advisory Panel asked for a revision of the second quarter release from 80 per cent. to 90 per cent. and for the same rate for the third quarter. He also proposed that the I.R.R.C. should advise the producing territories to consider internal re-distribution of their assessments and quotas to enable under-assessed producers to export more nearly in accordance with their potential capacity, as this would appreciably affect readily available supplies at high releases.

The Committee declared that chiefly owing to seasonal and labour difficulties an increase in the release for the second quarter would not result in larger supplies. They accordingly refused to raise the release for the second quarter ; for the third quarter the release was fixed at 85 per cent. A request for internal re-distribution of quotas was said to be outside the competence of the Committee, which was not concerned with the local administration of restriction. At a cost of some inconsistency, the Committee was prepared to recommend to the local governments that advance issues of second- and third-quarter rights should be made to producers capable of using them.

The Committee also agreed to the following addition to the usual formal communiqué announcing the rates of release : 'The Committee re-affirm their desire to maintain, at all times, a supply of rubber adequate to consumers' needs. They realise that producing territories, particularly those dependent on immigrant labour, must necessarily take steps in advance to organise themselves for increased production.' But as this communiqué coincided with the announcement of a compulsory tapping holiday of 28 days in Sarawak to keep exports from that territory within the permissible limits, it was hardly surprising that the Americans doubted the Committee's good faith. The price, which had declined to 10½*d.* just before the meeting, rose to 10¾*d.* By early March it reached 11½*d.* The assiduously spread view that the major producing territories would be found incapable of producing 90 per cent. or even 80 per cent. of their quotas, together with the continued decline in stocks and the increase in absorption, powerfully stimulated speculation.

No further steps were taken until the Committee's next meeting in March, at which the Advisory Panel again pressed for larger supplies. In particular they asked for an increase in the second-quarter release and repeated the request for internal re-distribution of the territorial quotas. These proposals were rejected.

The third quarter release was, however, raised from 85 per cent. to 90 per cent. and this rate was also fixed for the fourth quarter. The price of rubber rose again as soon as it became known that the second-quarter release was not to be raised. There were further increases during the last days of March, until 1*s.* 1⅜*d.* was reached, the highest price since 1927 when the Stevenson scheme was still in operation.[1] A reaction then developed and the price fell to about 1*s.*, declining further to 10*d.* in May and 9*d.* in June; it remained around that level during most of the summer. An important factor in the market reaction was the realisation that the producing territories as a whole could easily produce the exportable releases. It also appeared that manufacturers would not be forced to make large purchases at an early date. Labour troubles in America and some weakness in other commodity markets were contributory factors. After April large supplies, especially from the native producers in the N.E.I., relieved the shortage of spot rubber.

There was much criticism, especially in America, of the Committee's decisions between October 1936 and March 1937. The Committee was particularly criticised for not having raised the rate of release more rapidly, and for not arranging for the issue of rights to under-assessed producers, chiefly smallholders. Members of the Committee replied to this criticism with various counter-arguments. The chief contention was that higher releases than the 75 per cent. and 80 per cent. actually fixed for the first two quarters of 1937 would not have brought out more rubber, first, because February–April were the seasonally low producing months in the principal rubber-growing territories, and secondly because time was needed to recruit and train additional labour for the greatly increased production. Rapid increases in the rate of release would, it was claimed, have led to a scramble for labour and to unrest among workers, so that less rubber would have been produced. As one delegate said at the meeting of the Committee in January 1937: 'No measure, however drastic, would increase the flow of rubber from the trees. If the Committee decided to raise the rate of release for this quarter (January–March 1937) or

[1] The closing weeks of the commodity boom were accompanied by steep increases in rubber share values which lost all connection with earning power. The 2*s.* shares of one rubber company which had paid no ordinary dividend since 1926 rose to 2*s.* 8*d.* The estate of that company was on completely exhausted soil yielding under 200 lb. per acre, and no ordinary dividend could be expected except after a prolonged period of a price of 2*s.* 6*d.* per lb. By 1939 the ordinary shares had fallen to 2*d.* and by 1940 to 1*d.*; the company is now in liquidation.

the next, a very probable result would be that less rubber would be produced, since the higher rate of release would lead to competition for labour, higher wages, and probably less work on the plantations . . . They should not attempt to do something which in fact they believed to be impossible.'[1] In other words, output was unrestricted at a rate of release of 75 per cent.[2]

This argument is not easy to accept. There is a simple test of unrestricted output: the price of export rights falls to zero. So long as these have a market value some producers must pay for the right to produce, which they would not do if their exportable allowance represented actual capacity; nor would dealers bid for coupons unless the price of unlicensed rubber was below the market price for exportable rubber. During the first three months of 1937 the value of export rights, so far from being nil, was about one-half of the market price of rubber in Malaya, the N.E.I. and Ceylon.[3] The Sarawak tapping holiday in February, which was followed by another in April, provides an even simpler refutal of the view that output was at capacity level. The Committee's argument also implied that during the wintering months no producer could exceed 75 or 80 per cent. of his average monthly output. This again was difficult to justify; although the seasonal fall in estate production in Malaya and Sumatra was usually to about 80 per cent. of the average monthly output, this was an average figure, and could always have been exceeded by many producers. Moreover, in Java output is seasonally high during these months. Nor can the suggestion be accepted that higher releases would have failed to increase supplies through disorganisation of the local labour markets. The contention clearly did not apply to smallholdings. According to the Malayan press many estates there could have produced easily

[1] *I.R.R.C. Minutes*, p. 1244.

[2] There might have been a sounder case against a rapid and steep increase of the rate of production of which not much was heard. The authorities in Malaya, Ceylon and Sumatra would not have welcomed a substantial influx of immigrant labour to meet a purely temporary demand for larger supplies, as a subsequent reduction in releases would have necessitated the repatriation of the recent immigrants or their maintenance at public expense. But as a release of 85 per cent. had already been fixed for the third quarter when a request to raise the first or second quarter releases was rejected, these considerations did not apply to the conditions of early 1937.

[3] Cf. Statistical Appendix II, Table VII. Both in Malaya and in the N.E.I. smallholders' coupons in the early part of 1937 were worth well over one-half of the price of rubber. One member of the N.E.I. delegation argued at the I.R.R.C. meeting in January 1937 that an additional issue of rights to the native producers would result in less tapping, since the natives would sell the coupons, and the additional cash would reduce the incentive to tap. In fact, the additional issue would have resulted in a fall in the price of coupons relatively to unlicensed rubber, which would have stimulated tapping. This was amply borne out in 1941.

in excess of a 75 per cent. release early in 1937. In Java the estates had access to very large labour reserves in their immediate vicinity.

Nor is it easy to defend the refusal of the Committee to propose internal re-distribution of the quotas, or a special issue of rights to under-assessed producers, on the grounds that these matters were outside its competence. The Committee was concerned with supplies of rubber, and at high releases these were influenced by the internal distribution of quotas. If a country's basic quota is not greatly below its potential output at ruling prices and the quota is fairly distributed, a 90 per cent. or 100 per cent. release will generally elicit supplies of rubber equal to 90 per cent. or 100 per cent. of the quota. If one-half of the producers are under-assessed and the other half over-assessed, less rubber will be supplied, as the deficiency of exports from the over-assessed class will not be made up fully by the under-assessed group. Even if rights are freely transferable their price will increase the prime costs of the buyers, who will not therefore expand output as much as they would have done without this additional item in their costs. Moreover, producers who are under-assessed for considerable periods usually adjust their equipment to their assessment and would be unable to collect at short notice the rubber they could otherwise have produced.

It is difficult to resist the conclusion that the suggestion for an internal redistribution of the territorial quotas was rejected so flatly because of its awkward implications for the estates. Had the proposal been accepted, the under-assessment of the smallholders would have had to be discussed and its correction would have meant the loss to estates of valuable assessments. In the N.E.I. there was also the delicate question of the breach of the undertaking to transfer 28,000 tons from the estate to the native quota (discussed above, pp. 117–18), which was sure to come to light in any general review of the internal distribution of the basic quotas.

Two further factors contributed to the generally hesitant attitude of the Committee. First, there were doubts about the extent and the duration of the improvement in absorption ; possible repercussions of the American labour troubles were frequently cited as an adverse factor. The early fears proved largely unfounded and absorption during the latter months of 1936 and the first half of 1937 exceeded expectations ; when at last the doubts were set aside and a 90 per cent. release was fixed for the second half of 1937, the rapid American recession set in. Secondly, some members of the Committee were not altogether displeased with a period of

been made effective. It was also hoped that the American recession might last for only a few weeks or months.

World exports at 1,166,000 tons in 1937 were a record.[1] During the year there was some increase in stocks, which rose from about 465,000 tons at the beginning to over 530,000 tons at the end of the year. Almost one-half of the increase consisted of an increase in stocks afloat, the volume of which depends on the rate of exports which were much higher at the end of 1937 than at the end of 1936. Absorption at 1,095,000 tons was also a record, though U.S. absorption at 543,000 tons was below the 1936 level of 575,000 tons. The increase in stocks (including the rise in stocks afloat) equalled only slightly more than three weeks' absorption at the 1937 rate. The total was equal to 5¾ months' absorption at the average 1937 rate, but while at the end of 1936 the price stood at 11*d.*, with stocks at 5½ months' absorption at the 1936 rate, at the end of 1937 it was 7*d.* with stocks at 5¾ months' absorption.[2] The market was discounting conditions in 1938 and had undergone a change of sentiment for the worse.

The wide fluctuations in the American demand were again manifest in 1937–38. This is shown by the table on page 133.

In the late summer of 1937 the motor industry forecast U.S. automobile production for 1938 at 5½ million units or more; this figure was given by the American representative on the Advisory Panel of Manufacturers. By May 1938 successive revisions had reduced this to 1¾ millions. The actual total was just under 2½ million units against 4,800,000 units in 1937. Absorption of rubber early in 1938 fell below the 1932 level. These developments naturally played havoc with all estimates of consumption. In July 1937 the Rubber Manufacturers' Association of America estimated American absorption for the last quarter of 1937 at 145,000 tons while it turned out to be 102,000 tons. In November 1937 the estimate of American absorption for the first half of 1938 was 291,000 tons against an actual figure of 182,000 tons. The

[1] Exports at or near the rate of 90 per cent. were forthcoming from all the major producing countries. The Malayan estates found it difficult to produce at this rate and had to draw on stocks. To this extent the partial reassessment of 1937 did not suffice to offset the over-assessment of the estates.

[2] If absorption at the December rate is taken as a basis of calculation instead of the average monthly rate for the year, a different picture emerges. Stocks at the end of 1936 were only 5·0 times the December absorption, while for December 1937 the corresponding figure was 7·5. On the other hand, at the end of 1938 stocks were the equivalent of 5·3 times the December 1938 absorption and the price stood at 8*d.* Generally speaking the advantage of expressing stocks in terms of December absorption over using the average rate for the year is not substantial.

TABLE I

Absorption of Rubber and Index of Automobile Production in the U.S.A., 1937–38

(Seasonally corrected figures)

	Absorption of rubber (thousand tons)		*1938 as per cent. of 1937*	*Index of automobile production (1923–25 = 100)*		*1938 as per cent. of 1937*
	1937	*1938*		*1937*	*1938*	
Jan.	46·8	28·5	*60·9*	120	65	*54·2*
Feb.	53·3	25·9	*48·6*	120	62	*51·7*
Mar.	49·8	29·6	*59·4*	121	54	*44·6*
Apr.	50·2	28·6	*57·0*	130	54	*41·5*
May	51·1	30·2	*59·1*	135	49	*36·3*
June	52·5	32·6	*62·1*	130	46	*35·4*
July	47·4	36·9	*77·9*	129	43	*33·3*
Aug.	43·0	41·7	*97·0*	157	45	*28·7*
Sept.	46·6	42·4	*91·0*	135	46	*34·1*
Oct.	38·5	42·3	*109·9*	142	84	*59·2*
Nov.	34·3	49·1	*143·1*	92	96	*104·3*
Dec.	30·1	49·2	*163·5*	78	99	*126·9*

The automobile production index is from the *Survey of Current Business*. The absorption figures have been corrected for seasonal variations according to a new index prepared at my request by Mr. W. G. G. Kellett of the London Rubber Secretariat, as the figures of the Department of Commerce do not appear to be altogether satisfactory.

forecast for the full year was 565,000 tons; the final figure turned out to be 437,000 tons,[1] though meanwhile it had been estimated as low as 350,000 tons.

In September 1937 the price began to decline from the 9*d.* level and the fall soon gathered speed. In November 6¾*d.* was touched and the year closed with the price at 7*d.* The main cause of the reaction was the change of sentiment occasioned largely by the American recession; the ability of the producing countries to export 90 per cent. was a contributory factor. The release for the first quarter of 1938 was fixed in December 1937. A reduction from 90 per cent. to 70 per cent. was then announced, much the greatest single change so far. It was followed by a reduction to 60 per cent. for the second quarter of 1938. To mitigate the inevitable difficulties which were sure to arise in the producing territories, stocks which producers were permitted to hold were raised from 20 per cent. of their exports over the preceding

[1] The fall in world absorption from 1937 to 1938 was 162,000 tons (from 1,095,000 tons to 933,000 tons), of which the U.S.A. accounted for 106,000 tons. This time the secular rise in the demand for rubber outside the U.S.A. no longer sufficed to offset the effects of the industrial depression.

twelve months to one-quarter of their standard production.[1] The market was not satisfied with these severe cuts. The price drifted downwards and there were several sharp breaks in one of which (in March) the London spot price fell by 15 per cent. in one day and by 25 per cent. (from *7d.* to *5¼d.*) within twelve days; some positions had fallen by 20 per cent. within three days. This demoralisation of the market seemed unfounded since it was virtually certain that the Committee would succeed in raising the price to substantially higher levels.

The Committee decided on drastic measures and reduced the rate of release to 45 per cent. for the third quarter. Some members of the Committee wished for a reduction to 40 per cent., but the N.E.I. and Sarawak delegations asked for 50 per cent., emphasising the administrative difficulties in the East and the hardships inflicted on smallholders by this very rapid and steep reduction in the rate of release. Forty-five per cent. was the maximum release which the majority was prepared to concede; it was to be repeated for the last quarter.

In the East this rapid reduction in exportable amounts proved troublesome. Throughout the producing territories large areas were thrown out of tapping, both on estates and on smallholdings. The high coupon prices were again erroneously blamed for the failure of the smallholders to tap their trees and for the resulting rural unemployment, and demands were unsuccessfully put forward for a prohibition of the transfer of coupons.[2] The price of unlicensed rubber fell sharply; at times such rubber was unsaleable and the price of export rights represented almost the entire market value. In Java unlicensed estate rubber fell to 3–4 guilder cents per half-kilo; export rights were worth over 20 cents.

Acute administrative difficulties arose in Ceylon, where, on the authority of the Minister of Agriculture, the Rubber Controller had issued rights in excess of the permissible amount during the first three quarters of 1938 in order to soften the effects of the severe cuts on the economic life of the country. It was hoped that the very low releases would be raised before the end of 1938. This expectation did not materialise, and by September rights equal to the permissible amount for the whole year had been issued. The failure to issue any rights at all for the last quarter would have

[1] This provision was included in the renewed international agreement of 1938, which was anticipated by the Committee to enable estate producers to limit dismissals of labour.

[2] These demands did not go so far in rubber as they did in tin, where a scheme for the control of coupon prices was seriously proposed.

disorganised the economic life of several districts. Smallholders and the smaller estates would have been placed in a very difficult position and mass dismissals of labour would have been inevitable. The authorities decided to issue additional export rights equal to about 9 per cent. of standard assessments. This over-issue foreshadowed excess exports of over 5 per cent. The Ceylon Government hoped that the excess would be cancelled by the Committee on the analogy of the N.E.I. over-exports at the end of 1935. In the Committee's opinion, however, there was no analogy, as the cancellation of the N.E.I. excess exports had been part of the increase in the N.E.I. quota. After much discussion the Committee ruled that the excess could not be cancelled, but Ceylon was permitted to liquidate the surplus gradually over the next period of regulation. Meanwhile the Government, on learning that the excess exports would not be cancelled, had resorted to drastic measures. Producers and dealers were invited to surrender 1938 rights in exchange for 1939 credits, and a bill was rushed through the State Council empowering the Rubber Controller to force producers and dealers to exchange their present for future export rights. These powers had to be used as voluntary exchanges were few.

It would appear that the Committee paid insufficient attention to some of the consequences of its policy and extended little sympathy to the administrators who had to carry it out and still less to those who, like the smallholders or the under-employed labourers, bore the brunt of the severe cuts. A less severe reduction in the rate of release might have somewhat retarded the rate of recovery in the price but it would have eased the local situation. Several of the British members insisted that the Committee had full powers, without any limit set by administrative problems in the East; it was said that consideration of these difficulties would have transferred effective decision from the Committee to the Eastern governments. Somewhat unexpectedly, the strongest advocate of a reduction in the rate of release to 40 per cent. was an official representative, who argued from his experience in tin regulation that the local administrations were wont to exaggerate their problems; though he had been told by the government of the territory he represented on the International Tin Committee that 60 per cent. was the minimum feasible rate which could be operated, in fact a 33 per cent. release was successfully maintained for two years. He did not enlarge on the cost of such measures.

By the end of 1938 absorption was increasing, and the outlook was somewhat brighter. As the price was still considered unremunerative the release for the first quarter of 1939 was raised only to 50 per cent. The Advisory Panel asked for a higher release, but was overridden. There were also renewed arguments over the responsibility for the low level of prices and stocks. Once again the Committee rebuked manufacturers for having reduced their stocks, insisting at the same time that further reductions were necessary.[1] The Committee was greatly dissatisfied with the price, which averaged just under 7¼*d.* during 1938 and was around 8*d.* during the closing months of the year. In conjunction with low releases (averaging 55 per cent. for the year) these prices did not spell prosperity, but they were not so bad as was stated at the time. The prosperity of 1937 had led to a revision in the Committee's original ideas, and 9*d.* was now regarded as the minimum price yielding a reasonable return to the 80–90 per cent. of the estate producers generously admitted into the circle of efficient producers.

The first eight months of 1939 were marked by a continuous reduction in stocks to very low levels by the summer. The Advisory Panel unsuccessfully pressed for higher releases. The rate was fixed at 50 per cent. for the first half of the year and at 55 per cent. (subsequently raised to 60 per cent.) for the third quarter. The low level of stocks was admitted, but the Committee argued that price considerations pointed to the need for still further reduction as a price around 8*d.* was still unremunerative. At the February meeting of the Committee one of the members stated that the Committee was concerned only with the level of stocks and not with the price, but that the sufficiency of the stocks had to be interpreted according to prevailing price, which indicated the need for further stock reduction. By that time stocks at 4½ months' absorption were appreciably below the level which released the boom of 1936–37. They were also below the level (5 months' absorption) which had been assumed as a safe minimum for the smooth functioning of the machinery of production, shipment and absorption. The decisions of the Committee during this period finally disposed of the fiction that the Committee was guided by the level of stocks and not by the price.[2] The American member of the Panel emphasised the rapidly extending field of absorption in latex form, especially as sponge rubber in upholstery. He thought

[1] Cf. *History of Rubber Regulation*, pp. 108–10.

[2] The unsatisfactory level of past prices seems also to have weighed with the Committee: 'Having regard to the fact that the average price throughout the period of regulation from May, 1934, to the end of 1938 was only 7¼*d.* per lb. (15½ U.S. cents per lb.), it was natural that the Committee should adopt a more cautious release policy.' *History of Rubber Regulation*, p. 116.

that a substantial rise in the price would prejudice the successful development of this new field of absorption, which was one of the few in which the cost of the raw material represented the largest item in the total cost of manufacturing. This argument seems to have influenced the Committee in raising the release for the third quarter, though not sufficiently to prevent a further substantial reduction in stocks.[1]

Since the beginning of 1939 discussions had been under way between the British and American authorities for a barter exchange of cotton and rubber ; the British Government was to acquire a strategic reserve stock of cotton, and the U.S. Government was to receive rubber for the same purpose. The rubber involved amounted to some 85,000 tons, to be held as a revolving reserve stock for at least seven years, except in the event of a major national emergency, when it could be used.

The Committee disliked the barter proposals for various reasons the most important of which was the belief that the transactions would adversely affect the price of rubber, as speculators would be discouraged by a large stock in American hands, while the British Government was likely to object to a rise in price, which would inflict losses on the Ministry of Supply. As the governments had resolved on the plan the Committee had to yield, and on some pressure by the British Government and assurances that the stock would be firmly held by the U.S. Government, the release was raised to 70 per cent. for the last quarter, a few days before the outbreak of war.

Trading came to a standstill a day or two before the outbreak of hostilities and in a few markets rubber became unsaleable. The declaration of war was followed by a sharp rise in prices ; in Singapore spot rubber jumped from 29 cents to 40 cents per lb. within two trading days. The price of rubber, as that of other commodities, was depressed by the threat of war, while its outbreak raised it immediately.

[1] With stocks falling rapidly and the price beginning to creep up, the market reports were busy forecasting another boom and at the same time trying to engender it. One of these circulars—again by a leading firm—suggested that the Committee was aiming at a 9*d.*–9½*d.* price (against the price of 8*d.* actually ruling), but ' they no doubt realise that if such a price is to be maintained it will be necessary that a somewhat higher price should first be reached so as to leave room for some fluctuation '.

Before each meeting of the Committee the chorus of market reports would press for lower releases and higher prices. When stocks were high or rising the unfavourable statistical position would be emphasised ; when they were falling the Committee was reminded that statistics were the worst possible guide to market sentiment. The actual decision was almost always bullishly interpreted for the benefit of the speculators.

CHAPTER 10

ADMINISTRATIVE CHANGES AND THE RENEWAL OF THE SCHEME

I

ONCE regulation was established there were no important administrative changes in the major producing territories until 1937. In that year some important measures were taken in Malaya to expedite the flow of rubber and to ensure that the 90 per cent. release of the second half of the year should be met. On the recommendation of the I.R.R.C., the Controller of Rubber announced early in 1937 that estates able to produce in excess of their permissible exports during the first and second quarters could apply for an advance issue of rights which would be debited against their credits in subsequent quarters. Conversely, estate export rights were allowed to be carried forward from the first to the second and from the second to the third quarter ; this concession was granted only to producers who had no ready rubber to sell and who had made *bona fide* efforts to produce their full exportable amounts. Advantage was taken of these various facilities on only a very limited scale.

For administrative reasons the anticipation of rights was confined to estates. The smallholders would undoubtedly have taken advantage of such a provision, partly because they never hesitate to anticipate future income, but also since apparently many of them felt that the rubber prices ruling during the spring of 1937 were near the peak and that a decline was to be expected. According to a report of the Department of Agriculture : 'One result reported of the high prices is that smallholders are in constant fear of a major drop in the market and for that reason are tapping heavily and selling their rubber wet, to benefit as much as possible now.'[1] This sound view may have been due to the illiteracy of the smallholders which prevented them from reading market reports.

It will be recalled that estate assessments were based on the average annual production during the basic years (1929–32) together with scale allowances (limited to 500 lb. per acre for seedling rubber) for rubber untapped during these years, or for properties from which no production figures were available for

[1] *M.A.J.*, May 1937, referring to February.

that period. After the 90 per cent. release for the second half of the year was announced, the Malayan estate assessment authorities (assessment committees) concluded that without substantial changes in the method of assessment the Malayan estates would be unable to produce their permissible exports.[1]

The most important decision reached was the need to raise the assessments of estates able to exceed them.[2] The assessment committees proposed that they should be given power 'to increase assessments where this was obviously justifiable', in particular, to disregard basic years and scale allowances 'where current production clearly shows that the present assessment is incorrect'.[3] These powers were granted, and estates capable of producing in excess of their assessments were advised to submit production figures and claim increased assessments. These were to be based largely on crop figures from July 1937 onwards; where output figures were available for part of the year only, the annual total could be based on the best two months for which figures were available. Allowances for rested areas were also at a generous rate. On the other hand, estates which were selling rights were warned that their assessments might be cut unless they could give suitable reasons for these sales. These new rules were intended to bring assessments into line with potential production. The system again obviously and inevitably benefited chiefly estates with detailed records of production and producers able to present their case plausibly. The Asiatic-owned estates could take little advantage of the change.

Producers who did not wish to be re-assessed could continue on the old system, and as long as they did not sell rights they were not troubled. Estates with young, untapped, budded rubber, which was almost invariably over-assessed (in every sense) under the generous scale allowances, could leave these areas untapped and

[1] Most of the revisions introduced in 1937 and discussed in the next few paragraphs remained in force until the Japanese war.

[2] These were referred to as under-assessed estates. This term can be used in two entirely different senses. It may mean either that the assessment is below the normal capacity of the producer, or that it represents less than his fair share (based on some definite and recognisable principle) of the territorial quota. The two meanings coincide only if the territorial quota equals the normal potential productivity of the country. From 1937 onwards under-assessment in Malayan parlance usually referred to assessment below potential capacity. There was some justification for this loose terminology, as the Malayan basic quota was not very far removed from the normal productive capacity of the country and the assessment of most estates fully equal to their potential output.

[3] *Annual Report* for 1937 of the Controller of Rubber, Malaya. By 'incorrect' is meant 'below potential capacity'.

continue to draw the same allowances as before, for although the assessment committees were given a wide measure of discretion they were not allowed to reduce the scale allowances. Once such young rubber was tapped, or the producer sold rights, his assessment could be revised, though by giving plausible reasons for his failure to reach the standard assessment he could generally avoid a reduction. Producers who sold rights heavily during the second half of 1937 ran some risk of a cut in their assessments; accordingly they had to decide whether the cash proceeds of the rights were worth the risk, and as the price of rights was low after July 1937 some preferred to forgo the cash. Thus to some extent the change militated against the concentration of output on the lowest cost estates.

The chief beneficiaries of the change were estate producers with good seedling rubber untapped before 1933, and capable of producing well in excess of the maximum scale allowance. In no instance were owners of budded areas able to claim assessments in excess of scale allowances, which showed that these were excessive.

Altogether, after allowing for the few reductions in assessments, the total estate quota was raised by 4,000 tons. The sum total of assessments now definitely exceeded the Malayan basic quota, and small internal cuts which affected all producers, including smallholders, became frequent.

By far the most important discrepancy between assessments and productive capacity was not affected; there was no redistribution of the quota between estates and smallholdings, nor re-assessment of smallholdings. The solitary representative of the smallholders on the General Advisory Committee raised this matter in 1937, requesting that the smallholdings should also be re-assessed. He was sharply rebuked by the Controller of Rubber who stated that a general re-inspection of smallholdings was administratively impossible. The Controller also denied that the smallholdings were under-assessed: admittedly their theoretical maximum assessment was 500 lb. per acre (in practice 480 lb.), but the lower limit was some 250 lb. for smallholdings, while many estates were assessed at less. He added that the average assessment per acre of the smallholdings was almost the same as that of estates which, in his opinion, was evidence that they were fairly treated.

These are remarkable arguments. First, the relevant comparison was not between assessments per acre but per *mature* acre. According to an official letter from the Controller of Rubber to the I.R.R.C., the average assessments per planted acre of estates and smallholdings in 1936 were 396 lb. and 384 lb. respectively, while per mature acre the figures were 422 lb. and 399 lb.[1] Moreover, the experience of the five years before regulation had revealed beyond doubt that the normal output per acre of smallholdings was appreciably higher than that of seedling estates. Again, the general purpose of the re-assessment was to enable producers to harvest up to their capacity ; yet the assessments of smallholdings were quite out of line with the yields found by the smallholdings enquiry, which ranged up to 889 lb. and averaged 477 lb.[2] It was also generally held that the upkeep of smallholdings and the standard of tapping had improved since then. Assessments on an approximate capacity basis (at yields per acre at the general range of prices under restriction) would have increased the share of smallholdings in the Malayan quota from 38 per cent. to about 50 per cent.

The relative under-assessment of the smallholdings was freely discussed in Malaya in the spring of 1937. Considerable attention was nevertheless attracted by an outspoken leading article in the *Straits Times* in April 1937 which frankly stated that the smallholdings were under-assessed relatively to the estates and that their assessments were also clearly below productivity ; it was argued that the smallholders could easily produce at the rate of 100 lb. per acre in excess of their average assessments : 'It is useless to shut our eyes to the obvious fact that in the present scheme in Malaya, the European-owned estate receives preferential treatment in the matter of assessment, particularly where budded trees are concerned and that the Asiatic is restricted to maximum assessment of 500 lb., regardless of the possibility of his having the highest yielding trees in the country.'[3] This statement challenged the fairness of the entire control machinery. Three days later another leader was published which withdrew the argument of the former article, pointing out that the average assessment of the smallholders was about the same as that of the estates, which showed that they were generously treated ; the leader added that the previous article did not mean what it said, but meant something else, though what this was did not appear. A few months later a third article

[1] These figures differ slightly but not significantly from those shown in Ch. 7, Table II. The preferential treatment of estates revealed by a comparison of assessments per mature acre is clear from both sets of figures.

[2] Enquiries by the writer in Malaya in 1946 suggest that the findings of the smallholdings enquiry may have appreciably under-estimated the yielding capacity of smallholdings ; cf. p. 341, below.

[3] *Straits Times*, 23rd April 1937.

restated the argument of the first, thus by implication withdrawing the withdrawal. The argument was the same as that of the first, but was more cautiously worded.

II

In the N.E.I. the control of native rubber exports continued to be the dominant problem of the administration of rubber regulation, even after the increase in the N.E.I. quota in 1936. The export tax was increased steadily throughout 1936 from 29 cents per kilo in January to 37 cents by September. The rise in the guilder price following the Dutch devaluation in September necessitated steep increases in the special tax which was raised to 47 cents on 30th September and to 51 cents on 3rd October.[1] In October the special tax, at an average rate of 50·8 cents per kilo, was equal to four-fifths of the Singapore price of medium blankets and was over twenty times the price of rubber in the interior.[2] Further increases were, however, required, chiefly to counteract the rise in the world price which began to gather speed in November. In December the rate reached 59 cents per kilo, which was about six times the starting level in 1934 and four-fifths of the current Singapore price of medium blankets. But for the early introduction of individual restriction which was to come on 1st January 1937, the control of native rubber would have faced another crisis. The basic price (the difference between the Batavia price and the rate of the special tax) ranged during 1936 from 5½ cents to 8½ cents per half-kilo (about 1½*d.*–2*d.* per lb.); in the interior the price was some 4 cents less. At these prices the natives still exported some 150,000 tons of dry rubber.

The proceeds of the special tax were 47 million guilders in 1936, making a total of 82 millions over its two-and-a-half years of operation. These large sums proved too strong a temptation

[1] The time-lag in the introduction of the higher rates of duty on dry rubber was suspended between September and November, and the higher rates became effective immediately on announcement. This was an administrative necessity as otherwise very large quantities would promptly have been exported in response to the higher prices. The abolition of the time lag inflicted heavy losses on the processors of wet rubber who were paid compensation in a rough-and-ready way, apparently from the proceeds of the special export tax.

[2] Had a somewhat higher figure (actually more nearly in accordance with the majority of estimates) been assumed for the transport cost of native rubber from the interior to Singapore and for the processing charges in Singapore, the ratio of the tax to the average net return would on occasions have exceeded sixty to one, and the rate of tax risen above 6,000 per cent. against the maximum of 2,100 per cent. conservatively estimated here. Cf. the notes to Tables V and VI of Statistical Appendix II.

for the N.E.I. authorities, and part of the funds was diverted to general expenditure. The Government defended this policy on the grounds that the smallholders produced at such low cost that even the 1934–36 returns were profitable, while other sections of the N.E.I. economy, notably the rubber estates, were facing great difficulties.[1] This argument was not only a breach of the specific undertaking given in 1934, but it also disregarded the contributions of the natives to the general revenue through the payment of other taxes and dues.

The system of individual restriction introduced in January 1937 was based on a tree count carried out during 1934–36. The results of this tree census also greatly influenced the size of the quotas and the distribution of planting rights during the second period of regulation. The field work of the census was entrusted very largely to unemployed European planters, each of whom had eight to ten native tellers under him. The trees were counted by the tellers whose work was checked by the planters; the planting density of each holding was also estimated. Contrary to general belief, the area was not surveyed, and the published figures of the planted acreage were calculated by dividing the number of trees on each holding by the estimated density and aggregating the results. The count was confined to trees designated by the natives on their own, and no attempts were made to detect any concealment. The trees were grouped according to several classifications; they were divided into tapped, tappable but untapped, and immature trees; into six different density classes, ranging from 500 trees per hectare (202 trees per acre) to over 1,300 trees per hectare (526 trees per acre); and into good, moderate, indifferent, bad and neglected trees, or rather gardens. 'Neglected' referred to areas which could be rendered productive after being cleaned up; holdings so neglected as to be incapable of being brought back into tapping were omitted altogether. A series of tapping tests was also carried out to correlate planting density with output per tree and per surface unit.

A total of 582,365,735 [*sic*] trees was found; the planted area was made to total 1,683,328 acres[2] owned by 788,437 proprietors;

[1] An official spokesman, addressing the Batavia *Volksraad* in 1936, argued that the native producers had no costs, and that the price, even after the payment of the heavy export tax, was remunerative to them. He added that the world price, which was several times higher than the net return left to the natives, hardly enabled the estates to survive.

[2] Hectares and kilograms have been converted into acres and lb. for the sake of consistency, and in order to simplify a necessarily tedious account.

the over-all average size of the gardens was therefore 2·12 acres, and ranged from an average of 1·1 acres in South and East Borneo to an average of 6·9 acres in the Riouw archipelago ; 81 per cent. of the trees were on holdings with less than 1,000 trees each which seems a surprisingly low figure. The relation between planting density and output as ascertained by the tapping tests is reproduced in the following table.

TABLE I

Results of Tapping Tests carried out during the Last Quarter of 1936 in the Native Districts of the Outer Provinces of the N.E.I.

Density group	*Average no. of trees per acre*	*No. of tappable trees per acre*	*Average production per acre per tapping day (lb.)*	*Calculated annual output per acre assuming 160 tapping days (lb.)*	*Average annual output per tappable tree (lb.)*
Trees per acre :					
Under 202 .	162	157	2·97	476	3·02
202–282 . .	243	233	3·39	542	2·34
283–363 . .	324	308	3·82	611	1·98
364–444 . .	405	380	4·24	678	1·79
445–526 . .	486	455	4·58	732	1·63
Over 527 .	567	521	4·75	759	1·46

It will be noted that though the yield per tree falls with denser planting, the yield per surface unit rises—a point very frequently overlooked by European planters. The number of tapping days in a year assumed in converting daily production into annual output was almost certainly too low, being based on European estate standards ; smallholders generally tap over 200 days a year. The calculated annual yield figures are thus very probably too low.

The general average density over the whole of the native area was 346 trees per acre, and the calculated average output 545 lb. It was found that only 4·3 per cent. of the total area could be classed as good, with 17·8 per cent. fair, 40·3 per cent. mediocre, 21·5 per cent. poor and 16·1 per cent. neglected ; thus, mediocre, poor and neglected holdings accounted for 78 per cent. of the total area. These figures are paradoxical. The tapping tests found yields much in excess of expectations and far above the average yield on estates, while the compilers of the census maintained that four-fifths of the area was indifferent or worse.

The paradox was heightened when figures were published showing the estimated average yields per acre in the different residencies. These were calculated by applying the average yield per tree of the tapping tests to the average planting density in each residency as computed from the returns of the tree count. These calculated yields ranged from 432 lb. per acre for Acheen, to 637 lb. for Djambi, with the over-all average of 545 lb. The average calculated yield in Bengkalis was 555 lb., with 98 per cent. of the area indifferent, poor or neglected; for Tapanoeli the figures were 533 lb. and 98 per cent.; for Djambi 637 lb. and 81 per cent. On the other hand, in Benkulen the calculated yield was only 480 lb. though 93 per cent. of the area was classed as good or fairly good; thus the better the area the lower the yield.

This much-publicised census was obviously of little value; it may have served as an approximate basis of the relative number of trees owned by individual natives—on the assumption that the degree of concealment was the same throughout the native area—and thus furnished adequate data for individual assessments, which were only shares in a fixed quota. The tapping tests were also of some interest, but these were not an integral part of the tree count. A positive disservice was, however, rendered by the authorities in publishing the number of trees and of hectares to the last digit, since this suggested to outside observers that a painstaking survey had been taken whereas actually only a casual and approximate estimate was made. Little publicity was given to the fact that the published acreage figure was purely a calculated result which was moreover subsequently found to be quite inaccurate.

Lastly, the opinion that four-fifths of the area was found to be indifferent or worse was most misleading. The N.E.I. authorities themselves realised the worthlessness of the planters' views on the conditions of the native holdings; the N.E.I. representative on the Renewal Sub-Committee of the I.R.R.C. made this quite plain in an official memorandum: 'The brigade leaders (the planters) . . . were instructed to classify the gardens according to their general aspect. A certain amount of subjective judgment was inevitable; it must also be borne in mind that these inspectors were all former European planters who judged by estate standards. The Department of Economic Affairs realised that there was no connection between these classifications and the productive capacity of the gardens. This was fully corroborated by the test tappings, which showed no correlation between the yield per tree and the classification of the gardens. In fact the gardens overgrown with *blukar*, after some clearing showed high productive capacity.'[1] It may well be asked what was the point of publishing the results of the classification, or indeed of undertaking it.

In London and Amsterdam, however, the published results of the tree count elicited a crop of derogatory comments on native rubber. One of these is of particular interest. In June 1937 the results of the census were reviewed in the *Financial Times* by a former Malayan estate manager with many years' planting experience in the East, who was regarded as an authority on planting topics and who contributed frequently to the financial press and to periodicals in the East. The author declared that from the data and the classification of the planted area it emerged clearly that the smallholders were greatly *over*-assessed. Only 4·3 per cent. of the area had been classed as good ; this could be assumed to yield 400 lb. per acre, while fairly good native rubber (the next 17·7 per cent.) might yield 300 lb., the mediocre class 250 lb., poor rubber 200 lb. and neglected areas 100 lb. per acre. These figures, applied to the respective acreages, give a potential of 162,216½ tons (note the half ton), against the quota of 247,697 tons, an over-assessment of 86,480½ tons. The writer considered the assumed yields as generous. 'I doubt if any practical planter, basing his estimate on the census classification and his experience of native holdings, would give him higher figures of production . . . I shall be very much surprised indeed if the native succeeds in producing anything like the number of tons he has been awarded . . . with a stand all over of nearly 300 trees per acre, it is quite out of the question to expect yields of anything approaching a standard production as understood by the European planter, who has found out by experience that 80 fully matured trees are all that the soil can carry economically.' Thus the best 4 per cent. of native rubber may yield 400 lb. ; the author seems to have been unaware that *average* yields on smallholdings in Malaya had been around 480 lb. in 1929, and again 465 lb. in 1933 ; he had apparently not heard of the smallholdings enquiry which found an

[1] *Minutes of the I.R.R.C. Renewal Sub-Committee*, p. 413.

In July 1937 the late Professor Van Gelderen, the then leader of the N.E.I. delegation on the I.R.R.C., gave an interview to the Amsterdam *Telegraaf* in which he dealt with the condition of the native holdings. He pointed out that the dense planting seemed to have no adverse effect on the holdings ; growth and girth were somewhat retarded but the general health of the trees and the rate of bark renewal were not impaired. He thought that soil conditions on smallholdings were better than on estates, and that tapping was *less* intensive.

average yield of 477 lb. and individual yields up to 889 lb.; nor did he appreciate the elementary fact that yield per acre is higher with 300 trees than with 80 trees, even though the yield per tree is less.

The writer claimed to speak with special authority on this particular subject, since he had not only spent years in the East, *but had, under the Stevenson scheme, inspected and assessed scores of smallholdings in Malaya.* Here is a striking example of the outlook of the men who inspected or assessed Malayan smallholdings under two restriction schemes.

When N.E.I. native exports forged ahead of the permissible amount the author published a second article in the *Financial Times*, attributing the excess largely to over-tapping. In April 1938 he produced yet another article, this time in *The Planter*, criticising the increased quota proposed for the N.E.I. under the renewed scheme, the terms of which had been published. He referred again to the tree census and to the high planting density of native rubber. 'How such closely planted stuff can ever hope to qualify for an award even approaching that of "standard", is a problem which no planter would attempt to solve. He is well satisfied with about 80 mature trees to the acre. . . . 200 lb. per acre would be a liberal estimate for such closely planted stuff . . .' The author also took it upon himself to comment on the violent monthly fluctuations in native exports; the output 'drops suddenly coincident with the refusal of the ill-treated trees to aid and abet their owners'. In actual fact, the sharp fluctuations of native exports reflected the seasonal activities of rice planting and harvesting, the Mohammedan festivals and, above all, the exhaustion of the coupon issue.

When the N.E.I. native producers appreciated that failure to receive assessments deprived them of valuable coupons instead of reducing their taxes, additional claims began to pour in. By the spring of 1937 it was known that very large areas had been omitted; it is now known that the estimated acreage was only about one-half of the true figure.

The assessments of individual producers were based on the number of standard trees of each owner, in the computation of which number a mature tapped tree counted as a unit, a mature but untapped tree as one-quarter (except in South and East Borneo where the fraction was one-tenth), while immature trees were excluded. Various so-called 'correctives' were applied to the number of trees according to the average planting density and condition of each holding. In certain districts further coefficients were applied ; in particular, the larger producers were scaled down to enable all owners to obtain a share in the insufficient quota. Application of the various coefficients to the trees gave the number of standard trees, the quota of each residency being divided among producers proportionately to the standard trees of each. The share of each residency in the total native quota was itself fixed first in proportion to its average exports over 1933–35, with some correction and subsequent revision in favour of residencies particularly dependent on rubber.

For 1937 the average standard assessment was about 330 lb. per acre (approximately 350–360 lb. per mature acre) ; as this was based on the area calculated from the tree count, which was in fact about one-half of the actual area, the actual average assessment was only about one-half of these figures. The inadequacy of these assessments is particularly striking when set against the yields calculated from the tapping tests. The fractional assessments granted to ' tappable but untapped trees ' at only one-quarter or one-tenth of the assessment of tapped trees was in notable contrast to the treatment of the estates, whose untapped mature areas could claim scale allowances or even higher assessments on tapping results. These very low assessments were the inevitable result of the wholly inadequate aggregate native quota which for 1937 amounted to only 241,000 long tons. There was still much conjecture at the time about the potential supply of N.E.I. native rubber, but informed opinion generally placed it at between 400,000 and 700,000 tons (or about double or treble the quota), with London prices between 6*d.* and 10*d.* No attempt was made to redress even slightly the under-assessment of native producers by implementing the undertaking to transfer 28,000 tons from the estate to the native quota.

The machinery of control was comparatively straightforward. The natives were issued quarterly ' harvest permits ' (coupons) which were exchanged for export licences at ports of shipment. Harvest permits were freely transferable within each residency, but (with insignificant exceptions) not between residencies. Organised markets in coupons developed rapidly. In January 1937 native export rights fetched about 23 cents per half-kilo. As in Malaya, coupons were generally sold as soon as they were received, the smallholders producing unlicensed rubber subsequently. The introduction of individual restriction at a time of high rubber prices brought great prosperity to the natives, under-assessed though they were. Cash incomes in the principal rubber-growing districts were higher than at any time since the Stevenson boom. The sudden prosperity, together with the under-issue of coupons, caused a deficit of native exports during the first few months of 1937, but this was soon corrected, and by May the smallholders were already ahead of their permissible exports. By September the excess was almost 20,000 tons, but this could be only a temporary phenomenon as with individual restriction the system of control was firmly established.

An unusual and unexpected development was that large quantities of native rubber began to be shipped between districts instead of being sent direct to Singapore or to consuming countries. The reason for this development was soon discovered. The supply price of the exportable amount of rubber varied greatly between residencies ; generally it was lowest in those areas where the quota was least adequate, or where the natives were most dependent on rubber. Had coupons been freely transferable between residencies they would have moved to these under-assessed areas where coupon prices were highest. As rights were not so transferable, the rubber moved to the coupons, and districts where the price of unlicensed rubber was lowest shipped rubber to districts where the price was higher. This development served to reveal that the shares of the various residencies in the native quota diverged widely from their potential capacities and was partly responsible for a redistribution of the quota after July 1937 which reduced the inter-district shipments without eliminating them altogether.

The authorities were in two minds about the desirability of this trade. In the words of the *N.E.I. Native Report* covering the second half of 1939, 'The inter-residency transport exercises a certain levelling effect on the prices for uncouponed rubber and for coupons in the various districts, and may also prevent the forming of pools by exporters.' Powers were nevertheless taken to prohibit these shipments '. . . if it appeared that the trade made systematic use of price differences between districts, as this would violate the principle that each native district must produce its own export quota'. This principle could hardly be regarded as sacrosanct. Though the large-scale abandonment of rubber cultivation in certain districts would have had a dislocating effect, such a violent change was improbable. Inter-district shipments were prohibited in 1938 between a number of residencies, with additional restrictions in 1939 and 1940.

III

The continuation of regulation after 1938 had been envisaged by governments and by estate producers since the inception of the scheme. According to article 3 of the 1934 agreement, the I.R.R.C. had to submit, by the end of March 1938, a definite recommendation to the signatory governments for a renewal (with or without modifications) or abandonment of regulation at the end of 1938. From 1935 onward the R.G.A. spokesmen repeatedly insisted on the need to continue restriction after 1938, while Professor Van Gelderen, the leader of the N.E.I. delegation on the I.R.R.C. said in a press interview in July 1937 that he regarded regulation as essential for the welfare of the industry.

In March 1937 the I.R.R.C. remitted to a small Anglo-Dutch sub-committee the task of investigating the question of renewal and of submitting specific proposals. The discussions proved more prolonged than had been expected, the settlement of the quotas presenting the principal difficulty. These were tentatively fixed by taking the permanent basis (the average 1929–32 exports) and adding immature allowances for areas planted after 1924. The immature allowances were calculated on the same lines as on the earlier occasion ; 1925–27 plantings were again assumed to have made appreciable contributions to the output of 1929–32.[1]

The original basis of computation was retained fully for the calculation of the Malayan quota only. The others were essentially ' bargaining quotas '. The smaller territories were offered *ex gratia* allowances which had to be raised repeatedly (three times in some instances) to satisfy various demands. Siam, Sarawak and Ceylon appear to have fared best, in that their basic quotas were increased most compared with a computation on the basis of 1929–32 exports together with immature allowances. The bargaining position of these territories was strong since the larger countries were anxious to renew the scheme in a comprehensive form. Though the Ceylon quota was excessive and that of the N.E.I. inadequate, the ratios between the other basic quotas were probably not too far removed from what would have been the ratios between the unrestricted outputs at the prices visualised under restriction.

[1] For instance, an area planted in 1925 was seven years old in 1932 ; rubber of that age was assumed to yield 400 lb. under the international scale ; an area planted in 1925 was fully mature by 1939, and fully mature seedling rubber was entitled to 500 lb. per acre under the international scale ; 400 lb. were assumed to have been included in the permanent basis, so that the area received 100 lb. per acre as immature allowance.

The inadequacy of the N.E.I. quota was regarded as inevitable, as any attempt to do justice to the N.E.I. natives would have necessitated a quota so large as to be politically unacceptable to the other governments. Once this was admitted, the size of the N.E.I. quota became dependent on the outcome of prolonged bargaining. A host of figures, claims and estimates was debated by the renewal sub-committee. An N.E.I. official with special knowledge of native rubber estimated during these discussions that with a London price of 6*d*. the N.E.I. smallholders would export half-a-million tons. This was thought to be rather high, but there were several estimates around 400,000 tons. The results of the tapping tests at various planting densities applied to the native acreage as computed from the results of the tree count suggested a normal productive capacity of at least 380,000 tons. Several other possible methods of calculation were considered and their merits argued at length. In actual fact there were no acreage figures to serve as a basis for discussion since it was evident that the tree count had been altogether incomplete. Reliable acreage figures were available of the N.E.I. estate area ; on the basis of 1929–32 exports and immature allowances method, the estates would have been entitled to about 340,000 tons in 1939.

Agreement was eventually reached. In the words of the minutes of the decisive meeting : ' After a discussion which lasted two hours and covered every aspect of the N.E.I. basic quota, it was agreed that the following quotas should be recommended for the N.E.I. during the currency of the renewed agreement for the division of which, as between estates and natives, the N.E.I. Government alone was responsible :

1939	1940	1941	1942	1943
631,500	640,000	645,500	650,000	651,000

The basis of the calculation was not disclosed : ' Using all data available and making what the sub-committee believed fair inferences from known facts, the sub-committee are of opinion, after most careful consideration, that the quotas proposed are fair as between all the contracting Governments.'[1]

Although it was explicitly stated that the internal division of the N.E.I. quota was a domestic concern, the actual division was shown throughout 1939–41 in the *Statistical Bulletin* of the I.R.R.C., and estate and native exports were given separately. In 1939 the N.E.I. estate quota was 317,962 tons and that of the native producers

[1] *Minutes of the I.R.R.C. Renewal Sub-Committee*, pp. 230 and 251.

313,538 tons. The estates maintained a slight lead in quotas throughout, just as Malaya was allowed to retain a very small margin over the N.E.I. in total quotas ; these arrangements suggest that political and prestige considerations played a part in the negotiations in London and in the internal division of the N.E.I. quota in the East.

After some unsuccessful last-minute attempts by several territories to secure higher quotas, the following tonnages were proposed by the renewal sub-committee, accepted by the I.R.R.C., and submitted to the signatory governments all of which agreed to them. The quotas are shown in Table II.

TABLE II

Basic Quotas under the Renewed Regulation Agreement, 1939–43

(Tons)

	1939	1940	1941	1942	1943
Malaya	632,000	642,500	648,000	651,000	651,500
N.E.I.	631,500	640,000	645,500	650,000	651,000
Ceylon	106,000	107,500	109,000	109,500	110,000
India	17,500	17,750	17,750	17,750	17,750
Burma	13,500	13,750	13,750	13,750	13,750
British North Borneo	21,000	21,000	21,000	21,000	21,000
Sarawak	43,000	43,750	44,000	44,000	44,000
Siam	54,500	55,300	55,700	56,000	60,000
Total	1,519,000	1,541,550	1,554,700	1,563,000	1,569,000

The special position of French Indo-China under which her exports were virtually uncontrolled was maintained, and her free exports raised from 30,000 to 60,000 tons.

These quotas were substantially higher than those of the first period of regulation, and a given rate of release thus represented appreciably larger supplies.

Even more important than the revision of quotas were changes in the provisions controlling new planting and re-planting ; these are discussed in Chapter 12, below.

The revision of quotas was followed by only a few administrative changes in the East ; the existing machinery was maintained with revised assessments to reflect the new quotas. There was no general re-assessment, though 1937 output figures, or proved yields over a period, gradually supplanted the average 1929–32 outputs and immature allowances as the basis of the assessment of those estate producers who wished to be assessed on the basis of proved capacity. The quota changes did not call for any general re-assessment, as they broadly reflected the higher allowances resulting from young rubber reaching or nearing full maturity. Quota increases beyond the additional tonnages represented by the growing maturity of young rubber were absorbed in higher assessments or in reduced internal cuts.

In Malaya the maximum scale allowance for untapped budded rubber was reduced from 1,200 lb. to 1,050 lb. as the experience of 1937 had made it clear that the former figure was far too high. Even 1,050 lb. (still granted to some 130 clones, many of which were recognised failures) was excessive, especially as since 1937 producers could receive higher allowances if their claims were justified by tapping results. From 1939 onwards five-year-old untapped buddings with an average girth of 16 inches at 36 inches from the union of the scion and stock also received a scale allowance of 200 lb. This was a sheer gift to the fortunate owners, as such rubber is never tapped in estate practice.

The theoretical ceiling of Malayan smallholders' assessments was raised to 625 lb. per acre. According to the 1938 *Annual Report* of the Controller of Rubber the conditions of smallholdings were very unsatisfactory, and very few holdings were expected to qualify for the higher assessments.[1] No attempt was made in Malaya (or in any other major producing territory) to bring smallholders' assessments more nearly into line with productive capacity. Assessment on the basis of proved capacity was applied to estates only.

The appreciably higher quota of the N.E.I. natives made it possible to give less inadequate individual assessments than before. The realisation that very large areas had been omitted from the tree count convinced the authorities of the need for a proper survey, and this was begun in 1939.

[1] The Controller made no attempt to reconcile his views with the results of the smallholdings enquiry or the findings of the survey which had recently taken place in Sarawak. His remarks were also in notable contrast with some passages in the official *Malayan Smallholdings Report* covering July–September 1938. 'It must be remembered, however, that a great number of holdings, especially those owned by Indians and Chinese, are in excellent condition, while the presence of undergrowth, slashed on occasions, on many other holdings, is probably more of an advantage than otherwise as it protects the soil from erosion.' *M.A.J.*, November 1938.

CHAPTER 11

RUBBER REGULATION DURING THE WAR, 1939–41

I

ARTICLE 4 of the international agreement entitled any signatory government to disregard its obligations under the scheme (except the control of new planting) if it considered that national security was endangered. On the outbreak of war, the British and French Governments were thus entitled to withdraw. No such step was taken. For the first year of the war it was undoubtedly wise to continue the scheme. Its termination would have been followed by a slump in the price of rubber with various undesirable consequences, such as pressure on wages, a fall in Government revenues and a considerable reduction in the dollar proceeds of rubber.

On the reopening of some of the temporarily closed rubber markets early in September the price of rubber rose substantially above the August level, to about 10*d.* per lb. in London and 22 cents in New York. A discrepancy soon developed between the New York and London quotations. Just before the war the disparity between the two centres was limited by the cost of shipping rubber from one to the other to about one-eighth of a penny per lb. In the autumn of 1939 the New York price exceeded the London quotation at times by as much as 3*d.* per lb.

Stocks were low both in America and in Britain ; in the U.S. they were equal to about three months' absorption at the 1939 rate of consumption, and before the end of the year they had declined to just over two months' absorption. U.K. stocks, which represented about five months' absorption, cannot be considered solely in relation to British absorption, as they were habitually drawn upon by several European neutrals.

The U.S. Government now took a much closer interest than before in the rate of release and in available supplies ; the British authorities, notably the Ministry of Supply, also showed increased, though somewhat fitful, concern. In September the U.S. Embassy in London pressed for a substantial increase in the fourth-quarter release, stressing the political and psychological dangers of a runaway market, quite apart from the possibility of a definite shortage of rubber in America. The Advisory Panel also asked for a considerable increase in supplies, and a similar course was favoured, though somewhat intermittently, by the Ministry of Supply. At first the Committee greatly resented this increased interest, and several members threatened to resign if the Committee were to be subject to outside pressure. After much argument the release for the last quarter was raised to 75 per cent., which was to have resulted in some increase in stocks.

Estimates of absorption a few months ahead became even more hazardous than in peace-time. The military needs were certain to be very great ; on the other hand, Germany with her satellites and conquests would be deprived of supplies, while European neutrals would be rationed. More important still, civilian motoring throughout Europe was certain to be drastically curtailed, and as civilian cars were counted by the million, while tanks, planes and military lorries only in their thousands (according to the ideas of 1939), the net result might have been a decline in absorption.

There were also other secondary factors at work, though these did not directly influence the Committee. Rubber was an important source of exchange to the British exchange control which would have been adversely affected by a fall in price ; on the other hand the Ministry of Supply would have benefited from lower prices. Another consideration was the anxiety to avoid a speculative wave culminating in a runaway market, an ever-present possibility both in London and New York. The London price was gradually creeping up to the New York quotation, reaching almost 1*s.* per lb. in December, and there were signs that a speculative movement was developing. Administrative difficulties in the East had also to be weighed, though sometimes these were used as pretext rather than as basis of decisions. A temporary increase in the rate of release followed by a sharp reduction would have been particularly unwelcome to the local governments, especially in the territories which relied on immigrant labour and on imported rice.

The low level of stocks both in the U.S. and in the U.K. was, however, the overriding feature during the last few months of 1939 and the early part of 1940. Absorption, especially in the U.S., was running much ahead of expectations, and stocks were falling instead of rising. The Americans pressed for a retro-active increase in the fourth-quarter release, or alternatively an advance issue of 1940 export rights ; both these proposals were rejected as impracticable. A third suggestion was for a cancellation of excess exports, or at least for a deferment of their reduction. Substantial over-exports had been carried forward from 1938, were further increased during 1939 and totalled over 40,000 tons by the end of October. A rapid reduction of this excess would have substantially diminished readily available supplies—at 40,000 tons the over-exports were equal to 10 per cent. release for a full quarter—and the American suggestion was practical and appropriate. The Committee's adamant refusal on the grounds that cancellation, or even deferment, was *ultra vires*, was singularly unconvincing in view of the precedents of 1935 and 1938 when over-exports had been cancelled, or their reduction deferred, by resolution of the Committee.

At the end of 1939 world stocks had fallen to 335,000 tons, including about 150,000 tons afloat; stocks in the U.S. totalled only 124,000 tons, equal to 2½ months' absorption (at the end of October they were only 90,000 tons, less than two months' absorption), while U.K. stocks were only 50,000 tons. In spite of the conditions of semi-depression prevailing in America throughout most of the year, both world absorption at just under 1,100,000 tons and U.S. absorption at 592,000 tons were records so far.

The Panel and the British and American authorities suggested a release of 85 per cent. for the first quarter of 1940, but after long deliberation the Committee fixed 80 per cent. This rate was certain to add to stocks; the higher release had been requested only to accelerate their rate of accumulation. The authorities did not press their request, while the American manufacturers were pessimistic about business conditions to be expected in America for the second half of 1940, and freely volunteered the opinion that substantial reductions in releases would become necessary by the summer or autumn. This view quite naturally increased the Committee's reluctance to raise the release above 80 per cent. The 80 per cent. release was maintained for the second quarter, and although absorption continued to exceed expectations the stock position in America eased slightly; it remained serious in Britain. For most of the first three or four months of 1940 the price in London was around 11*d.*–1*s.* per lb. and in New York around 19–20 cents.

The higher outputs called for during the last few months of 1939 and the first half of 1940 were generally produced without any difficulty.[1]

[1] The output of rubber from Malayan smallholdings during the first quarter of 1940 was almost double that of the corresponding period of 1939. The official *Malayan Smallholdings Report* covering the first quarter of 1940 ascribed this to a variety of causes, such as the high prices and the intention to tap before the wintering season so as to reap the benefit of the exceptional boom. In actual fact there was a single simple reason which again seems to have escaped the authorities: the rate of release during the first quarter of 1939 had been 50 per cent., while in 1940 it was 85 per cent. (there had been

The meeting at which the releases for the second half of the year were to be determined had been fixed for 21st May 1940. Early in May the President of the Rubber Manufacturers' Association of America (the American representative on the Advisory Panel) informed the I.R.R.C. that in his opinion a 70 per cent. release for the second half of the year would meet the American requirements. The German offensive in the West was launched a day or two later, and before the meeting took place the Committee was informed that the American Government was contemplating the acquisition of a large reserve stock of rubber, and the Committee was asked to raise the rate of release to 90 per cent. from July onwards. This was far in excess of all known needs, and the Committee decided to maintain a release of 80 per cent. on the understanding that the decision would be reviewed when the plans of the U.S. Government became known.

To ascertain the intentions of the U.S. Government for the accumulation of a reserve stock of rubber, a representative of the Committee (one of the British members) went to America in June 1940. Agreement was soon reached with the American authorities on the terms on which the reserve stock was to be acquired by the U.S.A. The Rubber Reserve Company, a newly-formed subsidiary of the Reconstruction Finance Corporation, was to purchase not less than 100,000 and not more than 150,000 tons of rubber, to be bought for shipment before 31st December 1940, at prices between 18 and 20 U.S. cents per lb. c.i.f. New York for ribbed smoked sheet. The I.R.R.C. possessed no rubber; it undertook first, to raise the rate of release to the level needed to meet the stock requirements in addition to all other known demands, and secondly, to encourage producers to be ready sellers of rubber within the agreed price range of 18 and 20 cents per lb. The reserve stock was to be held intact until the end of 1943 unless it was required by the American Government for its defence programme, or supplies to the U.S.A. were interrupted by hostilities. The manufacturing industry was to maintain trade stocks at a normal level which was interpreted as 150,000 tons; if the manufacturers failed to do so the Reserve Company undertook to increase its purchases sufficiently above the proposed maximum to offset the decline in trade stocks.[1]

an under-issue of coupons during the last quarter of 1939 as the issue had been prepared before the release was raised and this was compensated by an additional 5 per cent. in the first quarter of 1940) and the 1940 rate applied moreover to a higher quota. There was no need to search for complex explanations.

[1] In view of the controversy to which subsequent developments gave rise it should be clearly understood that this last provision referred to the maintenance of trade

This agreement was followed by another in August, along broadly similar lines. The amount regarded as covered by the first agreement was now definitely specified at the higher figure of 150,000 tons, while a further 180,000 tons were to be bought for shipment during 1941. The purchases were to be made at a tapering rate, from 70,000 tons during the first quarter to 25,000 tons in the last. This clearly visualised 330,000 tons as the maximum reserve stock; it was also to protect producers from the effects of an abrupt cessation of purchases. The price fixed in the agreement was 17 to 18½ U.S. cents f.o.b. eastern ports, which, when allowing for freight and insurance costs, was fractionally higher than the price fixed in the first agreement. These prices were highly profitable to practically all estate producers.

The Committee met after the conclusion of the first agreement and raised the release for the second half of the year to 85 per cent. This was calculated to make available 137,000 tons to the Reserve Company after all other estimated requirements had been met, which complied with the terms of the first agreement but left no margin for contingencies. Another meeting was held after the second agreement was signed. As it referred only to rubber to be shipped in 1941, this agreement did not directly affect releases for 1940; there was, however, an indirect influence in that the danger of an abrupt fall in the rate of release at the end of 1940 was removed. Meanwhile the British Government had also signified its intention to acquire 20,000 tons of rubber to increase the dangerously low U.K. stocks. The Committee provided for this requirement by an additional 5 per cent. release for the last quarter, which though formally meeting requirements again left no margin to spare. This decision was preceded by a discussion during which some members of the Committee emphasised the danger which might arise in the producing territories through an intensified competition for labour at the high rates of release. The British member of the Advisory Panel rightly pointed out that these dangers were negligible compared to the peril which would arise if Britain ran out of rubber.

During the autumn the Committee was repeatedly informed that the Reserve Company was falling behind schedule with its purchases, finding it difficult to acquire rubber within the agreed prices. The American authorities also intimated that they wished

stocks at a *minimum* of 150,000 tons; an increase above this level did not affect the Committee's obligations to provide enough rubber for this, as well as all other demands. The provision was to protect producers against a possible price fall should the manufacturers allow their own stocks to run down. No one visualised an increase in trade stocks to an extent seriously interfering with the accumulation of the reserve stock.

to acquire the reserve stock at a much more rapid rate than originally contemplated; the Committee was accordingly urged to raise the rate of release. The American Government offered to conclude a third agreement at the Committee's option to cover the purchase of 100,000 tons on the terms of the second agreement; this offer was explicitly intended to avert the danger of rapid decreases in the rate of release after the completion of the second agreement.

These matters were reviewed by the Committee in November when the release for the first quarter of 1941 had to be decided. The representative of the Committee had returned from America and conveyed the growing sense of urgency felt by the American Government in the acquisition of the reserve stock. He supported the American request that the release for the first quarter of 1941 should be raised to 100 per cent. This proposal met with considerable opposition. Some members objected by emphasising the seasonally low output during the first quarter which rendered it improbable that supplies equal to a 100 per cent. rate of release could be produced. This contention appears to be an argument for higher rather than lower releases, to allow producers capable of higher outputs than those permitted by a release of 100 per cent. to make their maximum contribution. The strongest opposition came from the N.E.I. delegation, one of whose members laid stress on the power over rubber prices which would accrue to America through the possession of a large stock. He consented eventually to a rate of release of 100 per cent., on the understanding that the decision would not be regarded as a precedent for subsequent quarters of 1941, and 'that the rates in excess of 100 per cent. were non-existent so far as regulation went, and could never be put into force'.[1] Yet in the past the delegation had often (and rightly) argued that the N.E.I. native quota was far below capacity, and that the N.E.I. native producers could easily export in excess of a 100 per cent. release.

The rate of release was thus fixed at 100 per cent., as requested by the U.S. authorities. The Committee repeatedly claimed that this represented full production. This contention was incorrect, as is evident from the high prices of export rights throughout the quarter. In Malaya, for instance, smallholders' coupons during the first quarter of 1941 were worth about 50 per cent. of the Singapore price of first quality rubber.[2] An even simpler piece of evidence is supplied by the internal cuts which were still being imposed;

[1] *I.R.R.C. Minutes*, Vol. 16, p. 86.
[2] Cf. Statistical Appendix II, Table VII.

in Malaya these were at the rate of 2½ per cent. for two quarters in 1940 and for the first three quarters of 1941.

Total world exports in 1940 were almost 1,400,000 tons; absorption at about 1,085,000 tons was very slightly below the 1939 figure. World stocks rose by about 300,000 tons over the year; in America the increase was 160,000 tons and in the U.K. about 40,000 tons, while stocks afloat had risen by about 90,000 tons. American absorption totalled 648,000 tons and during the second half of the year was increasing very rapidly with the rising tide of prosperity. Those framing estimates of American consumption on both sides of the Atlantic found it difficult to adjust their ideas to conditions of full employment in the U.S.A., and though estimates were repeatedly revised the actual figures constantly exceeded expectations. As late as November 1940 the R.M.A. and the American member of the Advisory Panel forecast U.S. absorption for the three months October–December 1940 at 153,000 tons; the actual figure turned out to be 177,000 tons.

The Reserve Company's purchases were much behind schedule at the end of the year, and less than one-half of the 150,000 tons provided for in the American agreements to be purchased for shipment by the end of 1940 had actually been shipped. The excess of American absorption over the estimates and an increase in American trade stocks were contingencies which had not been allowed for in the Committee's policy of fixing the rates of release so as to leave little or no margin. The buying policy of the Reserve Company was also seriously at fault; the Company bought only spot rubber or rubber for near delivery, while producers and dealers regularly sold forward substantial amounts and had not enough spot or near rubber left for the Reserve Company. The Company was, moreover, frequently outbid by other buyers who either offered the upper price limit stipulated in the agreement at times when the Company hoped to obtain rubber for less, or actually paid more than the upper price limit, either openly, or under cover by buying lower grades without full discount. The Company's buying agents in the East were representatives of the large U.S. manufacturers, and rubber which should have reached the Reserve Company regularly found its way into private warehouses and was thus added to trade stocks, or went to swell the rising absorption figures. A further defect of the Reserve Company's buying policy was the insistence on f.o.b. or c.i.f. contracts under which the seller had to arrange for freight space (though under the former contract he was refunded the cost of freight) which was becoming increasingly difficult to obtain ; some of the Reserve Company's competitors were prepared to buy on an ex-warehouse basis under which the producer's obligation ceased on delivery of the rubber to a warehouse at port of shipment.

During the winter of 1940–41 a further factor appeared which was soon to eclipse all others. The exports from several producing territories were beginning to fall behind the permissible amounts. There were several reasons for this. In the hard bargaining which had preceded the renewal of the international agreement in 1938 the basic quotas of one or two territories were fixed at levels which either exceeded their capacity, or approached it so closely that exports at the rate of 100 per cent. could be expected only under most favourable conditions ; this applied particularly to Ceylon. Other territories, for instance Sarawak, suffered from a genuine shortage of labour as migration was greatly reduced with the outbreak of war. Labour, European supervision and the supply of materials were also becoming scarce in most of the producing territories, though the scarcity would not have been serious but for the repercussions of heavy taxation, notably the 100 per cent. excess profits tax.

A few days after the meeting of the I.R.R.C. in May 1940, the British excess profits tax was raised from 60 per cent. to 100 per cent. and the standard rate of income tax from 7*s*. 6*d*. to 8*s*. 6*d*. a few weeks later. It was expected that there would be a further increase to 10*s*. in 1941, and that profits made from the summer of 1940 onwards would be taxed at this rate. This taxation applied to sterling companies only, but affected these irrespective of the territories in which they operated ; profits on the substantial British-controlled estate output in the N.E.I. also attracted this heavy taxation.

When the excess profits tax was introduced in September 1939 at a rate of 60 per cent., rubber producers complained little, chiefly because the basic years for computing standard profits suited them well and permitted the retention of satisfactory profits. The much better prices and higher releases of 1940, coupled with the steep rise in the rate of tax, altered the situation and consequently the attitude of many British producers, as standard profits could now be secured by production much below permissible exports.

In gauging the effect which this taxation was likely to have on British estate output, some semi-technical considerations must be borne in mind. First, replanting expenditure was allowed by the inland revenue as a charge against taxable profits and no limit was placed on this expenditure. In normal times the revenue benefited by this arrangement, since replanting was not on an extensive scale and the claims were probably less than they would have been if depreciation at a fixed percentage had been allowed.[1] From about 1939 or 1940 the position was reversed, and producers who made high profits and also had substantial liquid funds available for replanting operations could and did spend large sums on replanting at the expense of the revenue. Secondly, the wear and tear involved in bark removal was not allowed for tax purposes. This would have been difficult to compute; moreover, estate producers very rarely tapped at a rate more severe than that which equated the rates of bark renewal and removal. It was also presumably held that in so far as the life of the trees would be shortened by severe tapping, the admission of replanting costs as a charge against taxable profit would cover any claim under this heading. This, however, was not always so, especially for young areas not due for replanting for many years. Thirdly, under the conditions of 1940–41 the standard assessments of producers whose exports fell behind the permissible amounts were practically never reduced even if they sold rights heavily. Reference to the shortage of labour or to the immaturity of replanted areas generally sufficed under war conditions to defeat any contention that the producer was over-assessed. Fourthly, as a bonus to stimulate replanting, the assessments of replanted areas were, throughout the East, maintained during the period of immaturity at the same level as before the felling of the old trees.

By the autumn of 1940 the boards of sterling companies widely realised that outputs of about 50 per cent. to 60 per cent. of their assessments would suffice to yield the standard profits of their companies, and while they were prepared to be patriotic up to a point, there was a growing restlessness at the sight of the heavy crops the proceeds of which were taxed away. The reaction of individual boards and agency houses varied considerably; some pursued a policy which disregarded excess profits tax altogether, and the properties were tapped to produce the permissible amount, or as near to it as possible; there were others who calculated to a nicety the output which secured their standard profits and restricted production to that level, which was easy once the price

[1] Thus so far from rubber producers not being granted any amortisation allowance (as has often been stated), producers willing to replant were permitted to determine themselves their rate of amortisation for taxation purposes. The loss of income on replanted areas was not allowed, but on balance the practice was of great advantage to producers who were able to take advantage of it.

was largely stabilised by the American agreements.[1] On the whole, however, the two extremes were rather exceptional, and the great majority of sterling companies produced appreciably more than the minimum necessary to secure standard profits, but not the maximum which their estates could have yielded. This manifested itself in various directions.

Some of the best rubber, especially young budded rubber, was left untapped. This particular policy was induced not only by the 100 per cent. excess profits tax, but also by the still generous scale allowances which, especially for five- to seven-year-old trees, were quite out of proportion to productive capacity. If it had been tapped much of this rubber would have yielded less than the scale allowances and its assessment might possibly have been reduced, while as long as it remained untapped it was entitled to scale allowances at full rates. On some properties unnecessarily light tapping systems were adopted, much below the rate at which bark consumption would have equalled bark renewal. As early as October 1940 the American Trade Commissioner in Singapore was told by a leading visiting agent that the group of estates which he supervised were, on instructions from London, tapped too lightly as the companies were liable to excess profits tax ; on the properties of several companies he advocated a tapping system 50 per cent. more intensive than the boards would allow.[2]

In Malaya the sterling companies soon became sellers of export rights to local producers not liable to excess profits tax, and this tendency was much enhanced in 1941. The price of rights was, however, fairly high in the autumn of 1940 ; to quote only one instance, the chairman of a locally-registered company stated in September 1940 that while their estate could easily produce 120

[1] The latter policy was supported, or at least expressed, by the chairman of the Malaya General Company, who stated in December 1940 at the annual general meeting of the company : 'For the coming year we have a standard assessment of 3,148,079 pounds, but to produce this crop would mean making the Government a present of well over 1,000,000 pounds of rubber . . . and although your Directors have every desire to help the Government and the war effort to the utmost, they do not feel that their responsibilities to the shareholders will permit them to tap to the fullest extent allowed under the International Rubber Regulation Scheme. Therefore, the output aimed at will be more or less on the lines of the present crop. . . .' This crop was about 69 per cent. of the company's standard assessment mentioned by the chairman.

This company is among the most prosperous rubber companies (it had paid dividends throughout the slump, as well as in 1942–43 and 1943–44) ; its secretaries and agents, Yule, Catto and Company, are also among the wealthiest secretarial firms.

There is good reason to believe that a similar policy was pursued by some other enterprises.

[2] U.S. Department of Commerce, Bureau of Foreign and Domestic Commerce, *Industrial Reference Service*, January 1941.

per cent. of its standard production, they were not prepared to pay 15 cents per lb. for export rights. In that the effect of the liability of the sterling companies to excess profits tax was tantamount to a reduction in productivity, it intensified their over-assessment relatively to local estate producers and to smallholders.

Perhaps most important in its influence on rubber supplies was the sudden increase in replanting during the second half of 1940 which continued at an increasing pace throughout 1941. In the conditions of 1940 and 1941 the companies liable to excess profits tax had everything to gain and nothing to lose by uprooting and replanting part of their acreage. In peace-time, replanting programmes had generally been drawn up years ahead and were so arranged as to secure by slaughter tapping the maximum output of rubber from the area about to be felled. In 1940–41 most of the replanting was carried out at short notice and little contribution was made to current supplies by slaughter tapping, which must be spread over a considerable period to be fully effective. The motives behind this sudden outburst of replanting, as well as its effect on rubber supplies, were widely known.

Under-tapping and large-scale replanting also affected rubber supplies indirectly by aggravating the scarcity of labour, supervision and material. Failure to tap the best areas tended to reduce the output per tapper and was thus wasteful of labour. The replanting operations withdrew much labour from current production. European supervision, which was getting scarcer every month, was being diverted from current output to replanting operations which require special care and which were given priority of attention on many properties. The shortage of manures was another constant complaint in 1940–41, but manures are not an essential requirement of current rubber production and available supplies were again diverted primarily to replanted areas.

In fairness to estate producers it must be said that the authorities revealed little sense of urgency. In the U.S.A., absorption broke new records every month until the phenomenal monthly figure of 85,000 tons was reached before any action came to be taken ; the Reserve Company watched with apparently little concern the diversion of large quantities of rubber into private warehouses. No indication was given until the summer of 1941 that the American authorities would go beyond a reserve stock of 430,000 tons ; in fact until March they seemed content with 330,000 tons. Meanwhile producers in the East were being assured by the authorities that Malaya would be held against any Japanese attack. These factors were not calculated to inspire urgency and self-denial.

From the second half of 1940 rubber supplies for the West were also adversely affected by the growing domination of Japan over French Indo-China and Siam. Some rubber from these territories continued to reach Malaya and the U.S.A., but the bulk went to Japan. Exports from India were also drying up with the rapid increase in internal absorption in that country. This was a long-term trend greatly accelerated by the war.

II

The year 1941 saw an intensification of the problems and trends of 1940. At the request of the American authorities the I.R.R.C. fixed the rate of release for the second quarter at 100 per cent. in February; the Committee stated again that this rate of release represented full production.

The decision was promptly followed by the announcement of a 2½ per cent. internal cut in Malaya, and the 100 per cent. release thus clearly did not represent full production. The effectiveness of restriction was confirmed by the continued high prices of export rights, especially of smallholders' coupons in Malaya and in the N.E.I. The N.E.I. administration actually took steps to maintain the price of coupons by issuing them in instalments as dislocation was feared from a too rapid fall in coupon values; this at a time when all-out production was said to have been achieved.

The Committee accepted the American offer to buy an additional 100,000 tons of rubber, and a third agreement was concluded in March. The terms were those of the second agreement, except for the absence of a time limit for the purchases, which were to take place in accordance with discussions between the Reserve Company and the I.R.R.C. with the aim of mitigating the effects of a steep decline in the exportable percentage. The U.S. Government subsequently signified its intention to purchase for shipment before the end of 1941 the full 430,000 tons covered by the three agreements.

Meanwhile the rate of accumulation of the reserve stock continued to fall behind schedule and absorption to exceed expectations. In February 1941 the R.M.A. estimated American absorption for the current (January–March) quarter at 166,000 tons, against the figure of 192,000 tons actually realised. Trade stocks in the U.S.A. were also rising, or more precisely appeared to rise until revised absorption estimates established that most of the intake believed to represent a net increase in trade stocks had again vanished into internal consumption. The Reserve Company, which continued to buy spot rubber or rubber for near delivery only, found it increasingly difficult to acquire supplies.[1] These supplies in their turn were adversely affected by the deficiency of exports compared to the permissible amounts under restriction, which was gradually becoming general.

During the second quarter it became evident that without important administrative changes the rate of accumulation of the reserve stock would fall progressively more behind schedule. U.S. absorption again reached new record levels ; it totalled 227,000 tons for the quarter, culminating in the June figure of 85,000 tons ; for the twelve months ending June 1941 absorption reached 756,000 tons. In addition to the very large second-quarter absorption, it was found that absorption in 1940 was not 618,000 tons as had been believed, but had reached 648,000 tons. Trade stocks at the end of June were found to be only 133,000 tons instead of some 170,000 tons as previously estimated. But while these stocks rose to 216,000 tons by the end of August, the reserve stock increased from 116,000 tons to 138,000 tons only.

The obvious step of centralising all American purchases was eventually taken in June, and exports to America were subject to licensing ; permits were given only for shipments against contracts with the official Central Buying Agency, or for rubber shipped in fulfilment of outstanding forward contracts. Shortly after this, rubber was declared a scarce material in the U.S.A., and manufacturers were rationed to a proportion of their previous intake.

These measures greatly improved the position of the Reserve Company against its buying competitors (who had sometimes been its own agents). Supplies were still affected by the mounting export deficits, which by the end of June exceeded 80,000 tons. The third-quarter release was again fixed at 100 per cent. with the customary reference that this represented full production. The decision was again followed by an internal cut in Malaya to 97½ per cent. ;[2] smallholders' coupons were still worth about half the market price of rubber.

In August unofficial information was received by the Committee that the U.S. Government contemplated a large increase in the

[1] In April stocks afloat to America were estimated at 140,000 tons, of which only 5,000 tons were for the account of the Reserve Company.

[2] There were also internal cuts in British North Borneo during most of 1941.

reserve stock. No specific proposals were as yet put forward, but an informal undertaking was given that the U.S. authorities would purchase all available rubber at the maximum price laid down in the second and third agreements (18½ U.S. cents f.o.b. eastern ports). At the same time the rising pace of war production in this country and the larger shipments to the Soviet Union following the German invasion of that country increased the demands on the failing supplies. Thus exports were sagging when, for the first time perhaps since 1919, all rubber which could be produced could be sold immediately at extremely profitable prices for many months to come. The export deficits affected not only the supply of an important war material, but also the dollar income of the British and Dutch exchange controls.

An important meeting attended by British and Dutch officials, as well as by some influential members of the I.R.R.C., was held at the Colonial Office in August to consider ways and means of increasing supplies. The representative of the Ministry of Supply suggested a temporary suspension of restriction in face of the pressing demands—not an unreasonable proposal at a meeting convened expressly to consider methods for increasing output. He was informed that this suggestion could not be entertained. A proposal for internal re-distribution of assessments was briefly mentioned and promptly rejected. It was finally decided to request the local governments to appeal to producers to export as much rubber as they could; the producing territories were also encouraged to make use of the 5 per cent. margin of over-exports allowed by the international agreement; lastly, where rubber could be produced in excess of 100 per cent. plus the 5 per cent. margin, the I.R.R.C. would be asked to increase retrospectively the permissible exportable amount of the territory concerned. These proposals were quite insufficient to meet the situation. Unlimited production was suggested to territories where internal cuts were in force to comply with the restriction scheme; unrestricted output was requested within the framework of rubber restriction. Prohibition of replanting, or substantial reduction in the assessments of producers falling behind their permissible exports, or the removal of internal cuts were not even mentioned.

The Committee met later in August and had to consider a definite American request for raising the release to over 100 per cent. in order to free any latent productive capacity and thus ensure genuine capacity working; it was also clear that for months ahead all rubber produced would be bought at the ruling prices.

Faced with an unlimited demand the Committee this time very nearly granted the request for unrestricted production. The release was raised to 120 per cent., and it was announced that excess exports would be covered by retro-active increases in permissible exports.[1] This announcement was followed by a sharp fall in the price of export rights throughout the producing territories. But exports of individual producers were still controlled through the issue of export rights and coupons, and as it was not stated that producers could export as much as they wished, the rights continued to command a price. No quotations are available in London beyond the first week of October 1941 when smallholders' coupons both in Malaya and in the N.E.I. still fetched about 1*d.* per lb. Moreover, while the restriction machinery remained in existence potential producers who had received no assessment at all were unlikely to produce any rubber, and there must have been many such producers among smallholders in the N.E.I.[2]

Shortly after this decision the Committee was formally informed of the intention of the U.S. Government to increase the reserve stock to 800,000 tons. It was also intimated that when this stock was accumulated manufacturers would again be free to use as much rubber as they wished; the Reserve Company visualised imports at the rate of 100,000 tons a month for some considerable time to come. This decision involved the conclusion of a further agreement, and the Committee's representative again proceeded to America. An agreement which never became effective was actually signed in December. On 2nd December the Committee met to consider the release for the first quarter of 1942, which was again fixed at 120 per cent. At the same meeting the prohibition of

[1] According to the *History of Rubber Regulation* it would have been simpler to allow unlimited production without fixing any rate of release but the Committee was prevented under its mandate from taking this step. There is a disconcerting tendency in that book, as there was in the Committee's decisions, to fall back on empty formal considerations in defence of steps taken for quite different reasons. On several occasions the Committee was prepared definitely to disregard the formal provisions of the agreement; in 1936 it cancelled the N.E.I. over-exports for 1935; in 1938 it agreed not to raise formal objections to the Ceylon excess exports of over 5 per cent. so long as these were gradually reduced. There were several other instances (not reviewed in this study because of their minor importance) when the Committee disregarded explicit provisions of the agreement. There were thus precedents for departing from the text of the agreement. All signatory governments would have certainly agreed, while if they had not the British Government could have taken advantage of the escape clause of the agreement and abandoned export restriction.

[2] The whole complex machinery of restriction was fully maintained; for instance, the local administrations continued to furnish (until January 1942) formal statements to the Committee that no undue accumulation of stocks (contrary to the provisions of the agreement) had taken place on smallholdings within their territories.

new planting was extended for the remaining years of regulation. These were the last decisions before the producing territories were overrun by the Japanese.

The Reserve Company's buying programme made considerable progress after June, and soon exceeded the schedule visualised in 1940. The 330,000 tons covered by the first two agreements were purchased by the end of August for shipment by the end of October, while 77,000 tons of the third agreement were bought for shipment by the end of November ; the Committee thus fully met its obligation to provide 330,000 tons for shipment by the end of 1941. More than 300,000 tons of reserve rubber were landed in America by the end of 1941. American stocks at the end of the year totalled 533,000 tons, excluding rubber afloat.

U.S. absorption in 1941 reached 780,000 tons and but for the restriction imposed after June it would have appreciably exceeded 900,000 tons.

III

While the acquisition of the reserve stock made headway, rubber supplies were still affected by the deficit of exports, which was becoming steadily more marked. By the end of November the total deficit reached almost 150,000 tons, as is shown in the table on page 170.

According to an official dispatch from the N.E.I. authorities to the Dutch Government in London, the N.E.I. natives were expected to produce 120 per cent. of their quota without difficulty. This official opinion, together with the performance of the N.E.I. smallholders in 1941, was ample comment on the fairness of the N.E.I. native quota and on the repeated statements that a 100 per cent. release (or sometimes less) represented unrestricted production. The text of an official telegram from the N.E.I. Government to the Netherlands Ministry of Colonies in London is also of interest : 'Native rubber coupons for last quarter will be fully issued in September. [On this becoming known,] price of coupons fell from around 25–30 cents [guilder cents per kilo, about *4d.*–4¾*d.* per lb.] to about 18–19 cents [2¾*d.*–*3d.* per lb.], while uncouponed rubber rose correspondingly and increased output is expected.' Thus a relative rise in the price of uncouponed rubber as against the value of coupons resulted in higher output.[1] It will be noted

[1] This obvious point was on several critical occasions denied in discussions at I.R.R.C. meetings ; an instance was given above, p. 128.

TABLE I

Permissible and Actual Exports of Rubber, January–November 1941.

	Exports (thousand tons)		Deficit	
	Permissible	Actual	Quantity (thousand tons)	As per cent. of permissible exports
Malaya	611	561	50	8
N.E.I. estates	312	275	37	12
N.E.I. natives	301	304	3	+ 1 (excess)
Ceylon	99	82	17	17
Sarawak	44	35	9	20
British North Borneo	20	18	2	10
India [a]	18	2	16	89
Burma	14	9	5	36
Siam	54	43	11	20
Total	1,473	1,329	144 [b]	10

[a] India was a special case, as her rubber manufacturing industry was developing so rapidly during 1940–41 that she became a net importer of rubber after mid-1941.
[b] The shipping shortage cannot be held responsible for the export deficit. Rubber was a high-priority cargo, and there was no excessive accumulation of port stocks. Moreover, Singapore and Penang were outside the export regulation area, and rubber despatched from the Malayan mainland to these shipping ports counted as exports under the regulation scheme.

that export rights were still worth about 40 per cent. of the f.o.b. price of rubber—and this after the rate of release had been fixed at 100 per cent. for eight months, which was said to have represented unrestricted production.

It was not until 13th December 1941 that the Dutch Government suggested to the N.E.I. authorities that all restrictive passages of the local rubber regulation legislation could be disregarded. From the records of the I.R.R.C. it does not appear that such a suggestion was made to the Malayan authorities before the Japanese occupation.

In Malaya, the production both of estates and of smallholdings appears to have fallen short of their permissible amounts by about the same percentage. The smallholdings thus did not produce at such a high rate as could have been expected from previous performances.[1] Too much weight should not be placed on this incomplete evidence. First, for various reasons, since the introduction of restriction, figures of Malayan smallholdings output for part of the year were much less reliable than for a complete year. Again, the output of Chettiar-owned holdings was credited to

[1] Which were much exceeded in 1946.

estate production, though many of these were assessed as smallholdings; accordingly, the output of smallholdings as a percentage of their quota was under-stated and that of the estates over-stated. This accounted for about 2–2½ per cent. of the smallholders' quota, and their output was approximately at the rate of 92–93 per cent., and not 89–90 per cent. as is suggested by the uncorrected figures. Moreover, after years of low releases and under-assessment the smallholders could not be expected to possess the equipment necessary to produce the large amounts called for in 1941 (which were, however, still below their rate of production towards the end of 1933 and the beginning of 1934). In some parts of Malaya they were also hampered by local shortages of share-tappers. To a certain extent their output was also influenced by the exceptional prosperity which descended on them in 1940 and 1941 and to which they had not yet adjusted themselves. In spite of these various adverse factors, the smallholders apparently still produced a somewhat larger proportion of their quota than did the estates.

The production of rubber by sterling companies was increasingly affected by the combined effects of over-assessment, 100 per cent. excess profits tax and unrestricted replanting. The cumulative effects of these factors are reflected in the following table in which the January–August 1941 rate of production of estates owned by sterling companies (as represented by the returns furnished by the R.G.A. to the I.R.R.C.) is contrasted with that of all other Malayan estates.

TABLE II

Rate of Production (as per cent. of aggregate standard production) of Malayan Estate Producers, January–August 1941

	R.G.A. estates	*Other estates*	*All estates*	*Internal rate of release*
January	91·5	95·0	93·1	97·5
February	82·3	93·1	87·4	97·5
March	78·0	87·0	82·2	97·5
April	74·7	86·6	80·3	97·5
May	76·6	95·6	85·5	97·5
June	87·4	95·8	91·1	97·5
July	89·4	97·8	93·9	97·5
August	87·9	98·5	92·9	97·5
Total, Jan.–Aug.	83·6	93·7	88·3	97·5

The divergent production trends cannot be attributed to shortage of labour or of materials as the locally-owned estates and those owned by sterling companies were equally affected. It is even possible to ascertain roughly the relative responsibilities of over-assessment and of 100 per cent. excess profits tax for the lower rate of production of sterling companies. During the first half of 1940 (when production is seasonally low owing to wintering) the average internal rate of release in Malaya was 78¾ per cent. (the international rate being 80 per cent., with an internal cut of 2½ per cent. in the second quarter). Over these six months when output was not yet affected by 100 per cent. excess profits tax, the R.G.A. estates produced at the rate of 72½ per cent. of their aggregate standard production and all other estates at 77½ per cent., which suggests that the R.G.A. estates already found it more difficult than the other estates to produce the permissible amount. During the first eight months of 1941, when the rate of excess profits tax was 100 per cent., the gap between the performances of the R.G.A. estates and that of the locally-owned estates was about 10 per cent. of standard production against 5 per cent. in the first half of 1940. From this it appears that the two factors (over-assessment and 100 per cent. excess profits tax) were about equally responsible in 1941 for the poorer performance of estates owned by sterling companies compared with other Malayan estates. The output of all estate producers was adversely affected by the shortages resulting from the wasteful use of labour and of materials by the sterling companies encouraged by 100 per cent. excess profits tax. At the end of October 1941, 5·8 per cent. of the mature estate area of Malaya was out of tapping, with a further 9·4 per cent. rested under rotational tapping systems. These figures exclude areas cut out for replanting.

In Malaya replanting was never prohibited; in the N.E.I. it was prohibited only in January 1942, after the fall of most of the Malayan mainland and of a large part of Borneo and only a few days before the Japanese conquest of Sumatra and Java. In Ceylon an official circular was issued in September 1941, which requested estates to produce higher crops without, however, 'over-tapping or damaging their trees'. The circular suggested that it would be helpful if estates postponed replanting and retained their trees in tapping for a little longer. Replanting was not prohibited in Ceylon until July 1942.

CHAPTER 12

THE PLANTING PROVISIONS OF RUBBER REGULATION

I

IN the 1934 agreement new planting of rubber was prohibited. Replanting (the uprooting of existing plantations and their replacement by new trees) was allowed up to 20 per cent. of the existing acreage of each owner, with a maximum of 10 per cent. in any year until the end of 1938. It has already been suggested [1] that these provisions jeopardised the future of the smallholding industry. An examination of the detailed record of the discussions preceding the 1934 agreement suggests that these provisions were drafted without consideration of this easily foreseeable long-term result. The planting provisions were discussed by the full Rubber Regulation Committee of the R.G.A., and the permission to replant opposed by some who accepted it only as a concession to the Dutch view. Thus it would appear that, at any rate at first, these measures were not a Machiavellian plot on the part of the estate representatives for the suppression of native competition. The officials whose duty it was to protect the interests of the smallholders were also somewhat unfamiliar with the economics of smallholders' rubber; the draft proposals were administratively workable and apparently equitable and were readily accepted. The operation, effects and implications of these provisions will now be examined in detail.

The essence of the matter can be put quite simply. On estates replanting is feasible and has been widely adopted; it is impracticable on smallholdings for economic and technical reasons. The gradual replanting of the estates with high-yielding material, combined with the prohibition of new planting (in spite of the existence of enormous areas of uncultivated land) might have led in the course of not more than 20 or 25 years (and might still lead) to the virtual elimination of the smallholders, however efficient they might have been at the outset, and however ready to take advantage of high-yielding material by new planting.

There are two principal reasons for the smallholders' unwillingness, or rather inability, to replant. There is first the lack of

[1] Above, p. 77.

capital required to pay not only the heavy expenses involved, especially the cost of manuring, which is necessary for successful replanting, but also to bridge the loss of income from the felling of old trees to the maturity of the new stand.[1] A rubber tree is tappable five or six years after planting and fully mature in another four or five years. The replanting of a stand of trees thus involves at least five years' loss of income and possibly several more years of reduced income, depending on the relative yields of the old and new stand of trees. Replanting can thus be undertaken only by producers with ample working capital, which the estates do, and the smallholders do not, possess. The issue is somewhat complicated by restriction without the substance being materially affected. Unless the rate of release under regulation is very high, or an abnormally large proportion of the property consists of immature replanted areas, the estate can produce the exportable allowance from the remaining mature part of the property. Such a course is not open to the smallholder who harvests his crop from all over his holding, tapping trees here and there and practising a rotational system of tapping by resting individual trees.[2]

The second reason for the smallholders' inability to replant is the technical impossibility of replanting successfully part of a holding of a few acres, as the area replanted would be closely surrounded by mature trees which would intercept the sunlight and whose roots would compete for food with the undeveloped rootlets of the newly-planted trees. Root competition may be reduced, or possibly eliminated, by the expensive and on smallholdings inconvenient device of cutting isolation drains. Nothing can, however, be done to prevent the stunted growth which results from shading out. The rubber tree is much more shade-resisting than most of its competitors but growth is greatly retarded when the sunlight is intercepted. From 1934 to 1938 individual producers were not allowed to replant more than 10 per cent. of their area in any one year, or more than 20 per cent. over the entire

[1] A planting manual of the Rubber Research Institute of Malaya estimated in 1938 that the loss of income and the cash expenses of replanting would be recouped only twelve years after the felling of the old stand.

[2] After 1935 in most producing territories either no reduction, or only a very small reduction, was made in the assessments of replanted areas whose owners thus had export rights to dispose of (except in British North Borneo where these were not transferable), which greatly reduced their loss of income. This concession was of little use to the smallholders, who were unable to replant for technical reasons given in the text. Nor could they be expected to speculate on the price of coupons and of unlicensed rubber several years ahead; twice during the restriction scheme (in the autumn of 1937 and again during the closing months of 1941) the price of coupons fell almost to zero.

period, and this rendered replanting on peasant holdings wholly impossible.

The official provisions governing replanting were never properly understood by the smallholders, who were handicapped by their inability to read and comprehend the somewhat complex rules and regulations insisted on in the various producing territories. Both in Malaya and the N.E.I. a detailed statement had to be submitted by each applicant for permission to replant, setting out in writing the exact acreage and location of the area to be replanted, the age of the trees, the material used, and certain other details (some of them quite complex) ; in writing be it noted, when the majority of the smallholders were illiterate. For these various reasons replanting was certain to be confined to estates.

The far-reaching effects of the planting provisions should now be clear. If the planted area was a wasting asset, the prohibition of new planting combined with the practical impossibility of replanting on smallholdings was bound to lead to the gradual elimination of the smallholders. Moreover, greatly improved planting material was constantly being developed, which enabled the estate to increase output per worker and per acre, while the smallholder was unable to take advantage of this and his competitive strength was greatly impaired. This was possibly of greater importance than the danger to the smallholders' position through the senescence of the trees or through the declining physical productive capacity of their holdings, since the productive capacity of these properties has much exceeded expectations.

It may conveniently be mentioned here that a ban on the alienation of land for rubber planting may have effects on the future of smallholdings similar to those of the prohibition of new planting combined with substantial replanting. Even if new planting is permitted, a refusal to alienate land may still endanger the position of the smallholders if on estates there is replanting on a substantial scale. If no land is being alienated for rubber, new planting is limited to owners of land already alienated but not yet under rubber, i.e. unplanted reserve land, or land carrying other crops which would be cut down for the purpose. Smallholders very rarely have unplanted reserve land, and in the circumstances most of their new planting could take place only by uprooting of fruit trees or food crops. This they might be unable or unwilling to do. Refusal to alienate land for rubber planting has thus in many instances much the same effect as prohibition of new planting on smallholdings. In Malaya, refusal to alienate land for rubber planting has been the official policy generally since 1922; its implications, both on the competitive position of Malaya as a whole, and on the relative position of estates and smallholdings do not appear to have been fully appreciated.

Replanting was not only permitted by the provisions of the scheme, but was also encouraged by the restriction authorities in various ways. In 1935, at an early stage of the first regulation period, on the recommendation of the I.R.R.C., assessments of areas cut out for replanting were reduced in Malaya and the N.E.I. by only 30 per cent. of the previous assessment; 70 per cent. of the old assessment was received during the immaturity of the replanted area as a bonus towards the cost of replanting.[1] The cash value of this bonus varied with the price of export rights but was generally substantial. Ceylon and several smaller countries made no deduction from the assessment of replanted areas and the bonus was thus 100 per cent. of the old assessment. The replanting bonus benefited chiefly the larger estate producers, as these alone replanted on a substantial scale. As these estates were most favourably assessed and were often over-assessed there were some protests, especially in Malaya, against the bonus.

By 1936 the complete absence of any replanting by smallholders was beginning to attract attention in the East. For example, according to the 1936 *Administration Report* of the Rubber Controller, Ceylon, not a single application for replanting had by then been received from smallholders. In February 1936 the *Straits Times* pointed out quite candidly that no replanting was to be expected from smallholders who had not the necessary capital, and that the estates were certain to gain substantial ground as a result of the planting provisions of the scheme. This was also becoming evident from the official planting statistics. About 240,000 acres were replanted between 1934 and 1938, practically wholly on estates; this was about 5–6 per cent. of the estate area. This replanting activity implied an increase of about 10–12 per cent. in the ultimate productive capacity of the estates, after allowing for the destruction of the old stand. There was, moreover, a gradual increase in the areas replanted annually, which was to be much accelerated during the second period of regulation.

In the discussions leading to the renewal of regulation in 1938

[1] In Malaya the reduction was 110 lb. per acre, while in the N.E.I. it was 30 per cent. of the last assessment.

This recommendation again refutes the contention of the Committee (above, p. 126) that the local administration of restriction was outside its concern.

it was recognised that some new planting would have to be conceded, but there was much argument over the amounts of new planting and replanting respectively to be permitted. By this time it had become quite clear that the smallholders and the smaller producers generally did not replant at all, and half-hearted requests were put forward by the local administrations for a modification of the planting provisions of the scheme which so obviously discriminated against the smallholders. Such proposals were not well received by the I.R.R.C., nor by its renewal sub-committee, one of whose members argued that new planting was demanded by those too lazy to face the careful thought and difficult decisions involved in replanting. This was hardly a fair statement of the position. For reasons which have already been stated, successful replanting was physically impossible on most smallholdings.[1]

The French delegate to the I.R.R.C. strongly opposed free, or virtually free, replanting. French Indo-China had very large areas available for the extension of the planted area, and as most of the plantations there were very young there was no reason for uprooting these. The French representative pressed for the interchangeability of new planting and replanting rights as, with the development of high-yielding material replanting also represented an increase in the productive capacity (though not to the same extent as new planting, which does not involve destruction of the old stand).

It was eventually resolved to recommend new planting during 1939 and 1940 of a total of 5 per cent. of the planted area in each territory, with unconditional replanting during the same period; the matter was to be reviewed again in 1940 by the I.R.R.C. After 1940 the power to decide on the permissible rate of new planting and replanting was to lie with the I.R.R.C.

The recommendation for 5 per cent. new planting during 1939–40 was announced in March 1938, and as the acceptance of the proposal was a foregone conclusion, preparatory steps were taken throughout the producing territories to enable planting operations to start

[1] An interesting official correspondence on the subject of renewal of regulation took place in 1937 between the chairman of the I.R.R.C. (the then Economic Adviser to the Secretary of State for the Colonies, and leader of the Malayan delegation on the I.R.R.C.) and the High Commissioner for the Malay States. The latter was advised to regard the Malayan delegation as his chief adviser on renewal matters, since the large estates were administered from London. 'There are of course the small Malay and Chinese producers who are not represented in London, but on the broad questions which will arise in regard to renewal their interests are not likely to diverge from those of the European estates' (*Minutes of the I.R.R.C. Renewal Sub-Committee*, p. 74). There was in fact a wide divergence of interest over the planting provisions, as well as over the division of the quotas.

early in 1939.[1] The general procedure was roughly similar in the more important territories. Producers were issued so-called 'share certificates' indicating the acreage they were entitled to plant; these documents were generally transferable. Their distribution was usually on the basis of 'to him that hath shall be given', and producers received certificates representing planting rights equal to 5 per cent. of their registered acreage. In view of the appreciable market price of the rights this amounted to a substantial windfall for the larger producers. In the N.E.I. planting rights were not transferable between estates and smallholders, which ensured that the smallholders should actually take up new planting to the extent of the full 5 per cent. of their 1938 acreage as calculated from the results of the tree census (which was of course only about one-half of their actual acreage). In the native rubber-growing districts of Sumatra and Borneo the authorities invited applications for new planting rights by the local population irrespective of ownership of a rubber holding. Although the majority of the population of the principal rubber-growing districts already had a holding, applications for new planting rights substantially exceeded the rights available, and the applications had to be correspondingly scaled down. This was a more satisfactory procedure than that adopted in Malaya which, as will be seen shortly, prevented the majority of the smallholders from participating in the new planting of 1939–40. In Ceylon, two-thirds of the available new planting rights were reserved for middle-class Singhalese and for Singhalese peasants. In Sarawak, too, some planting rights were distributed to smallholders who previously had not grown rubber.

There was a regular open market with widely fluctuating prices in the planting rights; in Malaya the price ranged from 18 to 50 dollars per acre in 1938. Early in 1939 the rights were worth 50–70 dollars per acre. In the N.E.I. the price of estate planting rights fluctuated between 100 and 160 guilders per hectare (40–70 Straits dollars per acre) in 1938–39. The 5 per cent. new planting permitted was fully taken up by 1940, and everywhere applications for new planting greatly exceeded available planting rights. This eagerness to apply for planting rights and their handsome prices suggest that rubber planting was not so unprofitable as was claimed at the time.

[1] The spokesmen of some of the weaker sterling companies protested against the 5 per cent. new planting which, it was said, would in view of the much improved planting material, represent a capacity increase of about 15 per cent. These protests implied that the industry should have continued for ever with estate yields of around 300–350 lb. per acre.

II [1]

While the producing territories took full advantage of the 5 per cent. new planting, in Malaya at any rate the smallholders were effectively prevented from benefiting from this concession. The reasons are semi-technical and require some detailed discussion.

The Malayan acreage statistics suggest at first sight that the 5 per cent. new planting of 1939–40 was taken up fully both by estates and smallholdings. The smallholding acreage even shows an increase of 8 per cent. from 1,264,678 acres at the end of 1938 to 1,361,128 acres at the end of 1940. This increase must include a substantial acreage revision, since according to the official statistics of the Controller of Rubber and of the Department of Agriculture, new planting by smallholders (owners of less than 100 acres each) totalled only 50,956 acres over this period; some 47,000 acres are stated to have been planted in 1939 and over 3,000 acres in 1940. From these latter figures it would appear that new planting by smallholders in 1939–40 totalled some 4 per cent. of their 1938 area of just over 1¼ million acres. Over the same period new planting by estates was 112,000 acres or 6 per cent. of their 1938 area. In fact, however, actual new planting by all owners of less than 100 acres was almost certainly less than 51,000 acres, and new planting by Malays and by resident owners generally was negligible.

The 1939 *Annual Report* of the Rubber Research Institute of Malaya (p. 252) summarises the approved applications for new planting by smallholders for the eleven months up to and including November 1939. The figures were supplied by the Controller of Rubber and cover all approved applications for new planting of 5 acres or less (5 per cent. of 100 acres, holdings over 100 acres being estates). There were 8,420 applications, totalling 16,649 acres. The remaining 30,000 acres of new planting in 1939 (the difference between 47,000 acres, which was the total new planting in 1939 by all owners of less than 100 acres each, and 17,000 acres, the total of approved applications for new planting of 5 acres or less) must thus all have been undertaken with the help of purchased planting rights, by owners who wished to plant more than

[1] In reading this section, it should be borne in mind that not only is more than three-quarters of Malaya still under jungle, but that very large uncultivated areas totalling millions of acres, can still be found in most districts of the western, highly developed, part of the country. A detailed discussion of this point will be found in the writer's *Report on a Visit to the Rubber Growing Smallholdings of Malaya, July–September 1946.* (In the press.) Cf. also pp. 187–190 below.

5 acres (5 per cent. of 100 acres). Owners who were in a position to plant 10 to 20 acres in 1939–40 with purchased share certificates were smallholders in name only, and probably some were not even smallholders in the statistical sense.[1] The figure of 50,956 acres newly planted in 1939–40 almost certainly includes some new planting by Chinese and Indian (mostly Chettiar) owners of over 100 acres. It very probably also comprises a considerable area of 'supplying' (the planting of a few trees on vacant patches within the existing holding), which was freely permitted under restriction and should not have been included in new planting. There may be other sources of error. New planting by smallholders was thus very probably less than 51,000 acres or 4 per cent. of their 1938 acreage. Moreover, Malays and the smaller Chinese holders undertook hardly any new planting, a fact which is masked in the statistics of total new planting by smallholders but is shown clearly by the figures of applications for new planting of 5 acres or less. Of a total number of applications of 8,420 only 3,033 were by Malays. The average new planting of individual Malay owners was certainly smaller than that of the Chinese or Indian owners and this would suggest that the aggregate of Malay applications for new planting in 1939 was almost certainly less than 8,000 acres. The Malays and the resident Chinese owners probably did not plant in 1939–40 as much as one per cent. and certainly less than 2½ per cent. of their 1938 acreage.

The failure of the Malay and of the smaller Chinese owners to use the new planting rights was due to several reasons, one of which was of over-riding importance. The planting rights, issued in the form of transferable share certificates in denominations and multiples of one-twentieth of an acre, entitled the owner to plant rubber to the extent of 5 per cent. of his 1938 registered acreage. Thus an owner of three acres would be entitled to plant about one-seventh of an acre, while the owner of a five-acre holding was entitled to plant one-quarter of an acre. These very small areas were whittled down considerably by a remarkable ruling of the restriction authorities by which one-twentieth of an acre was declared to be the equivalent of eight trees, so that one certificate or unit entitled the owner to plant eight trees. It is not clear whether this ruling applied throughout Malaya; it was certainly in force over considerable areas. As the smallholders usually plant over 200 trees per acre, this arbitrary ruling, based on past estate practice (planting is now much denser on estates than it used to be), reduced even

[1] For a discussion of the various classes of 'smallholder' cf. pp. 5–6 above.

further the fractional area which the smallholders were entitled to plant.

After the receipt of the share certificates, owners who had no unplanted reserve land (these were the great majority) had to apply to the land offices for the alienation of land on which to carry out new planting. The amounts involved were so small as hardly to be worth while to pay a visit to the land offices (often 15 to 20 miles away), and far too small to be worth carrying out new planting any distance from the existing holding of the owner. A smallholder is often prepared to operate a three- or four-acre holding a mile or two away from his house, but he cannot be expected to go far afield to plant or tap 16, 24 or 32 trees ; if these trees are any distance from his existing holding it would not be practicable to tap them, as the time lost in walking from one holding to the other (comprising a few trees only) would be prohibitive. Thus this fractional acreage of new planting was of no value to the individual smallholder, unless he had unplanted reserve land, or there was unalienated land available bordering on his own holding, where he could secure a small plot for planting. Moreover, only those areas could be of use where the few young trees would not suffer from shading or root competition. It was exceptional for all of these unusual conditions to be fulfilled simultaneously. New planting by the great majority of the smallholders was thus ruled out. Most smallholders who understood the purpose of the certificates therefore sold or gave them to friends or relatives who might have been in a position to use them. Many of the smallholders, however, were ignorant of the purpose and use of the share certificates, which were issued to smallholders along with a routine issue of export coupons without special explanation. As a result, some smallholders thought that they were an entitlement for supplying vacant patches or for replanting. Many owners gave the documents away or sold them at nominal prices, and some of these subsequently repurchased at much higher prices when they learnt the purpose of the documents.

Even the very small amount of new planting that actually took place was of doubtful value to smallholders. Much of this new planting was on unsuitable soil, or on silted or exhausted fields with a long previous history of food cultivation, or on eroded land or on steep hillsides liable to erosion ; no assistance had been extended to smallholders to help them to improve the soil or to choose suitable land. The 1939 *Annual Report* of the Rubber Research Institute of Malaya (p. 250) is unusually explicit on this matter: 'Unfortunately much of the land alienated for new planting is in districts where the population is high and cultivation intensive, is poor, being either old silted padi sawahs, or other areas where, owing to faulty methods of cultivation in the past, most of the soil has already been washed away. . . . (Where virgin land was bought) much of this land is undulating or very hilly and in some instances the slope is so steep that it does not appear practicable to advise the construction of terraces to minimise the soil erosion, owing to the excessive amount of excavation in the solid which would be required to make them.' Here again personal observation confirmed what could be inferred from easily accessible Malayan publications.

In contrast to the position of the smallholder, the renewal of regulation presented estates both in Malaya and in the N.E.I. with a gift in that the replanting bonus was raised to 100 per cent., and in neither territory was there henceforth a reduction in the assessment of an area cut out for replanting. The concession was of no value to the smallholders who continued to abstain from replanting. The N.E.I. authorities, though well aware of the reasons for the reluctance of the smallholders to replant, tried to cajole them by threatening to declare as 'degenerate' the older areas and to reduce their assessments unless the owners replanted. This, it will be noted, in the midst of the almost boundless uncultivated areas of Sumatra and Borneo.

In Malaya the Department of Agriculture was anxious to stress that some replanting was being undertaken on smallholdings. It was stated in one of the *Malayan Smallholding Reports* in 1938 that smallholders showed some interest in replanting; it appears from a subsequent passage that 'smallholders' referred to four Chinese and one Malay; three of the Chinese were on Penang Island, the poorest soil in Malaya. The number of smallholders in Malaya runs into six figures. By the end of 1938 less than 2,000 acres, or under one-sixth of one per cent. of the smallholding area was replanted in Malaya; replanting by Malays was less than 100 acres in the aggregate, against a Malay-owned smallholding area of 600,000–700,000 acres. Most of the small area replanted was owned by producers technically classed as smallholders but who were almost always Chettiar and Chinese owners who are not smallholders in the accepted sense of the term. In some instances they are not even smallholders in the statistical sense of being owners of less than 100 acres. Many Chettiar holdings are regarded as smallholdings for administrative and statistical purposes even though the aggregate area of one owner (which may consist of a dozen or more individual smallholdings belonging to the same owner) exceeds 100 acres. Again, as well as holdings registered in their own name, many of the larger Chinese smallholders have areas standing in the names of other members of the family, and when these are included the acreage actually owned by the head of the family exceeds 100 acres. Replanting by these two classes accounted for an appreciable proportion of the total replanting on smallholdings. But even where the individual Chettiar and Chinese (and his family) who replanted part of his area owns less than 100 acres in the aggregate, he is far removed from the typical smallholder in the sense of peasant proprietor.

III

It will be recalled that under the renewed agreement, 5 per cent. new planting and unlimited replanting were permitted for 1939–40 only. The I.R.R.C. was to review the position in 1940 and to decide on planting policy for 1941–43. Replanting was discussed in February 1940, and it was agreed to permit this unconditionally for the remaining three years of the currency of the agreement. This decision is recorded only very briefly in the official minutes : 'A general discussion followed, and it was agreed that replanting should be permitted unconditionally during the present period of regulation.'[1] It is known that the N.E.I. delegation drew attention to the disadvantages of the native under this system, and to the unsuitability of replanting to the needs and conditions of the smallholder.

New planting after 1940 was discussed at the next (May) meeting of the I.R.R.C. In view of the importance of the decisions to be taken, the secretariat of the Committee, assisted by the R.G.A. statisticians, had laboured for several months to prepare estimates of the trends of absorption and of future capacity. The data collected, and the results reached, were embodied in a special annex to the agenda of the meeting, and this was circulated as a memorandum to members of the Committee, their governments and to members of the Advisory Panel several weeks before the meeting.

Views on future absorption were clearly guesswork ; several different methods of fitting curves to past data resulted in estimated

[1] *I.R.R.C. Minutes*, Vol. 14, p. 120.

absorption of about one-and-a-half million tons for 1950, though the actual figure naturally varied with the choice of the base year.

Estimates of future capacity were based on certain assumed yields, varying with the age of the trees (allowing especially for the declining yield of old rubber), applied to the known acreage figures of estates and smallholders' rubber (the former sub-divided into budgrafted and seedling rubber). Two sets of estimates were drawn up, one on the assumption that the estates would replant 70,000 acres annually, while the smallholders would not replant at all, the other on the assumption that estates would replant 70,000 acres and smallholders 40,000 acres a year. The former was (rightly) stated to be more plausible. No new planting was assumed after 1940. No attempt was made to estimate the price required to elicit capacity output. The following results emerged :

TABLE I

Summary of Estimates by the I.R.R.C. Secretariat of Future Physical Productivity of Plantation Rubber

Year	Estates		Smallholdings		Total capacity (tons)
	Tons	Per cent. of total capacity	Tons	Per cent. of total capacity	
Assumption A: annual replanting of 70,000 acres by estates, no replanting by smallholders					
1939	812,000	53·1	716,000	46·9	1,528,000
1950	992,000	61·1	631,000	38·9	1,623,000
1960	1,037,000	74·2	360,000	25·8	1,397,000
Assumption B: annual replanting of 70,000 acres by estates and of 40,000 acres by smallholders					
1939	812,000	53·1	716,000	46·9	1,528,000
1950	992,000	61·7	617,000	38·3	1,609,000
1960	1,037,000	71·6	412,000	28·4	1,449,000

The divergent trends of the capacities of estates and of smallholdings reflect replanting by estates with high-yielding modern material, while the capacity of smallholdings declined with their advancing age. On Assumption A, one-third of the smallholding area would be over thirty years old by 1950, and over six-sevenths by 1960, and thirty years was believed to be the limit of the economic life of the holdings.[1] On Assumption B, the rate of decline was not so great, but some reduction was still postulated, as the small-

[1] Holding rather than tree, since a prime cause of the decline in yields with age is the loss of stand through disease and windfalls.

holders were assumed to use unselected seedling material for replanting, and this was not expected to offset the decline in yields from the older areas.

These figures revealed very clearly that the outcome of a policy which prohibited new planting, while permitting a large measure of replanting, would be a large reduction in the smallholders' share of total rubber production. The ratc of decline of the physical productivity of smallholders' rubber assumed for the calculations was almost certainly too great, and the estimates of future physical capacity unduly pessimistic. On the other hand, the relative competitive position of the smallholders was bound to deteriorate substantially as a growing proportion of the estate area was replanted with high-yielding material of which the smallholdings could not take advantage.[1] It might have been conjectural just how rapidly and to what extent the estates would have gained supremacy, but the trend was unmistakable.

By 1940 replanting by estates had increased much above the rate assumed in the memorandum of the I.R.R.C. secretariat which has just been quoted. According to the *History of Rubber Regulation* (p. 225) some 306,000 acres were replanted in 1939–40, which was appreciably more than the area replanted over the four-and-a-half years of the first regulation period. This was, moreover, before the further rapid increase in replanting stimulated by the excess profits tax. By mid-1940 estates were replanting at a rate of well over 100,000 acres annually, which was over 50 per cent. more than had been assumed by the I.R.R.C. secretariat. In Malaya the estates had replanted about 9 per cent. of their total acreage by the end of 1940 ; in the N.E.I. the proportion was about 15 per cent. and in French Indo-China about 8–9 per cent. These figures indicate a net increase of one-quarter or one-third in the productive capacity of estates as a result of replanting. By the beginning of 1941 several of the larger agency houses had worked out replanting programmes ten years ahead for the replanting of the bulk of the older rubber under their control ; by the end of 1941 some 13–15 per cent. of the Malayan estate acreage was replanted. But of course even the acreage replanted by 1940 represented a substantial increase in potential capacity in view of the much greater productivity of modern high yielding material.

Meanwhile replanting by smallholders continued to be very small or negligible. Some 25,000 acres, or 2 per cent. of the

[1] Smallholders employing outside labour on a piece-rate basis are affected particularly adversely ; cf. pp. 333 and 346 below.

Malayan smallholding area, was replanted by the end of 1940, practically all on Chinese and Chettiar properties of absentee owners, with a few instances of replanting by Malay owners with substantial interests outside rubber.[1] In the N.E.I. the native producers had replanted 45 hectares, or about 115 acres (out of a total planted area of several million acres) by the end of 1938. The acreage replanted by these producers in 1939–40 is not known in London, but it is certain that it was much less than one per cent. of their total acreage. In the smaller producing territories replanting by smallholders was also negligible. The comments by the leader of the N.E.I. delegation at the I.R.R.C. meeting are given in the minutes : 'He hoped that the memorandum, although unduly pessimistic, would bring home to the Committee the serious position of the native planter under the regulation scheme which limited new planting so severely, while allowing unrestricted replanting. Replanting did not accord with the psychology of the native rubber-grower or with his methods. He was wedded to the system of extensive new planting and would not take up replanting on a large scale for many years. His position was therefore becoming serious under the regulation scheme. The N.E.I. Government felt that this question required urgent and careful consideration, and he (the N.E.I. delegate) wished to reserve the right to raise the matter again at a later date. For the time being, he was in favour of allowing no new planting in 1941, except for experimental purposes, and reviewing the position next year.'[2]

The position of the smallholders in Malaya and Ceylon was far more serious than in the N.E.I. While over three-quarters of the N.E.I. native area was planted after 1924, the corresponding proportion in Malaya was under one-quarter and in Ceylon about two-fifths, and an early decline in the yielding capacity of smallholdings was thus more probable in these territories. Moreover, the policing of the prohibition of new planting was in all probability much more rigorous in Malaya and Ceylon than in the N.E.I. On the assumptions of the memorandum the smallholding industries both of Malaya and of Ceylon would have disappeared by about 1960.[3]

[1] It is candidly stated in the 1939 *Annual Report* of the Rubber Research Institute of Malaya (p. 251) that much of the small amount of replanting undertaken on smallholdings was unsatisfactory, owing to catch-cropping by smallholders short of cash, lack of manuring, and planting with unselected material, as well as for other reasons.

[2] *I.R.R.C. Minutes*, Vol. 15, pp. 76–77.

[3] A diagram showing the prospective trends of the physical productive capacity of Malayan estates and smallholdings will be found in Chapter 20 below, where the present (January 1947) position of the Malayan smallholders is discussed in face of the continued enforcement of the planting provisions of rubber restriction.

The proceedings were presided over by the then Economic Adviser to the British Secretary of State for the Colonies, who was the leader and voting member of the Malayan delegation. According to the minutes no word of protest came from any British members; yet rubber was the most important cash crop grown by smallholders anywhere in the Colonial Empire.[1] Nor was there any subsequent protest from any signatory government to whom the agenda, the annex and the official minutes were circulated.[2]

The only written criticism seems to have come from Mr. Walter Emery of the United States Rubber Company, who argued in a memorandum circulated to the Committee that no account had been taken of possible wide divergenees from the trend of absorption, nor of the possible high price which might be required to draw out all or most of the capacity output. The memorandum also emphasised that the prohibition of new planting would restrict the adoption of high-yielding planting material and limit its usefulness, since much of the existing acreage was planted on poor soil. Mr. Emery also thought that the Committee under-estimated the importance of reducing the price of natural rubber if this was to maintain its hegemony over synthetic rubber.

IV

While the respective merits of new planting and replanting were, after 1934, of academic interest only for the individual producer (since, with the exception of the 5 per cent. new planting in 1939–40, extension of the planted area was forbidden), the relative advantages of these two methods are of considerable general interest.

The need for replanting on estates arose from two different causes. First, by the early 1930's a substantial part of the older estate acreage in Malaya, Ceylon and to a lesser extent in the N.E.I., was showing signs of retrogression. In Malaya an appreciable part of the estate area yielded only 250–300 lb. per acre or even less. This retrogression was the result principally of soil erosion, of loss of stand through root diseases and of excessive thinning out. Secondly, the development of superior planting

[1] The absence of comment cannot be explained by preoccupation with the reverses of May 1940, as the agenda and the annex were circulated before the German offensive in the West. Moreover, the decision was, broadly speaking, the continuation of the policy which had been in force since 1934.

[2] There is some informal evidence to suggest that the N.E.I. Government might have strongly opposed the maintenance of these provisions for a third period of restriction (after the end of 1943).

material, capable of producing three to five times the annual yield of the old area, rendered the replacement of the latter profitable, even after allowing both for the capital cost and for the loss of income.

The cost per acre of replanting varied greatly on different properties. According to an estimate of the R.R.I.M. in 1935, the cost from felling the old stand to the maturity of the replanted area ranged from 140 to 230 Straits dollars per acre, with perhaps 180 to 200 dollars the most general figure. Costs were slightly lower in the N.E.I. and substantially (40–50 per cent.) higher in Ceylon, where the hilly country rendered planting operations more expensive.

The cost of new planting varied even more widely, as sometimes it was necessary to construct buildings, cut new roads and drains, and put up additional fences (and even to buy land where the producer had no suitable unplanted reserves). Speaking very approximately, the cost of new planting was of the same order, or slightly below that of replanting ; the heavier cost of felling and clearing and of the construction of roads and drains in new planting was generally offset, or more than offset, by the cost of manuring and disease control in replanting.

The yields to be expected from replanted areas are usually below those from newly planted jungle land. The soil under virgin jungle in Malaya and Sumatra is not particularly fertile, and the luxuriant growth reflects the rapid turnover of available plant food rather than inherent high productivity ; nevertheless, yields from such areas are better than those from land cultivated right up to the time of replanting, especially as much rubber has been planted on land which was previously under tapioca or other food crops.

This point leads to a consideration of an important disadvantage of replanting as a method of rejuvenating the industry. A replanted area is, by definition, tied to the soil of the previously existing plantation, and throughout the East much rubber has been planted on unsuitable land such as exhausted, eroded or infertile soils. Improved planting material, chiefly high-yielding budgrafts, as well as labour and manures, have frequently been wasted through replanting on infertile soil. Moreover, heavy manuring is generally necessary for successful replanting, while very little is required for new planting. This is because there is enough plant food in the soil in most producing territories to support the growth of one stand of rubber trees, but the quantity is insufficient to sustain adequate growth of a second stand. Hence the need for manuring in replanting, even though the annual latex crop removes very little plant food from the soil.

Smallholdings were less in need of replanting since they had not suffered from soil erosion and were less affected by root disease. Nevertheless, there were signs of retrogression in a few districts, while planting with high-yielding material was necessary, or at least desirable, for successful long-term competition with those estates which were being replanted with modern material. As we have seen, replanting (unlike new planting) is entirely unsuitable for the requirements of the smallholders, being virtually impossible on peasant holdings. Moreover, it was becoming increasingly evident that the extension of the smallholdings area presented no long-period danger either to the fertility of the soil or to the supply of land suitable for food cultivation. Malaya, Sumatra, Borneo and French Indo-China have vast areas still under jungle, and the supply of reserve land is thus almost unlimited. It will also be remembered that rubber cultivation by smallholders takes almost nothing out of the soil. A derelict smallholding reverts to secondary jungle with *Hevea* seedlings predominating, and in a few years' time is as suitable for native rice- or rubber-growing as before. In certain areas, especially in the N.E.I., a secondary jungle of rubber seedlings is actually beneficial, as it helps to keep out *lalang*, which once established over large areas is difficult to clear, and also because rubber forests are less liable to burn than most other jungle plants. A shifting cultivation by smallholders might have entailed some administrative inconvenience ; though it is certain that movement would have been on a small scale, since smallholdings continued to yield well for long periods, and the extension would have been required largely, although not wholly, in order to take advantage of high-yielding material. On smallholdings new planting thus appears to be socially, as well as individually, much more desirable than replanting. There might be exceptions in individual districts where land is scarce, particularly in Ceylon and in the Settlement of Malacca in Malaya.

The balance of the argument between replanting and new planting is less decisive with estate rubber, where past methods of cultivation had made greater demands on the soil and where, moreover, the construction of buildings and roads is also often required. It would appear, however, that in the territories with huge areas still under jungle suitable for cultivation, there is room for substantial new planting before the absorption of additional land could be regarded as sufficiently important to offset the disadvantages of replanting, especially where it involves the wasteful use of first-class planting material on poor soil. These conclusions are reinforced by the danger of a temporary shortage of rubber through large-scale replanting which materialised to a certain extent in 1941.

CHAPTER 13

THE CRITERIA OF REGULATION: NORMAL STOCKS AND EFFICIENT PRODUCERS

I

IN January 1936 the Rubber Manufacturers' Association of America (R.M.A.) formally addressed the I.R.R.C. for their ideas on, or definition of, normal stocks and efficient producers. By implication the manufacturers also wished to know the Committee's views on a price yielding a reasonable return to producers. The manufacturers' queries were reasonable, as these matters obviously affected their interests; moreover, the Committee's tasks were defined in the international agreement as a reduction of stocks to a normal level, and the establishment of a fair and equitable price reasonably remunerative to efficient producers. The R.M.A. letter was debated intermittently by the Committee for almost two years; yet the Committee was unable to provide the information.

From the very first meeting in 1934 until well into 1940, the Committee unsuccessfully tried to decide what were normal stocks. The attempts were not very serious since, while often maintaining the contrary, the Committee was concerned almost exclusively with the price of rubber rather than with the volume of stocks. This attitude is best illustrated by the decisions and discussions of the Committee during the first half of 1939. At that time stocks were low and were falling fast; the price at around or slightly below 8*d.* was considered unsatisfactory. In the discussion at the meeting in February 1939 it was argued that while the statistical position would justify higher releases than the 50 per cent. ruling during the first quarter, such a course would not be justified by the current prices. In the words of the voting member of one delegation: '. . . he had consistently maintained that price was not a primary consideration in fixing the rate of release. The only weapon in their hands was the effect produced by the reduction of stocks. Considering the general trading situation he felt that the price of rubber was unduly low and the Committee were entitled to interpret this low price in terms of sufficiency of stocks and to infer therefore that a further reduction in stocks was required.'[1]

[1] *I.R.R.C. Minutes*, p. 2005.

In short, the criterion of normal stocks was a price considered satisfactory by the Committee, though 'price was not a primary consideration' (as distinct from 'the effect produced by the reduction of stocks').

Several interrelated aspects of the question of normal stocks deserve discussion: a quantitative estimate or definition of normal stocks, their relation to the market price, the distribution of stocks (geographically and between different classes of holder) and its influence on the price, and lastly, the relative responsibilities of the Committee and of the manufacturers for the maintenance of a given level of stocks.

It is reasonably simple to estimate the stock of rubber needed at any given time to keep the machinery of production, shipment, distribution and absorption running smoothly, and capable of looking after seasonal variations and small disturbances. In the mid-1930's this stock figure, including stocks afloat, was very generally agreed to be an amount of rubber equal to five or six months' absorption. This stock is, however, compatible with widely different prices. The price may be such as to balance current absorption and exports, or it may be more nearly in accordance with underlying long period trends; early in 1929 exports and the absorption balanced with a London price of around 11*d*., but this level could not have been maintained for long as much additional low-cost capacity was nearing maturity. On extreme assumptions a state of affairs may be visualised under which any change in capacity would be reflected in the price (or rather in the structure of prices) without any change in stocks; the market would be unanimous on the new equilibrium price, or range of prices; stocks would remain unaltered, with part of the output supplied by the new low-cost producers. In practice the change in price would be accompanied by a change in stocks which market operators would blame for the price fall, even though the major factor was a permanent shift in the equilibrium level of prices. The position is not necessarily stable even if stocks are comfortably sufficient to keep the machine running smoothly and the price is not far from the equilibrium level. Some participants in the market may decide to develop speculative accounts and speculate say for a rise in price. With few exceptions, whenever a speculator buys forward rubber, a corresponding amount of physical rubber is frozen through the covering purchase of the dealer who has sold forward to the speculator. This diverts rubber from trade users and leads to a rise in price. The higher price should elicit more rubber and thus readjust the position; but long before this could happen the rise in price is likely to set up the expectation of a further rise, and a runaway market may develop.

Before the war, stocks of rubber were held by producers, dealers, speculators and manufacturers, and it was a matter of frequent argument at meetings of the I.R.R.C. and elsewhere as to whether the influence of stocks on prices depended on their aggregate volume only, or also on their distribution between various holders, in particular on the division of stocks between free and tied rubber. According to one school of thought, stocks of rubber influenced prices irrespective of their location and ownership; according to the other opinion, the price was influenced by free rubber only, as rubber held by manufacturers is practically never resold, and physical rubber held by dealers against forward contracts would be released only at extreme prices. Such firmly held stocks were thought not to influence the price save in exceptional circumstances. While this opinion is untenable, exclusive pre-occupation with a total volume of physical stocks may also be misleading. This can be illustrated by two examples. When tired bull speculators decide to liquidate their accounts they release a corresponding volume of physical rubber (probably lying in the U.K. or U.S. warehouses), and this will depress the price, even though the volume of stocks is no larger than before. Or again, manufacturers may decide to hold a larger (or smaller) proportion of their anticipated requirements in physical rubber and a smaller (or larger) proportion in the form of forward contracts, and any change in available physical stocks is offset by a reverse change in the supply of producers' free rubber available for the market.

The answer seems fairly clear. The volume of spot and near forward physical rubber is fixed within reasonably narrow limits, and this volume of rubber must be held by someone; the views of all the participants (producers, dealers, manufacturers and the public) determine the structure of prices of the various grades and positions of rubber. The process is not unlike that by which the structure of stock market values is fixed, except of course that a price differing from long-period equilibrium as determined by conditions of absorption and of supply cannot be maintained indefinitely. It appears that while there is an obvious negative correlation between the volume of stocks and the price of rubber, and while it is possible to ascertain a physical level of stocks which would normally suffice to keep the machinery of rubber production and absorption running at an even pace, this volume of stocks is compatible, at least for considerable periods, with a wide range of prices. Conversely, a price at or near the equilibrium rate may co-exist with different volumes of stocks. For example, at the end of both 1926 and 1929 world stocks equalled 3·3 months' absorption at the rates of these two years; but the price was about 1*s.* 7*d.* at the end of 1926 (average for the year 1*s.* 11¾*d.*), and about 7¼*d.* at the end of 1929 (average for the year 10¼*d.*).[1]

Although the Committee was explicitly charged with the task of reducing stocks, the minutes reveal frequent misunderstanding on where the responsibility lay for determining their volume. From June 1934 to mid-1936 the Committee repeatedly reproached the American manufacturers for maintaining large stocks, which were said to be evidence of the manufacturers' distrust of the Committee. In the autumn of 1936 the Committee decided on further stock reduction; yet when a boom developed a few weeks later, the manufacturers were held responsible as they had allowed their stock to run down. Instances can be found in the minutes of the Committee of one member blaming manufacturers for having reduced their stocks and at the same meeting another member declaring that the Committee would have to reduce stocks further.[2] On one occasion a member of the Advisory Panel asked the Committee to make up its mind on this subject and not to declare in the same breath that stock reduction was necessary and to blame manufacturers for reducing their stocks. There was some particularly acrimonious discussion between the Committee and the Panel in 1937, over the responsibility for the shortage of spot rubber in the winter of 1936–37. Several members blamed the manufacturers; had these not allowed their stocks to run down during 1935 and 1936 the difficulty would not have arisen. The Panel pointed out that the Committee had deliberately pursued a policy of stock reduction, and had urged this on manufacturers until the end of 1936. To this the Committee found no reply.

Here again the same answer should be plain. Changes in stocks result simply from differences between absorption and ship-

[1] The picture would be changed, but not very greatly, by setting year-end stocks against December absorption instead of the average yearly rate of absorption.

[2] At the sixteenth meeting of the Committee one member of the N.E.I. delegation blamed the manufacturers for having reduced their stocks by some 75,000 tons during 1935 and thus having failed to support the market. At the same meeting the manufacturers were reproached by a British member for maintaining excessive stocks.

The confusion also runs through the Committee's *History of Rubber Regulation*, where it is said on p. 122: 'During the early part of 1939 stocks were being reduced in spite of the Committee's suggestion to the contrary'; and on p. 123: 'The Committee . . . had (early in 1939) sound reasons for refusing the advice of the American Government and the Advisory Panel and for continuing its policy of stock reduction. . . .'

ments, both of which are outside the control of manufacturers. What puzzled and annoyed the Committee was the failure of low and falling stocks to result in better prices. They had expected stocks as low as, say, those of early 1939 to force up the price considerably, and thought that a brisker buying policy of manufacturers would have brought this about ; in fact it would have only transferred stocks from one warehouse to another. The manufacturers, together with all participants in the market, influenced only the price at which the stocks were held. The Committee could not easily blame manufacturers for not raising the price against themselves and thus reproached them for not increasing their stocks. Actually in 1939 the manufacturers had substantial forward contracts to make up for their somewhat lower physical stocks and they thus supported the market just as much as they would have done by holding larger physical stocks. The comparatively modest price [1] reflected the reluctance of the market to support higher prices at a time of great political uncertainty when, moreover, the supply was highly elastic, with the industry working at only a fraction of capacity.

II

The Committee was also unable to provide the R.M.A. with a definition in terms of costs and price of an efficient producer. The failure to provide a definition amounted to an admission of the arbitrariness of this concept, and of the mandate under which the Committee operated.

One member submitted a detailed memorandum to show that the mandate involved circular reasoning.[2] 'Efficient production is production at a reasonable profit ; but profitability depends on price and the duty of the Committee was to aim at a price level which was to be established by the efficient producer. . . . Supply was to be adjusted at (? to) a figure which would produce a price remunerative to efficient producers. . . . but if the price is . . . an artificial one there will always be some producers who can sell at that price and make a profit ; which those producers are cannot be ascertained until the price is determined. On the other

[1] Which was, however, still distinctly profitable to the majority of European-owned estates who were the highest-cost producers, with costs much inflated by restriction.

[2] The opening pages of Chapter 12 of the *History of Rubber Regulation* reproduce this memorandum. The quotations are actually from the book, pp. 145–46. One passage in the memorandum is not reproduced in the book : 'For some time to come it must remain an open question whether the estate is an efficient producer in competition with the native except under artificial conditions.'

hand it is impossible to define a price which will remunerate efficient producers until it is known what efficient production means. The Committee was therefore required to define efficient production in terms of price and to determine price in terms of efficient production.' [1] Apparently the circle can be squared after all: 'The Committee surmounted the price difficulty by concentrating on the stock and production side of its task. No attempt was made to control the price of rubber. . . . At the same time it used the prevailing price as a barometer; while a "fair" price was difficult if not impossible to define precisely, a price which was too low to be remunerative or so high as to produce excessive profits was within limits easy to detect.' [2]

This is hardly satisfactory. First, as we have already seen, it was contended that 'the Committee was entitled to interpret the sufficiency of stocks in terms of price'. A perusal of the minutes of the Committee leaves no doubt that the I.R.R.C. was influenced almost wholly by the prevailing prices and not by the volume of stocks. Whenever the price was thought unsatisfactory by the Committee this was regarded as synonymous with excessive stocks. According to the leader of one of the delegations: 'Price was the essence of the situation, and so long as this was maintained at a reasonable level, it furnished the best guide for the Committee.' Indeed, the Committee was so largely concerned with the price rather than with the total volume of stocks that whenever stocks were low but the price not high enough, stocks in particular countries or in the hands of particular owners were said to be the guiding criteria instead of total stocks. When American stocks declined but U.K. stocks rose this was instanced as evidence of the difficulty of selling rubber, and thus of excessive supplies; while an increase in the stocks of American manufacturers would be taken as a sign of ample supplies in the hands of consumers and a cause of the inadequate price. Nor was it so easy to define too high or too low prices as was implied. Eightpence was regarded as the minimum reasonable price by the Committee in 1935–36, but the N.E.I. natives had to be content with 1½*d.*–2*d.*[3]

In actual practice, the Committee did not act very differently from other organised controls of primary products. The members

[1] *History of Rubber Regulation*, pp. 145–46. It was also admitted that the circle of efficient producers would depend on the rate of release, since with a given price higher releases could reduce costs and increase the number of efficient producers.

[2] *Ibid.*, p. 147.

[3] Matters were not advanced by another attempted definition recorded in the minutes: 'Efficient producers are those who do not produce inefficiently.'

generally took a view of the economic situation and tried to secure a price which was profitable to the largest number of estates, and which could be maintained without danger from competing materials and, perhaps more important, without provoking too loud protests from the manufacturers or from the American authorities. It was realised that under restriction these were factors influencing the long-period elasticity of demand.

The monthly or quarterly cost returns furnished by the British, Dutch and French producers' associations, covering a large proportion of their membership, were frequently reviewed by the Committee when releases had to be fixed, or when a definition of efficient producers was attempted. The costs as returned were f.o.b. costs excluding depreciation and amortisation. A standard figure per lb. was added for freight, selling and head office charges. An average capitalisation figure was assumed as the capital cost of buildings and machinery, and another as the capital cost per acre of the plantation ; 7½ per cent. of the former and 4 per cent. of the latter were assumed as the annual charge for depreciation and amortisation ; one-twelfth of the resulting figures was divided by the monthly crop of each producer, and the result added to the other items to arrive at all-in costs. The returns covered some 50–55 per cent. of the Malayan, 35–40 per cent. of the N.E.I. and 70–75 per cent. of the French Indo-China estate output. Smallholders were not taken into account.

Some 75 per cent. of the output covered by the returns was produced at costs within 10 per cent. of either side of the average, and the median and the mode were close to the arithmetic mean [1] (weighted by output). Whenever the Committee had to decide who were the efficient producers a lenient view was taken ; it was generally estimated that some 80 per cent. or more of the Malayan and 95 per cent. of the N.E.I. estate output included in the cost returns came from efficient producers. Accordingly, the average cost of efficient producers was much the same as that of all estate producers. It was occasionally held that as the output of the marginally efficient producer was also required to satisfy the demand, the price must be such as to yield him a reasonable return too.

[1] It was not thought worthwhile to show the frequency distribution of costs for any one year for what is only one section of the higher-cost producers. As an indication of the order of magnitude, in December 1936 the all-in costs of Malayan estates included in the R.G.A. returns to the I.R.R.C. ranged from 4·50*d.* to 9·25*d.*, with the lower quartile around 5·20*d.* and the upper quartile at 6·60*d.* ; the arithmetic mean was 5·85*d.* If locally-owned companies and smallholders had been included the range would of course have been much wider.

Thus as well as the average costs of all estate producers, there were the costs of the average efficient producers and of the marginally efficient producers. The three figures did not differ greatly owing to the generous interpretation of efficiency and the large proportion of producers with costs near the average.

The following example, which refers to Malayan costs, illustrates the position in 1935. It was assumed that 80 per cent. of all producers were efficient.[1] The average cost of the efficient producers was almost exactly 6*d.*; that of all producers 6·25*d.*; that of marginally efficient producers 6·75*d.*[2] Cash costs absorbed some 4·50*d.*–4·75*d.*, depreciation charges about 0·4*d.*–0·5*d.* and amortisation about 1·0*d.*–1·10*d.* The yield for 1935 averaged 319 lb. per acre for efficient producers and 306 lb. per acre for all producers; for the marginally efficient producers it was 294 lb.; such deplorably low yields were an inevitable result of restriction. The average capitalisation of Malayan estates was assumed to be £45 per acre, and it was thus easy to calculate a 7½ per cent. return for the three classes of producer; 2½*d.* for the average efficient producer, 2·65*d.* for the average producer, 2·75*d.* for the marginally efficient producer; the prices indicated were thus 8½*d.*, 8·90*d.*, and 9½*d.*, of which cash costs accounted for about one-half. These figures referred to releases of 60–70 per cent. Throughout the years 1934–36 members of the Committee constantly referred to the ruling price as definitely unremunerative to the efficient producer; this at a time when three-quarters or more of this unremunerative price had to be taxed away to keep N.E.I. native exports within the permissible level.

These cost figures applied very closely also to 1936 and 1937; the releases in 1936 were slightly lower than in 1935, but applied to a higher basic quota, while in 1937 the effects of the higher release were offset by a rise in wages and the price of equipment. In 1938 the fall in wages was insufficient to offset the adverse effect of the greatly reduced releases, and costs rose by about a halfpenny per lb. In 1937 it was decided that 10 per cent. rather than 7½ per cent. should be taken as a fair return for a risky industry, and the quasi-pivotal prices were all raised by about one penny to 9*d.*–10*d.* per lb.

Producers' ideas of a fair price rose with every improvement

[1] The costs shown in the returns were much higher than those generally given in company reports, and a figure which covered the costs of 80 per cent. of the production shown in the R.G.A. returns would have covered the costs of a substantially larger percentage of all estate producers.

[2] These figures were subsequently revised slightly. The corrected average costs are shown below, p. 270.

in the market price of rubber. Just before regulation was introduced 6*d.* was thought a godsend ; on its establishment 6*d.*–7*d.* was regarded sufficient in the East and 7*d.*–8*d.* in London. The market price was below 7½*d.* for the first two years of regulation. When this level was reached in 1936, the manufacturers were told that it was insufficient to yield a reasonable return to efficient producers, and that the Committee would attempt to secure higher prices. The price rose sharply between October 1936 and March 1937. By May 1937 the High Commissioner for the Malay States stated in Kuala Lumpur that while he continued in office the Malayan governments would attempt to maintain the price of rubber between 9*d.* and 10*d.* This was approximately the average cost of all estate producers plus 10 per cent., as calculated by the I.R.R.C. from the R.G.A. cost returns. The American recession which set in during the autumn of 1937 put this price out of court for a year or two. By mid-1939, following the improvement of the early months of that year, 10*d.* was again considered the reasonable minimum. This figure was suggested, for instance, by the *Financial News* in July 1939. A few months earlier the *Pinang Gazette* had argued that by taking full advantage of high-yielding material and by economising on supervision, estates should be able to produce at 1½*d.* per lb. delivered Singapore. This may have been an exaggeration, but the contrast is nevertheless interesting.

A price yielding only a fair return to the average producer implies poor returns or losses to half the industry. For the whole of 1935 and part of 1936, on the showing of the returns to the I.R.R.C., the price was insufficient not only to secure ‘ a reasonable return to the average producer ’ but even to cover his costs. Yet the great majority of sterling companies, especially those operating in Malaya, were able to pay dividends. This led to some ineffective criticism by manufacturers of the cost returns.

The output per acre assumed in these calculations was usually the average production under restriction ; it was, however, explicitly stated in a memorandum submitted by the R.G.A. statisticians to the I.R.R.C. that the unrestricted output of the average efficient producer in Malaya around 1936–37 could be assumed as 400 lb. per mature acre.[1] It was not explained on what criteria these estates could be called efficient with an unrestricted output of 400 lb. and costs of 6*d.* and over, when the

[1] The same figure was also suggested by the late Dr. Rae in his paper ‘ Statistics of the Rubber Industry ’ read to the Royal Statistical Society in 1938, *Journal of the Royal Statistical Society*, 1938, part II.

smallholders could produce 450–500 lb. per acre or more, year in year out, at little or no cost. The Advisory Panel frequently asked that the costs of the native producers should be allowed in calculating those of the average producer. This suggestion was always rejected on the ground that no cost figures were available for smallholders ; it would have been more accurate to say that the majority had no costs, or at any rate costs which were only a fraction of those of the notional efficient producers.

The ' reasonable return to the average efficient producer ' was only another aspect of the maintenance of a profitable *status quo*, which was the primary purpose of rubber regulation, as of other restriction schemes. A ' fair and equitable price, reasonably remunerative to efficient producers ' cannot be defined or given any meaning which is not arbitrary. It is possible to speak of the supply price of a given quantity of rubber ; this, too, may be difficult to estimate quantitatively and would vary from year to year. But at any given time and in a given state of prosperity, it is a clear-cut and definite concept which the other formula is not. It is thus not surprising that the Committee never succeeded in answering the query of the American manufacturers, though it related to its primary function.

III

The perplexities of the I.R.R.C. in attempting to determine who were the efficient producers can be analysed from another angle. The Committee generally identified the industry with the estates, disregarding the fact that practically one-half of the world output of rubber was produced by smallholders with very different methods and costs of production. In particular, the smallholders dispense very largely or completely with the expensive and complex hierarchy on which the estates rely.

The following schematic list summarises the principal stages in the hierarchy of most European estates financed on a joint-stock basis and controlled from London or Amsterdam. Some of the functionaries listed would attend to the affairs of several companies and estates, but this does not greatly affect the issue.

Tappers, weeders, factory workers, sundry estate workers *Mandors* (foremen) Estate contractors and their labourers Conductor(s) ; estate clerks and dressers	Non-European

Assistant manager(s) Manager Visiting agent, visiting engineer, visiting medical officer, visiting accountant Agency firm Secretarial firm Board of directors Shareholders	European

In practice there are often further links in the chain. In the production of the same commodity the smallholder and his family are assisted at most by a few outside tappers, who may, in some instances, be supervised by a resident foreman or caretaker.

There is also a somewhat similar contrast between the amount of equipment and materials absorbed by estate and smallholders' production respectively. Estate requirements which are usually not needed on smallholdings include buildings for the housing of the labour force and the staff, as well as various sheds which are sometimes elaborate ; cars, lorries and petrol ; sheeting batteries for the production of sheet rubber, and small engines to operate them ; lighting equipment for staff quarters ; and many other items. In the use of coagulating acid alone is the position reversed, as the smallholder requires more acid per pound of rubber produced than does the estate. This, however, is a negligible exception.

It is often overlooked that differences in costs of production, particularly when associated with such widely different methods of production, reflect the different claims by the producers concerned on the available stock or flow of real resources, principally of labour and equipment. This point seems to be neglected in the frequent references to the excess capacity with which the rubber industry seems to be permanently saddled. This capacity is not homogeneous, and the operation of certain constituent elements of the total absorbs many more real resources in the production of rubber than are required when the output is derived from other producers. The indiscriminate references to excess capacity tend to obscure these issues.

The two principal weaknesses of estate production, or more precisely of production as organised by a large section of the estate industry, seem to be, first, the heavy overhead costs resulting from the maintenance of the elaborate hierarchy, and secondly, reliance on a large number of hired labourers for the performance of essentially simple routine operations. These disadvantages are not offset by higher yields. In fact, when production was unrestricted annual average yields per mature acre on Malayan smallholdings were 12 to 30 per cent. higher than on estates.

The ability of the smallholders to produce rubber with such limited expenditure of real resources reflects the comparative ease of rubber growing. All phases of rubber production, from the planting of the seed to the smoking of the sheets, are very simple and easy processes. Indeed, so easy is it to plant and maintain the trees, to collect the latex by a simple incision in the bark of the tree and to coagulate and mangle it that in Malaya even some of the aboriginal Sakais successfully produce sheet rubber. These considerations partly explain the often genuine perplexities of the I.R.R.C. and of others in trying to locate or define efficient producers.[1]

[1] In view of the critical tenor of this chapter, it should be stated in fairness to the I.R.R.C. that much of this criticism would broadly apply to several other organised monopolies of the 1930's.

CHAPTER 14

CRITICAL RETROSPECT

I

THE establishment, machinery and history of the international rubber regulation scheme well illustrate the political and administrative attractions of quota schemes. The objections to the necessarily arbitrary quota and assessment machinery were repeatedly urged before 1934, not only by outside observers and prominent administrators, but also by some leading representatives of the estates. Nevertheless in the end this machinery came to be considered the only administratively practicable and politically feasible plan promising an early return of prosperity to the rubber producing territories, together with a restoration of depleted government revenues. As such it was first cautiously accepted and soon definitely welcomed.

Regulation raised prices by restricting output and prohibiting planting; by eliminating competition it maintained the *status quo* and saved the high-cost producers. It thus resembled the numerous other national and international restriction schemes which marked economic policy in the 1930's. The exclusion of newcomers through the prohibition of new planting barred entry into an industry particularly suitable to the small man, whether European, Chinese or native.

The freezing of the industry was more complete in rubber than perhaps in any other major commodity. It was, moreover, particularly harmful, as the industry was virtually in its infancy, with costs on an unstable basis and with most major questions of technique and organisation still undecided. Some nine-tenths of the mature area under rubber in Malaya at the end of 1940 had been planted since 1910 and three-quarters since 1913; some form of organised restriction had been in force for at least some months every year between 1918 and 1928 and again after 1934, so that some nine-tenths of the 1940 area spent about two-thirds of its tappable life under restriction, and for three-quarters the proportion was about four-fifths. The corresponding proportions in the other territories was of the same order.[1] The uncertainty

[1] The Stevenson scheme did not apply outside Malaya and Ceylon, but a very large proportion of the area under rubber in other territories was planted after 1924 and reached maturity only shortly before the establishment of the 1934 scheme or actually after its introduction.

surrounding plantation technique and organisation was the combined result of the very rapid development of the industry, the longevity of the trees, the prolonged periods of compulsory restriction, and to a lesser extent of the very easy profits which were being made up to 1929 and in a certain degree after 1934.

The immaturity of the industry not only made restriction particularly undesirable but also emphasised its inherent arbitrariness. Restriction is particularly arbitrary where costs and technique are rapidly changing, and where a large proportion of the output during the years adopted as the basis for quotas is derived from high-cost producers who, in the rubber industry, already had been for several years sheltered from competition. The existence of estate and smallholders' production was a special feature of rubber regulation enhancing its arbitrariness. The crudest ideas have always been prevalent about the efficiency and soundness of the methods of smallholders, who were entirely unrepresented throughout the operation of the scheme ; their substantial under-assessment followed almost as a matter of course.

Quotas and assessments may be deemed fair if they are proportionate to the unrestricted outputs of the different classes of producer at the prices ruling under restriction.[1] Although they cannot be allocated on such a basis, a much closer approximation is possible than was ever attempted under regulation. Internationally the quota of the N.E.I. natives, and internally the quotas of smallholders in Malaya, the N.E.I. and British North Borneo were patently inadequate, whether on the basis of past performance and mature areas, or on any reasonable assumption about their probable outputs at the higher prices visualised under restriction.

A large measure of transferability of export rights and coupons was permitted in the major producing territories (though not between estate and native export rights in the Outer Possessions of the N.E.I.) in order to concentrate output on the properties of the lower-cost producers, and thus to mitigate the stereotyping effect of restriction. For various reasons this did not take place on any substantial scale. For instance, where larger companies owned several estates, although the concentration of production on some and the closure of others was sometimes considered, the fear of a

[1] It will be realised that fairness is here interpreted as equal proportionate reduction in output from the unrestricted level at the most probable range of prices, and does not take account of the dependence on rubber of different classes of producer or of their financial position.

reduction in assessments and the difficulties of transferring staff and labour, together with the contingency of a sudden rise in the rates of release, usually prevented such steps. Within each agency group there was even larger scope for similar measures, but the possibility of the loss of identity of the companies acted as an additional deterrent.

II

By the completeness of control over supplies (the scheme embraced some 97 per cent. of world exports) and by the notorious inelasticity of the short-period demand for rubber, the power of the I.R.R.C. was formidable.[1] American suspicions and the political importance of American goodwill were, however, restraining factors, and the Committee had to tread carefully between the pressure of high-cost producers for higher prices, and U.S. opposition manifesting itself in protests to the British and Dutch Governments and in a search for substitute materials.

The Committee was considerably influenced in its decisions by the cost returns of producers' associations, particularly by the costs of British producers, who, as well as being a majority on the Committee,[2] were still much the largest group of estate producers and had the highest costs. For the period 1935–39 the British figures showed average all-in costs of around 6*d.*–6½*d.*, the Dutch costs were slightly less, and the French figures lower again.[3] There is reason to believe that these data, especially the British figures, showed excessive costs, since dividends were regularly paid at times when the price was below the cost figures. The Committee, however, accepted the figures, and on occasions regarded them as understatements rather than the reverse.

The interpretation, or rather definition, of efficient producers (to whom regulation was to ensure a reasonable return) was

[1] The scheme was a complete monopoly superimposed on a perfectly competitive system, since each individual seller continued to produce only a negligible proportion of total supplies, and individual demand curves were shaped ┐.

[2] With two exceptions the voting members of the delegations were officials, but the practical importance of this was much less than is often assumed.

[3] Details are shown on pp. 270–71 below.

The French estates had, even before the successive devaluations of the franc, become the lowest-cost estate producers, while in 1930–32 their costs had still been the highest. This development largely reflected the gradual maturity of the best areas, and the fuller maturity of the young areas tapped in the early thirties. The rubber industry of French Indo-China seems to provide an authentic case of a very heavy subsidy enabling an infant industry to survive a slump and subsequently to become definitely competitive.

extremely generous. In 1937 the yields to be expected from the efficient estate producers were estimated at 400 lb. per mature acre in Malaya, 375 lb. in Ceylon, 450 lb. in the N.E.I., 400 lb. in French Indo-China, 350 lb. in British North Borneo, 230 lb. in India and 220 lb. in Burma.[1] It will be recalled that smallholders produced sustained yields of 450–500 lb. or more at little or no cost. Admittedly they probably could not have satisfied the entire demand, but the margin between their output and the quantity demanded could have been filled easily by genuinely high-yielding estates. To assume 400 lb. (at costs of 6*d.* per lb. and over) as the unrestricted output of efficient estate producers was to deprive efficiency of all meaning. Moreover, in order to give a 'fair return' to these efficient producers another 2½*d.* had to be added to the costs. Thus it was that after the N.E.I. natives had for two years been producing large quantities of rubber for a total net return of around 1½*d.*, the minimum which was regarded as yielding reasonable returns to the efficient estate was 8*d.*[2]

The passage of time did not bring about a revision of the definition of efficient producers. By 1938–39 the successful development of reliable planting material yielding over 1,000 lb. per acre was an accomplished fact, but the unrestricted yield of the efficient producer on whom the scheme hinged still stood at or below 400 lb. Meanwhile, the planting provisions of regulation severely restricted the use of high-yielding material. The successive investigations between 1931 and 1938 into yields and conditions on smallholdings in Malaya, the N.E.I. and Sarawak, had found average yields 25–30 per cent. above those of 'efficient estates' with very low costs and far lower bark consumption than had been expected. Nor was there any prospect of an early decline in these yields, since the life expectation of the holdings appeared

[1] The system of quotas and assessments vitiates any comparison of actual output per acre between different groups of producer over this period, while for the slump years the comparison is of very limited interest, as an appreciable proportion of the mature area was out of tapping everywhere during the depression. The 1929 yields and the results of special enquiries and investigations show clearly that the average yields of smallholdings in Malaya, the N.E.I. and Sarawak were definitely higher than those of seedling estates in any of the producing territories. As a group, the red soil estates in French Indo-China had probably the highest yields among estates, followed by the American plantations on the East Coast of Sumatra, and these by the Dutch estates there, with Malayan estates and other N.E.I. estates next.

[2] Estate spokesmen are understandably anxious to argue that their side of the industry is the only efficient section. Thus in a formal letter to the I.R.R.C., the R.G.A. representatives stated in 1937 that 'the efficiently organised part of the Industry, i.e. the Estates, could produce in excess of their quotas as envisaged under the renewed agreement.' *Minutes of the I.R.R.C. Renewal Sub-Committee*, p. 275.

very good. Again, every time a new *ladang* (dry rice clearing) was opened up by smallholders in Sumatra or Borneo, a new, high-yielding rubber plantation could be established without any additional cost. Thus the notional efficient producers were entirely non-competitive either against the smallholders or the high-yielding estates; they were using large quantities of labour and capital (their high costs reflected their extensive use of real resources) with which the smallholders could almost entirely dispense to produce an identical commodity.

It is often claimed on behalf of restriction schemes that they are conducive to stability. The establishment of rubber regulation did not serve to eliminate, or even to diminish greatly, the instability so characteristic of the industry. The following table illustrates some of the continued fluctuations.

TABLE I

Variations (a) in the London Price of Rubber, (b) in the Values of Malayan Domestic Exports of Rubber, (c) in the Earnings of 25 Rubber Companies,[a] *(d) in Malayan Rubber Estate Employment*

	(a)			(b)	(c)	(d)
	Highest	*Lowest* (*pence per lb.*)	*Average*	*Million Straits dollars*	£000's	*Thousand workers (end of each year)*
1934	7·6	4·2	6·2	208	360	302
1935	6·8	5·2	6·0	191	252	264
1936	11·1	6·5	7·7	208	505	277
1937	13·8	6·8	9·5	341	788	349
1938	8·6	5·2	7·2	199	315	296
1939	12·0	7·6	9·0	261	529	324
1940	14·0	10·9	12·1	450	1,078	351

[a] These 25 sterling rubber companies operated in Malaya, and all had financial years ending on 31st December. They have been chosen at random from *Rubber Producing Companies*. The figures shown are their aggregate gross trading profits.

Thus in three out of four calendar years of restriction before the outbreak of war the highest price exceeded the lowest price by over two-thirds, and in one year the maximum was over double the minimum. Again, the value of Malayan rubber exports after rising by over two-thirds from 1936 to 1937 fell by more than two-fifths over the next year. There were also very marked fluctuations in rubber estate employment; in Malaya the number of workers rose by over one-quarter from the end of 1936 to the end of 1937 only to fall by over one-seventh during 1938. These various figures do not suggest that the great disadvantages of restriction were compensated by stability.[1]

III

The years which have already elapsed since the effective end of regulation make possible a more detached discussion of some specific issues of rubber restriction, much debated before 1941 and in one instance even subsequently.

The equity of the operation of restriction between estates and smallholdings was frequently raised by the Rubber Division of the U.S. Department of Commerce, which rightly pointed out that this was a matter of concern to consumers since supplies at high rates of release were greatly influenced by the equitable internal distribution of the quotas. This issue was also often, but fruitlessly, brought up in the Batavia *Volksraad*. Before judging the equity of the scheme, two considerations must be remembered, whose weight or relevance may be disputed but which greatly influenced estate representatives.

First, the plantation industry was developed by the estates, whose representatives felt—and occasionally still feel—resentment against their increasingly effective smallholder competitors. The estates have often over-emphasised this point, since the real pioneers have mostly gone, generally after reaping a rich harvest during a number of profitable years. Again, in Malaya at least, the smallholders were so greatly under-assessed during the Stevenson scheme that any debt owed to the estates could be regarded as having been fully repaid by 1928. Moreover, the displacement of a given technique by an improved version, based originally on the first system, is a frequent development in industry and agriculture, though naturally always deplored by those who have to face successful competition. Secondly, restriction brought higher rubber prices and incomes to the smallholders (with the important exception of the N.E.I. native producers between 1934–36) for less work. For considerable periods Malayan smallholders could enjoy higher incomes by selling coupons than they could have earned by

[1] The I.R.R.C. had a difficult task because of the dependence of rubber on American prosperity. Yet, especially in view of its effective control of supply, it is difficult to agree with one of the alternate members of the Committee who thought that 'the regulation scheme had done wonders under extraordinarily difficult situations'. Discussion on Dr. Rae's paper, *Journal of the Royal Statistical Society*, 1938, part II, p. 368. Somewhat paradoxically the same speaker had stated earlier in the discussion that rubber was an 'extraordinarily controllable' industry.

tapping their trees in the absence of restriction. They also benefited in various ways from increased government expenditure on health and education services.[1]

These considerations do not, however, alter the fact that the benefits of restriction were very unevenly divided between estates and smallholdings, to the disadvantage of the latter. The relative under-assessment of the smallholdings in Malaya, the N.E.I. and in British North Borneo was beyond dispute. For Malaya this is obvious by comparing the shares of estates and of smallholdings in the Malayan quota with their respective contributions to output before the introduction of restriction, or by comparing their assessments per acre with their relative outputs per mature acre during 1929–33 ; or by contrasting the quotas of estates and smallholdings with their production during 1929–32, from which it emerges that in the early years of restriction the smallholdings received no immature allowances at all.[2] The under-assessment of the N.E.I. native producers was an internationally agreed feature, since it was explicitly stated in the course of the restriction negotiations that an N.E.I. native quota anywhere near their capacity at prices under regulation would be so large as to destroy any chance of an agreed scheme. The exports of the N.E.I. natives during the early months of 1934 compared with their actual quota make their severe under-assessment quite plain, and this was actually admitted by the N.E.I. authorities. This under-assessment again emerged clearly in 1941, when the N.E.I. natives, alone of all classes of producer, exported the full amount called for by the high releases of that year.

The relative merits of replanting and new planting were also bound up with the fairness of regulation as between estates and smallholdings. By prohibiting new planting after 1940 the Committee assumed a grave responsibility, since owing to the long period between planting and maturity a sudden shortage of rubber cannot quickly be rectified, and the demand for rubber is well known to be unstable. On all reasonable assumptions the potential physical capacity was in excess of demand, at least up to 1950 ;

[1] According to an American consular dispatch in 1939 : 'Malayan smallholders regard their export coupons as a pension . . . and would almost certainly object to the discontinuance of control.' *Rubber News Letter*, 15th December 1939.

[2] The whole regulation machinery in Malaya, the various additional assessments granted for rested areas, the system of scale allowances given on a girth basis, the mass of rules and regulations, and last, but not least, the inspection of smallholdings by planters ensured that the smallholdings should be under-assessed. The last point is of more than historical interest since the assessment (or inspection for assessment) of smallholdings by European planters seems an inevitable feature of rubber restriction.

but with a sudden increase in demand the price required to draw out a large proportion of the capacity might have been high. The prohibition of new planting also made sure that for many years to come rubber would be derived from existing plantations, many of which were poor. The yields on replanted soils are generally estimated at about 10 per cent. below those on newly planted soils ; moreover, estates frequently replanted on particularly poor soils. Again, many plantations, both estates and smallholdings, were tied by the planting provisions to the unsuitable soil on which they had become established. There was, of course, also the loss of income from the old stand, which together with the technical impossibility of replanting successfully part of a peasant holding, meant that this method of maintaining or expanding capacity was not open to the lowest-cost producers. There was a virtual prohibition of all new planting during regulation ; successful replanting is impossible on most smallholdings, while it was undertaken on a large scale on estates ; as has been shown in considerable detail earlier in this study,[1] there was implied here an acute threat to the position of hundreds of thousands of smallholders. Though it is difficult to say to what extent the planting provisions were definitely calculated to do so, they have gravely impaired the competitive position of the smallholders, and in fact threatened to jeopardise the whole future of the smallholding industry. *These provisions are still (January 1947) in force in Malaya and may yet endanger the whole future of the Malayan smallholding industry.*[2]

This discussion of the equity of rubber regulation may perhaps be fittingly concluded by a brief reference to the reaction of the Asiatics to their treatment under restriction, as revealed in numerous interviews with Malays, Chinese and Indians in Malaya in 1946. Several Chinese rubber dealers, as well as some Chinese and Malay rubber instructors (junior officials of the Rubber Research Institute of Malaya), said entirely without prompting (and of course in individual interviews) that the planting provisions of rubber regulation gravely threatened the future of the smallholders ; one of the Malays said he thought that with these provisions the smallholdings would be reduced to insignificance in about twenty or thirty years. They also said that these results of the planting provisions were common knowledge among educated Asiatics interested in rubber. One Chinese rubber dealer and one branch manager of a large crêpeing enterprise said that it was well known

[1] Chapter 12, above.

[2] They have been repealed very recently ; cf. p. 342, below.

that these provisions embodied an attempt to eliminate the smallholders in favour of the estates. It would have been gratifying to have been in a position to refute this contention. But it was impossible to do so, since this result of the planting provisions had been hinted at very broadly in a leading article of the *Straits Times* as early as 19th February 1936.

Nor did the under-assessment of smallholdings escape the attention of the more discerning Asiatics. There was much dissatisfaction among the villagers over specific aspects of the assessment machinery, notably the assessment of young trees on a girth basis, and the absence of individual inspection of the holdings. But the voicing of systematic and bitter criticism was confined to the more educated and alert individuals, mostly, but not exclusively, to Chinese. The writer was told on several occasions that it was widely realised by educated Asiatics throughout Malaya that the machinery had been operated in favour of the European estates and that the Asiatic properties, especially the smallholdings, had been grossly under-assessed. The unsatisfactory manner in which the restriction machinery had been operated in Malaya was attributed by several persons to the great influence of the General Advisory Committee, to whose one-sided composition reference has already been made. This particular criticism was not confined to Asiatics and was shared by senior European officers interviewed in Malaya.

The attitude of officials to the rubber-growing smallholder was strangely unsympathetic throughout the 1930's, especially in Malaya. This is particularly striking when it is set against the great administrative achievements in Malaya and against the anxious care of the administrators for the welfare of the Malays. A few examples may be briefly listed of the many instances of the unsympathetic official attitude towards the rubber-growing smallholder. We saw the Controller of Rubber, Malaya, rebuking the solitary representative of the smallholders on the General Advisory Committee for (rightly) requesting a re-assessment of smallholdings; the same official asserting that the smallholdings could not be under-assessed relatively to estates, since the average assessments per acre were about the same (above, pp. 140–41); the Malayan Survey Department instructing the inspectors of smallholdings in terms certain to result in the heavy under-assessment of smallholdings (above, pp. 94–95); the same department advising inspectors to disregard smallholdings under heavy natural covers (*ibid.*). We noticed the passive attitude of the authorities in face of the problems presented to the smallholder by restriction and the absence of any guidance through the maze of regulations. Indeed, in Malaya the administrative arrangements of the 5 per cent. new planting of 1939–40 were such as to exclude the great majority of the smallholders from the benefits of this small concession (above, pp. 179–82).[1]

Above all, we saw a former Economic Adviser to the Secretary of State to the Colonies, in his capacity as chairman of the I.R.R.C. and leader of the Malayan delegation, giving his consent to complete prohibition of new planting and to unlimited replanting, at a meeting of the Committee the agenda for which explicitly revealed the disastrous long-term effects for the smallholder of such a decision (pp. 184–87).

When discussing local conditions the I.R.R.C. also often appeared to move on uncertain ground, especially when smallholdings were under consideration. Thus, the leader of the N.E.I. delegation argued early in 1937 that an increased coupon issue to smallholders would lead to a fall in their output (above, p. 128), though it was clear that the contrary would happen, as lower coupon prices were bound to bring about a rise in the price of uncouponed rubber relative to coupon values and this would stimulate tapping, as was indeed amply proved in 1937 and again in 1941. This unfamiliarity with matters in the East also led the Committee repeatedly to assert on important occasions that output was unrestricted when smallholders' coupons were worth one-half of the market price of rubber. Ignorance of local conditions was also partly responsible for the frequent and fallacious assertions that the high prices of export rights were responsible for rural unemployment during periods of low releases.

Many of these examples show that officials, research workers and others closely connected with the industry still regarded the smallholder as a minor and rather inefficient factor in rubber production. The industry was too often regarded as synonymous with the estates. The estate representatives controlled the administration of rubber regulation, both on the I.R.R.C. and within the principal producing territories. The control which rested with the civil servants was nominal, for they were usually unfamiliar with the issues involved. But their presence on the various boards

[1] As will be shown in detail in Chapter 16 below, the officers of the Rubber Research Institute of Malaya were not only ignorant of the problems of the smallholder but actually hostile to this class of producer on whom the activities of the Institute inflicted considerable harm.

and committees absolved the estate representatives from responsibility for the decisions taken, and also acted as a protective screen. It is not improbable that the smallholders would have been less inequitably treated if the whole machinery had been administered by estate representatives without the semblance of official control and with the responsibility for equitable management clearly placed upon them.[1]

A few further specific controversial issues need be dealt with only briefly. The British and Dutch Governments and the Committee have frequently been blamed in America for the maintenance of regulation after the outbreak of war. Much of this criticism was ill-advised. Until the summer of 1940 the demand for rubber under war conditions was uncertain and the withdrawal of regulation would have caused much dislocation in the producing territories. It would also have resulted in a considerable fall in the foreign exchange receipts of the sterling area. Nor did the British and U.S. authorities seem at all anxious to build up considerable reserve stocks of rubber until after the German attack in the West in May 1940. During the second half of 1940, however, the Committee might with advantage have released more rubber, while from about mid-1941 onwards restriction could have been safely abandoned.

When after Pearl Harbour the U.S.A. found itself short of rubber the Committee was held responsible for the scarcity and again became the target of frequent attacks. Most of these were largely unfounded; by early 1942 America had accumulated a very large stock of natural rubber, far in excess of previous records, and also much larger than the quantities visualised when the reserve stock agreements were negotiated in 1940. The Committee's obligation under the first two agreements (June and August 1940) had been fully met; the third agreement (March 1941) did not stipulate a definite time limit, but over three-quarters of the quantity specified in that agreement had also been bought for shipment before the end of 1941. The Committee was, however, mistaken in its frequent references to full production during the first nine months of 1941.

It is difficult to see why, except for vague appeals to producers,

[1] The members of the I.R.R.C. were appointed to represent territories and not particular classes of producer; nevertheless, it was fully expected that the estate representatives would act as spokesmen for their constituents in the narrower sense. Two delegations of smaller producing territories (in both of which smallholders were of importance) consisted, however, of only one member each, both representatives of large estates.

no efforts were made during 1941 to deal with the deficiency of exports. There could have been few problems of war production admitting of a simpler solution than that of increasing the output of rubber in 1941. The first and most obvious step would have been to abandon restriction. As all rubber could be sold at the ruling highly profitable prices, it is not at all clear why restriction was maintained. A possible reason for its maintenance was suggested in one of the circulars of the Department of Commerce: the flood of native rubber which would have been elicited by the withdrawal of restriction would have shown up too clearly the inequitable distribution of the quotas and the under-assessment of the smallholdings. The second step would have been to prohibit replanting. By the summer of 1941 replanting was on a very large scale and absorbed increasing amounts of scarce resources. A British-Dutch prohibition of replanting would have met the case very well as it would have covered all territories except Siam (where there was no replanting) and French Indo-China, and thus no important group of producer would have been put at a relative disadvantage. At the very least the disallowance of expenditure on replanting for taxation purposes would have increased supplies. Thirdly, local governments could have been asked to legislate for a reduction for a period of years in the standard assessments of producers falling behind their exportable amounts by more than a given percentage, thus penalising over-assessed producers, or those who adjusted their production too closely to their excess profits tax standards. These measures would have certainly brought out all the rubber required; probably a veritable flood of rubber would have come from the N.E.I. smallholders. In the improbable event of these steps proving insufficient, more stringent measures would have had to be considered, such as compulsory minimum tapping intensities.

The self-perpetuating nature of regulation needs also to be mentioned. In 1933 restriction was still regarded as an emergency measure. By 1935 it was assumed that it had come to stay and by 1937 it was thought an essential feature of the industry. By 1938 the extension of restriction beyond 1943 was assumed. When the renewed scheme was debated in the Batavia *Volksraad* in 1938, the government spokesman expressed his hope of a more adequate quota for the restriction period of 1944–48. Some preliminary negotiations for a third period of regulation actually took place in 1941.

While the scheme effectively maintained the *status quo*,[1] it did not solve the long-period problem of excess capacity of high-cost producers which, in spite of years of prohibition of new planting and of greatly increased demand, was still considered sufficiently acute to warrant yet another period of regulation. Nor did restriction succeed in eliminating the very wide price and income fluctuations so characteristic of the industry. Restriction had become a permanent feature, no longer a stop-gap remedy to tide over a brief depression. There is an analogy here with the Stevenson scheme which was introduced after the 1921–22 depression had passed; the international scheme too was established after the great depression was largely over. The purpose of restriction had become the quasi-permanent maintenance of the high-cost producers. No progress was made towards their gradual elimination; the only class to be eliminated would have been the smallholders, and this through the operation of the planting provisions of regulation; the prospect of the gradual extinction of the lowest-cost producers can hardly be called a desirable aim of regulation. In all other respects the scheme, though bringing a period of prosperity to the producing countries after some very hard years, left unresolved the problems of the industry.

[1] Except for illicit planting by native producers in the N.E.I. and by producers in Siam.

PART IV
LABOUR AND TECHNIQUE

CHAPTER 15
PLANTATION LABOUR

I

FROM the earliest days of the rubber industry the most important producing territories depended on immigrant labour. The estates of Ceylon, Malaya and Sumatra were worked largely by Indian and Javanese labour (with Chinese labour for special purposes in Malaya), while some native districts in Sumatra and Borneo, as well as many estates in French Indo-China, employed migrant labour. Indeed, the comparatively easy access to the ample labour supplies of India, Java and China was an important factor in the establishment of the plantation industry in South-east Asia. The rubber industry was probably more successful than most other forms of tropical agriculture or mining in dealing with the special conditions created by this situation; nevertheless, the problems of immigrant labour still dominated the labour position in the 1930's.

Malaya will be dealt with first and in greatest detail. During the years 1929–33 the annual Malayan estate production approximately equalled the estate output of all other territories taken together, and was substantially greater than that of any other territory even after 1933, when its relative importance was reduced. Moreover, in Malaya the labour situation was dominated by the rubber industry, which accounted for over 90 per cent. of estate employment, while in the N.E.I. and Ceylon the proportion was one-fifth or less.

At the end of 1929 there were, according to the official Malayan statistics, 258,000 labourers employed on estates in the Straits Settlements and the Federated Malay States. These comprised 205,000 Indians, 42,000 Chinese, 6,000 Javanese and 5,000 others.[1] Malay and Javanese estate workers were thus few. The Malays were generally reluctant to accept regular wage-earning work. Sometimes Malays counted as members of the estate population

[1] The basis of these figures (which are subject to considerable limitations) is discussed below, in Statistical Appendix III.

were merely residing on the estates and working a few occasional days only. They were usually paid the same rate as South Indians [1] (about 50 Straits cents a day in 1929), and were recruited from, or returned to, their villages according to the state of the labour market. The wages of the Javanese estate workers were also generally the same as those of Indians.

For various reasons the official figures of the Chinese estate population considerably understate the number of Chinese estate labourers, and furnish a very inadequate idea of Chinese employment and interest in the Malayan rubber industry. According to the statistics of the Labour Department, Chinese estate labourers numbered 64,000 at the end of 1931. But according to the 1931 Malayan census the total number of Chinese gainfully employed in rubber cultivation in all capacities totalled some 182,000, while another 39,000 were engaged in 'other and multifarious' forms of agriculture, a term which certainly included many people connected at least part-time with rubber cultivation, e.g. tapioca and rubber, or pineapple and rubber cultivators. The census figures include the owners and tappers of Chinese smallholdings; but even allowing for this, the figures of Chinese estate employment are seriously incomplete. When working on European estates, Chinese were mostly engaged on special works, such as clearing, felling, or budgrafting. For such special tasks most European estates employed contractors who were small Chinese capitalists, or specially skilled workers who, with a gang of their compatriots, undertook the work. The workers were almost invariably paid by results, and were known as contract labourers.[2]

Much of the elaborate labour legislation in force in Malaya

[1] Throughout this study Indian estate workers in Malaya are referred to indiscriminately as Indians, South Indians or Tamils, in accordance with the general, though somewhat inaccurate, practice.

[2] This term is used in the rubber industry in several different senses. The original meaning is that of an indentured labourer, and a contract is simply an indenture. This is the sense in which the expression is used in the N.E.I. Secondly, a contract worker may be a labourer in the employ of a contractor engaged on some special work on the estate. The distinction here is between the contract worker and the labourer on the estate check roll, while the earlier distinction was between a contract worker, liable under criminal law for breach of his contract, and a free labourer whose liability was confined to civil law. From this use the term has spread to include in Malaya all tappers paid by results; for instance, Chinese tappers employed on smallholdings and paid by results (by the amount of latex collected) are referred to as contract workers, and the piece rate as the contract rate. Occasionally, the term contract labourer is used to refer to the fact that in Malaya most estate workers are on verbal monthly agreements and are supposed to be on a month's notice; in fact, when they wish to leave they usually abscond.

In this study wherever the term is used, its meaning will be clearly indicated.

applied only to Indians and Javanese, and with the exception of the deportation of undesirable elements, and a limitation after August 1930 on the total number of adult male Chinese immigrants, comparatively little control was exercised over either the movement or the working conditions of Chinese estate workers. Minimum health and sanitary standards were prescribed by the authorities, but in these matters the Chinese workers were on the whole fairly self-reliant and less in need of protection and guidance than were the other races.

Chinese wages were usually appreciably higher than those of Indians, as the Chinese worker is generally speaking stronger, more skilled and more careful than the Tamil estate labourer. Moreover, employers did not incur the health and education expenses, immigration fund contributions and other charges, which usually amounted to an additional cost of about one-third of the wages of Indian labourers. The earnings of Chinese in Malaya have always fluctuated widely, generally with the prosperity of the rubber and tin industries and to a lesser extent with the price of rice. The Chinese worker has definitely a profit-sharing outlook, even in wage-earning. He is prepared to work for food and lodging and perhaps only 5 cents a day when times are bad, but insists on his share in the prosperity of rubber and tin. The range of skill between various classes of Chinese workers was also much wider than among Indians, and it is not easy to speak of a general level of Chinese wages. In 1929 their daily earnings in manual occupations ranged from 80 cents to 1.50 dollars. On rubber estates they earned around 85–90 cents. Payment of Chinese estate workers was always by results.

Indian labourers were more docile and reliable, and were usually preferred for the day-to-day operation of European estates. Moreover, the larger estates, whose annual estimates were carefully prepared and which often had large forward contracts, preferred to employ labour whose wages were less liable to wide fluctuations. In 1933 (the first year for which this particular information is available), there were, on European-owned estates in the F.M.S., 10·2 Indians and 2·7 Chinese labourers per 100 acres of planted rubber ; Javanese and Malays were negligible. On Chinese-owned properties the figures were 1·2 Indians and 9·1 Chinese per 100 acres.[1]

Indian labour was first introduced into Malaya on any scale

[1] These figures are fairly reliable, and the criticisms of the Chinese employment figures (above, p. 218) do not apply.

in the 1880's, mainly to work on the sugar estates in Province Wellesley and Kedah. This was indentured labour, and that system was still in force when the expansion of the rubber industry suddenly created a very large demand for Indian estate labour. This situation resulted in a dilemma. The maintenance, let alone the large-scale extension, of indentured labour could not be tolerated, as in practice, especially in the early days, it often resulted in very bad labour conditions. On the other hand few employers were prepared to incur the heavy expenses of recruiting workers from India if there was the chance of losing their services in a few days' time should a neighbouring estate offer slightly higher wages. The sensible solution was devised of financing immigration through a central fund, the statutory Indian Immigration Fund, managed by the Indian Immigration Committee, which consisted originally of four members, two government officials and two employers' representatives. Such expenses as were incurred by individual employers in recruiting labour were reimbursed from the Fund, whose revenue was derived from quarterly assessments on employers of more than ten Indian labourers, with rates varying in accordance with the expected needs of the Fund. Established in 1907, it proved an immediate success; indentured labour had disappeared by 1914.

As the duties of the Indian Immigration Committee were originally envisaged as purely administrative—the management of the Fund fed from employers' contributions—there was no ground for objection to its one-sided composition. Although the Committee was established by statute, neither its functions nor its membership were statutorily defined. The original F.M.S. Enactment of 1907 defined the Committee as 'the Committee which shall, for the time being, be notified by the High Commissioner in the Gazette to be the Indian Immigration Committee'. The 1923 F.M.S. Labour Code defined the Committee as 'the Immigration Committee existing at the time of the passing of this Enactment, or hereafter notified by Order of the High Commissioner in the Gazette to be the Indian Immigration Committee'. It authorised, however, the High Commissioner to define the duties of the Committee and to appoint its members. In spite of this, neither its tasks nor the constitution of the Committee's membership have ever been formally defined. Both the functions and membership expanded steadily. Thus by 1928 the Committee was entrusted with the fixing of minimum wages. Its membership since the mid-1920's was generally sixteen: the Controller and Deputy-Controller of Labour, three other officials (at least two of these were heads of departments employing Indian labour on a large scale), nine representatives of various employers' organisations and two Indians.

With the exception of the slump years, the annual movement of labour between India and Malaya was considerable from the beginning of the century down to 1939. The migrants were South Indian labourers from Madras Presidency, almost entirely Tamils, Telugus and Malayalees, either going to work, mainly on Malayan rubber estates, or returning to South India on an occasional visit or permanently. They were all deck passengers on steamers plying between South India and Malaya. The deck passengers proceeding from South India to Malaya were either assisted or unassisted; the latter paid their own passages while those of the former were paid by the Indian Immigration Fund. Unassisted deck passengers included clerks, petty traders and artisans, as well as labourers; in the 1930's some 50–70 per cent. of the unassisted deck passengers were labourers, and an uncertain but appreciable proportion of these was available for estate work. Neither the Indian nor the Malayan authorities exercised much control over the movement of these migrants, whose numbers showed a marked long-period increase, again with the exception of the slump years.

Assisted migration, the most important factor in the supply of estate labour, was strictly controlled at both ends. It was subject to the Indian Emigration Act of 1922, and to the rules and regulations issued under it by the Indian authorities. The assisted emigrant traffic passed through camps at Madras and Negapatam, which were in charge of the Malayan Labour Department and inspected by officials of the Madras Government.

As well as paying the passages of all assisted labourers and of their dependants from South India, the Indian Immigration Fund was also responsible for the return fares of Indian labourers no longer fit for work. Before 1930 there was no provision for the return passages of able-bodied unemployed labourers. As every year until 1930 tens of thousands of workmen were assisted to take employment in Malaya, and work was always available, nobody conceived a state of affairs where the situation would deteriorate so greatly that not only would immigration have to be suspended, but that even after allowing for wastage there would still be thousands of able-bodied labourers unable to find work at all and others only intermittently without being able to earn a living wage. Even had the need for the provision of free repatriation of able-bodied labourers been suggested before 1929, it would have been rightly rejected while assisted immigration continued, and would have been considered by the labourers as an invitation to return to India at the expense of the Indian Immigration Fund whenever they felt inclined. However, the absence of provision for unemployed or under-employed labourers, as well as the lack of forethought of such a contingency, created great difficulties after 1929.

The labour situation on smallholdings need be discussed only briefly. On holdings employing outside labour for tapping, the workers were either Malay share tappers on Malay-owned holdings or Chinese contract tappers, mostly on Chinese properties ; there were a comparatively small number of Indian labourers on Chettiar holdings. Chinese tappers were invariably paid by results ; the rate varied inversely with the productivity of the holdings, and poorer-yielding properties had to pay higher rates than better holdings as otherwise they were unable to retain their labourers. As on estates, the piece rates generally fluctuated with the price of rubber and with the general prosperity of the industry. Earnings of outside labourers on smallholdings were usually of the same order as those of estate workers.

The pressure of the Indian authorities, the prosperity of the rubber industry, especially in the mid-1920's, the high administrative standards in Malaya, all contributed to the rapid improvement in labour conditions in the years before the depression. By the late 1920's Malayan labour legislation provided for minimum wages and maximum hours, free housing and medical attention for estate labourers and free elementary schooling for their children, and for the distribution of free milk-foods and rice to the infant children of estate labourers. For women workers a month's holiday with pay before and after confinement was also prescribed. Employers had to offer work on at least twenty-four days a month to all the wage-earners or pay minimum wages in lieu.[1]

The introduction of minimum-wage legislation was preceded by prolonged negotiations between the Indian and Malayan authorities. The 1923 Labour Code had already provided that the Indian Immigration Committee could determine standard rates of wages in certain areas to be paid for a day's work by able-bodied Indian labourers. There was, however, no legal sanction for these rates ; it was simply ' lawful for the Indian Immigration Committee to prescribe standard rates of wages '. In 1928 the payment of less

[1] According to a German observer writing in 1930 : ' die Britischen Gebiete scheinen das Problem Arbeit beinahe vorbildlich geloest ze haben.' F. Juda : *Organisation des Weltkautschukmarktes.*

than standard rates fixed by the Indian Immigration Committee was made an offence. The actual rates were prescribed by the Indian Immigration Committee only after the consent of the Indian authorities had been obtained. They came into force in February 1929, and were 50 cents a day for men and 40 cents for women, with 58 and 47 cents in certain less accessible and more expensive districts. These levels were designed to ensure that a labourer, after providing for his own and his dependants' expenditure at 1928 prices and standards of living, should be left with enough money to be able to save 12 dollars a year, as well as accumulate money for a return passage to India once every three years.

For some reason which has never been adequately explained, the minima had statutory force only in certain so-called 'key-districts'. These were Province Wellesley and the coastal districts of Selangor (50 and 40 cents), as well as certain inland districts in Pahang and Kelantan (58 and 47 cents). It was expected that the working of economic forces would ensure that these rates would be operative throughout Malaya. The Public Works Department and the F.M.S. Railways paid them as minima, and no recruiting licence was issued unless the employer undertook to observe them. By the end of 1929, rates of 50 cents were general throughout the country, though there were individual instances of task or piece rates being fixed at such levels as to render it difficult for a worker of average efficiency to earn the minimum wage. In view of the efforts made to ensure that the rates should become national minima it is difficult to see why the whole of Malaya was not covered by the statutory wage regulation. In actual fact, the most effective factor ensuring the general payment of at least the minima throughout the country was the support of the Planters' Association of Malaya, which recommended its members to pay them, a recommendation which was generally accepted.[1]

Tappers on Malayan estates, while being paid a full daily wage, worked some 5½–6½ hours only—approximately from 6 or 6.30 a.m. to 12 noon or 12.30 p.m. In 1929 when tasks were generally shortened to concentrate tapping into the early hours of the morning, tappers' hours were often even shorter.

While there were elements of instability in the situation, the

[1] Membership of the Planters' Association of Malaya accounted for a total planted area in 1929 of just over 1,200,000 acres: this was some two-thirds of the planted area of estates and over 90 per cent. of the European-owned rubber acreage. Some seven-eighths of Indian estate labourers were directly affected by the recommendations of the Planters' Association of Malaya.

conditions of South Indian estate labour in Malaya were definitely satisfactory in 1929. Labour conditions in Malaya were then probably the best enjoyed by agricultural labour anywhere in South or South-east Asia and were, of course, far better than in South India. Although data on earnings of agricultural labour in South India are inadequate, an estimate of the excess or real wages of estate labour in Malaya over those of agricultural wages in South India of at least 75–100 per cent., appears conservative, and this was for much shorter hours and lighter work. The 1929 *Annual Report* of the Madras Department of Labour on the Working of the Emigration Act of 1922 estimated the difference at between 50 and 100 per cent. in money wages, but this appears to have been an under-estimate.[1] Mr. Ormsby Gore wrote in 1928 : 'It is estimated that the real wages earned by Indian labourers in Ceylon are approximately 100 per cent. higher than their earnings as rural labourers in South India.[2] Wages in Malaya in the late 1920's were appreciably higher than they were in Ceylon. Again, in Malaya (and in Ceylon) wages had to be paid in cash, while in South India payment in rice and arbitrary deductions by landowners were still common. Perhaps most serious was the frequent lack of freedom of many agricultural labourers. The Whitley Commission found that in 1929 certain forms of bond service, practically indistinguishable from slavery, were still common in parts of Madras.[3] The thousands of South Indian emigrants seeking work in Malaya had good reasons for their choice.

II

During the depression of 1929–33 estate employment fell heavily. The table on page 225 summarises the available figures, which refer to the S.S. and F.M.S. only.[4] Because of their greater complexity the hardly less important migration statistics have been relegated to Statistical Appendix III.

On these figures estate employment was almost halved between 1929 and 1932. The statistics of Chinese workers are, however, not strictly comparable, and understate the decline in employment. The actual decline was fully 50 per cent., and the entire fall occurred between August 1930 and July 1932. No data are available of

[1] It was, moreover, a comparison between estate wages in South India and Malaya, rather than between rural wages or earnings in South India and estate wages in Malaya.

[2] *Report on a Visit to Malaya, Java and Ceylon during the year 1928*, p. 79.

[3] *Report of the Royal Commission on Labour in India* (1931) pp. 14–15.

[4] Cf. Statistical Appendix III.

TABLE I

Number of Labourers Employed at the end of each year on Estates in the S.S. and F.M.S., 1929–33

(Thousands)

	Indians	*Chinese*	*Javanese*	*Others*	*Total*
1929	205	42	6	5	258
1930	154	42	5	4	205
1931	121	37	3	3	164
1932	104	35	3	3	145
1933	111	39	3	7	160

the numbers employed on smallholdings. It is well known that the number of outside tappers employed on smallholdings was greatly reduced during the depression, and many owners who had previously relied on outside labour had to dispense with it.

In February 1929 when statutory wages came into force in the key areas, the price of rubber in Singapore was around 38 cents per lb. By April 1930 it had fallen to 24 cents, and by September to 12 cents. From the spring of 1930 wages began to be reduced outside key districts, and resolutions were passed by various district planters' associations for the reduction of wages in key areas. There were also demands for the repeal of the minimum wage legislation. As the rubber market went from bad to worse pressure for the reduction of wages increased, and following formal requests by the Planters' Association of Malaya, in July the Indian Immigration Committee decreed a 20 per cent. reduction in minimum wages to take effect in October. It was announced on behalf of the Planters' Association of Malaya and the agency houses that they would not object to a restoration of the minima to previous levels when market conditions returned to normal, which was explicitly interpreted as a Singapore price of 25 cents.

About the middle of August a mass dismissal of estate labour took place. In the F.M.S. alone the employed Indian estate population fell from 171,000 at the end of June to 134,000 at the end of December. Every week thousands of unemployed labourers besieged the offices of the Labour Department, which was entirely unprepared for such a contingency. Assisted immigration from India had been suspended at the end of July, and between August and the end of December some 67,000 South Indians, including 11,000 minors, were repatriated through the Labour Department. The repatriates were almost all workers who would have been prepared to remain in Malaya if work had been available at

40 cents a day.[1] As the slump progressed an increasing number of the Indians repatriated were workers unable to maintain themselves and their dependants on their greatly reduced earnings, especially as the issue of free rice, tea and milk-foods to dependants of estate labourers, frequent in 1929, was withdrawn.

For some time past there had been demands that the tappers should not be paid a full day's wage unless they were prepared to do two hours' field work in the afternoon. This proposal often involved hardship to the workers. Under Malayan conditions it was unreasonable to ask them to work for eight or nine hours without a long break. If on the other hand they returned to their homes at noon or 1 p.m., and turned out again for work in the afternoon, their spare time would be curtailed, particularly if, as often happened, the actual field in which they worked was a long way from their dwellings. During the autumn part payment for morning work was adopted on an increasing number of estates, particularly in non-key areas. In key areas the practice was almost certainly illegal. One section of the Labour Code provided that no labourer should be bound to work for more than six consecutive hours or more than nine hours in a single day. Although minimum wages were dealt with in a different section and the sections were not linked, a reading of the Code, together with the obvious intention of the minimum wage legislation to assure a definite minimum standard for all workers, makes it fairly certain that the practice would not have been upheld in court. It was, however, never tested in Malaya, though in Ceylon the practice was declared illegal in the courts.

By May 1931 the Singapore price of rubber fell to below 10 cents. Daily rates of wages outside key areas were being reduced, and the practice of paying only three-quarters of the daily wage for morning work became more and more widespread until by the end of the year it was universal. In July the Controller of Labour informed employers that no proceedings would be taken against estates in key districts paying only three-quarters of the minima for morning work. Moreover, the authorities no longer insisted on employers offering a minimum of 24 days' work a month; this also affected earnings adversely, as on many estates work was available on only four or five days a week. Most tappers refused

[1] Of 33,583 repatriates reaching Negapatam from Malaya in 1930, only 731 stated that their wages had been insufficient to maintain their families; 25,540 returned for want of work, and the rest for various reasons. Department of Labour, Madras Presidency, *Annual Report* for 1930 on the Working of the Indian Emigration Act of 1922.

to work in the afternoon; moreover, on many estates there was little afternoon work available, so that the tappers were not even given the opportunity of earning a full day's wage. Before the slump tappers comprised about one-half, or slightly more, of the Indian estate labour force, but with the great reduction and often suspension of cultivation work the proportion of tappers in the total increased considerably, and so did that of workers paid only at three-quarters of the nominal daily wage.

There is a studied vagueness in the majority of the official Malayan publications of 1931–33 dealing with the labour situation, including wages, earnings and the conditions of repatriation. Some official reports are quite misleading: for instance, the *Annual Reports* of the Colonial Secretary, S.S., for 1931 and 1932 stated that the minimum wage for Indian estate labourers remained at 40 cents, without mentioning that the minima were not enforced, and that by 1932 not even three-quarters of the minimum rates were being paid; the same was also implied in the *Annual Reports* for these years of the Controller of Labour, S.S. The principal exceptions are the *Annual Reports* for the early 1930's of the British Resident, Selangor, and the *Annual Reports* of the Agent of the Government of India,[1] which generally presented a reliable picture of prevailing conditions.

After assisted immigration was suspended in August 1930 estate labourers who were unable to find employment at standard rates and who applied for repatriation were repatriated free of cost until January 1931. As a result of this liberal repatriation policy and of the suspension of assisted immigration from India, the labour supply of Malaya was shrinking rapidly, and in spite of the depression there was some concern over the long-period consequences. Pressure was brought to bear on the acting Controller of Labour to suspend the repatriation of unemployed South Indians, and in January 1931 the Labour Department issued a circular to the effect that free repatriation would no longer be granted to able-bodied workers. This was an indefensible attempt to retain labourers who were either unemployed or dissatisfied with their earnings but could not afford a passage back to India. The circular was withdrawn after energetic representations by the Agent of the Indian Government and the stream of repatriation was promptly resumed. Workers unable to find regular employment at three-quarters of the standard wage and seeking repatriation

[1] This was an official appointed by the Government of India to watch over the interests of Indians in Malaya.

were generally given free passages. Repatriation was not usually granted, however, when work was available at three-quarters of the minimum wage, though many workers found it difficult to support dependants at these rates.[1] During 1931 some 56,000 labourers (41,000 adults and 15,000 minors) were repatriated and another 45,000 left paying their own passages, while only 20,000 unassisted immigrants arrived.

The policy of free repatriation of able-bodied unemployed workers was much criticised, chiefly on the ground that it endangered Malaya's future labour supply. Given the absence of any form of public assistance and the impossibility of settling the labourers on the land, repatriation was the best policy. The hardships undergone by the Indian unemployed who were repatriated were certainly not nearly so acute as those of the Chinese to whom free repatriation was extended only belatedly, or those of the unemployed Asiatic clerks who were not repatriated either, and for whom that would have been no solution, as they had lost touch with the land and with their villages.

By the end of 1931 Indian wages were generally 30 cents for morning work in key areas and 25–30 cents outside key areas. For workers with dependants the fall in earnings was substantially greater than the reduction in wages, as with the suspension of cultivation work most of the dependants lost their employment and swelled the ranks of the 'unemployed dependants' (non-working relatives) of the official classification. During the opening months of 1932 wages were fairly stable, but the wave of cuts and economies which followed the official communiqué announcing the failure of the Anglo-Dutch restriction talks in March brought about an acute crisis in wages, the worst during the slump. The reductions began outside key districts, but soon spread throughout Malaya. The 1932 *Annual Report* of the Indian Agent gives the summary of wages on a number of estates which he visited (see Table II, page 229).

Wages in 1913–14 had been around 30 cents, so that the morning rates just quoted were as much as 40 per cent. below those ruling before 1914, and 60 per cent. below those of 1930. Although it would appear that the larger and financially stronger estates paid somewhat higher wages, the wages shown by the Indian Agent

[1] This was freely admitted by the authorities. The Controller of Labour stated in the spring of 1931, in an address to the Standing Labour Committee of the Planters' Association of Malaya: 'The rates of wages now in force for male labourers, though adequate for single men, are not so for married men whose dependants are unemployed.'

TABLE II

Wages of South Indian Estate Labourers on certain Malayan Estates, January–May 1932

(Straits cents)

	Full day	*Morning work only*
January	40	Three-quarters of the rate for the full day
February	40	" " " " "
March	35	" " " " "
April	27	" " " " "
May	22–25	" " " " "

were received by many workers. Payment of less than 20 cents, even for morning work only, was rare, though not sufficiently so to be termed exceptional.

In judging the events now to be described it must be borne in mind that when the original minimum wages were negotiated the London price of rubber was around 1*s.* per lb. against 1¾*d.* in the spring of 1932, that the cost of living of Indian labourers had fallen by about 50 per cent. since 1928 and by about 35–40 per cent. since the end of 1929, and that a complete collapse of the rubber industry and of Malayan economy was widely feared. The procedure was nevertheless somewhat unorthodox.

The events can best be summarised in the words of the Controller of Labour himself, who reviewed them in an address to the Council of the Planters' Association of Malaya in June 1933 : 'In April 1932 the process of reducing costs tended outside certain key areas to bring about what neither you nor I would regard as reasonable wage conditions. I came before you then and got from you the unanimous declaration that starvation wages should not be tolerated in the Peninsula. You agreed to leave the fixation of a subsistence wage to the Indian Immigration Committee, and you and I bound ourselves to accept the decision. For all the Western portion of the country those wages were fixed at 7.20 and 6.00 dollars ; wages in standard rate areas to be paid at standard rates, wages elsewhere to be adjusted so that labourers would, in fact, earn every month the subsistence wage fixed by the Indian Immigration Committee. It was further agreed that failure to pay those wages would result in labour forces being mustered and informed that any person who did not earn this sum would be offered free repatriation.'[1] Thus the Indian Immigration Committee, on which the employers (the Planters' Association of

[1] *R.G.A. Bulletin*, August 1933.

Malaya) had a clear majority, had become not only a wage-fixing body, but also an arbitrator to whose judgment the Controller of Labour submitted himself in advance.

The rates fixed by the Indian Immigration Committee (7.20 and 6.00 dollars a month for men and women respectively) clearly visualised daily wages of 30 and 25 cents with a monthly employment of 24 working days. As the aim was the fixing of subsistence earnings the wage should have been paid even when the labourer was engaged on morning work only. It emerged from subsequent statements by the Controller of Labour and by others, that the majority of employers interpreted the award as referring to wages payable for a full day, and were not prepared to pay more than 75 per cent. of the award for morning work only. This was explicitly stated by the Indian Agent in his 1932 report,[1] and other evidence shows that many Indian workers were paid even less than three-quarters of 30 cents. By the end of 1932 matters had improved slightly and most Indian estate labourers were paid around 22–26 cents for morning work and 25–30 cents for a whole day, but there were still instances of labourers being paid 20 cents only for morning work.

The Controller's promise that labourers working on estates where they could not earn the subsistence wage would be mustered and informed of the conditions of free repatriation was not in fact kept. To quote his own words : 'After the agreement with the Planters' Association of Malaya and the Indian Immigration Committee was come to in May 1932, no action was taken up to October of that year to bring to the notice of the worker the conditions governing free repatriation, because the numbers offering

[1] Two paragraphs from the report may be quoted. 'I regret to have to state that the Indian Immigration Committee's decision was not being followed. Some employers taking the subsistence rates for a full day's wages, reduced them further by one-fourth or one-third. I brought all these cases to the notice of the Controller of Labour, but felt convinced that any insistence on the payment of standard rates would be most prejudicial to the best interest of the labourer, as it would result in further large-scale dismissals of workers who could not be absorbed in other industries here, and in the augmentation of the already heavy tide of repatriation. The offer of repatriation was also losing its value as a lever to raise wages, as most of the remaining labourers were reluctant to return to India.

'I must, however, record my opinion that whatever might have been the degree of success attained during prosperous times, the experiment of fixing standard wages in selected districts, and allowing economic forces to play their part in raising the level of wages in the rest of Malaya, has beyond doubt failed during the stress and strain of a prolonged slump, and the fixation of an irreducible statutory minimum for the whole of Malaya is an urgent desideratum.' *Annual Report* for 1932 of the Agent of the Government of India in Malaya, p. 9.

themselves were so big that it was highly undesirable still further to increase them.'[1] It is not clear why the workers should not have been informed of the conditions of free repatriation, as there was no case for retaining those who would have availed themselves of the facility. The situation is not easy to assess, as on occasions the Controller of Labour tended to contradict himself: 'In a small number of areas labourers have declined repatriation even where earnings did not come up to the desired level, but it can be taken as granted that it was widely known throughout Malaya that repatriation was available for those who did not receive a subsistence wage'[2]—which does not accord with the other statement just quoted. No doubt those very anxious to go were able to obtain free passages by stating their case energetically to the authorities, but many were ignorant of their rights or afraid of taking such steps.

There were, however, many instances throughout the slump, even in the summer of 1932, of workers being offered free repatriation before a reduction in wages, and electing to stay; these were particularly numerous on estates on which workers had good facilities for cultivating food crops, or where the manager had treated them especially well. Other frequent causes of the refusal to accept repatriation were the loss of ties with the worker's own village or the reluctance to return without savings. The Labour Department was thus on occasions faced with the difficult situation that estates were unable to pay subsistence wages, while the workers did not wish to be repatriated. The number of Indian labourers repatriated during 1932 was nevertheless very considerable, some 45,000 adults and 11,000 minors.

The following figures indicate the wages received during the slump years by a sufficiently large proportion of Indian estate workers (men) to be considered the mode: end-1929, 50–55 cents; end-1930, 40 cents; end-1931, 25–30 cents; mid-1932, 20–25 cents; end-1932, 25–28 cents.

In 1933, with the re-opening of smallholdings and of estates previously closed, the demand for labour was increasing. By June or July estates not paying 30 cents found it difficult to retain their workers. There was much movement of labour in the summer of 1933 and this led to the familiar outcry against crimping. By the end of 1933 estate wages were generally 30–35 cents for morning work only, while employment for dependants was more readily

[1] *R.G.A. Bulletin, ibid.*

[2] *Annual Report* for 1932 of the Controller of Labour, F.M.S.

available. By the autumn, share-tappers on smallholdings frequently earned 50–60 cents.

In his address to the Planters' Association of Malaya,[1] the Controller of Labour made two further points worth noting. First, he insisted repeatedly on the difficulties which had arisen out of the fact that minimum wages had legal force in certain districts only: 'Serious practical difficulties would have been avoided if standard rates had been in force over the whole country, and the Labour Department would have had an instrument which, used with foresight and discretion, would have enabled it the more easily to control and regulate wages in the dire emergency that existed. From the employer's point of view it is essential to have equal wage conditions in key and non-key areas, and this must be a cardinal plank in any labour policy.' Secondly, he frankly admitted that at times of stress, discussions with the Planters' Association of Malaya took the place of the Labour Code as the guiding factor in labour policy: 'In critical times the guidance of the law is never wholly adequate. Extra-legal action is called for, and in such circumstances no controller of labour is able to impose his will unless he has the support—the willing, active support—of the Planters' Association of Malaya.'

The fall in the wages of Chinese estate workers was even more spectacular than that of Indian wages. Starting from the much higher level of about 85–90 cents at the end of 1929 (Indian wages were about 50 cents), Chinese wages declined to about 50–60 cents by the end of 1930, and by the end of 1931 were almost level with those of Indians at around 30–40 cents. Moreover, unemployment was severe, especially after June when tin restriction was introduced. There was another sharp decline in 1932, and for most of the year Chinese wages were at approximately the same level as those of Indian workers. There were also many instances of Chinese workers accepting work for food and lodging with perhaps 5 cents a day in cash. Unemployment among the Chinese (to whom, it will be remembered, repatriation was not generally extended) continued to be severe. A notable improvement came in 1933, and by the end of the year Chinese workers on rubber estates again earned about 50 cents a day. There was some substitution of Chinese for Indian labour on estates in 1931–32, but this was on a smaller scale than could have been expected in view of the very severe fall in Chinese wages. The possibility of a large-scale replacement of Indian by Chinese labour was, however, always

[1] *R.G.A. Bulletin, ibid.*

in the background, and enhanced the difficulties of the Controller of Labour in his attempts to resist demands for wage cuts. The immigration of Chinese was also severely restricted from August 1930. There had been no organised assisted immigration of Chinese since before 1914, and the restriction was simply a drastic over-all limitation on the number of adult males who were allowed to enter the country from China.

While wage cuts were of obvious importance in view of their effects on the standards of life of tens of thousands of labourers and of their effect on the cost of production, mention must also be made of salary reductions. The salaries of estate managers and assistants were reduced usually by about 30–45 per cent.; on some financially weaker estates the reductions were even greater. In addition, there was also a total loss of commission (percentages on profits). Moreover, the acreage supervised by each manager was on the average doubled between the end of 1929 and the summer of 1932. After the slump rather more than one-half of the salary reductions were restored and commissions reappeared. It was, however, realised that before 1930 staffs and salaries had been excessive, and the staff reductions effected during the slump were reversed to a minor extent only.

III

During the second half of 1933 the improvement in the price of rubber, together with the imminence of restriction, led estates to replenish their greatly reduced labour forces. It seems paradoxical that the prospect of reduced output should have resulted in a higher level of estate employment. The explanation lay in the better profits—partly realised in 1933 and expected further to improve after 1934—which enabled estates to relax the more rigid economies of the slump, especially to make up certain arrears of cultivation. Once regulation was in operation employment varied directly, though not proportionately, with output.

In October 1933 the Controller of Labour and the chairman of the Planters' Association of Malaya left for India to discuss with the Indian Government the conditions under which assisted migration could be resumed. Early in 1934 the Indian authorities agreed to the resumption of assisted emigration to Malaya on a small scale. Not more than 20,000 would-be workers and their dependants could be given assisted passages during 1934. A system of bearer-letters to be obtained by immigrants was devised to ensure that both the numbers and the class of emigrants would be in accordance with the agreement. This did not operate entirely satisfactorily, chiefly owing to the unexpected pressure to emigrate. The bearer-letters became negotiable instruments and were bought, sold and forged on a large scale. The news that work was again available in Malaya spread rapidly through the recruiting districts of Madras where the monsoon had just failed, and the emigration camps were stormed by tens of thousands of applicants, some in possession of genuine bearer-letters, others with forged documents, and yet others with none at all.

Even allowing for the further deterioration of economic conditions in South India, it is remarkable that after the terrible experience of the slump and the starvation wages of 1931–32, which were well known in Madras, so many thousands should again have been anxious to return to Malaya at the first opportunity.[1] The attraction of Malaya surprised both the Indian and Malayan authorities and was undoubtedly a significant pointer to the economic and social conditions in the recruiting districts of the Presidency.[2] In addition to the applicants presenting themselves at the depots there were thousands of others who wished to emigrate, but did not proceed to the camps, as they were not in possession of the bearer-letters which they understood to be a necessary qualification for assisted passages. Throughout 1934 estate labourers in Malaya were bombarded with requests by relatives and co-villagers for bearer-letters. Many fewer workers than had been expected (actually only a few thousand) returned from Malaya to India for a holiday in 1934. The experience of 1934 and of subsequent years revealed that a large proportion—about one-half according to the estimates of the Labour Department—of Indian estate workers in Malaya had ceased to consider India as their home, and had come to regard Malaya as a permanent domicile.

A feature of the 1934 agreement between the Indian and the

[1] All observers were agreed that the news of conditions in Malaya and Ceylon had always spread very rapidly through the recruiting districts of Madras. Surprise has often been expressed how well informed was the illiterate Tamil of changes in economic conditions in Malaya.

[2] In the words of the 1931 *Madras Census Report*: 'One portion of the Presidency seems to have reached saturation . . . other adjoining areas are in the position that a strong and continuing emigration flow is necessary to maintain the population at a subsistence level. . . . Emigration has become markedly more popular in most parts of the Presidency during the last decade. The Tamil especially has long been a rover, and it is one of the problems of South India that his opportunities for roving seem likely to diminish' (pp. 45–47). According to the report, the desire to escape from caste disabilities also acted as a strong inducement to emigration. The experience of 1934 confirmed these observations.

Malayan authorities was the formal recognition by the latter of the Indian worker's right to free repatriation when no work could be found for him at a reasonable wage. No definition of a reasonable wage was apparently attempted ; its interpretation depended largely on the Indian authorities, who were guided, among other considerations, by the opinion of the Indian Agent in Malaya.

During 1934 Indian wages in Malaya were around 35–40 cents for morning work only. The standard rates in key areas continued at 40 cents for men (47 cents in less accessible districts) ; estate spokesmen occasionally advocated the payment of 30 cents only for morning work (three-quarters of the standard rate), but the labour market was sufficiently firm to defeat such proposals.

In the spring of 1934 some hurried new planting took place in anticipation of the expected prohibition. This activity, together with the clearing up and re-opening of some estates, resulted in a temporary shortage of Chinese labour. The stringent control of Chinese immigration was maintained, though the numbers admitted were raised slightly. The premium on quota passages continued so high as largely to exclude agricultural labourers and most of the immigrants were not prospective estate workers. In view of the likelihood that the shortage would be only temporary, the authorities wisely refused a substantial increase in the immigration quota. Chinese estate wages, or rather earnings, rose slightly to around 50–65 cents by the end of the year.[1]

During the year the fusion of the Planters' Association of Malaya and several minor planters' associations resulted in the formation of the United Planting Association of Malaya. This body was even more powerful than its predecessor and united the employers of virtually all Indian estate labour and of an appreciable, though numerically unascertainable, proportion of Chinese workers.

Rubber estate employment from 1934 to 1940 is summarised in the table on page 236.

After 1933 the Registrar-General of Statistics continued and extended the series, begun in 1933 for the F.M.S., of employment by race on estates owned by different nationalities. It appears that throughout the 1930's European-owned estates still relied very largely on Indian labour and even in 1940 four-fifths of employed workers on European estates were Indians. Conversely, over 90 per cent. of Indian estate labourers were on European-owned

[1] After 1934 Chinese wages were again consistently above those of Indian estate workers and fluctuated in the same direction but within much wider limits than the wages of Indian workers.

Table III

Workers Employed at the end of each year on Malayan Rubber Estates, 1934–40

(Thousands)

	1934	1935	1936	1937	1938	1939	1940
South Indians	179	175	184	236	209	214	218
Chinese	86	62	65	77	61	75	88
Javanese	12	9	10	13	9	12	14
Others	25	18	18	23	17	23	31
Total	302	264	277	349	296	342	351

Malayan labour statistics improved considerably after 1933; in particular, reports covering the whole of Malaya were issued by the Labour Department, and rubber estate employment came to be shown separately after 1934. The table above refers to employment on rubber estates of 100 acres or more in the whole of Malaya; Table I, p. 225 above, refers to employment on estates employing ten or more workers in the S.S. and F.M.S.

estates. Substitution of Chinese for Indian labour, though much discussed, did not take place on any significant scale. Chinese-owned properties continued to be worked almost entirely with Chinese labour.

The reduced level of production in 1935 and the prohibition of new planting adversely affected estate employment. To prevent the emergence of unemployment, the Labour Department greatly restricted the number of assisted passages, which were definitely confined to former estate labourers and to close relatives of Indians working in Malaya. There was, however, a substantial influx of unassisted passengers many of whom were labourers, and this resulted in some unemployment which was reflected in an increase in the number of non-working dependants. At the end of 1934 South Indians in all places of employment (including Government departments) numbered 229,000, with 92,000 non-working dependants; at the end of 1935 the figures were 231,000 and 106,000 respectively—some newly-arrived immigrants had not yet been absorbed in employment and swelled the number of unemployed dependants. Wages declined slightly during the year, and the payment of 35 cents (for morning work) became general. Some 6,000 Indian labourers were repatriated at their own request, mostly old, homesick people and some workers who were unable to find employment and preferred to return to India rather than wait for a vacancy. The liberal repatriation policy was attacked in Malaya on the grounds that it led to abuses by some people who succeeded in obtaining frequent free passages both ways, while in India it was criticised as evidence of the readiness with which Malaya discarded Indian workers after they were of no further use. In actual fact the Labour Department seems to have handled the repatriation of Indian labour with considerable discretion. There was no case for retaining Indians in Malaya against their wish solely because they were unable to afford a return passage.

There were some signs of a deterioration in the relations between the Malayan and Indian authorities. The 1935 *Annual Report* of the Malayan Labour Department was drawn up in a new form and carried a long review of the history of Indian migration to Malaya, which it ascribed predominantly to historical and political reasons. It was suggested that if need arose Malaya could easily obtain from China and Java all the labour she required. The comparatively favourable conditions of the Indian labourer in Malaya against Madras were also stressed, while the growing number of unassisted deck passengers, and the increasing proportion of labourers who looked on Malaya as their permanent domicile, were quoted as evidence of the views of those most intimately concerned on the relative amenities of Malaya and Madras.[1]

On the recommendation of the United Planting Association of Malaya (which had been pressed by the Controller of Labour), Indian wages were raised to 40 cents for morning work in March 1936. The increase was decided after the price of rubber had been firmly established at over 7*d.* It will be recalled that in July 1930 when standard wages were reduced from 50 to 40 cents, the agency houses undertook to restore the reduction when the price of rubber returned to 7*d.* As this level was actually exceeded for a short time in 1934, and again early in 1936, wages should accordingly have been restored to 50 cents. Admittedly output was restricted and the price of 7*d.* was thus less profitable than it would have been under unrestricted production; on the other hand, costs had been greatly reduced and the price was certainly more remunerative than it had been in July 1930.

In 1936 assisted immigration was further curtailed and confined to labourers returning from holidays in India. Thousands of applicants for assisted passages had to be refused. When the

[1] The revised form of the report was retained in subsequent years, with even greater emphasis on the relative conditions of Malaya and Madras. The 1936 *Annual Report* pointed out that much of the Madras criticism of free emigration came from interested parties, and reproduced a letter from a Madras paper in which an indignant *zemindar* complained that the purchase of workers together with the land was no longer a safe procedure as the labourer could escape to Malaya. The state of affairs implied had been noted in 1931 by the Royal Commission on Labour in India.

rubber boom during the winter of 1936–37 was followed by a period of high releases a stringency developed in the labour market. Indian wages were raised to 45 cents in January 1937, and to 50 cents in April, by which time rubber was over 1*s.* 1*d.*, which was almost double the price at which wages should have been restored to 50 cents. All these changes refer to *de facto* rates as paid throughout Malaya on the recommendation of the United Planting Association ; the standard wages in key areas had remained at 40 cents since 1930, losing all contact with reality.

Chinese earnings rose sharply to about 80 cents—one dollar by the spring of 1937. While wide fluctuations in Chinese earnings were a familiar feature in Malaya, more unusual—indeed unknown before 1937—was a series of lightning strikes, culminating in the cessation of work by about 10,000 Chinese tappers in March 1937. These strikes occurred principally on the smaller Chinese estates and on some medium holdings employing Chinese tappers. The workers felt that they were not being given a fair share in the prosperity of the industry, and struck for higher piece rates. Most of the demands were reasonable, officers of the Labour Department and of the Chinese Protectorate intervened, and a settlement was soon reached. The medium holdings were involved to a minor extent only, and the tappers' demands were largely informally conceded.

In comparing the wages and earnings of the mid-1930's with those of the late 1920's, the intervening fall in the cost of living should be remembered. Indian wages of 50 cents in 1937 represented substantially better real wages than the same rates fixed in 1929. The index of the cost of the Tamil food budgets on St. John's Island quarantine station which had been around 140–150 in the late 1920's (1914 = 100) stood around 85 in 1936–37. The price of rice continued low, and it was officially estimated at the time that an unmarried Indian labourer would spend only about one-tenth of his daily wage on rice. Many items in the Indian labourer's budget which were still luxuries in 1928 had become semi-necessities by 1937, and the Indian authorities suggested a recalculation of the original budgets on the basis of which the standard wages of 1929 had been fixed. This request was not unjustified, but it admitted implicitly that in spite of the severe setback of the slump the standard of life of the Indian labourer in Malaya had improved substantially between 1928 and 1937.

IV

In December 1936 and January 1937 the late Mr. Srinivasa Sastri, an Indian Privy Councillor, visited Malaya on behalf of the Indian Government 'to examine Indian labour conditions in Malaya and to make recommendations as to improvements desirable and whether assisted emigration should be permitted'. Mr. Sastri's report [1] is perhaps the best and fairest concise account on the subject. While emphasising the much higher standard of living of Indian workers in Malaya,[2] Mr. Sastri proposed certain specific improvements, the case for most of which seemed strong. He suggested a restoration of standard wages to 50 cents, the abolition of the distinction between key districts and the rest of the country, stronger representation of Indians on the Indian Immigration Committee, and a firm resistance by the authorities against the recurrent practice of paying only three-quarters of the minimum wage for morning work. Mr. Sastri also suggested the complete cessation of recruited assisted emigration which, in spite of all precautions, was still conducive to abuses.

The most important single issue reviewed was that of the continuation or cessation of non-recruited assisted emigration, and on this question the contentions of the Malayan authorities were largely, though not wholly, supported. Mr. Sastri concluded definitely in favour of the maintenance of this form of assisted emigration with certain safeguards, chiefly on the grounds that conditions on Malayan estates were so much better than in rural Madras. His words may be quoted in full: 'Where a man before whom all the facts have been placed as clearly as possible, elects to forgo the advantage of living in his own place in order to obtain certain other advantages in another place, I doubt whether any government can with propriety forbid him to make that choice so long as the government is satisfied that the new conditions are reasonably good. I have described the general conditions which I found in Malaya, and consider that there is no justification for preventing Indian labour from emigrating there. I have made certain suggestions, particularly with reference to wages, which should receive the close attention of the authorities in Malaya.

[1] *Report on Indian Labour Conditions in Malaya*, Delhi and Kuala Lumpur, 1937.

[2] 'Improvements can be suggested and effected, but allowing for the fact that the labourers are away from their own country, and that a new climate proves in many cases uncongenial, they are able to lead, particularly when accompanied by their wives and children, a healthy, respectable life, and aspire to a standard distinctly higher than they could attain in their own villages.' *Report*, p. 4.

If those improvements are forthcoming I am clear that permission to emigrate should be continued. That being so, it would be harsh as well as unreasonable that a man may go only if he is prepared to bear the cost of emigration himself. It is precisely those who are not in a position to meet their expenses who will be most anxious to emigrate.'[1]

The wages paid to Indian workers (though not legal standard rates) were raised to 50 cents soon after Mr. Sastri left Malaya, but the composition of the Indian Immigration Committee was left largely unchanged; nor was the distinction abolished between key districts and the rest of the country. The under-payment and under-employment condemned by Mr. Sastri reappeared in 1938. The abolition of recruited assisted emigration came about almost automatically through the severe curtailment of assisted immigration necessitated by the depression which set in towards the end of 1937, and which was soon followed by a complete prohibition of all forms of assisted emigration.

A few months after the publication of the Sastri report, Malayan labour conditions (as well as those in other rubber-producing territories) were again subject to outside examination, this time by Mr. H. B. (now Sir Harold) Butler in his capacity as Director of the International Labour Office.[2] He also was impressed by the exceptionally high labour and health standards of Malaya: '. . . the Government has been able to develop health and education to a point attained nowhere in the East except in Japan . . . and the country can afford to its inhabitants a standard of living substantially higher than in most Eastern territories.'[3] He referred explicitly to the contrast with conditions in India. But while the favourable standards of Malaya (and to a lesser extent of the other rubber-producing countries) were clearly and fairly set out, the precariousness of the position was also emphasised. Sir Harold Butler stressed the difficulty of maintaining or advancing social conditions in face of the periodic failure of the demand for primary products, and of the resulting price fluctuations of which rubber provided the outstanding example. As the repatriation of migrant labourers was often accompanied by hardship to workers who had lost touch with their villages, Sir Harold Butler urged an extension of subsistence farming for estate labourers.

Before the end of 1937 another slump had set in, lending topical

[1] *Report on Indian Labour Conditions in Malaya*, p. 24.
[2] *Problems of Industry in the East* (1938).
[3] *Problems of Industry in the East*, p. 48.

interest to Sir Harold Butler's remarks. The price of rubber was falling fast by October, and though rates of release continued high until the end of the year substantial reductions were expected. After November assisted immigration was sharply curtailed and assistance practically confined to workers returning from visits to India. In the face of the severe reduction in releases in 1938, this did not suffice to prevent unemployment, nor to maintain wages. Indian workers had again to be repatriated on a large scale; some 30,000 Indians (including minors) were repatriated during 1938. Unemployment was heavy among Chinese, and also among Indians unwilling to claim repatriation.[1]

In May 1938 Indian estate wages (men's) were reduced by 10 per cent. to 45 cents. The Controller of Labour also announced that he would not insist on employers offering a minimum of 24 days' work, and an offer of 20 days would be regarded as sufficient; this official toleration of under-employment was of course contrary to the labour legislation in force. The combined effect of these two decisions was a 25 per cent. reduction in earnings. A circular by the United Planting Association of Malaya in June called for a further reduction in wages to 40 cents in August, while the R.G.A. was pressing for a decrease to 35 cents; in conjunction with the reduction in days worked, this last demand implied a fall in earnings of about 42 per cent. since the beginning of the year. Demands were also put forward for a re-introduction of the payment of three-quarters of the daily wage to tappers.

No further measures were, however, taken after the 10 per cent. cut in wages and the official consent to under-employment,[2] chiefly because the Indian Government took drastic action, and without consulting the Malayan authorities prohibited emigration as from 15th June. The prohibition applied to persons wishing to emigrate for the purpose of unskilled work (defined as persons under contract to work for hire), or who were assisted to emigrate; under the Indian Emigration Act of 1922 the control of the authorities was confined to these emigrants. The prohibition therefore covered all would-be emigrants seeking assisted passages, as well as holders

[1] While little was done to alleviate distress among these classes, some public works were undertaken to relieve unemployment. Some of the local budgets (including that of the F.M.S.) were unbalanced (or rather no effort made to eliminate the deficit which was emerging), also with the definite idea of improving employment. Even though they did not prove sufficient, these were great steps forward since 1930–33.

[2] Outside key areas there were instances of part-payment for morning work. The Indian Agent obtained an early withdrawal of the official consent to under-employment, but for the remainder of the year there was a tendency to offer less than the statutory minimum number of days' work.

of bearer-letters or identification certificates from their estate managers even though they wished to pay their own fares, as such letters and certificates were held to be evidence of an agreement to work for hire. Workers returning from a holiday in India, frequently intending to rejoin their families in Malaya, were not allowed to leave, as many had identification certificates and were thus affected by the ban. Shortly after the imposition of the ban, legislation was passed in India authorising the Government to prohibit all forms of emigration. In practice this meant that the authorities could stop all deck passengers from proceeding to any specific destination; this, however, was not applied to Malaya. The Indian decision aroused much protest in Malaya. The authorities emphasised the hardship which was inflicted on many stranded workers who were not allowed to return to Malaya; they also stressed that the unilateral decision was contrary to the agreements (embodied in unpublished official correspondence) in force between the Indian and Malayan Governments. But while the Indian decision was abrupt and high-handed, so had been the action of the Malayan authorities in acquiescing in a severe cut in wages and earnings of Indian estate workers, without agreeing to an Indian request which was put forward at the time for prior discussion.

After some months of mutual recrimination, a Malayan delegation proceeded to Delhi early in 1939 to negotiate the conditions of a resumption of assisted emigration. The discussions covered a wide range, including standard wages, prohibition of the sale of liquor on estates, vernacular education of Indians, representation of Indians on the various legislative bodies, and the employment of Indians in government service. Agreement was not reached by September 1939, and some of the points at issue were still the subject of official correspondence at the outbreak of the European war, and were then left in abeyance. The ban on emigration was not lifted and the flow of emigrants was restricted to unassisted passengers among whom there were few workers after 1938.

The events of 1938 revealed an undue readiness on the part of employers and of the authorities to shift a large part of the burden of a depression on to those least able to bear it. A 25 per cent. cut in earnings was imposed, and a reduction of over 40 per cent. seriously pressed for, after a few months of unfavourable prices which followed a period of considerable prosperity; moreover, it was certain that the price would rise again soon, as supplies were firmly controlled. Had there been a danger of a long-period decline of the Malayan rubber industry, a general reduction in money incomes would have been unavoidable, as the Straits dollar, being linked to sterling, could not be devalued. This, however, was a remote contingency in 1938.

The emigration ban and the increasing Congress pressure both on the Madras Government and on the Central Government led the Malayan authorities and planters to search for other potential sources of estate labour. Javanese were being increasingly employed on estates,[1] and shortly before the Japanese war legislation was enacted providing for the extension of the organisation of the Indian Immigration Fund to cover Javanese workers. Various plans (notably a system of subsidised passages) were being unsuccessfully canvassed for the organised immigration of agricultural labour from South China. Estate managers found that the direct employment of Chinese on piece-rates (as distinct from indirect employment through contractors) was more practicable than had been believed, and this was spreading. A few estates, chiefly in the northern Unfederated States, tried to employ more Malays, in one or two instances with considerable success.

The high prices and large exports of the two years before the outbreak of the Japanese war resulted in a gradual increase in Indian wages and earnings, and in a more rapid rise in Chinese earnings. The general shortage of labour was enhanced by the requirements of replanting ; the 1940 *Annual Report* of the Controller of Labour referred to the large though unspecified number of workers employed on replanting operations in that year. Indian wages, which had remained at 45 cents since May 1938, were restored to 50 cents in October 1939, raised to 55 cents in January 1941 and to 60 cents in April 1941. The last two increases were at first regarded as cost-of-living bonuses, but eventually as definite wage increases. Standard wages in key areas still remained nominally at 40 cents, and were thus unchanged for eleven years during which actual wages ranged from 20 cents in 1932 to 60 cents in 1941. Chinese earnings rose from around 55–65 cents at the outbreak of the war to over one dollar by the summer of 1941. During 1941 estate workers, principally Chinese, drifted in growing numbers to smallholdings where daily earnings of over one dollar by Chinese tappers were frequent by the spring of 1941. When in the late summer the price of uncouponed rubber rose to levels not attained since the 1920's, instances of record earnings of 2–3 dollars a day

[1] This is not shown fully in the Malayan labour statistics where Javanese are often included in 'other races'.

were reported. The sustained high level of the demand for labour was accompanied by considerable industrial unrest, much of it of political origin, such as the anti-British Congress propaganda among Indian labourers, or anti-war propaganda by communists among Chinese workers, which subsided after June 1941. Legislation providing for the registration of trade unions and for the establishment of machinery for voluntary arbitration was enacted in 1940, too late to exercise any influence on the course of events.

V

In Java real wages had been low before the mid-1920's when the rubber boom and the rising prosperity of the sugar industry contributed to relieve economic conditions on the greatly over-populated island. During the second half of the 1920's Javanese labourers earned about 60–80 guilder cents a day working on sugar, rubber or tea estates. This they could do while continuing to live in their native villages, and either they themselves or members of their families still cultivated a rice-plot. The collapse of sugar and rubber after 1929 altered the situation, especially as after the spring of 1931 the sugar industry in east Java suffered both through very low prices and the reduction in output under the Chadbourne scheme. In 1930 rubber estate workers (men) still earned 50 cents in west Java; by 1932 this had fallen to 15–20 cents. According to a British consular report [1] wages in some overcrowded districts had by 1932 fallen to 10 cents for a working day of 10 hours. Sir Harold Butler actually instanced daily wages of 4–9 cents in the worst affected districts of east Java. The cost of living also fell sharply but not in proportion to wages or earnings. The official cost-of-living index of the native population in Java (1928 = 100) averaged 51 in 1932 and 42 in 1933. The crowded labour market of Java was fed not only by a rapidly rising population and dismissed labourers from rubber and sugar plantations and from various government departments, but also by the stream of returning labourers (indentured and free estate labourers, as well as share tappers from native holdings) from the Outer Provinces.

In the Outer Provinces (chiefly in the East Coast of Sumatra) estate wages declined proportionately somewhat less than in Malaya, and much less than in Java, from about 45–47 guilder cents at the

[1] *Report on Economic Conditions in the Netherlands East Indies*, Board of Trade, Department of Overseas Trade, 1933.

end of 1929 to around 30–32 cents by the end of 1932. There were different rates for free and indentured workers, for first engagements and for re-engagements, while there were a number of arrangements for payments for holidays and the issue of rice. A decline of about one-third would indicate the order of magnitude of the reduction in money wage-rates generally. The various measures by the plantations of the Outer Provinces to retain their labour forces (chiefly in order to save repatriation charges and the expense of subsequent recruitment should conditions improve), such as free allotments for food cultivation and the transfer of workers from rubber to palm-oil estates, could touch only the fringe of the problem, and large-scale dismissals took place almost without interruption for three years from June 1930.

Until its complete disintegration the indenture system acted as a brake on the fall in wages. In 1931 legislation was passed providing for the gradual disappearance of indentured labour by compelling estates to employ a steadily rising minimum percentage of unindentured labour. Actually the system disintegrated much more rapidly than was provided for by law. In view of the intensity of the slump the estates became anxious to reduce their labour forces, whose indentures stipulated wages and conditions which could not be met after 1930, and efforts were successfully made to induce the labourers to break their contracts. The N.E.I. authorities insisted, however, on maintaining the workers' rights to free repatriation. In 1937 another ordinance was issued to accelerate further the disappearance of indentured labour.

The table on page 246 summarises the official employment figures on estates in the Outer Provinces, and shows the fluctuations in total estate employment, as well as the disintegration of the indenture system.

Between 1934 and 1941 estate wages in the N.E.I. were largely stable at the levels to which they had been reduced during the slump ; some of the starvation rates in central and eastern Java improved, but these did not greatly concern the rubber industry. Men's wages in the principal rubber-growing districts of Java remained at 18–20 guilder cents for a full day's work. In Sumatra rubber estate workers (men) were generally paid 32 cents for a nine-hour day. There were slight variations with different types of agreement, but these were of small importance, and within each category rates remained stable until 1941. In 1936–37 the N.E.I. Government made some attempts to improve estate wages but the recession of 1937 put an end to these intentions. As before, estates

Table IV

Estate Employment in the Outer Provinces of the N.E.I. at the end of each year, 1929–39

(Thousands)

	Indentured workers	Unindentured workers	Total
1929	406	115	521
1930	353	126	479
1931	203	156	359
1932	54	209	263
1933	25	210	235
1934	16	215	231
1935	17	243	260
1936	19	258	277
1937	30	309	339
1938	19	313	332
1939	7	327	334

The numbers cover all estate employment, of which rubber estates accounted for about one-fifth. During the depression the decline in employment was heaviest on the rubber and tobacco plantations. The long-period upward trend in certain branches of tropical agriculture, notably Sumatran palm-oil, explains the comparatively slight decline in employment from 1937 to 1938, against the much steeper fall in Malaya between these years.

in the Outer Provinces provided free housing for their labourers, while in Java the workers continued to live in their own villages.

On the native holdings of Sumatra and Borneo share tappers in 1928–29 were still earning around 80 cents or even one guilder a day. It was expected that should earnings decline substantially from these levels, the great majority of these share tappers would return to Java. By 1932 many continued to tap with daily earnings of 15–20 cents. Earnings of less than 10 cents were referred to in several of the official *N.E.I. Native Reports*. In spite of the considerable reflux of labour from the native districts of the Outer Provinces to Java, thousands of Javanese share-tappers and unemployed estate labourers or workers dismissed by the Public Works Department remained in the rubber-growing districts, either as wage-earners under one or other of the numerous wage systems to be found in the Outer Provinces, or as proprietors who had themselves acquired smallholdings. There are no precise data on this subject.

Hired labour on rubber-producing smallholdings was of minor importance during 1934–36, as the operation of the special export duty limited production to owner-tappers and their families. There was a sharp rise in smallholders' incomes in 1937 following the introduction of individual restriction, and the increased prosperity, together with the higher output, led to the resumption of production with hired labour. Wages and earnings of share tappers were high in the early part of 1937 and daily earnings of 60–80 guilder cents were reported. But until the outbreak of the Japanese war the bulk of the native output was derived from owner-tapped holdings.

VI

The dependence of estates in Ceylon on Indian labour is even greater than in Malaya. As well as tapping and routine field work, special works such as clearing and felling are in Ceylon generally carried out by Indian estate workers. As in Malaya, Indian immigrants were until comparatively recently assisted or unassisted. There is also a large settled population of Indian labourers which acts as an important source of estate labour. The arrangements for financing the movement of immigrant labour were, around 1929–30, broadly similar to those in Malaya. The Board of Indian Immigrant Labour corresponded roughly to the Indian Immigration Committee in Malaya, but its composition was less one-sided.

The Ceylon rubber industry employs only a minor proportion of the total Indian estate labour on the island and in many ways is secondary to tea. Statistics of estate labour do not distinguish between rubber and tea estates, and the employment or migration figures are thus of much less interest for our purpose than they were in Malaya, where they refer almost entirely to rubber estate labourers. Moreover, when there was no restriction on migration, the proximity and easy travel facilities to South India encouraged much movement of labour, and estate labourers frequently returned to South India for an annual holiday; migration figures are, therefore, of smaller economic significance than those of movement between Malaya and South India. Employed Indian estate workers on estates of ten acres or over numbered 540,000 at the end of 1929 and, according to an official estimate, of these approximately 100,000 were on rubber estates. They were employed on some 300,000 acres of the planted rubber area. The many small estates and the hilly country explain the lower acreage per labourer compared with Malaya.

Real wages were in 1929–30 much higher than in South India. Proximity to India also offers certain advantages to the South Indian labourer which to a large extent offset the appreciably lower wages and standards of housing and sanitation in Ceylon compared with Malaya. Ceylon thus had little difficulty in attracting from South India sufficient labour for all estate requirements.

Negotiations with the Government of India resulted in the Minimum Wage Ordinance of 1927. This legislation covered Indians only. There was some anxiety that the minimum wages would be jeopardised by increased employment of Singhalese, but this turned out to be unfounded. The minimum wages, which came into force early in 1929, were at different rates for up-country, mid-country and low-country estates, the daily rates for men being 54, 52 and 50 rupee cents respectively, with lower rates for women and children. The cost of living at high altitudes was somewhat higher, and the work more strenuous, hence this particular differentiation. These rates were identical for tea and rubber estate workers, and were the rates actually paid, though tappers generally earned more than the minimum rates. In order to give a greater measure of stability to the real wage of the labourer, the estates also had to issue, at a fixed price, seven-eighths of a bushel of rice per month for each adult male worker, with three-quarters of a bushel for women, and five-eighths for each working child. There was also an obligation to issue free of cost one-eighth of a bushel of rice every month for each non-working child of an adult man or working widow. There was also a statutory obligation on employers to offer six days' work a week, or wages in lieu. The machinery for varying the minimum wages and the issue price of rice was comparatively inelastic and the procedure lengthy.

By the end of 1929, with a Colombo price of rubber around 36–38 rupee cents per lb., many rubber estates were already in difficulties. The number increased rapidly during 1930 with the price steadily falling to 18–19 cents by September. From the spring of 1930 there was continuous agitation for a reduction in the minimum wages. These demands came mainly from rubber planters; the tea estates were also less prosperous than they had been, but their difficulties were less acute. In May 1931 money wages were reduced by 5, 4 and 3 cents for men, women and children; at the same time the issue price of rice was reduced from 6.40 to 4.80 rupees per bushel.[1] As these changes left the

[1] Since the beginning of 1930 the retail price of rice had been appreciably below the issue price, and by 1931 the difference was so great that even the reduction from 6.40 to 4.80 rupees did not close the gap. There were two reasons why all estate workers did not buy their rice from outside; first, many were notoriously unmindful of the future and preferred to buy their rice through the estates, where they did not have to pay cash but had the cost deducted from their wages, and secondly, pressure was often brought to bear on the labourer to induce him to continue to buy his rice through his

cash balance available to the labourer after expenditure on rice unchanged, this was regarded as an adjustment and not a cut in wages, and this interpretation was accepted by the Indian authorities. The reduction or adjustment was, however, considered insufficient in view of the depression, and substantial further decreases in money wages were gazetted in December. Minimum wages of adult men on mid- and low-country estates were reduced to 43 and 41 cents (with roughly corresponding reductions for women and children), with an unchanged issue price of rice of 4.80 rupees per bushel. Wages on up-country estates were not altered. The practice of paying only three-quarters of the minima for morning work made its appearance in 1931 and was spreading until the beginning of 1932, when it was challenged in the courts by the Indian Agent. It was finally declared illegal in February 1932. The judgment resulted in a great outcry and in demands for the abolition of minimum wage legislation. Less than six days' work was also being offered on many properties, but this was tolerated principally to prevent the closure of many of the smaller estates.

The price of rubber fell sharply in February–March 1932 and that of tea in April, and heavy dismissals of labour were accompanied by widespread agitation for the termination of statutory wage regulation. These demands were refused and the planters had to be content with another formal application in April for a reduction in wages. After much discussion and argument in Ceylon and after prolonged correspondence with the Indian authorities, the minimum rates were reduced, the rates for men being fixed at 41, 37 and 35 cents, with a reduced issue price of rice of 4 rupees. These rates did not come into force until May 1933, by which time the position of both rubber and tea estates had improved substantially and rates higher than the minimum wages were widely paid. In November men's minimum rates were raised to 46, 40 and 38 cents, the issue price of rice being left at 4 rupees.

Workers who between 1929 and 1933 consistently bought rice from their estates suffered only a comparatively small reduction in their wages. It is, however, also evident that the surplus cash left after paying for rice was in 1929 and 1930 much less than

estate. Nevertheless, an increasing number went outside for their rice, and their employers were left with unsold stocks. This resulted in much dissatisfaction. Some employers argued that it was contrary to the spirit of the discussions leading up to the minimum wage legislation that while at the times of high rice prices the employers made heavy losses on the rice they issued to their workers, the latter should be free to buy their supplies from outside whenever the market price fell below the issue price. As the depression progressed this dissatisfaction naturally increased.

that of an Indian worker in Malaya. Generally, it appears that while in normal times the Indian estate labourer in Malaya is noticeably better off than in Ceylon, the relative positions were reversed between 1931 and 1933. This was due to the preponderance of the tea industry in Ceylon, assisted by a minimum wage legislation covering the whole country, and the judicial decision against the payment of wages below the minima for morning work only. The proximity and easy access to South India may have also played a part. It was officially estimated that employment on rubber estates was roughly halved during the slump, from about 100,000 to 50,000 estate labourers; total estate employment declined from 540,000 at the end of 1929 to 430,000 at the end of 1933.

During 1934–41 the estate labour situation in Ceylon was characterised by a gradual return of money wages to the 1929 level, and by the repercussions of the Indo-Ceylonese political conflict over the discrimination against Indians in Ceylon. In 1934 the minimum rates for men were increased to 49, 43 and 41 rupee cents from the previous rates of 46, 40 and 38 cents, with corresponding changes in women's and children's minima; the issue price of rice was raised from 4 rupees to 4.80 rupees. These rates remained unchanged until the spring of 1939. The greater stability compared with Malaya again reflected the preponderance of tea in the Ceylon estate labour market; while the tea industry did not enjoy the same measure of prosperity as the rubber estates in 1937, it largely escaped the severe setback of 1938.

There were, however, considerable fluctuations in earnings. In 1935–36 and again in 1938 many rubber estates offered less than the statutory minimum of six days' work a week. The Indian Agent protested against this practice, which was difficult to eliminate, especially on the smaller properties, where in 1938 four days' employment a week was frequent. On many of these properties the labour force was largely settled and the closure of the estate would have inflicted much hardship on the labourers. Suggestions for the payment of only three-quarters of the daily rates for tappers also recurred, but were successfully resisted by the Indian Agent, who was supported by some of the leading planters.

In 1939 men's minimum wages on mid- and low-country estates were raised to 47 and 45 cents without alteration in the issue price of rice. This increase restored minimum wages to the 1931 rates, which in turn represented the 1929 level, adjusted for the reduction in the issue price of rice from 6.40 to 4.80 rupees a bushel. Another increase in the minima was agreed early in 1940, when men's rates were raised to 54, 52 and 50 cents, which were the 1929 rates ; the issue price of rice was still left unchanged at 4.80 rupees.

The various changes were generally effected in agreement with the Indian authorities, and assisted immigration was resumed after the slump and continued until 1939. The immigrants were practically all returning estate workers and their relatives. Serious disagreement developed, however, over various discriminatory measures against Indians in Ceylon. When in 1939 the Ceylon Government dismissed many Indian employees and workers and replaced these by Singhalese, the Indian Government prohibited the emigration of unskilled workers to Ceylon. This step was welcomed by the nationalists in Ceylon, who had been pressing for some time for the exclusion of Indian immigrants. The rubber and tea estates, though apprehensive of the future, were not greatly concerned, as they were not short of labour at the time. The most immediate sufferers were the many workers on a temporary visit to Madras who were not allowed to return, whether or not they were prepared to pay their own passages ; the numbers stranded were much greater than those affected by the 1938 ban on emigration to Malaya.

The employed estate workers in Ceylon (of whom, it will be remembered, only about one-fifth were on rubber plantations) numbered 438,000 at the end of 1933 ; 477,000 at the end of 1935 ; 463,000 at the end of 1938 and 435,000 at the end of 1941. This last figure was one per cent. below that of 1933, the lowest reached during the depression. These fluctuations in estate employment were much less marked than those in Malaya. Rubber and tea restriction reduced the demand for labour, and even the high releases in 1937 could be satisfied by a comparatively small increase in the labour force, together with fuller employment of the existing force. Assisted immigrants were called on only to replace wastage, and even this was not possible after the ban on emigration in 1939. Estate labour was said by planters to have been sufficient for all requirements throughout 1940 and in the early months of 1941.[1]

The labour situation became tense towards the end of 1941. The virtual de-restriction of rubber and tea, together with the gradual wastage of the labour force, brought about an increasing stringency. The military reverses of January–March 1942, followed

[1] Ceylon rubber exports had fallen far below the permissible amount well before the development of the labour shortage, and the explicit admission that estate labour was not scarce until the autumn of 1941 was tantamount to admitting that the basic quota was in excess of Ceylon's capacity.

by air raids on Ceylon, resulted in heavy emigration from Ceylon to India and this aggravated the shortage. Negotiations were initiated for a temporary migration in 1943 of Indian estate workers to Ceylon but these again failed on the apparently intractable issue of the political status of Indians in Ceylon.

Money earnings had an impressive career. Following a special enquiry into Indian budgets in the autumn of 1941, men's minimum wages were raised by 3 cents to 57, 55 and 53 cents, with corresponding adjustments in women's and children's minima; the issue price of rice remained at 4.80 rupees. In 1942 the cost of living rose sharply; while basic wages remained unchanged, a special cost-of-living bonus was added, varying with the soaring official cost-of-living index. By mid-1944 the bonus for adults was at the daily rate of 46 cents; an up-country estate worker's (man) wage was 1.03 rupees, of which the bonus represented 46 cents; for women the bonus was about one-half of the wage. In August 1944 it was proposed to abolish the differentiation between up-, mid- and low-country wage-rates, and also to consolidate the basic wage and the cost-of-living bonus. The distinction between up-, mid-, and low-country wages was abolished as from August 1945. The basic wage and the cost-of-living allowance do not appear to have been legally consolidated, but they are regarded as consolidated in practice. At present (January 1947) men's wages are 1.34 rupees, of which the bonus accounts for 77 cents. The actual wages are very generally identical with the minimum rates.

The labour situation in the smaller producing territories approximated generally in various degrees to that in one or other of the major producing territories. In French Indo-China the estates relied largely on migrant Annamese and Tonkinese labourers; the situation was somewhat analogous to that in Sumatra. In the 1930's many of the labourers were still indentured. In 1932 the Government consented to a reduction of the minimum wage from 40 piastre cents to 32 piastre cents (from 4 to 3.2 francs) for labourers renewing their contracts. From 1932 to 1940 wages remained largely stable, with wage-rates around 32–35 piastre cents (3.2–3.5 francs) for a working day of nine to ten hours; free rice and other allowances, including a state-operated provident fund, represented another 8–10 cents.[1] The sparsely populated red-soil districts continued to

[1] One franc was worth about 10–12 Straits cents in 1934–36; the successive French devaluations brought it down to about 5 cents in 1938. Wages in the N.E.I. and in French Indo-China were much below the Malayan rates which were paid for a shorter working day.

rely on migrant Annamese and Tonkinese workers, many of whom were still indentured. The authorities exercised a close control over the working conditions of the indentured workers. The grey-soil estates were in densely populated districts and most of the labourers continued to live in their own villages.

In British North Borneo no completely satisfactory solution of the labour problem was reached before the outbreak of the Pacific war. No Indians were employed, and the estates relied on Chinese labour, or on Javanese workers recruited direct in Java or through Singapore, and in some districts on local Malay or Dyak labourers.

In India the estate labour situation is somewhat analogous to that in Java, with the labour supply close to the estates in the neighbouring villages.

CHAPTER 16

DEVELOPMENTS IN TECHNIQUE

AS already shown, the main processes of rubber production are essentially simple. Nevertheless, there have been important developments since the 1920's, some of which were a major factor in the reduction in estate costs during the depression of 1929–33. After 1934, however, regulation resulted in a retardation of the application of improved techniques to estate production, chiefly through restriction of output and the prohibition of new planting. At the end of the period, war conditions, excess profits tax at 100 per cent. and the fact that some of the experimental results were provisional, meant that little of the increased knowledge was applied. In the following discussion attention will be concentrated on estate practice, since (as will later be shown) no reliable information about technical progress on smallholdings is available, while the various research institutes and stations extended virtually no assistance to smallholders.

I

Some of the technical changes which took place in the rubber industry during the depression were intensifications of long-period trends towards greater efficiency ; there had, for instance, been a steady increase in the acreage supervised by each estate manager or assistant. Before 1914, 300–400 acres per European was regarded as a normal figure in Malaya ; by 1928–29 it was around 600–800 acres, while by the end of 1932 it had doubled again.

There were, however, other developments, which were more nearly changes in kind rather than of degree. Improved systems of tapping were of some importance, as tapping costs were about 75–80 per cent. of direct f.o.b. costs, and exercised a direct influence on the volume of estate output. A change widely introduced in 1929 and 1930 was the reduction in tapping tasks. This was based on the realisation that more latex could be obtained from a given area by the concentration of tapping into the early morning hours when latex flows most freely. It resulted in higher yields per acre and thereby in a reduction in indirect costs. Although it often meant slightly higher tapping costs per lb. (as the total latex brought in by each worker decreased slightly, and with the larger number of tappers the quality of tapping deteriorated), this was offset by employing the tapper on other work during the hour or two set free.

Much was expected from the introduction of rotational systems of tapping. The most popular was the ABC system under which one-third of the estate is rested while the other two-thirds are tapped. It enabled the estates to reduce the tapping force (and often the entire labour force) by one-third, and it was believed that after an initial fall the eventual decline in total yields would be only slight. Before 1933 there were, however, no carefully controlled experiments. A series of well-designed experiments was started by the Rubber Research Institute of Malaya in the mid-1930's to ascertain the economics of the reduction of tapping intensities, especially from the standard alternate daily tapping on half-circumference, to 'half ABC', i.e. alternate daily tapping on half-circumference with one-third of the estate rested. The Institute at first favoured the latter system, but subsequently reversed this recommendation, as it was found that the fall in yields was in most instances almost proportional to the reduction in tapping intensity. Double-cut tapping systems represented another attempt to reduce costs. By reducing the proportion of the time spent by the tapper in walking from tree to tree, substantial economies could be effected. By doubling the number of cuts on each tree whenever the tree was tapped and increasing the period of rest between the tapping days, the intensity of tapping (the total number of cuts of a given length per annum) remained unaffected. This system generally resulted in a slight loss of crop against a substantial saving in tapping costs per lb., particularly on hilly estates.

An interesting and potentially important development in the later 1930's was the notable success of a tapping system known as the 'fourth daily full spiral' under which the trees are tapped every fourth day, but the tapping cut—a spiral cut around the entire circumference of the tree—is double the length of the standard system, notably the half alternate daily method, under which the trees are tapped on one-half the circumference every other day. Bark consumption is equal under the fourth daily and the alternate daily systems; it may be less under the former when one or two months' rest is introduced. The method was evolved by the powerful and progressive Socfin Company (Société Financière des Caoutchoucs), and successfully practised on a commercial scale on its estates by the mid-1930's; by 1936 three-quarters of the mature estate area of French Indo-China was said to be tapped on this system. The system had been introduced into the experiments of the Rubber Research Institute, where it proved very successful. The worker tapped fewer trees daily, but spent more of his time in the actual tapping operations. Reflecting the higher output per worker, tapping costs per lb. on fully mature areas were generally 30 to 40 per cent. lower on the fourth daily than under the alternate daily system, while the actual yields per acre were higher. The method also reduced supervision costs, since the area tapped on any given day was only about one-half of that under the standard systems. The reduction in the size of the labour force required also resulted in savings in many other directions, such as medical and housing expenses. There were some doubts about the long-period effects of the system on the growth of the tree, and on the rate of bark renewal; the experiments of the Rubber Research Institute of Malaya suggested that the growth of tappable but not fully mature trees would be slightly retarded. It could, however, be safely recommended even on young trees for a few years, and on fully mature trees for longer periods. The system has considerable potentialities; in 1940–41 its more rapid acceptance was retarded by the operation of 100 per cent. excess profits tax and by the conservatism of the planting community and of the agency houses, but in 1946 the shortage of labour in Malaya led to its widespread introduction on European estates.

The changed attitude to weeding and eradication of disease resulted in important changes in estate practice, which contributed substantially to the reduction in costs during the depression. Until about the mid-1920's clean weeding was a cardinal article of faith of most estate managers. The serious adverse effects of this expensive system were beginning to be realised by about 1925, but as late as 1930 it was common on most Malayan estates. The disadvantages of clean weeding, particularly its effect on soil fertility, principally through erosion, have already been indicated in discussing the cultivation methods of smallholders.[1] It had been adopted by the estates in the belief that it would reduce the spread of disease (which turned out to be erroneous) and eliminate the competition of other growths for the available plant food (which was far more than offset by the adverse effects on the total supply of plant food). It was also held that clean weeding reduced the cost of supervision, and that it kept out noxious animals, which was true but could have been achieved by less costly and disadvantageous methods. When the deleterious effects of clean

[1] Above, pp. 58–59.

weeding, especially soil erosion, became evident, various devices were tried to deal with them but without much success and at considerable cost. Actually on many estates the results of clean weeding were so harmful that no remedial measure short of replanting held out any prospects. Eventually an increasing number of estates throughout the East adopted a policy of selective weeding, retaining such natural cover as sprang up between trees, and eliminating only definitely noxious growths, or those severely competitive with rubber. This was usually cheaper than clean weeding, and on most estates had distinctly beneficial effects.

A severe blow was struck against the theory of clean weeding (and its corollary clean clearing) when in 1932 the R.R.I.M. announced the preliminary results of some experiments which had been in progress since 1929. In the words of the Director, the results led to an overthrow of the established views on the deadly and widely prevalent root diseases, the worst enemies of the rubber tree in the East. The advocates of clean weeding and clean clearing had argued that the removal of growths other than the rubber tree would interfere with the progress of the diseases by reducing the points of contact through which these could spread.[1] The experiments revealed that this view rested on a misconception of the nature of the root diseases. These were now invariably found to spread most rapidly among the long, straight, interlaced roots of rubber trees on clean-weeded areas, while the mass of roots and rootlets of a dense cover barred the progress of the rhizomorphs (underground growths by which the disease spreads); it was found that the spread of the disease varied inversely with the quantity of living roots in its path. These findings also explained (though this was not stated) the lower incidence of root diseases on smallholdings, which had never spent money on combating them. Previous theories advocated by the Institute itself were shown to have been false, and the recommendations based on these as recently as 1930 to have been diametrically opposite to what now emerged as the correct treatment.[2] In the words of the 1933 *Annual Report*

[1] The following quotation from the 1929 *Annual Report* of the Institute provides an instance: 'It is well known that root diseases spread with greater rapidity when the soil is under cover crops than when such protection is not provided, owing to the moist conditions and to the fact that these diseases are spread by the root systems of the cover crop.'

[2] It also emerged that, in Malaya at any rate, the parasitic rhizomorphs were not saprophytic, that is they could not draw nourishment from dead tissue. This discovery was of considerable practical value, as it enabled producers to dispense with the practice of digging over at great expense at least the diseased patches and often the entire area to be planted.

of the R.R.I.M.: 'The progressive undermining of the classical root-disease theories which had marked the course of our root investigation in 1931–32 culminated during the year in a complete revolution in the views on the root-disease situation as a whole.'

The substitution of selective for clean weeding was carried a long step further by the advocates of the so-called forestry method of cultivation. These argued that the *Hevea* was essentially a forest tree and that therefore silvicultural methods were most suitable for its cultivation. This implied the toleration, and indeed the encouragement, of a dense natural cover from which only certain specifically undesirable growths would be eliminated. In practice the predominant cover would be a stand of *Hevea* seedlings, as seeds of *Hevea* would, naturally, be most numerous on rubber estates and, being shade-resisting, could grow under mature rubber. With care in thinning out the cover before it got out of hand and by selective weeding with attention to such factors as optimum conditions of humidity and soil temperature, it should be possible to reproduce very nearly the forest cycle of growth and decay characteristic of the jungle; in particular, the nitrogen supply of the soil could be fully maintained without expensive mechanical or chemical treatment. Thus ideal conditions for the growth of the rubber tree and of bark renewal could be ensured at far lower cost than on the majority of estates run on orthodox lines. Moreover, as some of the seedlings of the cover became tappable they would replace casualties among the old stand.

In certain directions the advocates of forestry overstated their case. The fact that the *Hevea* was originally a jungle tree was irrelevant, as all plant products of agriculture and horticulture had originally grown wild. This, however, reflected only on the presentation of the argument, and not on its merits. Again, two aspects of the forestry methods of cultivation require differentiation: forestry as a method of soil management, and as a system for ensuring the economic replacement of the old stand. The rejuvenation and replacement of the stand by tapping seedlings which had been part of the cover is of more doubtful value than forestry as a method of soil conservation and management. This method would probably result in low yields per tree and per tapper, as well as in slow growth, and might not be profitable with a high cash expenditure on wages, an aspect insufficiently emphasised by the supporters of forestry. Moreover, it might be difficult to obtain the advantages of high yields from budded stocks or selected seeds under such conditions. Again, the forester is concerned with a low-value crop of slow growth, the economic basis of whose production differs in many respects from rubber growing.

In the controversy the R.R.I.M. gave a large measure of qualified support to forestry methods. According to its 1931 *Annual Report*: 'There is every indication that the planting practice of the future will be along forestry lines, in which the nitrogen supply of the soil is nicely regulated through the effect on the selective growth of natural covers on the volume and nature of vegetable débris reaching the soil, and the light, heat and moisture conditions under which it decays. The pioneer work in this direction has been so successful that however long the establishment may take, we may regard ourselves at the point of a new departure.'

After 1934 with the prohibition of new planting, interest in the forestry controversy slackened, though the argument was rekindled intermittently. The issue was still unresolved in 1941. As a method of estate rejuvenation (the replacement of the old stand by the best seedlings from the cover crop), it was regarded with increasing scepticism, especially in view of the established success of high-yielding material which resulted in both high yields and low tapping costs. As critics of clean weeding the advocates of forestry rendered considerable service, and the validity of their criticism of past planting practices came to be freely admitted.

After prices recovered from slump levels, the manuring of rubber estates was much discussed, but the economics of the question still remain doubtful.[1] As the amount of plant food included in the annual latex output is negligible, the manuring of rubber presents features altogether different from that of annual crops, which each year remove large quantities of plant nutrients from the soil. But while the latex crop does not make substantial demands on plant nutrients. the growth of the tree absorbs appreciable amounts of plant food, The annual leaf formation also uses plant food, and if the leaf fall is washed away these nutrients are not returned to the soil. More important, at any rate in Malaya and Ceylon, is the loss of plant food through soil erosion. Apart from loss of plant nutrients,

[1] Those wishing to pursue this matter beyond the brief review of the following paragraphs may be referred to the various articles by Dr. W. B. Haines in the *Malayan Agricultural Journal* (especially in 1931), in the *Journal of the R.R.I.M.* (especially 1931–32), in the *Empire Journal of Experimental Agriculture* (especially January 1938), to the *Annual Reports* of the R.R.I.M., the *Quarterly Circulars* of the Ceylon Rubber Research Scheme, and to the frequent contributions of Dr. H. Ashplant to the *India-Rubber Journal* (especially in November 1937). Some of the best known manuring experiments were carried out by Mr. J. Grantham on the estates of the Sumatran plantation subsidiary of the United States Rubber Company, and the results published periodically in the *Archief voor de Rubbercultuur*.

the fertility status of estate soils may be low owing to an inherent lack of one or more of the main plant foods (nitrogen, phosphate or potash). The sustained high yields of smallholders' rubber, which is never manured, show that, apart from fertility losses through soil erosion or other results of unsuitable cultivation methods, manuring is not necessary. On smallholdings the dense ground cover has generally prevented soil erosion and the leaching away of nitrates through the direct impact of heavy rain, while the ample supply of vegetable débris restored the plant food absorbed by the growth of the trees and the annual leaf formation. The plant food requirements of rubber are much below those of annual crops, and the main task is to prevent loss of plant food through causes other than the annual harvest, and in this the smallholder has been more successful than the estate.

The still doubtful economics of manuring is bound up with the uncertainty of the physiological function of the latex in the tree. The rubber tree is grown not for its fruit, flowers, bark, roots, leaves, seeds or timber, but for its latex, an exceptional product whose place in the life of the tree is not clear, and this is a difficulty which affects many branches of plantation rubber research. Manuring does not directly stimulate the secretion of latex, but only improves the general condition of the tree, which in turn is likely to (but possibly may not) react favourably on the rate of bark formation, which in turn may result in better yields at a subsequent date. Bark renewal is most rapid during the year immediately following bark removal, and thus over the part of the tapping panel most recently tapped. In the normal course of events this only comes under the knife again after the conclusion of a full tapping cycle of about seven or eight years, so that the yield response cannot be fully gauged until then. In ordinary estate practice visiting agents and managers generally resolve on manuring when the annual girth increment has fallen below what they consider a standard rate for a given age of the trees, or if the foliage has an unhealthy appearance.[1] The experimental evidence on the economics of manuring gathered during the 1930's was conflicting, and the recommendations of the research stations on both the

[1] Moreover, under restriction, the cash value of the improved condition of the tree depends not only on the yield response and on the price and cost of rubber, but also on the methods of assessment and on future releases. As we have seen, in British North Borneo the estates secured higher assessments when using fertilisers; in Malaya no such provision was in force, but scale allowances were often granted to estate areas which though of less than minimum girth, showed a particularly healthy foliage. In such circumstances manuring could become profitable irrespective of yield response.

necessity of manuring and the actual contents of a manuring programme, were frequently reversed. All that could apparently be safely said by 1941 was that immature replanted rubber very generally needed complete fertilisers (manures incorporating nitrogen, phosphate and potash), while immature newly-planted rubber required little or none. The use of nitrogenous fertilisers appeared profitable on mature rubber on nitrogen-deficient soils, and that of phosphatic manures was probably remunerative through assisting the establishment of a leguminous cover. The last two propositions were somewhat tentative, while other recommendations for manuring mature rubber were so to an even greater degree. It is clear that the necessary use of manures is a weakness in estate practice [1] against the methods of smallholders, and is to a certain extent a confession of failure.

The relative merits of closer and wider planting densities received less attention than they deserved. There was a gradual tendency towards closer planting; the aim for fully mature seedling trees was a final stand of about 100–110 trees or even more, instead of 80–90 as formerly. The sustained high yields of the densely-planted smallholdings and the heavy losses of estate trees through root disease may have been responsible for the change. Both the R.R.I.M. and the leading N.E.I. experimental stations were conducting experiments to examine yields and tapping costs under different planting densities. It was noted that the relative profitability of the various planting densities depended on the relative yields over the life of the trees, on the price of rubber and on prime costs over the same period.[2] While the experiments had not been running sufficiently long (throughout the complete life of a stand of trees) to yield conclusive results, there was strong evidence that only on extreme and unrealistic assumptions of very low prices and high prime costs would areas planted as widely as was common in the 1920's prove most profitable.

In the 1930's a system known as avenue or hedge planting was developed in the N.E.I. This attempted to combine the high yields per acre of dense planting with the high yields per tree of

[1] Where applied on a large scale, manuring was often the heaviest item in the cost of cultivation and maintenance of the estate. In the future such high-yielding planting material may possibly be developed that the removal of latex will make such high demands on plant food reserves as to necessitate the use of fertilisers. Until such time it is difficult to accept the argument put forward in the *History of Rubber Regulation*: 'A more lavish expenditure on fertilisers to maintain the yield of old areas is also an increase in efficiency' (p. 150). Efficiency ought to mean the obtaining of results with least, not with most, expenditure of real resources.

[2] A more detailed discussion of this point will be found in Appendix D, below.

lower stands. Trees were planted very closely in rows, which in turn were far apart; in one instance, in each row trees were planted almost every three feet, while the rows (avenues) were 40 feet apart. This method gave a high density per acre (a final stand of about 300 trees), and it was expected that the roots would spread into the area between the rows, thus avoiding root competition and overcrowding, so that yields per tree would be high. Tapping costs would be lower as each tapper could also tap more trees than under more orthodox planting systems, since much less time was required for walking from tree to tree. Other, subsidiary, advantages were also claimed for this system, such as the reduction in the number of contour terraces to be constructed and kept up; again, the considerable distance between the avenues was expected to facilitate interplanting of food crops without interfering with the growth of the trees. This method certainly appears attractive, but no adequate yield data are available to support or disprove the claims put forward. Should it ultimately prove successful this planting method would strengthen the competitive position of estates against smallholdings (especially if combined with mechanisation; cf. p. 273, below), as it cannot readily be introduced on very small properties.

II

The establishment of superior planting material is the most important single branch of plantation research, since successful use of covers and of manures can at best raise yields (usually at considerable cost) only to the capacity of the trees as determined by their genetical constitution, while the development of high-yielding material affects the constitution of the trees. Moreover, for each individual planter the choice of planting material is the most important single decision, as it is irrevocable. Although the potentialities and importance of the selection and propagation of high-yielding material were becoming increasingly appreciated, progress was retarded by the depression, as most estates were more concerned with the immediate problem of survival than with long-term issues. In accordance with the wishes of the industry, the R.R.I.M., for example, largely suspended genetical research during the later stages of the slump. Some work on the selection and propagation of high-yielding material was, however, continued both in Malaya and the N.E.I.

The vegetative propagation of high-yielding planting material through budgrafting had been attempted since the early days of the industry. Substantial progress was recorded by 1930, even though many of the early clones were failures, either because the high-yielding properties of the mother tree could not be transmitted to the budded offspring, or because the latter developed undesirable secondary characteristics, such as poor bark renewal or poor resistance to wind or disease.

It is useful to recall the short history of the industry and the long life of the trees. The first clones in the N.E.I. were established in 1918, and a few trees tapped in 1922 ; Malaya followed three or four years later, and as late as 1929 very little was known of the performance under estate conditions of the various clones. Material capable of yielding 1,000 lb. per acre or more had been developed by 1928–30, but made no contribution to output before 1934. In 1932 the budded area of Malaya was estimated at around 150,000 acres and that of the N.E.I. at 260,000 acres. The great bulk of the area was still immature, and not more than one-fifth was expected to be in bearing even by 1935. Accordingly, comparatively few commercial tapping results from the newer budgrafted areas were available by the end of the 1930's. The clones developed around and after 1928 were a great improvement on the earlier types, but areas planted with these reached maturity only during and after 1934, and were generally left untapped for some years, since estates preferred to harvest the restricted crops from older areas. Available results show, however, that many of these newer clones were reliable and yielded very well, frequently 1,000–1,200 lb. per acre when fully mature, with occasional higher yields.[1] Throughout the 1930's better clones were constantly established in Malaya and the N.E.I. ; in 1938 the Head of the Botanical Division of the R.R.I.M. stated that several of the clones then developed would be capable of yielding 1,500–2,000 lb. per acre on maturity, while 1,000–1,200 lb. could be safely relied on from a number of well-known clones. Annual yields on good areas by the mid-1930's were around 1,000 lb. as against 500 lb. ten years previously ; rubber scientists were probably right in claiming that this was a unique achievement for a perennial crop, though, as regulation restricted output to about 300 lb. per acre, it was of somewhat limited immediate practical interest. The N.E.I. authorities were generally less confident ; in 1939 *De Bergcultures*, the journal of the West Java Rubber Experimental Station, still advised estates

[1] A useful and comprehensive review of the performance of budgrafted areas in Malaya and the N.E.I. can be found in the April 1938 *Quarterly Circular* of the Ceylon Rubber Research Scheme. An excellent and up-to-date summary of budgrafted yields is given in *Planting Material* (Kuala Lumpur, 1940) by R. O. Jenkins and R. J. Chittenden.

to use not less than twenty different clones in budgrafting extensive areas to reduce the risk of failure.[1] It was, however, clearly established that the poor performance of many of the earlier clones was due to inherent weakness of the clones, or to technical mistakes of planting or of budding, and not to the operation of grafting. Some clones had been established from trees the high yields of which were due to environmental reasons which could not be transmitted to their offspring, while others were planted on unsuitable soil, and yet others developed undesirable secondary characteristics. By the mid-1930's enough was known about the different clones greatly to reduce these risks.

The possibilities of genetical research were even greater than those of the development of budgrafting, since the latter attempts simply to propagate the best trees already in existence, while genetical work starts from the best available material from which it attempts to breed better types. Moreover, the planting of clonal seedlings (the genetically propagated offspring of high-yielding clones) requires no more attention than that of ordinary seedlings, and the budding operation is unnecessary. Much attention was therefore attracted in Malaya by the publication of a booklet [2] by the visiting agent and the resident scientist of the estates of the Prang Besar Company, in which the authors definitely favoured the use of clonal seedlings against budgrafts. This was a conclusion of particular interest as it came from the men responsible for the development of some of the best Malayan clones. The yields from clonal seedlings obtained on a Prang Besar property were striking. Average yields of about 900 lb. per acre were secured from six-year-old trees tapped according to standard commercial methods. The trees were clonal seedlings raised from seed from an isolation garden planted with the best Prang Besar clones. The authors contended that clonal seedlings from isolation gardens containing only high-yielding clones were not less reliable than the best budgrafted material, and that their freedom from undesirable secondary characteristics tilted the balance in their favour. The coefficient of variability in a population of clonal seedlings is much greater than in a population of budgrafts,[3] but it was claimed that the

[1] According to the R.R.I.M. there were about 10 clones which could be recommended with safety for large-scale planting in Malaya on suitable soils. It will be recalled that under the assessment rules in Malaya, scale allowances at the budgrafted rate were given to some 130 clones, which included many undoubted failures.

[2] *Planting Material*, by R. O. Jenkins and R. J. Chittenden.

[3] As the genetical constitution of all members of a clone is identical, yield variations among individual trees reflect environmental causes only, while among seedling trees variations may be due to heredity or to environment.

number of high-yielders was certain to be sufficiently great to ensure that selective thinning out would raise the yield of the area to that of the best budded rubber. The research stations, particularly the R.R.I.M., were reluctant to accept these claims. Planters were advised not to plant more than one-fifth of a new or a replanted area with clonal seedlings. The respective merits of the two classes of planting material (budgrafts and clonal seedlings) were still somewhat controversial in 1941. It is, however, certain that, whatever the commercial planting material of the future, scientific development will proceed along both lines ; new clones will be developed from high-yielding clonal seedlings, and clonal seedlings bred from high-yielding clones, and both sexual and vegetative propagation used to develop improved planting material.

III

There was considerable technical progress in directions other than planting and cultivation. Important economies in processing in estate factories took place during the depression. On most Malayan estates the cost of curing and smoking, which in the early 1920's had been around 5 cents per lb., was reduced from about 2–3 cents per lb. in 1929 to around 0·5 cents in 1932–33. This was again the combined results of wage cuts and of increased efficiency, the latter being more important. Inside the factory remarkable economies were achieved by the introduction of continuous sheeters, in which the latex coagulum passed without interruption from one pair of rollers to the next, the rollers being rearranged in line ahead formation, instead of side by side. By these and some other quite simple rearrangements great improvements were effected. Before the depression an hourly output of 500–600 lb. per battery was considered good. By 1932 about 2,000–3,000 lb. was not exceptional, and the factory labour force required for a given output was halved, or more than halved between 1930 and 1932. Further economies were achieved on many estates through the concentration in one central factory of processing formerly carried out in three or four separate buildings scattered over the property. In view, however, of the simple equipment used, the economies of large-scale operation are severely limited, and centralised factories for areas in excess of 5,000 acres have, so far, proved doubtful economic propositions. Higher transport costs of latex (which in its natural state consists of two-thirds water and only one-third rubber) from outlying fields to the factory and the additional expenses of the prevention of pre-coagulation seem to exceed any saving which would be achieved through large-scale operation. After the depression, there was further progress, chiefly through the general introduction of continuous sheeting batteries (often of improved models), and these ensured that in spite of the rise in wages, factory costs remained around 0·5 Straits cents per lb., against ten times that level in the early 1920's, when wages had been 10–20 per cent. lower.

As the result of the changes which have been reviewed, especially the abandonment of unnecessary methods of cultivation, there was a marked rise in physical productivity per worker on rubber estates. Quantitative estimates based on estate output and the employed population are subject to considerable limitations owing to the deficiencies of employment figures. For the F.M.S., however, it is possible to form a reasonably close estimate. Dividing the 1933 F.M.S. estate output by the official figure of employed workers on rubber estates (which became available for the F.M.S. from 1933), the annual output per employed worker was almost exactly 1·1 tons. This was an increase of about 60 per cent. over a 1929 figure of about 0·7 of a ton, calculated roughly from the somewhat incomplete employment data but reliable output figures of that year. As, however, the employment figure for 1933 was more complete than that of 1929, the actual increase in output per head was greater than shown by these figures; the increase in the average output per employed worker was probably of the order of 100 per cent. This is also indicated by the fact that while before the depression Malayan estates employed one worker to about five planted acres, by 1932 this had risen to about nine acres or more. The estimates of the average output refer to output per worker, not per tapper, and the employment figures include not only tappers and routine field workers, but also labourers engaged on new planting and replanting operations. In the 1920's probably only slightly over one-half of the estate labour force was engaged in tapping, perhaps one-eighth or one-tenth was in the factory, and with the exception of a few sundry workers, the rest were field workers, chiefly weeders. By 1932 tappers and factory workers comprised almost the whole of the labour force. Such field work as was still undertaken was carried out by these workers, mostly on days when tapping was not possible.

After 1934 restriction tended to retard the growth of output per head in varying degrees according to the rate of release, as the labour force could not be exactly adjusted to frequent changes in the degree of restriction. In this case output per worker depends largely on the permitted exportable amount. From July 1940 to June 1941, however, Malayan estate production (especially on European-owned properties many of which had part of their assessed acreage under immature replanted rubber) was nearly free from restriction at an average internal release of 92 per cent; and in spite of the effects of excess profits tax and of other special circumstances, it is of interest to calculate the output per worker on estates. Total Malayan estate production for the twelve months July 1940–June 1941 was 360,000 tons, while 351,000 workers were employed on rubber estates at the end of 1940. Output per worker thus averaged 1·03 tons, much the same as in 1933, when enforced economies were still general, whereas in 1940–41 labour was often wastefully used, there was much replanting (as well as some new planting in 1940) and European supervision was inadequate. Moreover, the returns of the employed workers had become somewhat more complete. These considerations suggest a strong underlying trend towards a higher output per employee.

IV

During the depression great efforts were made, chiefly through the R.G.A., to stimulate absorption of rubber, especially in uses other than tyres. In certain directions, such as rubber flooring, it was also necessary to make up for ground lost through the high prices of the 1920's.

Not much headway was made with rubber roads, in spite of efforts to popularise them. Even at 2*d.* per lb. rubber was still a more expensive material than asphalt, while the laying of rubber roads was also costly. Attempts to construct roads with a mixture of latex and cement, instead of laying rubber blocks, raised a number of technical difficulties. Moreover, the general adoption of the pneumatic tyre reduced an important advantage of rubber roads in that the task of shock absorption was transferred from the road to the tyre. Nevertheless, some of their advantages, notably reduced vibration and some diminution of noise, still remain and no doubt they will eventually become more widely adopted, especially in big cities. Greater success attended the publicity for extending the use of rubber in other fields, such as upholstery. This propaganda, together with the sharp fall in the price of rubber and the secular trend towards increased rubber consumption, helped to maintain absorption during the depression in uses other than tyres.

The absorption of rubber in latex form showed signs of development during these years. The dry rubber equivalent of latex exports totalled 3,300 tons in 1926, 5,000 tons in 1929 and 15,700 tons in 1933. By 1940 it was close on 45,000 tons. Increasing quantities were used in the form of sponge rubber, chiefly in upholstery which was the only significant new use of rubber (outside the military field) during this period, but one with great potentialities. At present (January 1947) latex shipments are severely limited by loss or destruction of the necessary equipment in Malaya and Sumatra, but there are indications of a further rapid increase in this demand.

The extended use of latex depended first on the development of colloid chemistry, and the rapid advances in this field during the 1920's were reflected in the rise in the number of patents taken out for the use of latex, which in Great Britain rose from fourteen in the three years 1920–22 to 289 for 1931–33. The cost of rubber in latex form is almost necessarily higher than that of sheet rubber, because the dry rubber content of natural latex is some 3½ lb. per gallon, and the freight on the dry rubber content is thus about treble that of the equivalent amount of rubber in sheet form. In 1939 the cost of rubber shipped in bulk in latex form was about 1½*d.* per lb. above that of rubber in sheet form, c.i.f. consuming countries. Various methods of concentrating latex had been evolved by the early 1930's and latex shipments of a much higher dry-rubber content became possible. Throughout the depression the premium on concentrated latex was in excess of the additional cost of preparing rubber in this form, and a number of estates, especially in Malaya, experimented with various methods of concentration. Unfortunately, the patents covering the processes already developed were so comprehensive as to make it precarious for newcomers to attempt to enter the field. If the cost of rubber in latex form could be brought down to the cost of sheet rubber in consuming centres, there would be a possibility of crude rubber regaining some of the ground lost to reclaimed rubber, chiefly because in some branches of manufacture, such as upholstery and dipped goods, the use of latex has considerable advantages.

Various special rubbers were devised and announced during the 1930's ; the aim was to suit the requirements of manufacturers of certain specific rubber products, to extend the use of rubber into fields held by other materials, and to counteract the competition of other products. Three of these special or modified rubbers may be mentioned. First, two British rubber chemists announced in 1933 the successful development of a softened rubber without the addition of any recognised chemical softener, the use of which often interferes with further processing. This promised appreciable savings in mastication costs over a wide range of rubber manufacture. Secondly, after years of experiments, a suitable rubber powder was produced by Dutch research workers and announced in 1938. This powder ('Mealorub'), the particles of which, it was claimed, did not stick together because they did not absorb moisture from the air, contained only a very small fraction of compounds, mostly chemicals which would be added to rubber in most forms of manufacture. This powder would thus be free from the two principal weaknesses of its various predecessors—excessive water absorption and admixture of foreign materials. The wide range of potential uses of this powder include many moulded products. Lastly, in 1942 the U.S. Rubber Company announced that it had evolved a flocculated natural rubber which was said to be softer, cleaner and more uniform than coagulated rubber. Considerable hopes are attached to the success of this product.

V

The fall in costs during the depression resulted from improved technique and severe reductions in wages.[1] From 1934 to 1940 costs were relatively stable; restriction partly removed the incentive for the introduction of technical improvements and severely limited their application, while wages were relatively stable compared to 1929–33. Variations in costs reflected principally changes in the rate of release, partly offset in Malaya by a rise in wages in 1937 and a fall in 1938. After 1939 costs were inflated by war conditions.

The table on page 270 summarises estate costs in Malaya, the N.E.I. and French Indo-China as returned to the I.R.R.C. after 1935 by the British, Dutch and French producers' associations.[2]

There are occasional data on the constituent items of these costs. For Malayan estates separate figures are available of f.o.b. costs, all-in cash costs (f.o.b. costs, freight and selling charges, and head office expenses) and of all-in costs (all-in cash costs plus

[1] Details are shown in Appendix E, below.

[2] The method of compilation of these costs and their scope are described on pp. 197–98, above.

TABLE I

Annual Average All-in Costs of Production of Estate Producers in Malaya, the Netherlands East Indies and French Indo-China, 1935–41

(Pence per lb.)

	Malaya	*N.E.I.*	*French Indo-China*
1935	6·05	6·66	5·79
1936 [a]	6·18	6·20	5·51
1937 [a]	6·17	5·20	5·49
1938 [a]	6·68	6·46	4·71
1939	7·13	6·26 [b]	5·30 [b]
1940	7·13	not available	
1941	7·70 [b]		

[a] The 1936–38 figures show the effects of the Dutch devaluation of 1936 and of the successive French devaluations. The rise in Malayan and N.E.I. estate costs between 1937 and 1938 reflects the steep reduction in releases. The greater rise in N.E.I. against Malayan costs was due partly to an appreciation in the guilder against sterling in 1938, and also to the extension of the N.E.I. cost returns in 1938 to some higher-cost estate producers previously excluded.

It will be recalled that in French Indo-China output was unrestricted.

[b] First six months only.

amortisation and depreciation charges). Until the outbreak of war, freight and selling costs were about 0·6*d.* per lb. and head office charges about 0·3*d.* per lb. After 1939 freight and selling costs (including war risk insurance) rose steeply and by mid-1941 were about double the pre-war figures. Amortisation of the estate represented about 1*d.*–1·10*d.* per lb. and depreciation of buildings and equipment about 0·4*d.*–0·5*d.* per lb. The incidence of depreciation and amortisation costs varied inversely with the average rate of release only slightly from year to year.

A detailed subdivision of estate costs during the second half of 1937 or during 1940,[1] both periods of high releases and good wages, may be of interest, since the relative importance of the various items may serve to give an idea of the possible reduction in costs to be derived from some of the proposed measures for improving the efficiency of the industry. Fortunately a detailed subdivision of Malayan estate costs [2] is available for the calendar year 1940 (Table II, page 271).

Consideration of these items throws much light on the cost reductions to be expected from amalgamation. Direct f.o.b. costs and freight and selling charges (the latter not shown in the table) would not be reduced at all by amalgamation, while cultivation

[1] For various reasons 1941 costs were frequently distorted.

[2] Compiled on the same basis as the R.G.A. returns to the I.R.R.C.; i.e. the figures are arithmetic means, weighted by output.

TABLE II

Sub-Division of Malayan Rubber Estate Costs: Average 1940 f.o.b. Costs of 157 Estates with a Mature Area of over 400,000 acres, as furnished by the Rubber Growers' Association to the London Rubber Secretariat[1]

	Straits cents per lb.		*Per cent of f.o.b. cost excluding export duty*	
Local inspection and direction	0·52		3·90	
Supervision of estate	2·56		19·20	
Sundry labour charges	0·89		6·68	
Sundries	0·19		1·42	
Quit rent	0·69		5·18	
Total general charges	——	4·85	——	36·38
Repairs and upkeep of buildings and machinery	0·45		3·38	
Upkeep of mature rubber	1·19		8·93	
Manuring	0·82 [a]		6·16	
Total maintenance and cultivation	——	2·46	——	18·46
Collection [b]	4·30		32·76	
Manufacture	0·74		5·55	
Packing	0·68		5·10	
Sundries (ex estate)	0·30		2·25	
Total direct charges	——	6·02	——	45·16
Total f.o.b. cost excluding export duty		13·33		100·00
Export duty		1·40		
Total f.o.b. cost		14·73		

[a] As all other items listed in this table, the manuring cost shown represents a general average. The deviation from the mean was, however, widest in this item, as many companies spent little or nothing on manuring, while in some other instances this item accounted for as much as 2½ cents per lb. or even more.

[b] Almost entirely tapping costs.

expenses are most unlikely to be affected. Some items in general charges would be reduced by uniting contiguous areas, but here again it must be remembered that on most properties above 3,000–4,000 acres, as well as on many smaller estates, additional supervision would be required on every additional 1,500 acres. On estates belonging to agency groups there is generally little waste of European supervision through excessive reserves of manpower, as such reserves are carried centrally and not by each estate or company. Several other cost items, while not varying proportionately with increased acreage, would vary in the same direction, and the reduction in costs per lb. would be very small.[2] Larger

[1] This is the statistical and information service which survived the defunct I.R.R.C.

[2] The large proportion of fixed charges seems sometimes to have misled observers about the potentialities of cost reduction by amalgamation. By definition, fixed charges do not vary with output, but they often do with acreage.

units would result in some saving in head office charges, but these are generally small; this would almost certainly be the only economy to be derived from the amalgamation of non-contiguous properties. The economies to be derived from this kind of amalgamation are certainly far below those which would result from the replacement of European by Asiatic supervision.

Evidence on the relation between size and costs[1]—a consideration relevant to amalgamation—remains inadequate. The optimum size of the productive unit is still in dispute. The very large estate, whether cultivated intensively and planted with continuous areas of budgrafts and clonal seedlings, or extensively along forestry lines; compact estates of 4,000–5,000 acres; small estates of a few hundred acres owned by professional men, civil servants, business men or proprietary planters, entrusted to an Asiatic conductor and visited occasionally by the owner, or by an estate manager on a part-time basis; Chinese-owned smallholdings or medium holdings of 15–25 acres each, worked by two or three labourers; native smallholdings of three or four acres each, with virtually no cash costs—all these have claims. The smallish 1,000–2,000 acre estate, financed on a joint stock basis and cultivated intensively, is probably least likely to prove the optimum unit. Yet this is still the most usual type of European estate in the East.

Some material has very recently become available for a correlation analysis between the size of estates and costs per lb. Analysis by Mr. W. G. G. Kellett of the costs and mature acreages of the 157 estates for which data were given in Table II, p. 271, shows a negative but not significant correlation between size and cost. When the analysis was confined to 138 units of up to 5,000 acres each there was still no significant correlation, but the negative correlation between size and cost was appreciably more marked than without this limit (−0·17 against −0·12). Data for a correlation between yields and costs were incomplete, but some evidence suggests a significant negative correlation which is indeed highly probable. It appears that the economies of scale, especially above 5,000 acres, are small compared to those of high yields.[2]

This, however, might be modified if plantation technique were

[1] Cf. also above, p. 14.

[2] Mr. H. Fairfield Smith, statistician of the R.R.I.M., working on some figures, extracted by Mr. H. Ashplant from the 1938 edition of Rickinson's *Rubber Companies Position* (a well-known reference book of the industry), found a significant negative correlation between size and the 1937–38 costs of sterling companies (*I.R.J.*, 27th June 1939). But the underlying data were unsuitable for this type of calculation and the results accordingly vitiated.

to be revolutionised by mechanisation. In September 1940 a large Malayan engineering firm invited planters to a trial of a machine designed for the felling and clearing of the jungle before planting, or of the old stand of trees before replanting. It was claimed that with this machine the felling and clearing of an area could be completed in about one-sixth of the time usually envisaged for these operations, and at lower cost.[1] As felling and clearing are generally heavy items in the cost of planting (even where trees are first killed by poisoning), the new device is of considerable practical interest. The experience gained during the war in the design and use of bulldozers is likely to be of service in perfecting this technique. Another somewhat similar proposal, but with little experimental backing, was also put forward at about the same time. In March 1940 an anonymous writer in *The Planter* advocated the use of a special light plough in estate practice for turning in the leaf-fall which would improve the fertility of the soil without recourse to manures, assist in weeding the property, thus economising manual labour, and facilitate the raising of food crops between the planting rows without competing with the main crop. The value of this proposal is difficult to assess in the absence of practical tests. The mechanisation of tapping would be the most important advance. Although a number of proposals have been put forward, some highly ingenious, none has as yet been found practicable, and there are substantial technical difficulties to be surmounted. Thus, the basic estate operations have so far remained largely unaffected by mechanisation. In particular, the use of much unskilled labour on simple, repetitive operations with little or no mechanical assistance, is almost as much a feature of the industry in 1946 as it was thirty years ago. In the absence of mechanisation it is doubtful whether there is any real economic justification for the survival of much of the estate area.[2]

Though amalgamation into very large units is unlikely to lead to significant reductions in costs, greatly increased yields through the use of high-yielding planting material are in a different category. Some 55 per cent. of all f.o.b. costs would be reduced in inverse ratio to the higher yields. Moreover, an additional reduction would follow in tapping costs, the most important item in direct costs, when the tapper was in receipt of a fixed daily wage, or

[1] 'Mechanised Replanting', *The Planter*, October 1940.

[2] The development of latex shipments or of special rubbers, though it may favour the estates for some time, is unlikely to do so permanently, as co-operative shipments by, or on behalf of, smallholders, or purchases of smallholders' latex by dealers, would probably follow very soon.

whenever piece rates vary inversely with the productivity of the trees, as they generally do. More workers would be needed to collect the larger quantity of latex, and tapping tasks (the number of trees tapped daily by each worker) would have to be reduced, but there would still be an appreciable net saving in tapping costs, as a smaller proportion of the tapper's time would be taken up by walking from tree to tree.[1] Speaking broadly, if yields per acre were trebled, which is quite feasible in the absence of restriction and with planting material already solidly established before the war, cash costs per lb. would be approximately halved, or more than halved.

To emphasise the limited scope of the economies of scale in rubber production is not to deny that very many estates are too small or badly sited for efficient operation. Many companies with an area of two or three thousand acres or less, own three or four estates of a few hundred acres each, often so far apart that centralised supervision or centralised processing of latex are impossible. The provision of amenities for the workers, especially of open spaces for food cultivation and cattle grazing, is often impeded by the multiplicity of small, badly laid-out estates under different ownerships. These deficiences apply chiefly to the smaller properties operated on a joint-stock basis, and their elimination would not necessitate units larger than, say, 4,000–5,000 acres. As already stated, very little could be gained from the amalgamation of companies with non-contiguous properties.[2]

The economics of the group system (of company-owned estates managed by secretarial and agency firms of whose group the companies are members) was no clearer by 1940 than it had been ten years earlier. The rapid changes in plantation technique in themselves provide an important justification of this much criticised system. It is virtually impossible for individual estate managers to keep abreast of technical progress by constant reading of the

[1] The reduction in the size of the labour force would also affect several other important items, such as capital charges, supervision costs and medical expenses.

[2] An important advantage generally claimed for very large units is their ability to finance research work and to attract first-class research workers. In the rubber industry the example sometimes cited, and often implied, was the outstanding work on the Sumatran estates of the subsidiary of the United States Rubber Company, where on N.E.I. soil, developed by American capital, research workers of several nationalities (some of the most successful being British) contributed to the progress of plantation technique. But the number of first-class research workers is small, and there are certainly not enough available for a substantial number of individual companies, however large, and the great bulk of the estates must rely on the advisory services of research stations, while members of agency groups share the services of scientists, such as mycologists and geneticists.

publications of research stations. In practice these are read and sifted by the planting advisers (visiting agents) of the agency houses, and material of value to estates in the group is embodied in letters circularised to all managers, who are also informed by the same method of the progress made within the group. Another substantial economy of the group system is a great reduction in the reserve staff to be carried by individual estates or companies. This was of particular importance after the acreage supervised by each manager or assistant had greatly increased and there were fewer Europeans on each estate, often one or two where there had been three or four. It would have been difficult to continue with the greatly reduced staffs had there not always been available within the group managers or assistants capable of acting for others in emergencies, of which illness was the most frequent. Against these economies must be set the continuation or recrudescence of the practice of forcing managers to obtain supplies through the agency house and not from the cheapest sources; restoration of agency house charges to levels ruling before the depression, which were often excessive; obstruction to amalgamations even where these would have resulted in undoubted economies; and artificial multiplication of units through the method of 'other investments'.[1] Though the agency system, perhaps even more than most other controversial features of estate technique and organisation, would require a prolonged period of price competition before its merits could be fully tested, there is a stronger case for it than is often believed. Shorn of its abuses, the system is more likely to survive on its merits (with those estates which could maintain themselves in free competition with smallholdings) than its critics assume.

VI

The discussion of technical progress has so far referred almost exclusively to estate practice. Largely owing to the lack of interest of the research institutes and stations in the problems of the smallholders, there is a dearth of reliable information on technical progress on smallholdings in the years before the Japanese war. Monsieur R. Soliva suggested in 1942[2] that there had been a substantial increase in the daily output per tapper on smallholdings

[1] Cf. p. 11, above.

[2] *Rev. Bot. Appl.*, 1942, p. 47. Monsieur Soliva is a former manager of the Singapore branch of the Banque de l'Indochine. He is the author of *Economic Aspects of Rubber Planting* (Singapore, 1931), a well-known and useful booklet on the rubber industry as it was around 1930.

in the N.E.I. between the late 1920's and 1940, resulting largely from more careful and more selective tapping. This was no doubt a contributory cause of the unexpectedly high output of the N.E.I. native producers in 1935–36 in face of the very low internal prices. The *Malayan Smallholding Reports* also hinted periodically at considerable improvements in the methods of smallholders. In Malaya in July–August 1946 daily output per tapper on smallholdings was about two-thirds or three-quarters of the daily output on estates, which suggests a substantial reduction in the margin compared to the 1920's, when output per tapper on Malayan smallholdings was believed to be less than one-half of the output per tapper on estates. The preparation of smallholders' rubber both in Malaya and in the N.E.I. improved considerably in the years before the war, partly as a result of official propaganda. The R.R.I.M. adapted for the use of smallholders a smoke-house seen in a Malay village. This smoke-house may perhaps have served occasionally to keep down the smoking charges of the Chinese dealers,[1] but it was not generally economic for individual smallholders. It may have helped to improve the quality of smallholders' rubber, though this was usually quite satisfactory. In the N.E.I. the improved quality of native exports was the result partly of the working of the export tax and also of intensive official propaganda.

Compared to their efforts on behalf of the estates, the assistance given by the research stations to the smallholders was of a minor order. This was a substantial handicap to the smallholders in view of the importance of centralised technical research in plantation rubber, an industry with very rapid technical progress and where owing to the small size of the individual unit centralised research is particularly economic. The discrimination against the smallholders can best be illustrated by a somewhat detailed survey of the activities of the R.R.I.M. The picture presented by the work of the Institute would, however, apply broadly to the activities of other research organisations in the principal producing territories.

Before 1941 the Institute was financed from the proceeds of a specific export tax on all Malayan rubber exports. At present

[1] The response of the smallholders to this new smoke-house revealed once again that within the factual knowledge available to him the outlook and policy of the rubber-growing smallholder were distinctly rational. It was found that while he freely used the smoke-house when the dealers' charge for smoking rubber was over one dollar *per pikul* (0·75 cent per lb.), the smoke-house was less popular when the cost was around one dollar, and altogether neglected when the dealers offered to smoke substantially below that price, which was apparently the smallholder's estimate of the cost of smoking his own rubber himself.

(January 1947) it is financed out of general revenue, of which the heavy export tax on rubber is a major source. Until 1934 some 45–50 per cent. of the revenue of the Institute was contributed by smallholders. The advent of restriction reduced the share of smallholders in the total Malayan output (chiefly through under-assessment) and thus their relative contributions to the revenue of the Institute, which between 1934 and 1940 ranged from 32 per cent. to 40 per cent. ; over the whole decade of the thirties the proportion was about 40 per cent. Moreover, for the purposes of its Smallholders' Advisory Service the Institute classed as smallholdings all Asiatic estates under 500 acres and occasionally even all Chinese estates. On this basis over one-half of its revenue was derived from the producers catered for by the Smallholders' Advisory Service. At present about one-half of Malayan rubber output is derived from smallholdings (over three-fifths from all Asiatic-owned properties), and a corresponding proportion of the export tax is contributed by this class of producer.

In 1933 the affairs of the Institute were investigated by a small commission presided over by Professor (now Sir Frank) Engledow. After a review of existing arrangements, in the course of which it was stated that no advice was available to smallholders, the Commission recommended the establishment within the Institute of an advisory service for smallholders. This was established in 1934. Only a very minor part of the activities of the Institute has, however, been directed towards assisting smallholders. The 1934 *Annual Report* of the Institute barely referred to the smallholders ; the 1935 *Annual Report* devoted four out of 160 pages to them, and by 1939 this rose to 21 out of 277 pages. Summaries of the budget of the Institute were regularly published in the *Annual Reports*, and from these it appears that in 1934 two per cent., in 1935 five per cent., and in 1939 about 10 per cent. of the total expenditure was spent on the Smallholders' Advisory Service. Until 1937 no European officer was assigned to the Advisory Service. In that year the personal assistant of the Director supervised the service on a part-time basis. In 1938 one full-time European officer (out of 21) was entrusted with this work. This officer was one of the most junior (possibly *the* most junior) amongst the European officers of the Institute, and was apparently on a special salary scale lower than that of other European officers.

The obvious *prima facie* objection might be advanced that the general work of the Institute has benefited all producers, smallholders as well as estates, and that this vitiates such comparisons as those just made. This objection is not valid. A large part of the time and activities of the officers of the Institute has always been devoted to advisory work for estates, in the form of visits to estates, analysis of soil and plant samples sent by estates, correspondence with estate managers, lectures to planters' associations, and conducting planters around the experimental station of the Institute. The analysis of the work of each division used to be given in detail in the *Annual Reports* of the Institute, including the proportion of his time devoted by each qualified officer to advisory and to research work; advisory work was generally about one-third or more of the total. To take a random example: according to the 1937 *Annual Report* (p. 72) officers of the Soils Division of the Institute visited estates on 262 occasions during that year, and of these visits only 113 were connected with research work. Moreover, most of the research was not fundamental but applied, or economic, research on such matters as manuring, disease control, replanting or tapping systems, and most of these were of interest to estates only. Lastly, all experiments were carried out on the basis of estate technique and most of the results are of little value to smallholders.[1]

More remarkable than the somewhat one-sided nature of the activities of the Institute is the unfamiliarity of the officers with the conditions and problems on smallholdings. Here it is possible to quote published, easily accessible, material. A number of examples will be quoted lest it be thought that isolated or unrepresentative instances have been chosen.

In April 1935 the then Head of the Chemical Division of the Institute, as one of its most senior officers, addressed the Rubber Division of the American Chemical Society on the preparation of Malayan rubber; his views were widely reported in trade journals. This is how this officer described to their main customers the produce of the Malayan smallholders: 'The rubber from average smallholdings is no better than it was six years ago. It contains, as it always did, dead spiders, leaves, sand, dirt and betel-nut juice

[1] It has been suggested to the writer by an officer of the Institute that experiments must necessarily be carried out on estates as no proper control is possible on smallholdings, and that this consideration explains the almost exclusive interest of the Institute in the estates. This does not, however, explain why the advisory work of the European officers has been so largely confined to the estates, or why the research work has been concentrated on problems of interest to estates only. Moreover, some experimental work could almost certainly have been carried out on smallholdings. At least yield records could have been collected from smallholdings on the performance of seedling rubber and of some of the better-known clones. Such records would very probably have yielded material of interest.

and is manufactured in a haphazard fashion. Most of it is bought in the U.S.A. in the form of Singapore blanket, which finds a ready sale.'[1] Actually it is N.E.I. native rubber that is sold as Singapore blanket. As is common knowledge in the industry, Malayan smallholders' rubber has always been marketed in sheet form; on the Singapore market it is sold as Chinese smoked sheet. Chinese smoked sheet grades nos. 2–4, which comprise the bulk of the output from Malayan smallholdings, are generally quoted at prices which are only between 3 and 5 per cent. lower than those of first-quality estate smoked sheet. With the exception of a small quantity of very low-grade rubber produced in the remote areas of Kelantan and Trengganu, the great bulk of Malayan smallholders' rubber was throughout the 1930's sold in Singapore at prices only 3–6 per cent. below those of first quality estate rubber, which is sufficient to refute the remarkable statement just quoted. Moreover, even medium blankets (N.E.I. native rubber) fetched only about 10 per cent. less than first quality estate rubber in Singapore.[2] It remains to be added that the Chemical Division of the Institute has always been responsible for research into and advice on the preparation of Malayan rubber. According to the 1938 *Annual Report* of the Institute, the officer just quoted adjudicated prizes at the Malayan smallholders' rubber competition that year.

Another remarkable opinion by the same officer can be found in a paper 'Brown Bast: Some considerations as to its nature'.[3] The paper deals with the incidence of this bark disease: 'The average smallholding contains infinitely more permanently dry trees than the average estate . . . the smallholding presents fewer brown bast cases because it has so few even reasonably vigorous trees.' In other words, so few trees are diseased because most of them are already almost dead. Yet the yield per mature acre of smallholdings at that time exceeded estate yields by about one-

[1] *R.G.A. Bulletin*, September 1935.

[2] These facts and figures can be verified from easily accessible sources such as the *Malayan Agricultural Journal*, where the percentages of smallholders' rubber sold as smoked and unsmoked sheet respectively used to be stated regularly for all the principal producing areas; at least 90 per cent. of smallholders' rubber was marketed in sheet form. The market prices of smallholders' and of estate rubber in Singapore were also quoted and the fine margin between these grades was clearly shown. Through the courtesy of the United Baltic Corporation the writer was given access to the records of their transactions on the Singapore market in the early 1930's; the prices paid by that firm for Chinese smoked sheet nos. 2–4 were generally between 3 and 5 per cent. below those of first quality estate rubber. In Malaya the writer was shown the price quotations of two large Chinese dealers in August 1946 and these showed even smaller discounts.

[3] *Journal of the Rubber Research Institute of Malaya*, vol. 2, 1930.

quarter. In the course of the smallholdings enquiry of 1931–33 only eight out of 9,000 trees examined were found to be dead. It would be interesting to know the basis of the article just quoted.

The views of the Institute on the tapping methods of smallholders are also of interest. Overtapping and excessive bark consumption have always found a place among the few paragraphs devoted to smallholders in the annual reports. No evidence was put forward in support of these statements, which were in such marked contrast to the findings of the smallholdings enquiry of 1931–33. On occasion references to excessive bark consumption on smallholdings were coupled paradoxically with references to rural unemployment caused by sales of coupons. According to the 1938 *Annual Report* (p. 197), 'The average smallholder still cares little for the rate at which his bark is being consumed, which may be as high as three or four inches per month, and is quite unmoved by warnings as to what may happen if he continues to tap as wastefully as at present.' This last statement would certainly have needed some supporting evidence. In 1938 the rate of release under rubber restriction averaged only 55 per cent. (the lowest during the regulation scheme), and the smallholders were moreover under-assessed. Their output totalled some 115,000 tons in that year against 175,000–200,000 tons during the years covered by the 1931–33 smallholdings enquiry, which found *annual* bark consumption to average 4·92 inches on a full circumference; the 1938 production equalled about 200 lb. per mature acre, against 385–465 lb. over the period covered by the smallholdings enquiry. The 1939 *Annual Report* observes (p. 247) : 'Many tapping panels on smallholdings would, on estate standards, probably be considered untappable.' This might have been so, but it was irrelevant as the economics of estate and smallholders' production are different, and a tree untappable by estate standards may be tappable by a smallholder without cash wage costs. The remark confirms the suspicion that the acquaintance of the Institute with the economics of production on smallholdings was inadequate.

It is instructive to contrast with other sections of these documents the sections or passages devoted in the *Annual Reports* of the Institute to the smallholdings. In other parts facts are clearly stated, tables well presented, evidence is marshalled and the basis of facts, figures and arguments is carefully set out. The few pages dealing with smallholdings are a collection of frequently carelessly prepared tables, casual remarks, unsupported statements, often quite obviously based on hearsay evidence derived, presumably, from conversations with planters. A characteristic instance is the reference to bark consumption, quoted in the preceding paragraph, which does not even specify whether the reference is to bark consumption on full, one-half, or one-third circumference.

When discussing smallholders' rubber with officers of the Institute, in the course of a visit to Malaya in 1946, it was found that they were even less familiar with the subject than could have been expected from their published work. A very senior officer told the writer that the smallholding area was less than 30 per cent. of the Malayan rubber acreage; the actual figure is 40 per cent., as used to be shown regularly in the *Malayan Rubber Statistics Handbook*, the *Annual Reports* of the Controller of Rubber, the *Annual Reports* of the Adviser on Agriculture, and many other easily accessible publications. Another officer asked how it was possible to quote figures of the total annual production on Malayan smallholdings, since it was impracticable to collect the data from the tens of thousands of smallholders who do not keep records. In fact, total production is easily calculated without reference to individual output figures; the formula by which it used to be calculated by the Department of Statistics was published every month in the monthly *Malayan Rubber Statistics* and was reproduced again every month in the *Malayan Agricultural Journal*. One officer also said that he could not see why any special research, experiment, or apparently even thought, was required for analysis of the smallholders' problems, since 'the behaviour of the tree is not influenced by its ownership'. This argument disregards some essential aspects of smallholders' rubber cultivation, such as the greater planting density, the absence of close supervision of tapping, the soil conditions different from those prevailing on estates, the difficulty of replanting, and so forth.

While in Malaya, the writer asked two senior officers of the Institute, both heads of divisions, each of whom had been in Malaya for more than ten years by 1941, whether they had ever been on smallholdings. One officer said that some years ago he had on one occasion visited two smallholdings, by accident rather than design, when on his way from one estate to another. The other officer said that he could not remember how many smallholdings he had visited, but the number was certainly below ten. Thus two heads of divisions of the Institute, with a combined service of well over twenty years, had been to fewer smallholdings than were visited by the writer on the average every day while on tour in Malaya. The work of these particular officers was concerned with the field rather than the laboratory, and the number of their visits to smallholdings would be above the average for all officers. Each of these officers had over the same period paid over a thousand visits to estates.

It cannot be formally proved that the work of the Institute actually impaired the position of the smallholder ; but the evidence is very strong. There was the regular annual toll in the form of the specific export tax whose proceeds were expended on advisory and research work on behalf of the estates, thus strengthening their competitive position against the smallholders. More important than the actual taxation of the smallholders for the benefit of the estates was the suggestion inherent in the name, constitution and financing of the Institute, that a responsible body was actually looking after the interests of the smallholder, when nothing was in fact being done. The development of high-yielding material benefited only the competitors of the smallholders, so that even fundamental research was of little help to them ; applied research and advisory work was carried out almost solely for estates. While the Institute liberally assisted the estates in their replanting programmes, attention was not drawn to the potentially disastrous results for smallholders of the planting provisions and of the extensive replanting activity of estates. More important still, the statements in the publications of the Institute on the alleged excessive bark consumption on smallholdings served to give credence to views on this subject which gave spurious justification to the under-assessment of smallholdings. Opinions such as those expressed by a former Head of the Chemical Division, quoted earlier in this section, naturally also served to discredit the smallholders and their product. There is no evidence of any protest by the Institute against the planting provisions of rubber regulation which so gravely jeopardised the position of the smallholders, nor against the under-assessment of the smallholdings, nor against the crass official suggestion that smallholdings under secondary jungle growth should not receive assessments. On a narrow interpretation of its functions these matters might have been regarded as outside the scope of the Institute, but they were of a semi-technical character, and the Advisory Service of the Institute was intended to watch over the interests of the smallholders generally. No officer of the Institute appears to have enquired at the time whether the methods of distributing planting rights to smallholders in 1938–39 were appropriate to their circumstances, whether suitable land was available near the villages, whether the smallholders were in need of guidance, and above all, whether an individual smallholder could turn to any good use a permission to plant 5 per cent. of his existing area. Meanwhile the officers of the Institute gave valuable help to estates for the new planting programme. The *Annual Reports* of the Institute for 1938 and 1939 provide interesting details of the hundreds of visits to estates (actually over 1,000 in 1938) by officers of the Institute and of the thousands of samples and of letters received from estates; most of this activity was advisory and not research work.

No interpretation of the Institute's functions can explain its failure to assist the smallholders by providing high-yielding planting material for the 5 per cent. new planting of 1939–40, or for the small amount of replanting by smallholders who, it will be recalled, contributed some two-fifths of the revenue of the Institute. As a result, the bulk of the small area newly-planted or replanted on smallholdings in the course of the last ten or twelve years has been planted with unselected seedling material. In the 1939 *Annual Report* of the Institute a few paragraphs (p. 253) are devoted to this topic; when stripped of the verbiage it becomes clear that nothing was in fact done. One passage is of special interest: 'Unfortunately, distribution of some of the most valuable clones is restricted, owing to the fact that they are owned by private companies who will sell only on the completion of a legal agreement that material will not be multiplied for resale. As a result, these clones are not in general available to smallholders.' This is most misleading. First, the passage does not explain why clonal seed was not made available to smallholders, or why the Institute's own clones were not used for the purpose. But the statement is open to a graver objection. Much the most popular clone in Malaya was the celebrated Tjirandji 1, while Tjirandji 16 was also among the six leading clones. Tjirandji 1 is particularly suitable for planting on smallholdings. It is an excellent all-round clone, and its only defect is slight liability to windbreak, a risk which on the densely-planted smallholdings is much diminished. All Tjirandji clones are free and can be multiplied for resale. The use of these clones had been recommended by the Institute on several hundred, and possibly on over a thousand occasions; the clones were also used on a large scale on the Institute's own experiments. Those responsible for the *Annual Report*, the most important publication of the Institute must have known that the Tjirandji clones were free.

The attitude of the Institute towards the smallholders is particularly surprising in view of its scientific achievements in other directions. Sir Frank Stockdale wrote in 1939: 'The Institute is performing work of the highest quality and value to the industry. The Malayan rubber industry is now being served, as far as technical guidance is concerned, better than any other agricultural industry in the Colonial Empire. I was particularly pleased to note that the emphasis which the Engledow Commission laid on the importance of any policy of applied research being determined by economic considerations is being fully recognised.'[1] This may have held for the estate side of the industry, but certainly did not apply to the smallholdings.

An important reason for the one-sided attitude of the Institute must be sought in the constitution of its governing body. The Board of the Institute comprises the Director of the Institute, the Director of Agriculture, Malayan Union (formerly the Adviser on Agriculture, Malay States), the Financial Secretary, Malayan Union (formerly the Financial Secretary, F.M.S.), five estate representatives and two representatives of smallholders. The active part of the governing body is the Permanent Committee of the Board, whose membership comprises the Director of the Institute, the Financial Secretary and three estate representatives.[2] It is very doubtful whether the representatives of the smallholders (both of whom were Malays) attend Board meetings with any regularity, and it is even more doubtful whether they understand the implications of the proceedings, or whether they have ever been in a position to press their case. Neither the Director of Agriculture nor the Financial Secretary can give much time or attention to the matters of the Institute; in particular, the activities of the Financial Secretary (who is the only government official on the Permanent Committee) are far removed from rubber research. The significance of these arrangements follows from the fact that the expenditure of the Institute is controlled by the Board and in practice by the Permanent Committee. This probably serves to explain the almost exclusive attention paid by the Institute to the estate side of the industry.

Had there been no restriction, and had the smallholders been able to share in the technical progress, the benefits of which were

[1] *Report on a Visit to Malaya, Sumatra, Java and Ceylon in 1938*, p. 16.

[2] The membership of the Permanent Committee (which is in fact the active Board of the Institute) thus reflects the view that the industry can be taken as synonymous with the estates. In this the membership of the Permanent Committee is analogous with the composition of such bodies as the Rubber Regulation Committee (Malaya) or the General Advisory Committee on Rubber Regulation, which have been discussed in earlier chapters.

so largely reserved for the estates, they would have gained substantial ground. There were signs of their competitive strength in the early 1930's, such as the high yields of Malayan smallholders' rubber, the good conditions of smallholdings discovered by the smallholdings enquiry, and the gradual improvement in the price of their grades against estate rubber. These were viewed with concern, and inspired the sentiments which found expression in a remarkable leading article in *The Planter* in June 1930. This referred to the success of native methods of planting, and suggested that if the natives also mastered the comparatively simple technique of budgrafting, the long-period outlook for the estates might be well-nigh hopeless : 'In the hands of the producers of budwood lies the decision whether rubber planting will, in the far from remote future, become a native industry or remain an asset of immense value to those European races to whose administrative skill and financial acumen the development of Malaya and of the Dutch East Indies has been due . . . it is the honest, unbiased opinion of many leading men outside the rubber industry that the less the smallholder has to do with rubber the better it will be in the long run for himself, and for all others engaged in rubber production.'[1] The development of clonal seedlings has made even the mastery of this simple technique unnecessary.

[1] Similar sentiments were expressed in a letter addressed at that time by a rubber shareholder to the *Financial Times*, and reproduced in the *India Rubber World* of September 1930. 'Is it not time the governments concerned faced the position and prohibited the cultivation of rubber by smallholdings? Briefly, my argument is to eliminate the smallholder by legislation and then introduce a generally accepted restriction scheme. Only by this means can the rubber industry be protected and assisted to better times. The alternative is survival of the fittest, who in the long run is sure to be the native smallholder.'

PART V

THE THREAT TO THE MONOPOLY OF NATURAL RUBBER

CHAPTER 17

THE RISE OF SYNTHETIC RUBBER

I

IN the spring of 1942 stocks of rubber in the U.S.A., though higher than ever before, were insufficient to meet total requirements for more than a very limited period. The shortage of natural rubber, together with the indispensable part played by rubber in modern industry, and especially in the American economy,[1] led to one of the most spectacular industrial achievements of recent times : the establishment within less than two years of a synthetic rubber industry in the U.S.A. capable of supplying the great bulk of the essential civilian and military requirements of the Allies. Before considering this, a brief review of synthetic rubber up to 1941 is desirable.[2]

The value of rubber arises from a variety of physical properties

[1] In the words of the Truman Committee : 'The hard fact facing the Office of Defense Transportation today is that private automobiles run about nine times more passenger miles than buses and railroads combined . . . The second hard fact is that many areas in the country are not served by any public means of transportation, and what is even more crucial, military considerations have dictated that many of the munitions and weapons of war are to be made in factories well outside city limits and off the routes of the common carriers . . . War production is dependent on an economy geared to rubber.' Second *Annual Report* of the Special Committee Investigating the War Program (1943), p. 37.

[2] The literature of synthetic rubber is extensive and growing fast, most of it necessarily technical. Some of the less specialised publications include : U.S. Tariff Commission, War Changes in Industry Series, No. 6, *Rubber* (1944) ; *Report of the U.S. Rubber Survey Committee* (Baruch Committee, 1942) ; *Report on Rubber* of the Special Committee Investigating the National Defense Program (Truman Committee, 1942), and the *Hearings* before that Committee ; *Hearings* before the (Gillette) Sub-Committee of the U.S. Senate Committee on Agriculture on the Utilisation of Farm Products (1942) ; Rubber Reserve Company, *Report on the Rubber Program, 1940–1945* ; War Production Board, Rubber Bureau, *1944 Year-End Report* and *Final Report* (1945) ; *Reports of the U.S. Rubber Director* (1943–44) ; *Synthetic Rubber*, a Report by the Research Unit of the Procurement Division of the U.S. Treasury (March 1938) ; Melvin A. Brenner, *The Outlook for Synthetic Rubber* (National Planning Association, Planning Pamphlet No. 32, 1943) ; K. E. Knorr, *Rubber After the War* (Stanford University, Food Research Institute, War-Peace Pamphlet No 4, 1944) ; Dr. H. Barron, *Modern Synthetic Rubbers* (London, 1942).

In view of the rapid changes in the total output, in the costs of production and in the manufacturing and processing technique of synthetic rubber, it needs to be stated that most of this chapter was written in the summer of 1945 with some revisions at various times in 1946–47.

of vulcanised and compounded rubber. The most important are: high elasticity, resilience and tensile strength, high abrasion and tear resistance, low hysteresis (loss of energy through internal heat), very low permeability by gas and water, high resistance to oxidisation (good ageing qualities), good electrical properties (especially high di-electric strength), and substantial resistance to the action of oil and heat. Rubber also has certain desirable processing qualities: it can easily be reduced to a plastic state in which various compounding materials can be introduced and the product moulded to any required shape, while vulcanisation (the combining of rubber and sulphur, usually under conditions of heat) restores its elasticity lost in plasticising. Another important processing characteristic is its adhesiveness ('tack'), which facilitates the production of articles constructed with several plies or sheets. The most characteristic property is elasticity, and rubber is generally defined with reference to this.

The chemical structure of the commodity is rarely discussed in the ordinary course of business, though it inevitably comes to the forefront when the synthesis of rubber is considered. For about three-quarters of a century natural rubber has been known to be a polymer of isoprene (a butadiene [1] derivative), a liquid hydrocarbon boiling at low temperatures, which can be obtained from rubber by distillation. Early unsuccessful attempts at synthesis aimed at the production of a substance chemically identical with the natural product by synthesising isoprene and polymerising [2] this material. Shortly before 1914 interest shifted from isoprene to other butadiene derivatives and to butadiene itself, and elastic rubberlike materials were derived from butadiene and di-methyl butadiene.

[1] Butadiene, a hydrocarbon (C_4H_6), is a gas at ordinary temperatures but can easily be liquefied by cooling.

[2] Polymerisation is the process by which molecules are linked to form larger, longer and more complex molecules or molecular chains, possessing the same chemical composition, but exhibiting different physical properties from the original material (the monomer). When two materials are involved whose molecules are thus linked, the process is known as co-polymerisation. A high polymer (or co-polymer) is a substance the molecular chains of which consist of a large number of molecular units.

While the work of building up rubber from its constituent parts has not been really successful much was learned which led to some of the most important advances in rubber chemistry on which depends the whole technique of modern rubber manufacturing. At the same time the chemical structure of natural rubber is still the subject of much speculation, and the relation of the hydrocarbon to the other substances in rubber is not yet understood clearly. This is of some practical importance; for example, the development of efficient modified rubbers, such as oil-resisting natural rubber, depends largely on the success of further fundamental research in this field. Again, the nature of the chemical process which occurs when carbon black is incorporated into rubber, or when sulphur and rubber are combined, is still far from clear. The solution of some of these problems might radically alter the prospects of rubber consumption.

The research work was largely of academic interest until the pressure of the British blockade forced the Germans to turn to synthetic rubber (methyl rubber), which they produced in small quantities after 1915. The product, though useful for U-boat batteries, was much inferior to rubber in its physical characteristics, and manufacture was lengthy and expensive. Production ceased after 1918.

In 1922 an elastic rubber-like substance was accidentally discovered by an American chemist in search of an anti-freeze material. The ultimate raw materials for this substance were petroleum, salt and sulphur. The material was christened Thiokol, and first appeared on the market in 1931. The various grades are generally highly resistant to oils, greases and solvents, but lack some of the most useful physical properties of rubber. In 1940 the output of all Thiokol types was about 700 tons, and the selling price about 45 cents per lb.

The du Pont de Nemours Company became interested in the development of synthetic rubber in the 1920's. In the du Pont process, acetylene—obtained from calcium carbide—is combined with chlorine to yield chloroprene, a substance closely akin to butadiene but with a higher boiling point, and this is polymerised into a rubber-like material. A feature of the process is the very heavy consumption of electric current in the production of calcium carbide from coal and lime. This rubber was also announced in 1931 under the trade name of Duprene, subsequently changed to Neoprene. Neoprene (or rather most Neoprene types) is superior to natural rubber in resistance to age, heat, oil and solvents, and is also non-inflammable ; its resilience and tensile strength are inferior to those of the natural product. Small but increasing quantities of Neoprene found a market in America as a speciality product in uses where oil and solvent resistance were important. In 1940 the output was around 2,000 tons and the price about 65 cents per lb.

Another American synthetic rubber was Butyl, a co-polymer of iso-butylene (a gaseous by-product of petroleum refining) and of butadiene, with the former providing 98 per cent. and the latter 2 per cent. of the co-polymer. Exceptional impermeability to gas and to liquids was claimed for this rubber. Its development was announced by the Standard Oil Company in 1941 ; no manufacturing capacity was in existence at the time of Pearl Harbour.

In Germany, work on synthetic rubber started again during the 1920's, partly under the stimulus of the high rubber prices of 1925–26. A straight butadiene polymer possessing rubber-like qualities was developed by 1933. This was the first Buna (from butadiene and natrium, sodium being used to facilitate polymerisation). The butadiene was derived ultimately from coal and lime (through calcium carbide and acetylene), requiring a lavish expenditure of electric power. Shortly afterwards an improved version was developed : Buna N (or Perbunan), a co-polymer of butadiene and acrylonitrile. This latter material is generally obtained from petroleum or other hydrocarbons, and from atmospheric nitrogen. Buna N is outstanding for its resistance to oil, age and heat, and is largely a speciality. Small quantities were sold shortly before the war at around 3*s.* to 4*s.* per lb.

The next step forward was of considerable practical significance, and largely shaped the future progress of synthetic rubber. In 1936 the development of a successful general purpose synthetic rubber was announced in Germany, the celebrated Buna S, a co-polymer of butadiene (about 75 per cent.) and of styrene (about 25 per cent.). The latter is a liquid derived principally from ethylene (from hydrocarbons, usually petroleum) and benzene (obtained from coal-tar). Buna S was intended as a direct substitute for the natural product, and was to be used principally in the manufacture of tyres. Measures for its manufacture on a large scale were taken almost immediately on its announcement. In 1939 the output was 14,000 tons ; in 1940 it was 41,000 tons and eventually it rose to a peak of 115,000 tons in 1943. This rubber was not marketed before the war, but it is believed that the price charged to manufacturers in 1939 was the equivalent of about 2*s.* to 3*s.* per lb. Little was known outside Germany of its performance under service conditions. In the important properties of resistance to abrasion and age it was understood to be superior to natural rubber, but its adhesive qualities, resilience and tear-resistance were believed to be somewhat inferior. On the whole it appeared to provide a fairly efficient, though costly, substitute for natural rubber.

Synthetic rubber was also produced in the Soviet Union after 1933, but information is scanty both about the processes employed and the performance of the products. The principal types of Soviet synthetic rubber were believed to be S.K.A. and S.K.B., both straight butadiene polymers, one based on petroleum, the other on agricultural alcohol. These are general purpose synthetic rubbers whose chemical composition approximates more closely to natural rubber than that of any other synthetic rubber produced on a large scale. Soviet sources have claimed at various times that the service performance of these rubbers was equal or superior to that of natural rubber, but there has been no impartial examination of these claims.

Sovprene, akin to Neoprene, was another synthetic rubber produced in the Soviet Union by the late 1930's, while several other types may have been manufactured in small quantities. Around 1939–40 the Soviet Union with an estimated annual output of about 80,000 tons was the largest producer of synthetic rubber.

There was no other synthetic rubber production on any scale before the outbreak of the war. The development of several other varieties was announced, and some were produced on a very small scale in several industrial or semi-industrialised countries, but the aggregate output of these was below 1,000 tons. None of these minor synthetic rubbers has achieved any prominence since, though Butyl rubber was developed from one of the minor synthetics. Thus in 1939–40 there was no synthetic rubber production of quantitative importance outside Germany and the Soviet Union whose economies were largely geared to military needs; the small Neoprene and Thiokol output in the U.S.A. covered about one-third of one per cent. of American absorption of rubber. It is often said that synthetic rubber was gaining ground before the war; this is formally true, but these figures help to put the matter into proper perspective.

The reason for the negligible synthetic production before 1940 was quite simple. Quite apart from certain important qualitative defects, the synthetic product cost over 2*s.* per lb., while natural rubber was selling around 8*d.* Leading technical experts, and indeed champions of synthetic rubber, repeatedly stated between 1937 and 1942 that without a heavy government subsidy general purpose synthetic rubber had no immediate, and little prospective, chance of competing with natural rubbers.[1] A complex patent situation probably slightly retarded the development of one or two types in America, but this was of secondary importance. Development work on synthetic rubber, particularly the special purpose types, was progressing rapidly, especially in America, but this was altogether different from large-scale production of general purpose synthetic rubber.

This is the answer to those [2] who ask why Great Britain, for example, was without a synthetic rubber industry at the outbreak

[1] Authoritative pronouncements on this subject include an address by Dr. W. J. S. Naunton (of I.C.I.) to the Institution of the Rubber Industry in January 1937; the emphatic evidence by Mr. W. S. Farish, President of the Standard Oil Company of New Jersey, before the Truman Committee; as well as many articles and statements during this period by leading rubber chemists in this country and in America, especially by Dr. P. Schidrowitz, Professor E. A. Hauser and Mr. E. R. Bridgwater.

[2] For instance, Dr. H. Barron in *Modern Synthetic Rubbers.*

of the war. After the fall of Malaya and the N.E.I. the absence of a British synthetic rubber industry was deplored, and there were frequent suggestions that the influence of rubber growers had retarded the establishment of the industry in Britain. These allegations were quite untrue, and this country, which is a heavy importer of refined petroleum and of grains, and which is without an abundant supply of hydro-electric power, appears particularly unsuited for the large-scale production of synthetic rubber. A synthetic rubber industry would have been of very little use to the British war economy; rather the reverse, since (if it could have been operated at all) it would have entailed a substantial waste of resources.[1]

II

Suggestions for the establishment of a government-owned synthetic rubber industry in the U.S.A. date from the summer of 1940, when after the fall of France the military preparedness of the U.S.A. was subject to general review. Four government co-polymerisation plants, with a total annual capacity of 40,000 tons were to be erected by the end of 1941. After Pearl Harbour the government programme was repeatedly revised, and by April 1942 an annual capacity of 800,000 tons was the ultimate goal. It was clear at the outset that no substantial output could be expected until the second half of 1943 at the earliest, and that on the most favourable assumptions full-capacity working could be expected only by 1944. Soon after the expansion of the programme to a projected annual capacity of 800,000 tons, considerable technical and political difficulties emerged among which those arising over the supply of butadiene deserve some consideration.

Practically all modern synthetic rubbers are derived either from butadiene, or in a few instances from chloroprene which is chemically closely related to butadiene. This is the key ingredient of synthetic rubber, and while its production is often complex and expensive, it can be based on a large number of different raw materials. It can be produced by several processes from a number of petroleum

[1] In modern conditions the chief advantage of a blockade is the enforced waste of resources, especially of labour and of basic raw materials; a hot-house synthetic rubber industry would have amounted to the renunciation of an important differential advantage of this country's economy over that of Germany. The correct insurance would have been the accumulation of a large stock of natural rubber, sufficient for several years' requirements. The policy pursued, though very belatedly, was along these lines but on an inadequate scale.

fractions [1] and from natural gas ; from acetylene, and thus ultimately from coal and lime through calcium carbide ; and from alcohol which in turn can be derived from grain, potatoes, soya beans, sugars, molasses, and indeed virtually all starchy agricultural products. The wide range of agricultural commodities suitable for the production of butadiene explains the demands for the establishment of a synthetic rubber industry which have often accompanied agricultural surpluses. In 1941 some 70 per cent. of the production of alcohol in the U.S.A. was derived from molasses, just under one-quarter from petroleum fractions, and only 6 per cent. from grain. Before 1942 was far advanced it had become clear that these proportions would be drastically altered, as the shipping (especially tanker) shortage would necessitate a sharp reduction in molasses imports, while the direct military demand for petroleum fractions would be very large. It became clear that for some time to come the bulk of American alcohol production would be based on grain. Here were the makings of a first-class lobby.

Two-thirds of the butadiene capacity envisaged under the April 1942 programme for the prospective output of 800,000 tons of synthetic rubber was based on petroleum, and about one-third on alcohol. At the time there were still considerable agricultural surpluses in the U.S.A., and this fact, together with the not unnatural desire for a dominant share in what promised to become a lucrative and important industry, led to great pressure by the farm bloc for an increased share of alcohol butadiene. Further complications arose as a result of conflicts over the allocation of scarce materials and of certain technical difficulties. The combined effect of these various adverse factors threatened to disrupt the entire programme.

At this critical juncture the Rubber Survey Committee (Baruch Committee) was appointed by President Roosevelt in August 1942, and within three weeks produced a report remarkable for lucidity, terseness, correct analysis and the ruthless frankness with which it exposed the situation. The Committee bluntly stated that unless the synthetic programme was carried to a successful conclusion in time, the U.S. economy would collapse, and the war be lost. The Committee recommended an expansion of the programme to an annual capacity of over one million tons, as well as some revision of the types to be produced, but insisted that the time for fundamental modifications had passed, since ' any weapon on the battlefield is better than the best weapon on a blueprint '. The appointment

[1] Crude oil consists of a mixture of substances with different boiling points ; petroleum fractions are the derivatives of heating petroleum to different temperatures.

of a Rubber Director with almost dictatorial power within the field of rubber production and rubber plant construction was also recommended. Apart from the specific suggestions, the general tenor of the report and the sense of urgency which ran through it, must be credited with an important share in the subsequent success of the synthetic programme.

The recommendations of the Baruch Committee were immediately accepted. In 1943 it became necessary somewhat to scale down the programme, chiefly because of the shortage of material and labour for the construction of the plants for producing butadiene from petroleum. As, however, the actual output of most of the plants, especially the alcohol butadiene plants, was shortly to exceed their rated capacities, the over-all quantities visualised by the Committee were largely attained. The following table summarises the capacity position by the end of August 1944.

TABLE I

Comparison of U.S. Government Synthetic Rubber Programme in 1944 with the recommendations of the Baruch Committee

(Long tons)

	Rated Annual Capacities			*Estimated ultimate capacity of 1944 plants U.S.A. and Canada*
	Baruch U.S.A. only	1944 *U.S.A. only*	1944 *U.S.A. and Canada*	
Buna S	845,000	705,000	735,000	1,000,000
Butyl	132,000	68,000	75,000	75,000
Neoprene	69,000	63,000	63,000	70,000
Thiokol	60,000	Programme suspended		
Total	1,106,000	836,000	873,000	1,145,000

Sources: *Special Report of the Office of Rubber Director* (1944), and Tariff Commission, *Rubber* (War Changes in Industry, No. 6).

Thiokol was included in the programme as an emergency product to provide quickly available supplies for tyre recapping. The success of an intensive rubber scrap collection campaign, together with difficulties in the processing of Thiokol, led to the suspension of this programme. Unexpected difficulties also arose in the construction and operation of the Butyl plants and the programme was halved.

The Baruch Committee broadly confirmed the existing plan for a two-to-one ratio of petroleum and alcohol based butadiene.

From 1942 to the end of 1944 most of the output was supplied by alcohol butadiene, chiefly because the construction of petroleum butadiene plants was much delayed through shortage of materials, and also because the raw material supplies available for these plants were curtailed, as some of the required petroleum fractions had to be diverted to the production of aviation petrol. The bulk of the alcohol was derived from grain. There was little difficulty with the styrene programme as this ingredient had been produced before the war and no controversial issues or difficult problems were involved. The co-polymerisation phase also involved fewer technical difficulties than had been feared in the early stages.

The structure of the industry and the interests involved are broadly as follows: practically the entire butadiene capacity (96 per cent.) and styrene capacity (98 per cent.) are government-owned, as are all Buna S (co-polymerisation) and Butyl plants, and over 80 per cent. of the Neoprene capacity. In all, some 95 per cent. of the total investment in the synthetic rubber industry has been derived from public funds. Though the government thus owns practically the entire industry, the plants are operated by private concerns at a management fee. The butadiene from alcohol and the styrene plants are operated by chemical companies (the alcohol being largely supplied by distilleries), the butadiene from petroleum plants by oil companies (which also supply the petroleum fractions required), the Buna S plants by rubber manufacturers, the Neoprene plants by the du Pont Company, and the Butyl plants by subsidiaries of Standard Oil of New Jersey. The operating companies have no specific rights in the plants, except that of first refusal at any given price should the government dispose of the plants.

As well as producing large quantities of synthetic rubber, American technical ingenuity performed the equally important feat of processing this rubber into serviceable products. This aspect of the programme is often overlooked. In the early years of the century a rubber tyre lasted about 2,000–3,000 miles at speeds around or below 20 miles; by 1940 it was expected to have a useful life of 25,000–30,000 miles at speeds of 50–60 miles, while the cost of a tyre per mile had been reduced by over 95 per cent. These improvements reflected the progress of rubber technology, especially of rubber chemistry. The chemistry of synthetic rubber differs in important aspects from that of natural rubber, and some branches of rubber technology had almost to be learnt afresh within a space of a few months.

The following table summarises the success of the synthetic rubber programme.

TABLE II

Output of Synthetic Rubber in the U.S.A. and Canada

(Thousand long tons)

	Buna S	*Neoprene*	*Butyl*	*Buna N*	*Total*
1939	—	1·8	—	0	1·8
1940	—	2·5	—	0	2·5
1941	—	5·4	—	2·5	7·9
1942	3·7	9·0	0	9·7	22·4
1943	184·8	33·6	1·4	14·5	234·3
1944	702·3	58·1	21·7	16·8	798·9
1945	756·0	45·7	56·5	7·9	866·1

In official American parlance, Buna S is known as GR-S (Government rubber—styrene based), Neoprene as GR-M (Government rubber—monovinylacetylene based), Butyl as GR-I (Government rubber—isobutylene based), and Buna N as GR-A (Government rubber—acrylonitrile based). The absence of any reference to butadiene in these initials is due to the fact that this chemical forms the basis of most of these rubbers and is thus not suitable as a distinguishing mark. The more familiar international terminology has been retained here for the sake of consistency.

The figures include the small Canadian output (some 4–5 per cent. of the total from 1943 onwards) ; most of the basic materials for the Canadian production are supplied by the U.S.A. The production of the few private plants is also included, but the output of Thiokol and of other minor synthetics (less than 1 per cent. of the total after 1943) is omitted. Owing to certain unsatisfactory physical characteristics, Thiokol, though used for certain special purposes, is no longer classed as synthetic rubber by the American authorities. The different treatment of these small items accounts for frequent minor discrepancies between various figures of the American synthetic production.

A virtually brand-new industry capable of supplying the enormous rubber requirements of the allies was thus created in about two years and in the face of formidable technical difficulties.

III

In comparing the properties and costs of natural and synthetic rubbers it is necessary to distinguish between general and special purpose synthetics.[1] The former (Buna S types) are substitutes for the natural product intended to replace it in the most important uses, principally motor tyres. The latter (Neoprene, Buna N, Butyl [2]) are superior to natural rubber in certain particular characteristics and tend to displace it in some of the less important uses, notably where oil and chemical resistance is specially desirable ; but they also extend the field over which rubber products can be

[1] The distinction is, however, often drawn too sharply. Cf. Ch. 19, pp. 312–13 below, for a discussion of the competition between synthetic and natural rubber.

[2] Butyl is halfway between special and general purpose synthetic rubbers.

used. These rubbers would not normally compete with natural rubber on a price basis ; their superior qualities would ensure them a market for special purposes, even at prices appreciably in excess of the natural product. The price of rubber is usually a small proportion of total cost in such items as tank linings, oil hoses, pipe rings, and in these uses the lengthened life of the product would more than offset the higher cost.

The general purpose synthetic rubber *par excellence* is Buna S, which accounts for seven-eighths of the American capacity. Certain of its properties (both in processing and in use) differ, however, notably from those of the natural product, and some of its deficiencies caused much trouble, especially in the early days of the U.S. synthetic programme. Buna S was found to be more difficult and expensive to process than is natural rubber. More serious is its poor adhesive quality (lack of tack), which necessitates the cementing (special bonding) of plies of the tyre casing or of belting made from this rubber, an operation unnecessary in the processing of natural rubber. In 1942–43 the cost of manufacturing a tyre from Buna S was about one-third higher than when natural rubber was used ; in 1945 the discrepancy was about 15 per cent. Some of the service properties of Buna S are superior, others inferior, to natural rubber ; the latter still seem to outweigh the former. The resistance to age and abrasion of Buna S are somewhat better, while its resilience, tensile strength and tear-resistance are poorer. The lower resilience of Buna S tyres results in the generation of excessive internal heat when the tyres are driven at heavy loads, or over poor roads, or at high speeds ; at high internal temperatures synthetic rubber loses strength even more rapidly than does natural rubber and tyre failures are numerous. The internal heat also puts a severe strain on the cords of the tyre carcass, with a resulting rapid deterioration in the cotton fabric. These defects are particularly important in the manufacture of bus and lorry tyres, and though substantial progress has been made in this field, most of the fundamental difficulties still remain. Some of these difficulties are also experienced in the use of Buna S in inner tubes. Medium and heavy tyres must still be given an admixture of about 30–50 per cent. of natural rubber, and rayon fabric must be substituted for cotton ; even under these conditions the tyres must not be overloaded or driven at high speeds. Heavy lorry and military tyres, especially when likely to be used on bad roads, must contain an even larger proportion of natural rubber. Small passenger tyres, however, can be made entirely from Buna S, and will function fairly satisfactorily if not driven at high speed. For most other general purposes where no special resistance to chemicals, oil, and solvents is required, Buna S is an adequate substitute for natural rubber, though its processing costs are usually somewhat higher.

Butyl is sometimes classed as a general purpose rubber though its performance in tyres has so far been unsatisfactory. Its outstanding property is impermeability to gases, and it is used for gas masks, barrage balloons and other fabrics. Its use for inner tubes is also envisaged. It still exhibits certain undesirable processing qualities (notably it is wasteful of machinery) which may retard its wider adoption.

In appraising the costs of the synthetic rubbers produced under the U.S. government programme, it must be remembered that the industry had to be established at very short notice, during a period of acute shortages of constructional materials and of railroad equipment. Long-period considerations of operating efficiency and cost had to be sacrificed to speed ; processes known to be out-of-date and in a long-period sense inefficient, were at times deliberately adopted as existing equipment could be adapted to these more quickly and at less immediate cost in materials. Whenever possible, standard methods of construction and operation were adopted, and in some instances the cheapest method was set aside as it could not have been generally applied. Again, the shortage of tank wagons dictated a location of plants such as would minimise the movement of butadiene ; normally somewhat different considerations would have weighed more prominently, as butadiene is cheap to transport. Above all, the choice of alcohol based butadiene was dictated by the overriding importance of early supplies, while the production of alcohol from grain was the result of the wartime shortage of molasses. All these factors tended to inflate costs. The actual results are all the more remarkable.

Some of the most instructive official figures published in detail and available at the time of writing, relate to mid-1944. The actual data are complex as they relate to a number of different processes and to plants working at different rates of capacity, and the following table merely summarises some of the relevant data [1] ; it is reproduced from the report of the Tariff Commission, which has already been quoted.

[1] For details, cf. Tariff Commission, *op. cit.*, pp. 7–8, 80–82, and *Special Report of the Office of the Rubber Director* (Aug. 1944). Less detailed but more up-to-date figures will be found on pp. 316–17 below.

TABLE III

Estimated and Actual Costs in May 1944, of Buna S Synthetic Rubber of U.S. Government Programme

(Cents per lb. of rubber)

	Butadiene	*Styrene*	*Co-polymerisation*	*Total*
Alcohol process, with price of alcohol:				
95 cents per gallon				
Based on advance estimate	37·1	4·6	7·9	49·6
Actual May 1944	35·7	4·8	7·4	47·9
15 cents per gallon				
Based on advance estimate	10·4	2·6	7·9	20·9
Actual [b]	8·8	2·9	7·4	19·1
Butene-butane (petroleum) process:				
Advance estimate	8·1	2·3	7·9	18·3
Actual May 1944	12·7	2·4	7·4	22·5

[a] The actual price paid by the plants was of that order in 1944.

[b] That is to say, what the actual costs would have been if alcohol could have been bought at 15 cents per gallon.

Source: Tariff Commission, *op. cit.*, p. 7.

The cost of alcohol is by far the largest item in the production of butadiene from alcohol; processing costs are only about 2 cents per lb. It had been expected that alcohol (with a pre-war price of 25 cents per gallon) would be available for the synthetic rubber programme at about 50 cents per gallon. Its actual cost, owing to the high grain prices, was around 95 cents in May 1944. Over the next few years the cost of alcohol butadiene is generally expected to be from 12–20 cents per lb., generally nearer the higher figure. This would have to be alcohol derived from molasses, or synthetic alcohol. The cost of grain alcohol would be much higher.

The excess of the actual over the estimated cost of petroleum butadiene was due almost entirely to the low capacity working of some of the plants early in 1944. Approximately 70 per cent. of the cost of this process are overheads, hence the inflation through working below capacity, the reasons for which have been given earlier in this chapter. The costs in the table include full provision for amortisation within five years; if a ten-year basis had been adopted, costs would have been lower by about 2–3 cents, and without amortisation they would have been 5–6 cents less. Five-year amortisation seems definitely too conservative, since the capital cost on which the amortisation is calculated includes in many instances the construction of roads, public utilities and in some instances even the cost of land.

The butene-butane process (dehydrogenation of butylene) was the cheapest of the various butadiene from petroleum processes in May 1944, and is likely to be the most economic in the future. The following table elaborates the figures given in the last line of Table III to show the range of costs of this process, as well as the influence on actual costs of amortisation charges and of capacity working.

TABLE IV

Buna S Rubber: Range of Costs in May 1944 using Butadiene from Dehydrogenation of Butylene, and Styrene from Coal-Tar or Petroleum Fractions

(Cents per lb. of rubber)

Item	*Co-poly-merisation*	*Butadiene from dehydro-genation of butylene*	*Styrene from coal-tar or petroleum fractions*	*Total cost*
Amortisation of investment in 5 years				
Lowest cost in each category	6·68	8·22	2·24	17·14
Highest cost in each category	8·78	15·59	2·82	27·19
Average cost . . .	7·36	12·72	2·40	22·48
Amortisation of investment in 10 years				
Lowest cost in each category	5·63	6·60	1·77	14·00
Highest cost in each category	7·73	11·67	2·48	21·88
Average cost . . .	6·31	9·87	1·99	18·17
Without provision for amortisation				
Lowest cost in each category	4·58	4·98	1·30	10·86
Highest cost in each category	6·68	7·75	2·14	16·57
Average cost . . .	5·26	7·02	1·58	13·86
Number of plants in average cost	15	3	3	—
Percentage of rated capacity operated:				
Plants having lowest cost .	102	149	117	—
Plants having highest cost.	58	57	97	—
All plants included in average cost . . .	96	80	114	—

Source: Tariff Commission, *op. cit.*, p. 81.

Thus by May 1944 some petroleum based synthetic rubber was actually produced at a cash cost below 11 cents[1]; the average

[1] This very low figure was, however, reached by one plant only for a short time. Cash costs below 12 cents per lb. have been exceptional to date (June 1946).

cash cost of the most efficient process was below 14 cents, and this figure was still inflated by under-capacity working.

The cost of the special purpose synthetics, notably of Neoprene, have also been reduced from the pre-war figures of over 40 cents per lb. The following figures for May 1944 are given by the Tariff Commission [1]; they refer to one plant only.

TABLE V

Neoprene Rubber: Estimated Cost of Production and Actual Costs for May 1944

(Cents per lb.)

Basis of cost	*Estimated in* 1943	*Actual May* 1944
Amortisation of investment in 5 years . . .	30·45	30·87
Amortisation of investment in 10 years . . .	26·43	27·33
Without provision for amortisation . . .	22·41	23·78

The actual cost of Neoprene was based on acetylene costing about 11·7 cents per lb.; according to the *Special Report of the Office of the Rubber Director*, this intermediate material might cost only 7 cents per lb. in the future, and this lower figure would reduce the cost of Neoprene by about 4 cents per lb.

None of the Butyl plants was operating at more than a fraction of rated capacity by mid-1944, and actual costs are of little interest. It is generally held that Butyl will be one of the cheapest, or probably the cheapest, of all synthetic rubbers, with cash costs as low as 10 cents per lb., or even less.

Early in 1945 the Rubber Reserve Company forecast that the cash costs of Buna S would ultimately be reduced to 11 cents, and according to the Company's *Report on the Rubber Program 1940–1945* (issued in 1946), cash costs of 11–12 cents per lb. were being regularly obtained in one plant. In 1946 petroleum based Buna S was produced at a cash cost of 13–16 cents per lb. in a number of plants.

Most of these cost figures—both those actually realised and the estimates of competent authorities—differ notably from the ideas of 1939; the discussion is now in terms of costs of 12 to 20 cents per lb., instead of 45 to 75 cents. This change has come about partly through the pooling of all the important patents in 1942, and through the free exchange of information and of technical staffs. But it chiefly reflects the particular stage of progress reached

[1] *Op. cit.*, p. 82.

around 1939–40, when a number of important processes (in the production both of synthetic rubber and of its ingredients) had been developed in the laboratory and had reached small-scale experimental production ; the translation of these into large-scale operation for an unlimited market brought about a steep reduction of costs. Under normal conditions this process would have taken many years, but in 1942–44 it was, as it had to be, compressed into a matter of months.

CHAPTER 18

NATURAL RUBBER, 1941–45

I

ALTHOUGH the growth of the American synthetic rubber industry overshadowed all other developments after 1941, energetic steps were also taken to increase the supply of natural rubber for the Allies. Ceylon and India were the only Far Eastern producing territories which escaped Japanese occupation. By the middle of 1941 India had become a net importer of rubber, as the rapid growth of her rubber manufacturing industry had temporarily outstripped the capacity of her plantations. In spite of severe restrictions on rubber consumption and of the high price offered for the product, only comparatively small quantities were exported after 1941.

Net exports from Ceylon in 1941 (excluding 'amounts placed under customs control at 31st December 1941 ')[1] were 86,000 tons. In March 1942 a bonus scheme was announced by the authorities under which producers were to be paid in addition to the basic f.o.b. price of 61 rupee cents (11*d.*) per lb., 30 rupee cents per lb. for output over 90 per cent. of standard assessment, and 60 cents per lb. for production over 100 per cent. This scheme proved difficult to administer and was withdrawn in April when the basic price was raised to 1*s.* 2*d.* per lb. f.o.b. Colombo. Appeals were also issued to producers to increase output, but some of these were distinctly ambiguous. In 1942 a circular of the Ceylon Rubber Research Scheme requested producers to ' take such steps to effect an immediate increase in output as may be compatible with the preservation of the capital value of the property . . . this is a patriotic duty as well as good business '. The chairmen of several sterling companies operating in Ceylon stated in 1942–43 that their tapping policies were strictly compatible with the maintenance of

[1] Under the regulation scheme, rubber placed under customs control before midnight of 31st December in any given year could, at the option of the territory, be debited against the exports of that year, even though it was not shipped until the subsequent year. In Ceylon all rubber lying in any warehouse in Colombo at the end of 1941 was declared to have been placed under customs control, and was to be counted against 1941 exports. This was a device to diminish, in appearance only, the heavy deficit of 1941 exports below the permissible amounts. The quantity involved was about 16,000 tons, and reduced the under-exports from 23,000 tons (21 per cent. of permissible exports) to 7,000 tons (6 per cent.).

the well-being of the trees. The regulation machinery, including the issue of coupons and of export credits, was maintained until the end of May. It was abandoned on energetic representations by the Commander-in-Chief, who suggested that the 400 men engaged on rubber and tea control work could be more usefully employed on other tasks. There was some opposition in London but this was overruled, and the restriction machinery was abandoned as from 1st June 1942.

Production in 1942 was 101,500 tons.[1] New proposals for securing further increases were announced early in 1943. Producers were invited to slaughter-tap 20 per cent. of their tappable acreage in return for a governmental undertaking to pay the cost of replanting up to £45 per acre. To be eligible for the payment the trees had to be so exhausted as to be incapable of economic yields. Participation was voluntary, and the scheme was confined to areas approved by the authorities. Acceptance of the offer was of obvious advantage to many estate producers whose old rubber stood little chance of competing successfully with Malaya or the N.E.I. Up to the end of 1944 some 95,000 acres were earmarked for slaughter-tapping. In 1944 producers were offered differential prices varying from 2*d.* to 6*d.* over the ruling price of 1*s.* 2*d.* for output in excess of an agreed basic quantity. This bonus plan was again unsuccessful and was withdrawn in 1945 in favour of an increase in the basic price to 1*s.* 6*d.*[2]

Yet another stimulus to output was an agreement reached between the British inland revenue and the R.G.A., admitting as a charge for taxation purposes the additional wastage of assets resulting from intensive tapping. The basis adopted was the average tapping intensity during 1935–37, which was assumed to have been equivalent to fifty full circumference cuts. Tapping in excess of this rate qualified for liberal allowances based on the R.G.A. contention that at the assumed standard rate of tapping rubber trees would last for twenty-five years. The underlying idea, the admission of 'extra wear and tear' as an allowable expense was sound, but the allowances were generous. The average rate of release during 1935–37 was 71 per cent. and the Ceylon quota was then inadequate, and it is difficult to accept the assumption that at the intensity of tapping then current the trees would wear out

[1] Export figures are summarised on p. 306.

[2] This was a net price; export duty, medical and research cess and several other small items, totalling altogether some 1¼*d.* per lb. were borne by the Ministry of Supply. To this extent the rise in the price was greater than appears at first sight, since in the past these items had been paid by the producer.

after twenty-five years. According to all available evidence, the need for replanting arises from loss of stand through root disease, or of loss of soil through erosion, or from the obsolescence of unselected planting material, and not from the wear and tear of tapping ; but even if it were otherwise, 100 half-circumference cuts would not impose any real strain on the trees. However, the concession was fully justified if it stimulated production at a time when every ton of natural rubber was urgently required.

The efforts of the authorities, chiefly of the U.S. Rubber Reserve Company, to obtain natural rubber from the Western Hemisphere and Africa, received far greater publicity than did the measures to increase supplies from Ceylon and India ; but the results were on the whole disappointing, and generally in inverse ratio to the initial publicity given to the numerous schemes. The supply of wild rubber increased notably under the stimulus of the very high prices offered ; more rubber was also forthcoming from the Firestone plantations in Liberia, largely as the result of the increasing acreage reaching maturity. The large Ford plantations in Brazil still failed to yield rubber in commercial quantities, seventeen years after the start of the venture. It was expected that wild rubber exports from Brazil might reach some 80,000 tons a year, but actual exports were only around 25,000 tons, though the f.o.b. price offered was at first around 2*s*., subsequently raised to 3*s*. ; moreover, large sums were spent by the Rubber Reserve Company in providing transport and medical facilities, such as ships and entire hospitals. The extended planting in the U.S.A. of guayule (*Parthenium argentatum*), a shrub indigenous in Mexico, yielded a small quantity of rubber ; the results of this project fell short of expectations, and the programme was sharply curtailed after 1943. Another much publicised venture, large-scale planting of *Cryptostegia grandiflora*, a vine yielding some rubber, proved a complete failure. Increasing but still very small quantities of natural rubber were produced in the Soviet Union from kok-saghyz (*Kok-saghyz taraxacum*), a perennial shrub yielding about 150 lb. of rubber per acre. The efforts, chiefly by the British colonial authorities, to increase supplies of African wild rubber received little publicity but were more successful.

The table on page 306 shows natural rubber exports for the years 1942–45.

The experience of 1942–45 strongly suggests that no source of rubber can yield appreciable quantities in excess of pre-1941 exports at prices even remotely competitive either with American synthetic

TABLE I

Natural Rubber Exports, 1942–45

(Thousand tons)

	1942	1943	1944	1945
Ceylon	116	99	103	95
India	– 0·6	0	8	4
Liberia	12	14	18	20
Other Africa	18	31	37	34
Latin America and Oceania	23	32	41	41
Total	168	176	207	194

The 1942 Ceylon exports include shipments from 1941 stocks. The Indian production drive had not yet got under way in 1942, while some rubber reached the country from Burma and Malaysia before the fall of these areas, hence the net imports of that year.

rubber or with exports from the Far East, and discussion of the post-war outlook can be confined to synthetic and Eastern rubber.[1]

II

Although after mid-1942 there was no restriction on rubber production in the territories outside Japanese occupation, the regulation scheme, and with it the I.R.R.C., remained formally in existence. In 1942 the Committee received requests, or more nearly ultimata, from India and Ceylon, for permission to undertake new planting. As the Indian authorities had already taken measures to arrange for new planting, the discussion by the Committee was of formal interest only. Actually the regulation scheme was frustrated by the loss of most of the producing countries, and there was obviously no way of enforcing the prohibition of new planting in the Japanese-occupied territories. The permission granted to India and Ceylon, though couched in somewhat involved language, was in fact for unlimited new planting. Owing to shortage of materials and labour the actual new planting was on a relatively modest scale. The exact figures are not available in London, but it is understood that the total area planted in India and Ceylon from 1942 to the end of 1944 was below 60,000 acres.

This extension of the planted area is insignificant compared

[1] It is assumed that at all probable prices of crude rubber, reclaim will play about the same part as it did before the war, and that the ratio of reclaim to crude will be of the same order as during the 1930's.

Some South American rubber (in excess of 1941 quantities) may perhaps be bought by the U.S.A. for political reasons, but the amounts are unlikely to be substantial.

with the revised estimate of the N.E.I. native area, which was made public by the Dutch authorities in 1943. The survey of the native area begun in 1939 had progressed considerably before the outbreak of the Japanese war, but the analysis of the data is said to have required some time, which is the official explanation of the delay in announcing the result. The native area is now said to be 3,179,092 acres [*sic*] against the previous official figure of 1,806,516 acres. No further data have been published; in particular, no estimate has been given of the age composition of this huge area which, it will be noted, is almost equal to the entire planted area of Malaya, estates and smallholdings together. On this basis the N.E.I. natives are easily the largest single class of producer; within the N.E.I. their acreage represents over two-thirds of the planted area. Here indeed is the legacy of the Stevenson scheme.

The revised figure has received little publicity in this country. Those sceptical about the feasibility of the control of new planting in the N.E.I. will no doubt ask how much of the additional acreage was planted after 1934 in contravention of the provisions of the regulation scheme, which were rigorously enforced elsewhere. Moreover, as the additional acreage must have come to light gradually since 1938, it may be asked why the N.E.I. native quota was not increased, especially as these producers were the only known class who did not fall behind the permissible exportable amount in 1941. The revised figure is thus not without awkward implications.[1]

III

Under the provisions of the 1938 agreement, the I.R.R.C. had to make a formal recommendation to the signatory governments by the end of 1942 for the continuation or the withdrawal of regulation after 1943. After considerable discussion, it was decided to recommend an extension of regulation until eighteen months after the end of the Japanese war. The purpose was to keep in being the formal framework of the scheme until at least the broad outlines of the post-war position could be ascertained.

The British Colonial Office vetoed the suggestion, ruling that rubber regulation must lapse. On 29th December 1943 an official

[1] The inadequacy of the N.E.I. native quota (based on the earlier estimate which was also used for calculating the distribution of new planting rights in 1939–40) is particularly striking in the light of the new acreage figures; with an area approximately twice that of the estates (and one which had a higher yield per surface unit), the native quota was slightly lower than that of the estates.

communiqué was issued which stated *inter alia* : 'They (the British, Dutch and Indian Governments) have for some time past been considering the possibility of constituting a new and more widely representative Committee for consultation and the collection of information. Such a Committee should, in their view, have no powers of regulation of exports, production or planting . . . Unfortunately, in the time available, it has not been possible to bring these discussions to a conclusion, and the three Governments have therefore decided, in the hope that it may be possible to form the proposed Committee with a wider membership, to extend the existing agreement for a short period of four months.' [1] Thus plantation rubber, which was the first industry to receive official British support for a compulsory restriction of output in 1922, seems to have been the first to lose it twenty-one years later.

The period of grace expired on 30th April 1944, and the scheme formally ended on that day. Later in the year a Rubber Study Group was formed with British, Dutch, American and eventually French participation ; the actual members are British, Dutch, American and French civil servants, British, American and French rubber manufacturers, and British, Dutch and French estate representatives. The study group has held several meetings, but the conversations have so far been confined to exchange of information only, and no issues of policy have as yet been discussed. Thus so far as policy is concerned there seems to be a clean slate.

[1] The communiqué also stated : 'During the first two years of the war the quotas of release under the agreement were raised to a level which removed any effective restriction.' This, as we have seen, was not so.

PART VI

THE PRESENT POSITION AND PROSPECTS OF THE INDUSTRY

CHAPTER 19

PROSPECTS AND POLICIES

FOR obvious reasons the future of the rubber industry is very uncertain. The political situation in the principal producing territories is unsettled ; the resumption of migration to restore the depleted labour forces of Malaya, Sumatra and southern Indo-China is still doubtful ; supplies of consumer goods and even of elementary necessities are in places very scarce ; the prospects of food supplies are doubtful ; the cost of living and money wages are high and unstable. Meanwhile a brand-new synthetic rubber industry has been created in the U.S.A. and its competitive position against the plantation industry is to a certain extent a matter for speculation ; nor is it known as yet what the official policy will be on the future of this industry. Yet there are certain factors amid the general uncertainty which justify a review of prospects and possibilities, and even some tentative practical proposals. It should be remembered, however, that much of the argument of this chapter, as well as of Chapter 20, rests on less secure foundations than does the analysis of the rest of the book.

I

Estimates of the trend of total rubber absorption are necessarily hazardous. If a continuation of the pre-war rate of increase is assumed and various curves are fitted to the absorption data of the 1920's and 1930's, the extrapolated figures show an estimated absorption of between 1¼ and 1¾ million tons around 1950. This is a result of limited value ; even in the absence of a war whose advent and prolonged duration have rendered such estimates even more precarious, the actual figures might have diverged widely from the projected trend, and this for several reasons. Long-period changes in the demand for motor travel, which is almost certain to remain a predominant factor in the absorption of rubber will depend on many and varied factors. Economic conditions in the U.S.A. are also likely to remain an important influence. In the early part of 1938 American absorption was running at an annual rate of just over 300,000 tons. In 1941 it reached 780,000 tons, and without some compulsory reduction after June it would have approached one million tons. Although fluctuations of this magnitude alter the entire picture over a few years, it is doubtful whether they would greatly affect the long-period trends. Certain technical changes, already much canvassed though not yet translated into practice, are likely to diminish the replacement demand for motor-car tyres. One specific instance is the development of a composite tyre with Buna S tread (and possibly Buna S side-walls) and natural rubber carcass, which might much enhance the life expectation of tyre casings, since the better resistance to age and abrasion of Buna would not be offset by internal heat which develops in the carcass.[1]

Though for a considerable period to come tyres and tubes are likely to represent the bulk of the absorption of rubber, the possibility of very substantial increases in certain other forms of absorption cannot be ruled out. Responsible officers of the U.S. Rubber Company stated in private discussion in 1943, that should the price of natural rubber remain reasonably stable at around 12 U.S. cents per lb. (7*d.*), they expected a large extension of the use of rubber and of latex in road construction and in rubber flooring. The potentialities of sponge rubber upholstery were beginning to be appreciated before the war, sizeable quantities already being consumed, and there was every reason to expect rapid increases.[2] The various improved rubbers developed in the few years before 1941, the increasing use of liquid and concentrated latices, all suggest the possibility of extending the use of rubber into new directions. Even wider horizons would be opened up by a successful combination of rubber with materials other than sulphur. Hitherto rubber has been demanded solely for the physical characteristics of the vulcanised rubber compound. In the future, it might possibly be used for its chemical rather than for its physical properties, and compounded with substances other than sulphur, it might serve as the basic material for products quite unlike the rubber compounds of the present day, much as nitrocellulose differs from cotton, or glycerine products from the fatty oils from which they are derived.

[1] A composite tyre of this kind necessitates the use of two different rubber ' mixes ' (rubber and chemical compounds) in the manufacture of each tyre, a natural and synthetic mix. This, in turn, requires the use of more equipment, labour and time than the use of one mix only, and has not been adopted on any scale in the American emergency programme. There is, thus, little experience of the cost and potentialities of the production and performance of such tyres.

[2] Complete rubber upholstering of a passenger car requires some 40 lb. of crude rubber, which is about the amount used in two or three passenger car tyres.

A substantial increase in the absorption of rubber for military requirements can safely be assumed, as rubber has proved its worth, and indeed its indispensability, in modern warfare. A steady though unspectacular increase in the absorption of rubber in civil aviation, in agriculture (especially on farm vehicles), and in footwear, is also highly probable. Absorption in 1940 and 1941 was 1·1 and 1·2 million tons respectively, so that the generally suggested figures of 1·5–1·8 million tons for absorption over the next few years allow a generous margin for expansion. The data available at the time of writing (January 1947) confirm these figures.

Estimates of the order of magnitude of the potential capacity can be made more safely. Synthetic capacity in North America is at present around 1·2–1·3 million tons annually, with another 150,000–200,000 tons in Europe and the Soviet Union, say a total of between 1·3 and 1·5 million tons. The physical capacity of the Eastern rubber plantations has certainly not been reduced appreciably below the basic quotas under the regulation scheme. The smallholdings have suffered hardly any damage, and the great bulk of the mature estate acreage will be tappable after a comparatively short period of cleaning up ; preliminary surveys have established that the areas destroyed since 1941 do not exceed 7–8 per cent. of the estate area in Malaya and 10 per cent. in the N.E.I. These considerations suggest that the physical productive capacity of plantation and synthetic rubber is around three million tons annually.

For another year or perhaps two years, while the restocking demand is considerable and the Far Eastern plantations are coming back into production gradually, every ton of rubber will be readily marketable, and indeed badly needed ; subsequently, however, excess capacity is likely to emerge on a far larger scale than at any time before the war. If the synthetic plants in the U.S.A. were operated at capacity, and the estates and smallholdings in the more easily accessible areas in the East were tapped at a rate at which bark consumption about equals bark renewal, rubber supplies would be far in excess of all reasonable estimates of prospective absorption.

II

Before reviewing the policies which may be adopted to deal with this situation, it seems worth while to discuss the probable competitive position of synthetic and natural rubber, and to consider the most probable outcome of free economic competition. Although it is both usual and useful to distinguish between special and general purpose synthetic rubbers (broadly speaking between Neoprene, Buna N and Butyl on the one hand and Buna S on the other) this distinction is often drawn too sharply. It is certainly true that under free competition the special purpose synthetics would be far more likely to hold their own against the natural product than would Buna S ; it is also true that the field in which they compete with natural rubber is quantitatively much less important than that of the rivalry between Buna S and natural rubber. But the economic principles underlying the choice between natural and synthetic rubber are the same whether general or special purpose synthetic is to be used, and most of the analysis of the next few paragraphs, though primarily concerned with general purpose synthetic rubber (which accounts for over four-fifths of the American capacity), applies also to the other types.

The unit cost of the raw material to the rubber manufacturer is not the only factor determining the competitive position of synthetic and natural rubber. First, the densities of natural and synthetic rubber differ, that of the latter being somewhat higher, so that a tyre of a given volume requires a greater weight of Buna S than of natural rubber. Processing costs must also be taken into account. In the manufacture of tyres these are still about 15 per cent. higher for synthetic than for natural rubber. Far more important are the qualitative differences in the use of natural and synthetic rubbers, which can be best expressed in terms of the life expectation of the manufactured product.[1] In this context it should be remembered that the cost of crude rubber is only part of the cost (and *a fortiori* of the selling price) of the final article. Accordingly the use of a more expensive raw material will be found profitable if the service life of the manufactured product is prolonged. The special purpose oil-resisting synthetic rubbers show this best. The life of certain products in which the limiting factor is the life of the rubber used may be so greatly lengthened by the use of Buna N or Neoprene that the saving will probably exceed any likely additional cost of these rubbers over the natural product. But while these rubbers present an extreme instance, the same principle is at work in the competition between Buna S and natural rubber. The following equations summarise the main considerations affecting the competitive position of synthetic and natural rubber in tyre manufacture.

[1] In some minor uses this presentation somewhat over-simplifies the argument without affecting it substantially.

Tyre casing based on natural rubber	*Cost in pence*
Cotton C lb. @ c pence per lb.	Cc
Rubber R lb. @ r pence per lb.	Rr
Other ingredients	A
Labour	L
Other expenses	Z
Total cost $= (Cc + Rr + A + L + Z)$ pence	

Tyre casing based on synthetic rubber	*Cost in pence*
Cotton C' lb. @ c pence per lb.	$C'c$
Rubber $(1-k)\ R'$ lb. @ r pence per lb.. . .	$(1-k)R'r$
Synthetic kR' lb. @ p pence per lb.. . . .	$kR'p$
Other ingredients	A'
Labour	L'
Other expenses . . .	Z'
Total cost $= (C'c + (1-k)R'r + kR'p + A' + L' + Z')$ pence	

C', A', L', Z' are all functions of k, which is the proportion of synthetic rubber used. An important instance of the higher costs of ' other ingredients ' in the use of synthetic rubber results from the necessity of a partial substitution of rayon for cotton in the manufacture of lorry and bus tyres.

Assuming that one natural rubber tyre casing gives the same performance as q synthetic-rubber casings, then q is also a function of k, and if synthetic rubber is to be as valuable as natural rubber, the following relationship must hold,

$$Cc+Rr+A+L+Z=q(C'c+(1-k)R'r+kR'p+A'+L'+Z')$$

from which by transformation

$$qkR'p=(C-qC')c+(R-q(1-k)R')r+(A-qA')+(L-qL')+(Z-qZ'),$$

or

$$p=\frac{1}{qkR'}[(C-qC')c+(R-q(1-k)R')r+(A-qA')+(L-qL')+(Z-qZ')]$$

As the life expectation of the tyre varies with the proportion of Buna S in the rubber compound, the value of p is also a function of that proportion, conceivably exceeding the price of natural rubber at lower values of k, and falling to a fraction of the price of natural rubber at very high values of k.[1] It appears that single rubber compounds only are being used for the manufacture of tyres under the U.S. programme, and synthetic and natural rubbers are mixed in different ratios for light, medium and heavy tyres. Should it prove economic eventually to use separate compounds for tread and carcass (if this should so improve the quality of the tyre as to

[1] A similar relation holds for the relative values of crude and reclaimed rubber in tyre manufacture. In small proportions, say up to 10–12 per cent., reclaim is almost equivalent to natural rubber, but at higher ratios its usefulness and value decline rapidly.

offset the higher cost), then any given *k* would result in different, and almost certainly higher, values for *p* than if one mix only were used.

The equilibrium price, or rather price ratio between synthetic and natural rubber, varies in different products, heavy, medium and light tyres being different products for this purpose. In any given state of technique it should, however, be possible to obtain the values of *p* as a function of *k* for the most important rubber products, at least for the U.S.A., and by aggregating these to find the equilibrium ratio between the prices of synthetic and natural rubber, as a function of the proportion of synthetic rubber used. At present secrecy surrounds the actual figures, though it is known that for tyres the leading manufacturers have calculated the equilibrium price ratio as a function of the proportion of synthetic rubber used. It would be useless to attempt to make estimates; first, because technical conditions are changing rapidly, and secondly, because the general outlines of the present position are sufficiently clear to allow some broad conclusions.

There is a measure of agreement on the prospective competitive position of the special purpose synthetic rubbers, and it is generally held that much of the American Neoprene and of the small Buna N capacity might be able to survive without any government assistance. Their excellent resistance to oil, solvents and chemicals may assure them a market. The American capacity for the production of these special purpose rubbers is about 90,000–100,000 tons a year. Even if the entire capacity were to continue in production, it does not follow that an equivalent amount of natural rubber would be displaced, since some of these rubbers would act as substitutes for other materials. Altogether, these rubbers are likely to displace an absorption of natural rubber in the U.S.A. of perhaps about 50,000 tons annually. The position of Butyl is more uncertain, partly because most of the output has been for specialised military uses. Owing to its impermeability and expected low cost of production, Butyl has been regarded as a potential competitor of natural rubber in the manufacture of inner tubes. It is, however, suggested below that the plantation product could be sold at prices substantially lower than the most sanguine forecasts of Butyl costs, and its large-scale use in tubes is accordingly improbable under competitive conditions. Rubberised fabrics are likely to be the chief outlet for Butyl; before the war about 1½ per cent. of American absorption (6,000–8,000 tons) was in these uses.

Much the most interesting and important issue is that of the competitive position of Buna S against natural rubber. While details are not available, it was stated in 1944 by one manufacturer that for bulk use in tyre manufacture the value of Buna S was still appreciably below that of natural rubber, and that if the cost of Buna S to the manufacturer was around 15 cents per lb. that of natural rubber had to be at least 18 cents to justify the use of substantial quantities of Buna S. In 1945–46 the leading American trade journals still frankly admitted that in large-scale use (especially in tyre manufacture) Buna S was still inferior to natural rubber, an opinion which seems to be shared by both British and American manufacturers when not addressing popular audiences. This view was also expressed by Sir George Beharrell, chairman of Dunlop's, at the annual general meeting of the company in June 1945 : 'The qualities of the two products, natural and synthetic rubber, are hardly comparable. I do not think that at present synthetic rubber can compare at all in quality with natural rubber for the manufacture of tyres, and I do not believe that any manufacturer would willingly use synthetic rubber if natural rubber were available.' It thus appears that so far the superior resistance to abrasion and age of Buna S has been insufficient to offset the lower resilience, adhesiveness and tensile strength of Buna S compounds ; moreover, the processing costs of synthetic tyres are still higher than those of natural rubber tyres. Buna S has so far also been found to be more variable than the plantation product, whose variability has frequently been criticised by manufacturers.

The compounding of synthetic rubber is, however, in many ways still on an experimental basis and substantial improvements are certain. It will be argued below that the plantation rubber industry is still in its infancy quite as much as the synthetic industry, if not more so ; but this similarity does not extend to the compounding of natural and synthetic rubbers. Rubber chemists and technologists possess forty years of experience with the plantation product, against less than five years with synthetic rubber. It is sometimes implied by protagonists of natural rubber that it is necessarily superior to the synthetic ('artificial') product. There is no ground for such a presumption, since even the most ardent believer in a benevolent Providence must hesitate before assuming that nature has so contrived the isoprene polymer secreted by the tree *Hevea brasiliensis* as to suit uniquely the requirements of the American motorist. The very versatility of natural rubber is more likely to be a liability than an asset in an era of functional specialisation. With much further progress in the technique of producing, compounding and processing the synthetic material, a whole range of specific rubber compounds could be developed even within the general field of Buna S, each of which might be superior to natural rubber in some particular use. This, however, is not yet in sight. At present natural rubber still has a comfortable lead on an equal price basis, and if Buna S and the plantation product are marketed at approximately the same price, the latter will rapidly recapture the bulk of the market for tyre and general purposes. The probable range of prices of the two products under competitive conditions must now be considered.

There are a number of forecasts of prospective costs of general purpose American synthetic rubber, ranging generally from 14 cents to 20 cents per lb.; more recently there has been a tendency to reduce the estimates, and figures of 13–15 cents have become more usual. So far as is known, there is no responsible estimate of less than 10 cents, excluding amortisation and selling costs. By 1946 much petroleum-based Buna S was produced at cash costs of 13–15 cents per lb.

Colonel Bradley Dewey, U.S. Rubber Director in 1943–44 and a strong champion of synthetic rubber, stated in December 1943 [1] that some Buna S was already being produced at a cash cost of under 14 cents; as we have seen, this figure was substantially reduced by mid-1944. Colonel Dewey predicted post-war costs at between 14 and 16 cents, including full depreciation allowances for efficient plants working at full capacity.[2] The authors of the *Special Report of the Office of the U.S. Rubber Director* (August 1944) suggested after a careful review of the main factors likely to affect costs that after the war the cash costs of petroleum based Buna S could be expected to be about 11–12 cents per lb. c.i.f. Akron (the leading rubber manufacturing centre in the U.S.A.); their estimates were based on reasonable, though somewhat optimistic, assumptions. Though they are subject to a margin of error, these estimates are not altogether conjectural. Sufficient experience had been gained of the most important operations by August 1944 to suggest reasonable ideas of the order of magnitude of the prospective costs of production; this applies particularly to petroleum based operations where plants were working at, or near, rated

[1] *Chemical and Metallurgical Engineering*, Dec. 1943.

[2] Estimates of the same order of the prospective costs of Buna S over the next few years were put forward in 1944–46 in public statements or articles by several leading U.S. rubber manufacturers, notably by Mr. P. W. Litchfield, chairman of Goodyear, Mr. John L. Collyer, president of Goodrich, and by Mr. R. P. Dinsmore, vice-president (in charge of research) of Goodyear.

capacity, since the costs of these processes are much less influenced by variations in raw material prices than those of the alcohol butadiene operations.

Amortisation charges are hazardous to estimate, as the economic life-expectation of the plants is difficult to foretell. A piece of capital equipment should be written off by the time the market for the product disappears, or the total cost of production from new equipment is less than the prime cost of output from the existing asset. Amortisation costs as high as 6 cents per lb. have been suggested for synthetic rubber, on the basis of an investment of about 600 dollars per ton of annual capacity and of a five-year amortisation. This figure appears excessive, as the life-expectation of the whole investment (including roads, public utilities, etc.) is certain to be more than five years. Moreover, under normal conditions the cost of construction is certain to be less, while improved design would lengthen the life of the plants. Amortisation costs are nevertheless unlikely to be below $1\frac{1}{2}$ cents per lb. on any reasonable assumption, while another half-cent is a conservative estimate for selling charges, management fees and royalties, so that for these items at least 2 cents must be added to the estimates of cash costs given in the preceding paragraphs.[1]

It would thus appear that estimated all-in costs of 12–13 cents per lb. ($7\frac{1}{4}$*d.*–$7\frac{3}{4}$*d.*) of Buna S are the lowest which can be reasonably expected in the next few years; such low-cost Buna S is more likely to be based on petroleum than on agricultural alcohol. The estimate allows for an appreciable further reduction of costs from present levels as a result of technical progress; the majority of responsible estimates in the U.S.A. visualise all-in costs of around 13–16 cents ($7\frac{3}{4}$*d.*–$9\frac{1}{2}$*d.*) per lb., excluding a return on capital. A liberal allowance for the effects of technical progress is clearly justified in such a very young industry. In the more distant future, further reductions might be possible, and even revolutionary changes

[1] Discussion of the amortisation charges of synthetic rubber plants is often unnecessarily confused by speculation about the price at which the U.S. Government will eventually dispose of the plants. Whatever price is charged for these, it will not affect depreciation and amortisation costs as part of the long-period supply price of synthetic rubber, since when a plant comes to be renewed the operator will estimate prospective profits and capital charges at that time in deciding whether or not to continue production. The price (or rental) charged by the authorities would, however, affect costs and the supply price during the period between their disposal by the government and the first replacement. The importance of this matter seems exaggerated, as the difference between giving away the factories and charging any reasonable price is unlikely to represent more than $2\frac{1}{2}$ cents per lb. on the output to be expected over the economic life of the plants.

in technique may have to be envisaged, but such contingencies cannot be expressed quantitatively.

III

It is now necessary to attempt to form an estimate of the approximate price which would, under competitive conditions, elicit sufficient natural rubber to satisfy world demand ; in other words to estimate the supply price of the required quantity of natural rubber. Even allowing for the uncertain conditions in the Far Eastern territories, it appears possible to frame an estimate which would suffice to indicate the competitive prospects of natural rubber against Buna S. This opinion appears to be justified when adequate weight is given to two obvious considerations : first, that smallholdings account for over one-half of the total planted area, and thus well over one-half of the capacity of the industry (as unrestricted yields on smallholdings exceed those on seedling estates) ; secondly, that the plantation industry is still in its technical infancy.

When the importance of the smallholdings is recognised it will be appreciated that the costs of production of over one-half of the productive capacity of natural rubber are certain to be very low, or almost nil. A large part of the smallholding acreage, even in the N.E.I., can be tapped without recourse to outside labour. The majority of the *ladangs* which reached maturity in Sumatra and Borneo in the mid-1930's were tapped or were at least tappable by the owner and his family, and it was gradually being realised that the dependence of the garden owners on outside labour had been greatly over-estimated. It was explicitly stated in 1934 in an official *N.E.I. Native Report* that exports at an annual rate of 300,000 tons in the spring of 1934 were produced almost wholly by family labour. The substantial native exports of 1934–36 when the penal special export tax was in force made it clear that the larger part of the native productive capacity in Sumatra and Borneo was in the hands of owners with hardly any costs of production. Moreover, even when the holding was tapped by outside labour it was generally on some kind of share basis, not involving any cash expenditure, and at the same time sufficiently attractive to secure the required labour. The purchase of coagulants, the hire of a mangle, and local transport to the market, may involve very small cash costs, but even these can, if necessary, be largely dispensed with. Thus, many smallholders could almost be referred to as no-cost, rather than low-cost, producers. The owners of the larger smallholdings or medium holdings very frequently rely on outside labour. But they generally require labour for tapping only (often paid on a share basis) and their cultivation costs and overhead costs are very small.

Although the smallholder incurs few or no cash costs the supply price of smallholders' rubber is positive, since at very low prices the gardens in the interior are not worth tapping, or the cultivation of other crops becomes more profitable to the owner or to the tapper. An examination of past performance will help to form an idea of this supply price. For this purpose it is necessary to look back to the period immediately preceding the introduction of regulation in 1934. It will be recalled that in the spring of that year N.E.I. native exports were at an annual rate of 300,000 tons and were rising rapidly; these exports were the product of family tapping only. At that time the London price was around 5*d.*–5½*d.* per lb. with a sterling-guilder exchange rate less favourable to sterling than the present rate (7.30 against 7.60). The Malayan smallholders also produced at an annual rate of 300,000 tons at these prices. The combined exports of Siam and Sarawak (almost entirely smallholders' rubber) at the time were at the rate of 30,000 tons a year and were also rising very fast, while the production of smallholders in Ceylon and British North Borneo during the early months of 1934 can be conservatively estimated at an annual rate of 35,000 tons.

The early part of 1934 thus saw smallholders' output at very nearly 700,000 tons with a London price of about 5*d.*–5½*d.*, and production was still rising rapidly. Moreover, huge areas of N.E.I. native rubber reached maturity only after 1934, again largely in holdings whose owners, according to official statements, had next to no costs, or no costs at all. In Siam and Sarawak, too, much rubber was still immature in the early part of 1934. The capacity of smallholders' rubber expanded substantially after 1934, and its supply price declined—in the instance of the N.E.I. natives so greatly as almost to destroy the whole regulation machinery. It can be very conservatively estimated that, in the absence of restriction, a London price of 4*d.*–5*d.* per lb. during the mid-1930's would have resulted in annual exports of smallholders' rubber of at least 750,000–800,000 tons, and probably in much larger exports.

The supply price of smallholders' rubber need not be substantially higher in the future. Much of the capacity can be operated without outside labour, and is thus largely unaffected by changes in wages. Similarly, very many smallholders, possibly the majority also produce their own food requirements and their output is largely independent of the price of rice. Though this does not hold for most smallholders in Malaya, Borneo and Siam, many of whom need to buy rice, rubber cultivation has been so attractive to these producers that they can be expected to return to it as soon as the commodity is marketable again. This has already proved to be the case in Malaya and in the N.E.I. By the late summer of 1946 Malayan smallholders' production was at an annual rate of about 310,000–320,000 tons in spite of a shortage of labour, an acute shortage of coagulating acid, very high prices of equipment and of consumer goods, and of strong official pressure to cultivate foodstuffs. N.E.I. native exports were by then also at a rate of 300,000 tons annually, in spite of the dislocation of transport throughout Sumatra and Borneo ; moreover, a large part of these exports had to run a Dutch naval blockade. Admittedly, the price of rubber was much higher (about 10*d.* per lb. f.o.b. ports of shipment) than the levels visualised in our discussion. But the price of rice was about fifteen times the 1940 level owing to a short-period scarcity which should not extend beyond 1948–49. Moreover, many N.E.I. producers received much less than the Singapore price as the shippers had to be compensated for the risk and cost of running the blockade.

Very high prices of rice and of other agricultural products, especially of vegetable oils, may divert some resources of both labour and land from rubber to other cultivation, but this is unlikely to be of quantitative importance. Rubber is certain to remain a crop ideally suited for cultivation by smallholders ; as before, it will be largely non-seasonal, free from weather risks, easily marketable, and require less sustained work than most alternative crops. With prices of 4½*d.*–5½*d.* per lb.[1] c.i.f. consuming countries (including freight at about 1*d.* per lb. against about ½*d.* before the war), rubber should still be attractive to smallholders. It is naturally assumed that the simple commodities on which the smallholder usually spends his income will become available, which is again probable within a few years at the latest. The smallholders may be temporarily handicapped if the authorities

[1] *These approximate estimates of prospective supply prices throughout this chapter assume broadly the maintenance of the purchasing power of sterling and the dollar at approximately the* 1945 *levels. They would require obvious modification if this assumption breaks down with a violent fall in the purchasing power of money in Britain and the U.S.A. Such a general rise in prices would, however, also affect the cost and the supply price of synthetic rubber ; it is unlikely that it would greatly affect the estimates of the relative competitive strength of natural and synthetic rubber, the principal concern of this chapter.*

give preferential treatment to estate labour in the distribution of foodstuffs and of consumer goods. This is the policy pursued in Malaya at present (early 1947) but it is not likely to be a factor of long-period quantitative significance.

Lastly, on a longer view, a further factor of great potential significance needs to be remembered. The supply prices so far given refer to the unaided efforts of the smallholders ; indeed, these producers have been handicapped by an unsympathetic official attitude, of which many examples have been given throughout this study.[1] Should high-yielding planting material, especially clonal seed, be made available to them, the supply price of their rubber would be substantially reduced. Output per tapper and per acre would be doubled or trebled, and every time a new rice clearing was opened in the N.E.I. a high-yielding small rubber plantation would be established at no individual or social cost. In Malaya too (three-quarters of which is still under jungle), ample land is still available for the extension of the planted area. With high-yielding material the smallholders would find it worthwhile to produce very large quantities of rubber (possibly several hundred thousand tons) at, say, 1*d.*–2*d.* per lb., delivered Singapore ; the incredulous are referred to the unsuccessful attempts to control N.E.I. native exports during 1935–36, by taxing away almost the whole of the price.[2] It was suggested to the writer while in Malaya that the government should fell and clear large areas, preferably by mechanical means, establish small, high-yielding plantations, and sell, lease or give these to smallholders as part of a policy of raising the efficiency of the Malayan rubber industry, as well as improving the standard of living of the local population. Such a policy would greatly strengthen the competitive position of the smallholders, and also that of the whole plantation industry.

Estimates of the prospective supply price of estate rubber are

[1] At the time of writing (January 1947) the official policy in Malaya is more unfavourable to the smallholders than ever before, with the maintenance of the planting provisions of rubber restriction and the preferential treatment of estates in various ways ; these matters are discussed in the concluding chapter of this study. If such policies are allowed to prevail much longer, the argument of the text would require modification, as a sufficiently unfavourable official policy might even destroy the smallholding side of the industry, after first impairing its competitive position. Both in Malaya and in the N.E.I. official policy will be a crucial influence on the supply price of smallholders' rubber and on the prospects of the smallholders.

[2] At such low prices the freight to consuming centres becomes an important factor, and it is safer to estimate the supply price in terms of the Singapore price. At higher levels, say above 4*d.*–5*d.* per lb., the estimate is not likely to be seriously affected by the rise in freights which do not press very heavily on rubber unless exorbitant levels are reached.

much more hazardous, particularly because of the unsettled labour conditions in the East. Yet it seems possible to form reasonable estimates, even though they are subject to a wide margin of error. The areas destroyed or ruined as a result of the Japanese occupation are now known to be small. The cost of rehabilitation of large areas may prove heavy, though it is not likely to be crippling. Some kind of compensation is likely to be forthcoming from the government, while many sterling companies have substantial cash reserves. While rehabilitation costs vary very greatly between different areas and properties, they are unlikely substantially to affect the supply price of large quantities of estate rubber, and they need not be discussed.

Wages and salaries have already risen substantially above 1941 levels. In the autumn of 1946 wages in Malaya were about double the 1941 rates. The cost of living has risen greatly. In the autumn of 1946 the price of rice, which varied greatly between different parts of the country, was everywhere several times the 1940–41 level. In the open market the cost of rice bought by Indian workers outside the ration was about ten to fifteen times the 1940–41 level. These high prices reflected the shortage of a necessity ; they were charged on the basis of what the market bore, and were quite unrelated to the cost of production. There is as yet no migration of labour from India, and the Indian Government is likely to insist on various improvements in the conditions of Indian labour as a prerequisite of the resumption of emigration. But unless the Indian Government proposes to prohibit emigration altogether, Indian labour should become available at broadly the present rates, as it is difficult to visualise so great an improvement in economic and social conditions in rural Madras as to render emigration unattractive. The Malayan authorities may also be in a position to supplement the labour resources of the country by migration from South China and from Java. Moreover, the Malays themselves seem also less reluctant to accept estate employment than they have been in the past. In the N.E.I. and in French Indo-China, estate operations have not yet been resumed on a substantial scale, and there is at present no migration from Java to Sumatra, or from Annam and Tonkin in northern Indo-China to the rubber-growing districts of Cochin-China and Cambodja in the south. The resumption of internal migration, and therefore the level of wages, in these territories is likely to be influenced by the political settlements still to be reached ; the cost of rice and the price of rubber are also likely to be factors. Judging from Malayan experience, and from the limited alternative occupations in the densely populated areas of Java and northern Indo-China, it may be suggested that money wages in these territories may settle down within a few years at about double or treble the 1940 or 1941 rates expressed in Straits cents or in pence, though in view of the political uncertainties throughout these territories this estimate may be wide of the mark.

As was to be expected on general grounds, the increase in salaries has been much less. The general presumption was strengthened in the rubber industry, as a number of former planters were likely to be attracted by the prospect of playing a part in the reconstruction of the industry. Moreover, the recruit for a planting billet is usually of specialised qualifications and inclinations, who, if the industry is not prosperous, is prepared to, and may have to, accept a salary which does not reflect fully the general rise in wages and salaries. It is thus not surprising that in the autumn of 1946 planters' salaries and allowances in Malaya were only some 10–25 per cent. above the 1940–41 levels. Further increases can be expected, but these are certain to lag behind the increase in wages.

It is now necessary to return again to 1933–34, since costs under restriction are of little value for a discussion of costs under competitive conditions. At that time many company chairmen stated that with a London price of 3*d.*–3½*d.* their companies could make a fair profit; in 1932 several stated that they could do so at 2½*d.* The average cost of production of the sterling companies furnishing returns to the Commercial Research Department of the R.G.A. was below 3*d.* per lb. in 1933 [1]; this figure (which included a small allowance for depreciation) was an over-all average of the costs of several hundred companies with a total output of about 100,000 tons. A price of 3½*d.* actually released a Stock Exchange boom even before restriction negotiations had started. The costs of 1932–33 were based on very low salaries and on impossibly low wages. On the other hand, the entire output was derived from unselected seedling trees and harvested before the development of more economic tapping systems introduced in the mid-1930's. It was repeatedly stated at the time by the highest authorities [2] that the introduction of high-yielding planting material could be confidently expected to absorb the inevitable rise in salaries and wages, and that in the long run estate costs need not rise above 1933 levels. A rise in wages such as has occurred since 1941 was clearly not contemplated in 1933, nor, however, were the further

[1] Cf. Appendix E, below. [2] *Ibid.*

improvements in planting material and technique reported by 1940.[1]

Estate wages and salary rates may be very roughly estimated to settle at about 3½–4 times the 1933 levels; wages will probably have risen by a somewhat higher proportion while the increase in salaries will probably be substantially less. This does not, of course, imply that wage and salary costs per lb. will have risen in anything like the same proportion. Quite apart from the technical improvements reviewed in Chapter 16, the increase in wages and salaries has in itself already led to important economies in labour and personnel in Malaya. The full spiral fourth daily tapping system has been widely adopted, with substantial economy in labour. In November 1946 estate production was at about three-quarters of the 1941 rate of output, with only about one-half of the 1941 labour force on the estates. There are also signs that the increase in salaries is likely to lead to wider employment of Asiatics in responsible positions; there is scope here for appreciable economies.[2]

These considerations suggest that if a period of price competition were introduced for some years in the plantation rubber industry, and output thereby concentrated on the most efficient properties, with no unnecessary cultivation methods nor inflation of staffs, then it is highly probable that within a few years after a political settlement in the N.E.I., the estates will be able to produce at least half-a-million tons at about 5*d.*–5½*d.* per lb. (say 8–9 U.S. cents) c.i.f. U.S.A. ports. It will be noted that this estimate is not based on an over-all average of estate costs, but on those of the more efficient part, say the more efficient half of the estate industry.[3] This qualification is most important, as it definitely postulates concentration of output on the cheapest producers, whose identity can be established only by competition.

On these estimates of smallholders' supply price and of estate costs, it would appear that if price competition is established, then

[1] It will be recalled that the *Pinang Gazette* suggested in March 1939 that if estates took full advantage of technical improvements and economised on supervision, the more efficient properties should produce at 1½*d.* per lb. delivered Singapore.

[2] When in Malaya, the present writer was shown a European-owned estate of 400 acres supervised on a part-time basis by a Eurasian manager, whose main charge was an 1,800-acre property in the same neighbourhood. The estate was in excellent condition, and the cost of supervision far lower than on most European estates.

[3] It will be appreciated that these considerations do not bear on conditions of 1946, a period of governmental price-fixing and of partial resumption of production. But it is of interest to record that in the summer of 1946 a leading representative of Chinese estate interests in Malaya suggested figures of very much the same order as those given in the text as the supply price of rubber under competitive conditions from the better estates under his control.

a dollar price of about 8–9 cents per lb. c.i.f. consuming countries should, within a few years, elicit about 1·3–1·4 million tons of rubber, the greater part from smallholdings. Rounding off the figures, a total annual supply of 1·5 million tons may be assumed in response to a price of 10 U.S. cents or 6*d.* per lb.[1]

Taking a longer view, further considerations need to be borne in mind. As we have seen, in 1941 the plantation rubber industry was still in its technical infancy, quite as much as was synthetic rubber. Technical progress, especially the development of high-yielding planting material, was extremely rapid throughout the 1930's, but because of restriction only a small trickle could percolate into actual practice. Some important developments were announced in 1940 only, or even later. The distribution of clonal seed to smallholders, combined with extensive new planting, possibly on a mechanised basis, holds out the possibility of large quantities of rubber at very low prices indeed. It is therefore entirely gratuitous to assume that the possibilities of reducing the cost of production are less in natural rubber than in synthetic rubber. While further reductions in the cost of the latter are possible below the level of 12–13 cents for Buna S mentioned earlier, it is not easy to see the scope for such revolutionary changes as are pregnant in the present stage of plantation technique.

It thus appears that within a year, or perhaps two years, plantation rubber can easily under-sell Buna S, even assuming a very substantial rise in estate wages above the 1941 level, a further significant measure of cost reduction in synthetic rubber, and without allowing for the effects of further technical progress in plantation practice beyond a wider adoption of improvements already realised by 1941. It is probable that the plantation product could be delivered in America at about three-quarters of the prospective price of Buna S.[2] This assumes, however, that unrestricted price competition [3] will be allowed, and that full advantage

[1] But broadly assuming the maintenance of the purchasing power of the dollar and of the pound at roughly 1945 levels; cf. p. 320, above.

[2] The view that on all reasonable assumptions the plantation product would oust Buna S under competitive conditions, is also held by Mr. K. E. Knorr (*op. cit.*), by Mr. Melvin A. Brenner (*op. cit.*), and by the leading trade journals such as the American *India Rubber World* and the British *India-Rubber Journal.*

The following quotation from the New York *Rubber Age* (Jan. 1945) confirms that this view is shared by the American manufacturers: 'Few manufacturers are interested in purchasing and operating the synthetic rubber plants in open competition with the British and the Dutch, unless some form of Government assistance is forthcoming.'

[3] Including the absence of covert or indirect restriction through compulsory cultivation of alternative products; cf. p. 347, below.

will be taken of known advances in plantation technique. It is also assumed that a political settlement will be reached in the N.E.I.

When the merits of an infant industry tariff for the protection of synthetic rubber are debated in America, it is a relevant consideration whether the supply price of the required quantities of natural rubber is around 4½*d.*–6*d.* (say, 7½–10 U.S. cents) per lb., at about the 1945 purchasing power of money or about twice that level. Though it is understood that no issues of policy are being discussed by the Rubber Study Group, which is only a fact-finding organisation, some of the most important facts, including the supply price of rubber, may well be distorted if the atmosphere of discussion were again to be that of pre-war regulation. For example, the *History of Rubber Regulation* (published as recently as mid-1944) regards 8*d.* as a reasonable minimum pre-war price. As we have seen, this was based on the false concept of 'the average cost of efficient producers' with neglect of the smallholders, from whom it was stated that no cost returns could be obtained. The truth was that the world's needs could have been amply met at a price of 3½*d.*–4*d.*[1]

IV

It is impossible to assess the likelihood of substantial government assistance being extended to Buna S. But a brief review of the considerations and arguments underlying what is likely to become an outstanding political controversy in the U.S.A. may serve to put the matter in perspective. Almost no vested interests have been created directly by the establishment of the Buna S, butadiene and styrene capacities, as over 95 per cent. of the total is owned by government agencies, the operators having only the right of first refusal should the government dispose of the plants. The production of petroleum fractions and of alcohol are, however, in private hands, as these were peace-time activities; the government interest starts at the conversion of these materials into butadiene and styrene. The greatest pressure for a tariff or a subsidy is likely to come from those interested in the production of the raw materials.

The stakes are not so great as is sometimes suggested or implied. If the entire butadiene output were based on petroleum fractions, it would absorb less than one per cent. of the annual crude oil output of the U.S.A. Grain alcohol is most unlikely to be a competitive source of butadiene. According to an estimate quoted

[1] This estimate of the supply price does not reflect on the 1940–41 agreement between the I.R.R.C. and the Rubber Reserve Company, as entirely different considerations prevailed then.

by Mr. Knorr, the pre-war price of grain would have had to be below 30 cents per bushel to be competitive with molasses as a source of industrial alcohol.[1] The average price of grain during 1930–39 was around 60 cents; by 1943–44 it was around 1.40 dollars. Mr. Knorr has estimated that even if 240,000 tons of Buna S were produced from grain alcohol butadiene, this would absorb only two-and-a-half per cent. of the average annual production of wheat and corn in the U.S.A. A more specialised and not altogether uninfluential interest in the synthetic rubber programme is that of the chemical companies, who have a large interest in the production of industrial alcohol and of numerous other intermediate materials. They are also important producers of styrene and they operate (on behalf of the government) the styrene and the butadiene-from-alcohol plants. The direct employment afforded by the synthetic rubber industry is a very minor factor in the American labour market. The co-polymerisation, butadiene and styrene plants together employ only some 25,000 workers, less than one fair-sized aircraft plant.[2]

Thus a contraction of the synthetic rubber industry would affect the U.S. economy far less than would appear from some public pronouncements. The matter cannot, however, be evaluated in such simple terms. There is an intense and justified enthusiasm in America over the outstanding achievements of the synthetic rubber industry. The technicians and chemists point with pride to these and emphasise the potentialities of the industry. Members of the farm bloc are not likely to weigh exactly the financial advantages to their constituents from a maintenance of the synthetic industry; the fact that it appears as a potential outlet for an undefined quantity of grain is a sufficient inducement to press for government assistance. Another imponderable is the lingering dislike of rubber growers (especially of the British producers), which is partly a legacy of the Stevenson scheme.

[1] Moreover, even the cheapest alcohol is very unlikely to be competitive with petroleum as a source of butadiene. In the words of the Batt Committee (whose membership and functions are reviewed on p. 330 below): 'Since 1929 the average annual price of fermentation alcohol has never been below 20 cents per gallon when made from molasses, and it has been considerably higher when made from corn. There is ample evidence to demonstrate that alcohol would have to be made available to the butadiene producers at a price substantially below 15 cents per gallon to enable it to become competitive with the low-cost petroleum butadiene plants. It appears that substantial volumes of alcohol at this price level can be obtained only through subsidies.' *Report of the Inter-Agency Policy Committee on Rubber*, p. 38.

[2] The effect on employment of changes in the income of the producers of raw materials, and the repercussions on employment in the export industries of a cessation of rubber imports, would also have to be considered in a detailed appreciation of the position.

The merits of granting government assistance to the synthetic industry are already much canvassed in the U.S.A. The participants in the debate seem to fall into two more or less distinct groups. There are those who insist that the greater part of U.S. rubber requirements should be home-produced. The arguments of this school of thought are not easy to summarise, and generally assume the conclusion they wish to reach: the U.S.A. must be made independent of imports of a vital raw material, which so greatly affects the country's everyday life, as well as the efficient functioning of its industry. The demand for government assistance is often coupled somewhat paradoxically with categorical assertions that synthetic rubber would hold its own under free competition. Others contend that valid arguments for a measure of independence from far-away sources of rubber do not involve exclusion of the bulk of pre-war imports.

It is probable that if the synthetic industry were to be assisted, the tariff (or rate of subsidy) would have to be high—in the opinion of the present writer much higher than is often assumed. A tariff of at least 40–50 per cent. is likely to be needed if it is intended to continue in operation the bulk of the American synthetic industry in face of free competition from the plantation industry.[1] But if the American consumer, taxpayer or motorist (who of course is often the same person), is prepared to pay the price, the bulk of natural rubber imports can be excluded, though for years to come it would result in slower, more expensive and more troublesome motoring.

If the entry of the natural product were severely restricted by a prohibitive tariff, or by severe import quotas, or by a heavy subsidy to the synthetic product, the plantation industry would be deprived of half its pre-war market at a time when the other half has been impoverished. Whether price competition is restored, or a new restriction scheme is introduced, the industry would have to

[1] This is not often realised, as the long-period supply price of the plantation product is almost invariably greatly overstated because discussion is so largely concentrated on the estate side of the industry and because there are so many misconceptions current about smallholders' rubber.

A notorious instance of the habitual over-estimate of the supply price of natural rubber occurred quite recently, in the summer of 1946. A price of 50 Straits cents per lb. f.o.b. Singapore (from which, in Malaya, a heavy export tax of 4 cents per lb. was deducted, which had to be borne by the producers) was fixed by inter-governmental agreement; specific tonnages were allocated to the various consuming countries by international agreement, and the British authorities undertook to act as residual buyer for all Malayan rubber forthcoming, should total supplies exceed the official allocation. It was believed that the surplus would not exceed 10,000 tons at most for the second half of 1946; it was actually over 200,000 tons, to the acute embarrassment of the authorities.

operate at a fraction of its capacity. On either alternative the difficulties would be very great, and a re-establishment of regulation would not solve the problems of an industry whose capacity would be many times in excess of absorption for many years to come. A buffer stock scheme, advocated below for more prosperous conditions, may still prove the best solution. The blow to the economies of the Far Eastern territories would, however, be so great that a restriction scheme might have to be accepted to compensate both producers and their governments with higher prices for the loss of most of their market. It should be accepted only in an extremity, since there are few industries which need a period of price competition more than does plantation rubber. The closing of the U.S. market and the resulting contraction of the industry, would sooner or later confine operations to the geographically more favourably placed smallholders and to the lowest-cost estates; for the latter, rubber would probably become a sideline to tea, palm-oil, or coffee cultivation.

The political and economic consequences of such an American policy would be far-reaching, and would necessitate, both through their direct effects and their symptomatic significance, important changes in British trade policy. These cannot be discussed here, but the wide range of repercussions should be remembered.[1] There would have to be a re-shaping of the economic structure of the rubber-producing territories, and the costs and stresses of such a change would provide the principal justification of a restriction scheme.

The advocates of what may be called the moderate policy in the American synthetic rubber discussions admit that past events justify a reduction of America's dependence on imported rubber supplies. The adherents of this view point out, however, that the establishment of a huge synthetic industry was essentially an emergency measure, akin to the expansion of the aircraft industry; they add that a recurrence of the 1941–44 rubber crisis could be avoided without the domestic production of all, or most, of American requirements. The general suggestions are for the maintenance in the U.S.A. of a large revolving physical stock of rubber, equal to at least one year's absorption, and preferably to be expanded at times

[1] The economic effects would be largely the same if natural rubber lost the U.S. market through successful competition of the synthetic product or through exclusion by tariff or quota; but there is little doubt that the political reactions would be different. Moreover, the very doubtful contingency of successful synthetic competition would always hold out the chances of at least a partial reversal of fortunes, while the determination to maintain a large domestic synthetic industry would be quasi-permanent.

of international tension, together with the continued production and use of, say, 200,000 tons of general purpose synthetic rubber annually, if necessary with the aid of a government subsidy; for the maintenance of a further reserve capacity capable of resuming operations at short notice; and for intensive research into the production and processing of synthetic rubber. These measures, together with the experience gained during 1941–44, notably the necessity for early action in times of danger, would provide ample security. Such a policy would also put a ceiling on rubber prices and ensure that the U.S.A. could not be charged exorbitant prices for its rubber imports; this would remove another cause of American apprehension.

A policy broadly along these lines has recently (July 1946) been recommended by the influential U.S. Inter-Agency Policy Committee on Rubber (Batt Committee), on which all interested government agencies were represented; Mr. William L. Batt, a former chairman of the War Production Board, was chairman of the Committee. The lucid and well-reasoned report of the Batt Committee is a document of considerable interest, to which full justice cannot be done here. The principal recommendations are for a continued production and use of about 250,000 tons of general purpose synthetic rubber annually, and for the maintenance in standby condition of an annual capacity of a further 350,000 tons. The Committee assumed that enough special purpose synthetic rubber would be produced without government assistance to satisfy the requirements of national security, but that little or no general purpose rubber would be produced without such support when natural rubber was freely available.

If a moderate policy prevails in the U.S.A. the prospects of the plantation industry are reasonably hopeful. A higher level of U.S. industrial activity than in the 1930's would compensate for most of the loss to synthetic rubber; it is clear from the experience of 1940–41 that in a prosperous year the U.S.A. could easily absorb as much as 850,000–900,000 tons of rubber. Even without greater American prosperity, the secular rise in the demand for rubber is soon likely to offset the partial loss of absorption of natural rubber, though it would be rash to dogmatise, since the effects of the devastation in Europe and the attitude towards natural rubber imports of the Soviet Union and of the Soviet bloc generally are difficult to evaluate. Synthetic rubber production in North America and the Soviet Union may total between 400,000 and 500,000 tons annually, and this may represent an annual loss of natural rubber absorption of about 250,000–400,000 tons. Combined natural and synthetic rubber absorption is at present (January 1947) at an annual rate of about 1·3 or 1·4 million tons, and the best estimates over the next few years suggest an annual absorption of the order of 1·5–1·8 million tons. Assuming a synthetic rubber production of about 400,000–500,000 tons, absorption of natural rubber is likely to be at an annual rate of about 1·1–1·3 million tons, which would be approximately equal to the high rate of absorption of the years 1940 or 1941.

This is not to imply that the difficulties of the industry will not be great. Quite apart from the physical, economic and political problems of reconstruction, there will still be much excess capacity and many high-cost producers to deal with. Nor will the main factors underlying the instability of the industry have disappeared. The two developments likely to bear on this last point are the rise of the American synthetic industry, and the acknowledged huge expansion of the acreage and capacity of the N.E.I. native producers. The substantial Buna S capacity in the U.S.A. is likely to set a ceiling to rubber prices. The rise of the N.E.I. natives to unchallengeably the largest single class of producer is likely to increase the elasticity of the total supply, since the output from these producers is fairly responsive to price changes. These considerations suggest some diminution of the price fluctuations which would occur under uncontrolled price competition. The liability to price fluctuations is, however, likely to remain very considerable. The dependence of rubber on the American motor industry, the instability of the U.S. economy, the irrationality of organised rubber markets, the plasticity of wages and salaries in the producing territories and the inelasticity of supply of a large proportion of the total capacity can all be expected to continue, with the political uncertainties in the East an added factor making for instability.

V

The major problem of rubber policy thus remains: the elimination of excessive instability without stereotyping the industry. The 1934–41 regulation scheme not only failed to resolve the difficulty but it actually secured the worst of both worlds: it froze the industry while permitting wide and rapid fluctuations to continue. The attitude of the producers has altered little since 1933. Addressing the annual meeting of the R.G.A. in April

1942 the retiring chairman said : 'There will be room for both (natural and synthetic rubber) in co-partnership with our friends in the United States by post-war agreement on much the same lines as the International Rubber Regulation Scheme.' In October 1943 Mr. Eric Miller put forward the same suggestion at the annual general meeting of Messrs. Harrisons & Crosfield ; this he did twenty-one years after the Stevenson Committee, of which he had been a prominent member, had declared that 'a policy of restriction can only be a temporary palliative'[1] ; restriction was in operation for most of the period since the Stevenson report, and its resumption is again proposed.

The blunt truth is that a period of price competition is long overdue, partly as a spur to efficiency, but also for a classification of the relative efficiencies, in terms of long-period supply prices, of different classes of producers. The importance of the last point will be appreciated by considering some unresolved issues, such as the supply prices of natural and synthetic rubber ; the relative competitive strength of estates and smallholdings, of large and small estates, of the different producing territories, and of various methods of cultivation.

The probable tendencies likely to emerge from several years of competition deserve some consideration. The competitive position of natural and synthetic rubber has already been reviewed in this chapter, and repetition would be superfluous. Within the plantation industry the smallholdings would almost certainly gain considerable ground at the expense of the estates unless discriminated against by adverse official policies. Estate methods of production are so much more expensive in terms of money, as well as of labour and capital, that under competition the smallholders would make substantial headway. They gained much ground until the advent of regulation, but for whose introduction they would have made further progress against the estates. This is obvious from a consideration of the methods and costs of these two major classes of producer, and the conclusion is confirmed by such empirical evidence as the rapid increase in smallholders' production after mid-1933, the performance of the N.E.I. native producers in 1934–36 and again in 1941. The steep rise in estate wages and cost of supplies since the 1930's has further weakened the position of the estates. Considerable sections of the smallholding industry, especially owners with poor-yielding properties relying on outside labour, may find their position further weakened as they may have to offer

[1] Cmd. 1678 of 1922, para. 14.

high piece-rates to attract tappers; owners who rely on outside labour for cultivation work may also find themselves adversely affected.[1] But these considerations do not alter the conclusion that the long-period competitive position of smallholders as a class has been strengthened against that of the estates by the rise in wages and salaries, and in the cost of supplies and of equipment.[2] But the estates are not likely to be eliminated, since the supply price of part of the capacity of smallholders' rubber is likely to be above that of substantial quantities of estate rubber.

The actual extent of displacement of estates by smallholdings cannot be foretold with any degree of accuracy (though it would almost certainly be substantial) as it depends, among other factors, on the trend of wages, the introduction and possibilities of mechanisation, the distribution of high-yielding planting material to smallholders, and possibly the most important factor, the official attitude towards the rubber-growing smallholder. It may be tentatively suggested that under conditions of free competition the share of smallholdings in total output would be not less than 60–65 per cent. over the next few years (against about 45 per cent. in 1940), with a probable long-period trend to increase.

Among geographical groups of producers, on pre-war showing, the British estates in Sumatra, the estates in Ceylon and British North Borneo, together with India and Burma, seem worst placed to face competitive conditions. The position of producers in Ceylon has been strengthened by their freedom from Japanese occupation, by the exceptional prosperity they have enjoyed since 1941, and by the capital compensation scheme mentioned in Chapter 18. These advantages have, however, been reduced and may even have been offset by the steep rise in wages since 1940. Indian producers are very likely to secure tariff protection against competition from Malaya and the N.E.I.

A widely canvassed issue in discussions about the rubber industry is the prospects of large and small units within the estate industry. Confusion is rife on this subject. It is generally stated, usually without examination, that amalgamation, if necessary by compulsion, into larger units is the most important step towards the reduction in estate costs. As has been shown earlier,[3] the problem is far from being so simple. It is obvious that the economies of

[1] A disadvantage which would be enhanced by restriction on planting or on the alienation of land.

[2] Adverse official policies might, however, destroy the competitive advantage of the smallholders; cf. Chr. 12, above, and Chr. 20, below.

[3] Pp. 271–72, above.

scale can only play a relatively minor part in rubber production, as otherwise the smallholders could not be such formidable competitors. Though it might be argued that among the estates the larger producers are more efficient, it would appear, first that generalisations about the economies of large-scale production in rubber growing are unsafe and that some of the proposals for reorganisation are undoubtedly quack remedies; secondly, that only several years of free competition could really establish the relative economic merits of the many different types and units which comprise the estate side of the industry; and thirdly, that it is most improbable that spectacular cost reductions would be achieved by increasing the scale of operations, and probably no economies at all through operating units over 5,000 acres.

The really important technical economies which may prove essential for the survival of a substantial part of the estate industry must be sought in other directions: development and use of very high-yielding planting material (which would reduce costs per pound by 50 to 70 per cent. compared to costs on unselected seedling estates); or some radical changes in plantation technique, such as the possible introduction of avenue planting, the mechanisation of important phases of operations, careful choice of tapping methods, and possibly the adoption of forestry methods of cultivation.[1] But whatever view in detail is taken of these controversial issues, the case for a period of price competition seems very strong in what is essentially an undeveloped industry.

There are, however, some *prima facie* objections to price competition. Under competition the estates would find it harder to accumulate the liquid funds needed for rehabilitation than they would under regulation, in that profits are likely to be lower. But in any case, with the large synthetic capacity in America, profits are most unlikely to be at a rate which would enable the accumulation of very large reserves in a few years. Where rehabilitation requires heavy expenditure the funds must come either from the cash resources of the companies and/or government compensation.

Under competitive conditions the dollar receipts accruing to the British, Dutch and French economies will be smaller than under regulation. Here again, a return of the halcyon days of the past cannot be expected; with restriction, however, prices

[1] Under a régime of price competition the average cost of estate output would, of course, also be substantially reduced through the concentration of production on the more efficient estates at any given stage of technique.

might still be raised above competitive levels without bringing the synthetic capacity into play. The required aim (if politically practicable) could, however, be attained without regulation, for instance by the imposition of export taxes to raise the market price of rubber to any required level. Such a tax would presuppose an agreement between the governments concerned, as the competitive power of any territory imposing it unilaterally would be considerably impaired.

Another possible argument against price competition in rubber would be a reference to the general trend towards the suppression of competition envisaged in the plans for post-war industry. In spite of all fair phrases about expansionist economics, whenever a specific plan is published on behalf of an industry, price maintenance, organised control of output and restriction of entry are almost invariably postulated; in Britain this applies from heavy steel to retail fruit distribution. The rubber producers may ask why they alone should submit to price competition when apparently no other industry contemplates doing so. It should, however, be remembered that before it became widespread elsewhere, compulsory restriction of output had been a feature of the rubber industry, and it would be a measure of somewhat rough justice if rubber were to remain competitive for a while in a quasi-monopolistic world. Should organised control of output and entry become a general feature of the economic system, the rubber industry must be expected to follow suit, but it should not do so without a few years of competition.

VI

Free price competition without any intervention would very probably result in wide price fluctuations, in spite of the somewhat greater elasticity of supply introduced by the huge native acreage in the N.E.I. and by the large synthetic capacity in the U.S.A. The adverse effects of such fluctuations are familiar, and have been discussed earlier in this study. It may, however, be possible to reconcile price competition and a large measure of stability by means of a buffer stock or pool, aiming at the elimination of short-period fluctuations, while allowing long-period trends to work themselves out.

A proposal along these lines was put forward by Mr. Ormsby Gore (Lord Harlech) as early as 1928, as being specially suitable for the rubber industry: 'The form that rationalisation might eventually take in the rubber industry seems to me to be a powerful disinterested corporation, with sufficient financial resources to build up large reserve stocks in times of depression, which would be used to prevent or mitigate the temporary booms that cause such disturbance.'[1] Since then many similar suggestions have been put forward. Lord Keynes has dwelt more than once on the wide price fluctuations of primary products (of which rubber presents the extreme case), and has advocated special government storage facilities—a variant of a buffer stock scheme—as the most suitable solution.[2] Authoritative support for a buffer stock scheme also came from the British Government delegation at the Hot Springs conference of 1943. More recently (April 1945) a League of Nations expert committee reported in favour of buffer stocks, and this opinion has been incorporated in some League proposals for post-war economic stability.[3] The list could be extended. Though for some years past there has thus been a considerable body of opinion in favour of such a policy, it has not yet been put into effect. The case for it in the rubber industry is particularly strong, as being the only device for combining a period of greatly overdue competition with a reasonable measure of stability. There seems no reason to doubt its practicability, provided pressure is resisted for prices higher than would be justified by considerations of long-period equilibrium.

If the initial price is fixed at a level not far removed from the equilibrium price over the first year or two years of the pool's operations, and the managers are prepared to carry stocks up to 300,000–400,000 tons, there is no reason why the plan should not work smoothly, with quarterly or half-yearly price changes of a minor order compared to past fluctuations.[4] In conducting day-to-day business the pool would act as any large dealer, with the outstanding difference that it would be prepared to maintain a large open position. The managers would quote a series of buying and selling prices (with a turn of perhaps one-eighth or one-sixteenth of a penny) for different grades of rubber (including even general purpose synthetic rubber if found desirable, though

[1] *Op. cit.*, p. 147.

[2] 'Government Storage of Foodstuffs and Raw Materials', *Economic Journal*, Sept. 1938.

[3] *Economic Stability in the Post-War World* (1945).

[4] Lord Keynes calculated in 1938 that 'there has only been one year in the last ten in which the high price of rubber exceeded the low by less than 70 per cent. The average excess of the year's high over the year's low has been 96 per cent. In other words, there is on the average some date in every year at which the price of rubber is approximately double its price at some other date in that year.' 'Government Storage of Foodstuffs and Raw Materials', *Economic Journal*, Sept. 1938.

this is unlikely), and for different positions, from spot rubber to, say, twelve months' futures. Experience would show how often the prices would have to be revised. The pool would probably do an appreciable volume of business in physical rubber in competition with other dealers. The bulk of the physical stock would probably be held in the U.S.A. as the most important consuming country.[1] On the analogy of the various national exchange equalisation accounts, it may be suggested that the initial capital could be made available by the issue of treasury bills, or similar securities of the participating governments. The necessary capital would be much less than is required to finance the exchange equalisation accounts. £25 millions would be ample on all reasonable assumptions since this would carry more than a quarter of a million tons of rubber even at 1*s*., and only part of the capital would be locked up in physical rubber at any given time. The pool would probably make a substantial profit on current account; if pressure for high prices is resisted there is no reason for expecting losses on capital account. Should there be any deficit, this could easily be financed by a very small tax on all rubber exports, which the manufacturers would gladly accept as a means of abolishing the violent price fluctuations.

These are only the rough outlines of a scheme which could no doubt be greatly improved. It is, however, not easy to see why it should be inherently impracticable. In the past, rubber producers have objected strongly to any suggestion of a buffer stock, even to the modest proposal for a stock held by the I.R.R.C. to prevent runaway markets such as had occurred in 1936–37. But before 1941 the producers always had available the much more profitable alternative of restriction. When the alternatives are only variants of price competition, complete non-intervention or a buffer stock, they may reconsider their attitude, although prejudices often die hard. Leaders of the industry are wont to argue that owing to the special circumstances of rubber growing, especially the low elasticity of the supply of the commodity, a buffer stock scheme would not suit the requirements of the industry and would be unworkable. This argument is difficult to accept, since the low elasticity of supply is one of the principal causes of the price instability of rubber, and thus an important justification for a buffer stock plan.

It was, however, from the market, from the brokers and dealers,

[1] This stock would be a part only of the total held there as an insurance against the recurrence of a rubber crisis.

that the strongest opposition to buffer stock proposals has come in the past, and will no doubt come again in the future. The reason is not hard to see : the speculative business of the market would vanish, and its activities shrink considerably. But none of its useful functions would disappear. The ready marketability of rubber would in no way be impaired ; it would continue to be easily saleable in the interior of Malaya and the N.E.I. As before, the shipping, grading and sorting of rubber would be largely performed by dealers. Some dealers would close down as there would not be enough business to go around in the absence of speculation, but others would continue their activities. As has been shown, the rubber markets have not in the past reduced the violence of the price fluctuations, and the professional participants were often engaged in misleading the public in order to obtain more business. As the buffer stock scheme visualised here would enable the market to carry on all its legitimate functions,[1] there would be no need to regret the disappearance of activities which were of negative social value.

VII

Thus the policy suggested (after the end of the temporary scarcity) is for a period of price competition, coupled with a buffer stock for the elimination of excessive price fluctuations. Conditions can, however, be visualised under which regulation would have to be introduced again. Two contingencies which might necessitate the resumption of restriction have already been mentioned. The virtual closure of the American market might justify a temporary control scheme, though in such an eventuality a subsequent early acceptance of competitive conditions would be desirable. Again, if the economic system of the future turns out to be largely monopolistic, it would be unreasonable to ask the rubber industry to pursue a different course, and after a period of competition a renewal of restriction would have to be accepted.

There is another contingency which might force a return to restriction. In the past the official American attitude to formal international commodity agreements has varied from indifference to strong opposition. During the last few years, the U.S. authorities have given their official support to several international commodity agreements, including at least one (coffee) covering a major U.S.

[1] Including the provision of hedging facilities for manufacturers by quoting forward prices.

import. The U.S.A. was a party to the 1942 international wheat agreement, while an international cotton regulation scheme was being officially discussed in 1944–45. Press reports suggested in August 1944 that for political and economic reasons the State Department favoured post-war inter-governmental regulation of commodities in which surplus capacity has emerged as a result of the war ; this would clearly apply to rubber. These reports were confirmed when Mr. Bernard Haley, Chief of the Office of International Trade Policy of the State Department, gave a large measure of qualified support to commodity regulation in an important address to the American Academy of Political Science in April 1945. A day or two before Mr. Haley's address, the New York *Rubber Age* (April 1945) actually proposed a resumption of regulation after the war, to cover both natural and synthetic rubber. Thus it appears that just when the U.S.A. has the power effectively to veto any plan for rubber restriction and to enforce competition among producers, the authorities may be more inclined to favour an all-embracing restriction scheme under which the sheltered high-cost producers are likely to be the synthetic plants ; or the U.S. authorities may press for restriction among natural rubber producers to raise the price of natural rubber. These measures, while enhancing the cost of rubber to the American motorist, would enable the authorities to maintain in operation an appreciable proportion of the synthetic rubber capacity without a tariff or an expensive subsidy. It is even possible that the free entry of natural rubber into the U.S.A. may eventually be conditional on the acceptance by the natural rubber producers of a restriction scheme, either for natural rubber alone or for both natural and synthetic rubber.

The details of the most suitable machinery could be decided only at the time of the re-introduction of regulation. The lessons of the past indicate only too clearly that without special protection the smallholders are certain to be harshly and unfairly treated. Whatever scheme is adopted, the quotas and their internal distribution should frankly recognise that at prices likely to prevail under regulation the normal output per acre of smallholdings, without any overtapping, appreciably exceeds that of seedling estates. Again, if planting is to be restricted and replanting permitted, a special issue of new planting rights to smallholders will be required to offset their inability to replant. An important factor ensuring fairer treatment of smallholders would be a general reconsideration, long overdue, of both official and unofficial attitudes towards these producers. A resumption of restriction would suggest the desirability of periodic impartial investigations into estate costs of production. These would be largely unnecessary under competition, but would be useful under restriction, especially if the prices envisaged were to be once again linked with the 'average cost of efficient producers'. Lastly, whatever form of regulation is adopted, the free transfer of export and production rights would be desirable.

The advent of synthetic rubber and the lavish governmental and private expenditure on research into production and processing, will force the plantation industry, whether competitive or controlled, greatly to increase its expenditure on organised research. The industry will not be able to expend sums comparable to those spent in America, since the resources of the producers and of the local governments are much smaller. Nevertheless, research on a more ambitious scale than before the war will be necessary if the plantation product is to continue to compete successfully with synthetic rubber; unremitting efforts will be required to improve the quality and to reduce the supply price of natural rubber. The widest distribution of the results of research will also have to be ensured; as already emphasised, high-yielding planting material must be made available to the smallholders, since it is probable that the answer to synthetic competition lies in rubber at the lowest possible price, which means smallholders' rubber together with the output of the more efficient estates, supplemented by a reliable supply of latex and possibly by some modified or special rubbers.

CHAPTER 20

THE POSITION AND PROSPECTS OF THE MALAYAN RUBBER INDUSTRY[1]

I

THE previous chapter discussed the factors affecting the future of the rubber industry generally. We shall now consider certain features specifically in relation to Malaya, where the volume of production had, by the autumn of 1946, reached the peak level of 1941. The intrinsic importance of the Malayan rubber industry in the economy of the British Empire is very considerable, as it is a highly important source of foreign exchange, and the economic basis of one of the most prosperous colonial territories ; Malayan smallholders' rubber is also the most important cash crop grown by any local population in the colonies. The brief review of the following pages may also throw some light on the problems of the other producing territories.

The destruction of plantations as a result of the Japanese occupation was very small. Between 3 and 5 per cent. of the smallholding area and about 7–8 per cent. of the estate area was felled. Some immature areas planted by the estates in 1941 are so overgrown that they may have to be replanted or abandoned. In all, not more than 5–7 per cent. of the total area has been lost.

The labour force is very seriously depleted. By the late summer of 1946 only about one-half of the 1941 estate labour force was available,[2] while there was an acute shortage of labour on those smallholdings which rely on outside assistance. The shortage was clearly noticeable where cleaning-up operations were necessary. In the autumn of 1946 Indian wage rates were about double, and earnings of Chinese about two-and-a-half times those of 1941. There is a growing practice of paying piece-rates in place of share-tapping on many smallholdings. Another recent development is a greater willingness on the part of Malays to accept wage employment on estates. The price of rice and of simple manufactured goods is generally high, and in some places very high. It is, however, widely expected that prices will fall (there was already a slight decline in the autumn of 1946).

[1] For reasons stated on p. 309, above, the degree of reliance which can be placed on parts of this chapter differs considerably from that which the earlier parts of the book can bear.

[2] By the late spring of 1947 the estate labour force was, however, largely restored.

By September 1946 the smallholders were producing at an annual rate of over 300,000 tons, which was higher than at any time since the eve of restriction. This was in spite of shortage of outside labour, and (partly because of this shortage) the fact that somewhere between one-quarter and one-third of the mature acreage was wholly untapped, and part of the rest only lightly tapped. The estates with only one-half of their labour force, were by September–October 1946 producing at an annual rate of about 270,000 tons, or three-quarters of the 1941 level. They also had very large areas, including some of the best budded rubber, still untapped. Considerable economies in labour had been achieved compared with 1941.

Experience suggests already that these large yields cannot be wholly ascribed to flush production (the result of the resting of the trees) either on smallholdings or on estates. In a few districts yields on some smallholdings have reached an annual rate of 1,200–1,500 lb. per acre. Though these very high yields are partly due to flush production, the length of time which has elapsed since these areas were re-opened, and the observed condition of the trees, suggest that previous ideas of smallholders' capacity may need further substantial revision, possibly well beyond the levels suggested by the results of the smallholdings enquiry of 1931–33.

Against this rapid recovery of output, both on smallholdings and on estates, the official policies at present being pursued are such as to threaten not only the future of the smallholding industry but also the survival of the Malayan industry against that of the N.E.I. They also jeopardise the social stability of Malaya.

By far the most important element is that *the planting provisions of restriction are still (January 1947) in force, and are being enforced.* In other words, the low-cost producers are still being prevented from expanding by new planting.[1,2] This is tantamount to unilateral restriction for Malaya. Some of the effects of unilateral restriction have already been seen in the operation of the Stevenson scheme. This, however, was not the only instance. The alienation of land for rubber planting was severely restricted in Malaya from 1930

[1] The purpose can only be to maintain the position of the high-cost producers. Economy of labour in the interest of the food production campaign cannot be adduced as an argument, since on these grounds replanting should also be prohibited. Moreover, replanting requires sustained manuring which is unnecessary for new planting and it is thus particularly wasteful of resources required for food production.

[2] Since this paragraph was written the ban on new planting has been lifted in Malaya. Restrictions on the alienation of land for planting still remain, and these may have long-term effects similar to the ban on new planting; cf. pp. 175–76, above.

to 1934 (as well as during the Stevenson scheme), while her principal rivals did not place themselves under this restraint. After 1934 the prohibition of new planting applied formally to all eastern territories, but it is very doubtful whether the prohibition was as effectively policed in the N.E.I. or Siam as it was in Malaya. As a policy of unilateral restriction is again being pursued in Malaya, the results of similar policies in the past deserve a brief review.

Between the end of 1925 [1] and the end of 1940, the area under rubber in Malaya increased from 2,450,000 acres to 3,480,000 acres, while in other countries in the East the increase was from about 2,430,000 acres to approximately 6,780,000 acres, so that the share of Malaya in the total declined over this period from approximately one-half to about one-third.

Over this period there was a striking increase in the planted areas of some of the low-cost territories; in Sarawak from 90,000 acres to 240,000 acres, in Siam from 50,000 acres to 420,000 acres, in French Indo-China from 90,000 acres to 330,000 acres. Most important of all, in the N.E.I. the area under rubber increased during this period from about 1,800,000 acres to nearly 4,800,000 acres, with the native area alone rising from about three-quarters of a million acres to around 3¼ million acres. Not only did these territories make very rapid headway against Malaya, but the age composition of the planted areas has become much more favourable than in Malaya, with a larger proportion of their rubber in the young age groups.

The following table epitomises the position:

TABLE I

Changes in Areas under Rubber, 1925–40

	1925 (Thousand acres)	1940 (Thousand acres)	1940 *as per cent. of* 1925	*Percentage of* 1940 *area over* 15 *years' old*
Malayan estates	1,559	2,107	135	65
Malayan smallholders	1,082	1,374	127	79
Total Malaya	2,641	3,481	132	70
Ceylon estates	321	359	112	82
Ceylon smallholders	176	280	159	63
Total Ceylon	497	639	129	74
N.E.I. estates	980	1,567	160	49
N.E.I. natives	750	3,200	425	23
Total N.E.I.	1,730	4,767	275	32
All other territories	540	1,370	254	38

[1] The peak year of the Stevenson boom.

Between 1925 and 1940 the smallholders in Malaya increased their acreage by 25 per cent. against 325 per cent. in the N.E.I.; by 1940 four-fifths of the smallholdings acreage in Malaya was over fifteen years' old against less than one-quarter in the N.E.I. Although rubber cultivation was bound to have spread in any event in the native areas of the N.E.I. and in Sarawak, Siam and French Indo-China, the rapid growth of the productive capacity of these countries was much stimulated by the policies pursued in Malaya.

On any reasonable assumption the prospective demand for natural rubber over the next decade or so can be entirely, or almost entirely, satisfied from the four low-cost producing territories already specified (the N.E.I., Siam, Sarawak and French Indo-China) if their mature areas are fully tapped. It is a striking reflection on the deterioration of the relative position of Malaya (and of Ceylon) over the last two decades, that in a few years' time it should be possible to meet the normal peace-time demand for natural rubber without any contribution from the two territories which less than twenty-five years ago considered their monopoly position sufficiently powerful to operate a statutory restriction scheme without co-operation from any other territory.

The long-term competitive position of the low-cost producers, particularly the N.E.I. native smallholders, is very strong. The basis of this strength lies in their planting methods described earlier,[1] and in the favourable age-composition of their holdings. It is reinforced by recent political changes in the N.E.I. For the first time since its establishment, the native industry of Sumatra and Borneo will cease to be governed by an administration in whose rubber policy the maintenance of the capital value of the European estates was a prime consideration. In due course this political change is bound to be reflected in such matters as planting policy, or the distribution of high-yielding planting material to smallholders. The position of these producers would be likely to carry some influence even under restriction, since the future government of the N.E.I. would almost certainly stake a claim for a quota commensurate with their acreage and competitive strength.

In these conditions, unilateral restriction must prove disastrous to Malaya. In the face of overwhelming historical evidence and in defiance of categoric governmental assurances this policy is again being pursued in Malaya, with a planted acreage less than one-third of the total area of the principal producing territories,

[1] Above, pp. 67–68.

and substantially less than the acreage under rubber in the N.E.I. where there is not even nominal control of new planting.

Replanting is quite inadequate to enable Malaya to retain, let alone to strengthen, her position, because as has been shown in detail in Chapter 12 above, the lowest-cost producers cannot take advantage of it, and also because many plantations, both estates and smallholdings, are on unsuitable soil. In fact, the smallholders will be gradually eliminated unless they can plant on new land. Earlier discussion of this question related to smallholders generally. In Malaya there is the added factor that the higher average age of their properties than in the N.E.I. means that the smallholders are much more acutely threatened. This is shown in Diagram I (overleaf).[1] The main assumptions of the diagram are as follows: new planting is prohibited; estates replant annually 80,000 acres or 4 per cent. of the 1941 Malayan estate area [2]; yields on seedling estates already planted average 400 lb. per mature acre and on budded estates 800 lb. per mature acre; yields on estates to be replanted in the future will rise from 100 lb. per acre at five years from planting, to 400 lb. seven years and to 1,200 lb. twelve years from planting (which is very conservative, and particularly for the earlier years is definitely below most current estimates); yields on smallholdings average 600 lb. per mature acre up to thirty years from planting and then gradually taper off until they drop to zero at forty-one years. A note showing the assumptions in detail is appended to the end of this chapter.

Thus if this restrictive policy is continued, or resumed, then on the assumptions of the diagram the smallholdings will be eliminated in about twenty years. The underlying estimates probably understate the physical productive capacity of smallholdings (though the yields assumed are still much higher than the *maximum* assessment under rubber restriction before the war, and about treble the average assessment of smallholdings under the Stevenson scheme), and may also exaggerate the decline in the physical capacity of the smallholdings, but they do not overstate the decline in the competitive

[1] Prepared by Mr. W. G. G. Kellett, Statistician of the London Rubber Secretariat.

[2] This is likely to be conservative, as there are good reasons for expecting a high level of replanting on estates. The effective administration of the majority of the plantation-companies lies with the agency houses; the independence of the companies is purely nominal. The agency houses (which have no substantial shareholdings in the operating companies) are usually much more concerned with lengthening the life of the estates than with maximising of dividends. Once the advantages of replanting are recognised by the agency houses they can be expected to maintain a high level of replanting even if from the shareholders' point of view a different use of funds would be profitable.

position of the smallholders through the absolute and relative decline in the yields per acre on smallholdings against estates.[1] Moreover, the yields assumed on replanted areas are definitely conservative, and those assumed on smallholdings up to 30 or 35 years of age are reasonably generous.

It has already been shown that rubber is a crop highly suited to the smallholder, who is in fact a very efficient producer. It is an industry where, statutory restriction apart, the small man was able until recently to start on his own, and make a decent, as well

Diagram I

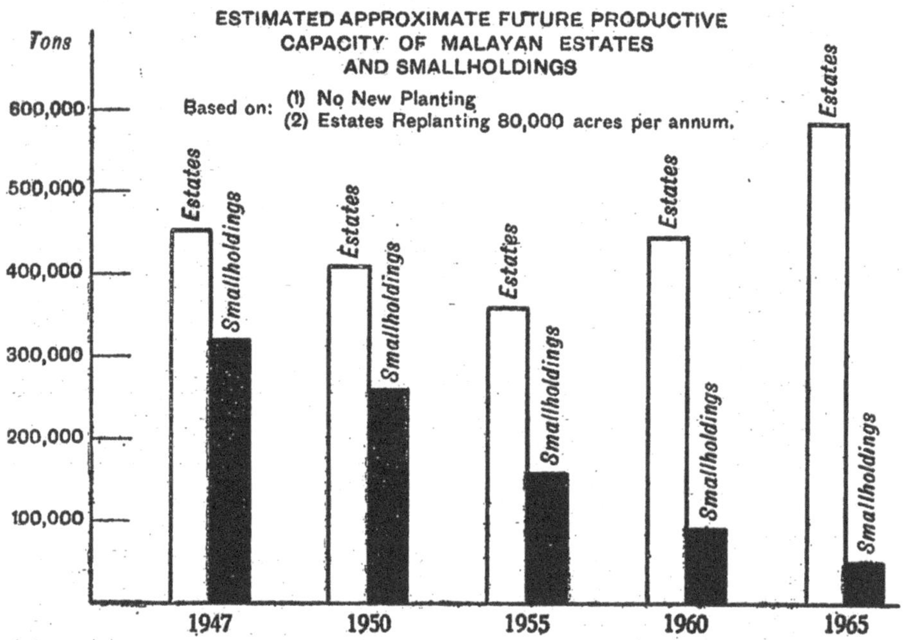

as an independent, living with the possibility of rising to higher levels. There are throughout Malaya quite a few small and medium-sized holdings owned by former estate labourers who branched out as independent planters when new planting was possible. Had it not been for the statutory restriction prevailing in Malaya almost without interruption since 1922, the number of these small and medium owners would to-day be considerably larger than it actually is. Such an extension of small individual ownership would have conduced to the social stability of the country. Thus the policies

[1] This affects especially smallholders relying on outside labourers for tapping to whom higher piece rates have to be offered to offset the lower yields per tree than on estates. Inability to plant with high-yielding material would enhance the relative disadvantage of this section of the smallholding industry.

pursued involve discrimination against one of the best forms of peasant proprietorship in favour of production (at a high cost), which is dependent on large alien labour forces. It involves the substitution of landless labourers for independent agricultural producers. This hardly seems in accord with declared British colonial policy.

Apart from the major element of the planting provisions there are other elements of official policy and administration detrimental to the smallholder. First, there is the failure to distribute supplies and equipment needed for the production of smallholders' rubber. The Malayan Rubber Estate Owners' Company was much more successful in providing supplies and equipment to the estates than was the Rubber Buying Unit which acted as the agent for the Colonial Office in distributing supplies to smallholders. This agency very largely failed in its task,[1] so that once again specific pledges given in London were not honoured. This has had the result that in the summer of 1946 some supplies (for instance, acetic acid) were unobtainable, while others (for instance, tapping knives and latex cups) could be obtained only at exorbitant prices. The immediate effects on the smallholder were a financial loss, and in some cases contraction of new indebtedness.

Secondly, the authorities are already making available to estate workers some foodstuffs and textiles at controlled prices, and a further extension is planned. Meanwhile the smallholders and their workers frequently have to pay very high prices for essential commodities as these schemes are not extended to them. Apart from immediate hardship, their competitive position is again weakened.

Thirdly, the burden of the official drive to increase food production falls largely on the smallholder, who is often compelled to grow padi and tapioca on soil yielding only nominal crops, and to forgo the production of rubber which is his best crop, even at the present very high prices of food. Official pressure for food cultivation has by the early part of 1947 become an important handicap to the rubber-growing smallholder compared with the estates.

II

The main changes in policy which are necessary will be clear. Most obviously there is the need for a very early removal of the

[1] Readers who consider this an exaggeration are referred to *Report on a Visit to the Rubber Growing Smallholdings of Malaya*, Chapter III (to be published shortly), for a detailed discussion and examples of the negligence and ineptitude on the part of those entrusted with the task.

restriction on new planting. In order to make new planting feasible, there must also be liberal alienation (and on easy terms) of land. There are various other possibilities as well of assisting the smallholder to take full advantage of such a change in official policy. Reference has already been made to a suggestion made by a temporary officer in Kuala Lumpur, that the Government should fell and clear, preferably by mechanised means, large areas suitable for rubber cultivation, establish small high-yielding plantations, and lease or sell these on favourable terms to actual or prospective smallholders. Short of this, loans could be made to suitable applicants to enable them to meet the expected cost of establishing a new plantation ; particular attention should be given to the encouragement of small ownership. It is axiomatic that high-yielding planting material, above all clonal seed, should be freely available to all who undertake new planting. This means that the material must be brought to the notice of, and distributed to, smallholders. Other measures would be arrangements for the more efficient and equitable distribution of supplies and equipment for rubber production, and of foodstuffs and textiles, as well as for a more equitable sharing of the burden of the food production drive.

The position of Malayan rubber research will also need early consideration. In the years before 1941 the R.R.I.M. was rapidly making up ground lost through its belated start, and it served the estate industry well. There will, however, have to be a substantial increase in the scale of rubber research, and no doubt the activities of the Institute will also expand. The potentialities of mechanised rubber cultivation should claim early attention. The Government might follow the example of the N.E.I. Government and own some rubber estates, operating them on commercial lines. They might go even further and operate a number of estates of different sizes ranging from, say, 1,000 to 30,000 acres, specifically with a view to comparing the working costs of different sized units. These estates could be considered the commercial counterpart of the work of the Research Institute in the scientific field. Even the largest of these estates would be well below one-half per cent. of world acreage, and would not affect competitive conditions ; on any rational assumption, the optimum size of the operating unit in rubber production is fully compatible with perfect competition. Some economic aspects of rubber research, such as optimum planting density, the economics of avenue planting, and the optimum size of estates, will require more attention than they received before 1941.

The needs of the smallholder will not, however, be met without drastic re-organisation (including the control and administration) of the Institute. It may be that even this would prove inadequate, and that a new organisation would need to be established concerned solely and specifically with the problems of production on smallholdings.[1] Such measures are required not only in the interests of the smallholders, but also in order to strengthen the competitive position of the Malayan rubber industry as a whole.

Although neither the estates nor the smallholdings have suffered as much damage as was feared from the Japanese occupation, and the supply price of Malayan rubber will not be appreciably affected, there have been considerable individual losses by deterioration or destruction of both plantations and equipment. There is little known publicly about official plans for compensation ; meanwhile, some of the producers will have difficulty in restoring or maintaining production, and it is therefore desirable that a policy covering both principles and methods of administration should be announced soon.

The competitive position of the Malayan rubber industry is likely to be influenced by the taxation system. The tax system of Malaya embodies some legacies of the early days of imperfect administration ; for instance, the export taxes were a mainstay of the revenue before 1914 as they were easy to collect. In the general re-examination of the country's fiscal system which will no doubt be undertaken, the influence of the principal sources of revenue on the competitive position of the export industries will need to be remembered.

The authorities might also consider establishing stations for buying and smoking smallholders' rubber, or for purchasing and shipping their latex. This would be done in competition with other dealers. There is precedent for such action in Malaya, since the Government owns some rice mills, which purchase and process Malayan padi in competition with Chinese millers. The need for such action in rubber was not particularly urgent before the war, as buying competition among dealers was generally brisk. There were occasional exceptions, and these might become more numerous in the future, especially as Japanese dealers are likely to be eliminated. The development of bulk latex shipments is also likely to reduce buying competition.

In 1941 the conditions of Malayan estate labour were by general consent among the best, or actually the best, anywhere in the

[1] Specific proposals will be found in *Report on a Visit to the Rubber Growing Smallholdings of Malaya*, Chapter III (to be published shortly).

East. The chronic persistence of certain deficiencies and abuses —in spite of repeated and fair criticisms—stood out all the more vividly. The suggestions for reform in Malaya have already been implied or stated explicitly: extension of minimum wages to the whole country and abolition of the 'key districts'; reconstitution of the Indian Immigration Committee, or preferably the establishment of a small wages board with one representative each of employers and workers, with a judge as chairman; energetic steps to prevent the recurrence of the evasion of the minimum wage legislation through part payment 'for morning work only', or through the offer of less than the minimum number of working days; increase of subsistence food production by migrant workers on estates; public works during a period of depression. The extension of the minimum wage legislation to Chinese workers may also have to be considered.

Although it is impossible to estimate accurately the future dependence of the Malayan rubber industry on immigrant labour, Malaya is unlikely to be able to dispense with it in the next few years. Though the economic future of the country is uncertain, it would appear that unless the rubber industry were to collapse, Malaya, if in need of immigrants, will be able to offer wages and conditions which will attract large numbers, unless the would-be emigrants are barred from departing. The Malayan authorities may, however, be faced with difficult decisions. Migration from South India will be subject to the discretion of the Indian authorities, and with Congress firmly established in Madras, the *zemindar* and the *bania* may not be content to watch passively a movement which tends to raise the wages and status of agricultural labour in the recruiting districts. Large-scale immigration of agricultural labour from South China may be politically unwelcome in Malaya. Javanese labour appears at first sight the ideal solution, since the Javanese are racially and politically much nearer to the Malays than are the Chinese or the Indian migrants; they are also excellent estate workers, and the supply is unlimited. There would be an important drawback: by relying on Javanese labour, the costs of the Malayan estates would be at the mercy of the N.E.I. administration, which could inflate Malayan costs simply by varying the minimum conditions stipulated for Javanese immigrants, and this might be a precarious position.

III

Some of the proposals in the preceding section are designed to strengthen the competitive position of the Malayan rubber industry. It may be objected that the acceptance of new planting, which is the most fundamental of these proposals, would enhance Malaya's already great dependence on rubber, with all the attendant risks. There is an understandable reluctance on the part of the authorities to commit Malaya further in this direction. The substantial advantages are, however, easily overlooked : the prosperity of Malaya (in spite of the poverty of her soil), the high administrative, educational and health standards all have their source very largely in money derived from rubber. In any case, it is probable that for years to come the rubber industry will remain the mainstay of the Malayan economy, even though the structure of the industry may differ from its present form ; hence the importance of bringing the industry to a high degree of efficiency, for which new planting is an essential condition. The dangers inherent in the reliance of a country on a few staple exports depend not only on the international competitive strength of the producers, but also on their ability to turn to alternative sources of livelihood. The case for new planting by smallholders, low-cost producers growing an appreciable proportion of their food requirements, or capable of producing these within a reasonably short period, is thus stronger than it is for new planting by estates whose costs are high and whose large labour forces depend almost entirely on purchased foodstuffs. But in any event extensive new planting need not compete to any great extent with the attempts to develop suitable industries or crops other than rubber. The search for these can continue while new planting of rubber is permitted or even assisted.

There is one particular feature of rubber cultivation which suggests strongly that an extension of the planted area would not seriously hamper the development of other forms of economic activity, nor permanently increase to any great extent the reliance of Malaya on rubber. This is the very small demand which rubber makes on plant food. As has been shown earlier,[1] the annual crop of latex takes next to nothing out of the soil, and on smallholdings much of whatever plant food is removed is returned by the decomposition of the natural cover and of the heavy leaf fall.

Even a very large extension of the area under rubber smallholdings would not, moreover, represent an irrevocable commitment

[1] Above, pp. 259–260.

in the direction of greater dependence on rubber, since an abandoned smallholding reverts to *blukar*, with rubber seedlings predominant, and in a few years is again perfectly suitable for opening up for other cultivation. At worst, a slight tendency toward shifting cultivation may develop but with comparatively little movement and over very long cycles. The administrative inconvenience which would be caused if such a movement did in fact take place would be a small price to pay for the enhanced competitive strength of the Malayan rubber industry. In view of the long life of the rubber tree and of the sustained yields of smallholders' rubber, it is certain that movement would be small; its actual extent would depend on the rate of decline and obsolescence of rubber smallholdings, the location of land alienated for new planting, the availability of capital and labour for new planting, and the willingness of smallholders (and of landless people) to take up land some distance from the existing holdings.

Although a policy of extensive new planting would divert some labour into the industry and to this extent may be said to enhance Malaya's reliance on rubber, the actual diversion would be much less than would appear at first sight. There are thousands of share tappers and casual labourers working on rubber smallholdings for low incomes which they have to accept as they possess no rubber holdings of their own. If these people became small owners the number of rubber smallholders would increase, but there would be no change in the number of people dependent on rubber for their livelihood. The real change would be the substitution of small owners for wage-earners and casual labourers.

Whatever may be the detailed merits of the proposals which have been made, decisions on these matters cannot be postponed much longer. At the present time (January 1947), in spite of all the obstacles put in their way, the N.E.I. native producers are exporting at a rate of 300,000 tons a year; in French Indo-China production is expected to reach an annual total of 100,000–120,000 tons within a year or two of the political settlement. In face of the policies which have been so persistently pursued, and which still permeate official opinion in Malaya, the implications are serious not only for Malaya but also for the whole of British colonial economic policy.

Note on the Assumptions of Diagram I

Diagram I is based on the following assumptions:

(*a*) There will be no new planting.

(*b*) Estates will replant with high-yielding material at a rate of 80,000 acres per annum.

(*c*) Yields on existing seedling rubber will average 400 lb. per acre per annum.

(*d*) Yields on existing budded estates will average 800 lb. per acre per annum.

(*e*) The following yields are assumed for estates to be replanted in the future.

Age (years)	*Yield (lb./acre)*	*Age (years)*	*Yield (lb./acre)*
5–6	100	9–10	700
6–7	200	10–11	900
7–8	400	11–12	1,100
8–9	500	12–13	1,200

(*f*) The following yields have been assumed for smallholdings:

Age (years)	*Yield (lb./acre)*	*Age (years)*	*Yield (lb./acre)*
7–30	600	36–37	400
31–32	575	37–38	300
32–33	550	38–39	200
33–34	525	39–40	100
34–35	500	40–41	50
35–36	450	Over 41	Nil

APPENDICES

APPENDIX A

THE VALUE OF THE AGRICULTURAL AND MINING OUTPUT OF MALAYA, 1929 AND 1932[1]

THE F.M.S. Retrenchment Commission (1932) in its report (pp. 2 and 3) produced an estimate of what it termed the national income of the F.M.S. for 1931. In fact, the calculation is a rough estimate of the gross value of agricultural, mining and manufacturing output. It is not stated how the figures were calculated, nor whether agricultural produce consumed by the growers was fully allowed for. Gross and net output are not differentiated, services are omitted altogether, except for retail distribution which figures as 'difference between wholesale and retail prices', and gross profits of foreign trade which are represented by the difference between retail prices (ex import duty) and declared import values, 'and we have assumed this difference to be 25 per cent. of the declared value'. The Commission omitted to say that much of the rubber and tin was produced by companies domiciled outside the F.M.S., and the gross proceeds should not therefore be included in the F.M.S. national income. The Commissioners were generally somewhat unorthodox on invisibles, as can be seen from the following statement: 'Profits on external investments and other invisible imports [*sic*] entering into individual incomes, rank, of course, for inclusion into gross National Income . . . accretions of this sort are, in some respects, fortuitous in character and might, if they occur, be regarded as bonuses.' The Commission's calculations of certain elements in the gross agricultural output, such as livestock and forest produce, may, however, be useful.

The sole purpose of the rough calculations which follow is to indicate the importance of rubber and tin in the Malayan economy in 1929 and 1932. From the scanty data available, nothing more ambitious than an approximation to the orders of magnitude can be expected.

The calculation of the value of mining output—138 million dollars in 1929 and 46 millions in 1932—is based on figures in Sir Lewis Fermor's *Report upon the Mining Industry of Malaya*. There is no reason to doubt the accuracy of his careful work. Some of the figures have had to be estimated, but the totals are unlikely to have a margin of error above 2 per cent.

The estimate of the gross value of agricultural output is much more hazardous, although acreage figures of the areas under the most important crops are available, and the annual production of rubber and padi was

[1] Cf. p. 15, above.

officially estimated. Only very approximate yield figures are, however, available for other crops, and these not year by year but as *ad hoc* estimates published by members of the staff of the Department of Agriculture, whenever they investigated the conditions of production of individual commodities. These are found occasionally in the *Annual Reports* of the Director of Agriculture, or in articles in the *M.A.J.*

Estimates of prices at which the output is to be valued are even more approximate. For rubber and tin, export prices calculated from the F.M.S. trade returns furnish reasonably accurate figures. For our purpose, these are preferable to any given set of market prices, since export prices are calculated by dividing total net exports by the quantity exported, and no further allowance need be made for the different grades of rubber produced. For padi, neither the Singapore price nor any other market index can be used, as these all refer to imported rice or padi. The price paid by the government rice mill at Bagan Serai in Perak for Malayan padi is probably the best single price to take. For coconuts, coffee and tapioca the prices used are those in the *Annual Reports* of the Director of Agriculture or in the market reports published occasionally in the *M.A.J.* As rubber, for which accurate figures are available, was by far the most important item in agricultural output, the comparatively large errors in the estimated value of the other items do not affect the total results very greatly. Nor is the calculation of agricultural output much affected by discussing gross figures only, as the value of purchased fertilisers and of draught animals was negligible.

The estimates of 430 $\pm$ 20 millions and of 130 $\pm$ 15 millions for the agricultural output of Malaya in 1929 and 1932 are based on the following calculations[1]:

Rubber. The Malayan output of rubber for 1929 and 1932 can be estimated at 446,000 and 417,000 tons respectively. The 1932 figure is official, as are most of the component elements in the 1929 total, which is subject to a margin of error of not more than 1–2 per cent. The value per ton of net rubber exports from the F.M.S. was 772 dollars in 1929 and 159 dollars in 1932. On this basis the total Malayan output in these two years can be valued at 344 and 66 million dollars.

Padi and rice. The output of padi and of the rice derived from it used to be officially estimated. The official figures for 1929 and 1932 were: padi 126,229,000 and 197,103,000 *gantangs* (gallons), rice 180,000 and 291,000 tons. The 1929 figures were probably under-estimated and should be raised by about 7½–10 per cent. The average price

[1] The data have been taken from various articles in the *M.A.J.*, as well as from a number of official publications, including the *Annual Reports* of the Director of Agriculture, S.S. and F.M.S., of the Registrar-General of Statistics, and of the F.M.S. Department of Trade and Customs; from the *Malayan Rubber Statistics Handbook*, from the *Report of the Rice Production Committee* (1930), and from the *Report of the F.M.S. Retrenchment Commission* (1932). Some of the data were found in the semi-official *Outline of Malayan Agriculture* (1936), by D. H. Grist.

paid for padi at the government mill was 7·5 cents per *gantang* in 1932. According to the Malayan trade returns, the unit value of padi in 1929 was just under double the 1932 figure. Padi has been valued at 14 and 7·5 cents per *gantang* and rice at 110 and 60 dollars per ton for the two years. For 1929 the output of padi and of rice may be valued at 20 and 22 million dollars, and for 1932 at 15 and 17 millions. The value of rice output only has, of course, been included in our calculations of the value of agricultural output.

Coconut products. The 1930 coconut census estimated the area under coconuts at 600,000 acres, of which 460,000 acres were mature, 120,000 acres on estates and 340,000 acres on smallholdings. These are rough figures, particularly because the returns from the Unfederated States were unsatisfactory. According to *ad hoc* enquiries by the Department of Agriculture smallholders derived an income of about 30 dollars per acre of mature coconuts in 1932. On the basis of a mature area of 340,000–360,000 acres, 10–11 million dollars seems a reasonable estimate of the value of smallholders' coconut produce in that year, including the value of coconuts consumed by the growers. The yield on estates in the early 1930's was around 10 *pikuls* copra or slightly less. The average price of estate copra was around 5½ dollars per *pikul* in Singapore in 1932, and the mature estate area about 120,000 acres. The estate output of coconut products (virtually all of which was exported in copra form) in 1932 may accordingly be valued at 6 million dollars. The total Malayan output in 1932 may thus be taken at 16–17 millions ; net exports of coconut products in that year were 13 million dollars. Net export of coconut products totalled some 22½ millions in 1929 and the output may therefore be valued at 26–27 millions. These results tally closely with the estimates of the Malayan Vegetable Oil Commission of 1934.

Pineapples. The 1929 area was estimated at between 40,000–50,000 acres and the yield at around 3,000–4,000 fruits per acre. Prices received by growers fluctuated substantially, but an average of 1.60–1.80 dollars per hundred fruit appears reasonable. On this basis, the 1929 pineapple crop may be valued at about 4 million dollars. In 1932 the acreage was larger but prices somewhat lower ; an approximate estimate of 60,000 acres, and an average price of 1.30 dollars results in an estimate of 3 million dollars.

Palm oil and kernels. In 1929 the entire production was exported with a total value of 500,000 dollars. In 1932 some 10 per cent. of the poorer quality oil and kernels were retained for local soap manufacture. Exports in that year were 1·2 millions, and the total output may be estimated at 1·3 million dollars.

Areca nuts. For this commodity net exports are a rough indication of production. They were 6·2 million dollars in 1929 and 2·7 millions in 1932. To allow for the small local consumption of Malayan nuts, these figures may be rounded off to 6½ and 3 millions respectively.

Tapioca products, coffee, gambier, tobacco, tea, other spices, fruit and vegetables. Some of these were historically associated with the early development of Malaya but were of little importance by 1930. The output of tobacco was negligible in 1929 but developed rapidly during the slump years. The output of vegetables also expanded substantially between 1929 and 1932. The cash value of the output of all these products was small: $10 \pm 2\frac{1}{2}$ million dollars for both years appears reasonable.[1]

Live-stock, fishing output and forest products. The only way to estimate the value of live-stock produce and of the output of fisheries and of forestry in 1929 and 1932 is to start from the F.M.S. Retrenchment Commission's estimates for 1931, compare the numbers engaged in these pursuits in the F.M.S. and in Malaya (largely on the basis of the 1931 census) and to allow for price changes between 1929, 1931 (the year to which the Commission's estimates referred) and 1932. For live-stock produce the results have been checked roughly with a few figures of the live-stock population in the various Malayan administrations. The following estimates resulted: live-stock and milk 16–18 million dollars for 1929, 12–13 millions for 1932; output of fisheries 24–26 millions for 1929, 14–16 millions for 1932; forest produce 8 millions for 1929 and 6 millions for 1932. These figures, especially those of the output of fisheries and forestry, are subject to a wide margin of error.

The estimates given earlier of the gross value of Malayan agricultural output in 1929 and 1932 excluded fisheries and forestry; additional amounts of 30–35 millions and of 18–22 millions would cover these for the two years.

[1] Impressions formed after a visit to several hundred smallholdings in Malaya in 1946 suggest that this item may have been considerably undervalued. The general order of magnitude of the estimates of the agricultural output as a whole is not affected, and as no reliable figures are available for a calculation of this item the original estimate has been retained.

APPENDIX B

SUPPLEMENTARY DATA ON THE RESPONSE OF PRODUCERS TO SLUMP PRICES

THE following two tables show in some detail the response of different classes of producer to the fall in prices after 1929. They supplement Tables II and III of Chapter 3. The first table has been calculated from Dr. Whitford's *Reports on Plantation Rubber*, the second has been taken from his 1933 report. In the light of subsequent information, notably the revised figures of the N.E.I. native acreage, and Malayan smallholders' production in 1933–34 and in 1946–47, it is thought that Dr. Whitford's capacity estimates, especially of smallholdings, were too low.

TABLE I

Potential Capacity (Dr. Whitford's estimates) and Actual Output of various Groups of Producer, 1929–33

(Thousand tons)

		1929	1930	1931	1932	1933
Average London price: pence per lb.		*10·3*	*5·9*	*3·1*	*2·3*	*3·2*
Malaya:	Capacity	464	477	498	520	533
	Production—quantity	446	443	437	417	461
	,, as % of capacity	*96*	*93*	*88*	*80*	*86*
N.E.I. estates:	Capacity	160	165	177	200	229
	Production—quantity	151	152	164	149	170
	,, as % of capacity	*94*	*92*	*93*	*74*	*74*
N.E.I. natives:	Capacity	122	162	212	264	308
	Production—quantity	107	88	87	61	113
	,, as % of capacity	*88*	*54*	*41*	*23*	*37*
Ceylon:	Capacity	81	82	82	84	85
	Production—quantity	80	76	62	49	64
	,, as % of capacity	*99*	*93*	*76*	*58*	*75*
Sarawak:	Capacity	12	14	21	30	40
	Production—quantity	11	11	10	7	11
	,, as % of capacity	*91*	*79*	*48*	*23*	*28*
British North Borneo:	Capacity	9	10	11	13	14
	Production—quantity	7	7	6	5	8
	,, as % of capacity	*78*	*70*	*55*	*38*	*57*
India incl. Burma:	Capacity	14	14	14	14	15
	Production—quantity	13	12	10	4	5
	,, as % of capacity	*93*	*86*	*71*	*29*	*33*
Siam:	Capacity	6	6	7	11	16
	Production—quantity	4	5	4	3	7
	,, as % of capacity	*67*	*83*	*57*	*27*	*44*
French Indo-China:	Capacity	11	13	15	22	28
	Production—quantity	9	10	11	13	17
	,, as % of capacity	*82*	*77*	*73*	*59*	*60*
Total:	Capacity	879	943	1,037	1,158	1,268
	Production—quantity	828	804	791	708	839
	,, as % of capacity	*94*	*85*	*76*	*61*	*66*

TABLE II

Index of Rubber Production, 1930–32

(1929 = 100)

	1930	1931	1932	*1932 output as per cent. of capacity*
Malayan estates	97	98	98	*83*
N.E.I. estates	100	108	100	*75*
Malayan smallholdings	101	97	89	*75*
Sub-total	99	100	95	*80*
Ceylon	97	79	63	*59*
N.E.I. natives	83	82	57	*23*
India (including Burma)	86	64	30	*27*
Sarawak	94	89	62	*23*
British North Borneo	96	82	63	*40*
Siam	100	100	68	*31*
Others (chiefly African and South America)	69	54	32	*16*
Sub-total	83	78	52	*23*
French Indo-China	102	119	143	*59*
Grand Total	96	94	84	*59*

APPENDIX C

THE DATA UNDERLYING THE RUBBER-RICE COMPARISON

THE following notes summarise the sources of the data for Tables I and II of Chapter 5.

The spread between the Singapore price and that received by the Malayan smallholder for the bulk of his rubber was generally narrow, especially at times of low prices. The margin may be taken as 4 cents for 1929 (a year of good prices), 2½ cents for 1930, 2 cents for 1931, one cent for 1932 and 1½ cents for 1933.[1] No strict accuracy is claimed for these figures, but they show the general order of magnitude; they are in accordance with the observations of the late Dr. Whitford in his various *Reports on Plantation Rubber*, and are also in rough agreement with the prices published in the market reports of the Malayan Department of Agriculture. The figure of one cent as the average margin for 1932 was also confirmed by some remarks of an unofficial member in the F.M.S. Federal Council in the autumn of 1933. The keen buying competition of European and Chinese dealers (and after 1934 of Japanese merchants as well), together with the proximity of the most important smallholdings districts to the larger towns, explain the remarkably low margins.

The price of padi for 1929, 1932 and 1933 is the average price paid for Malayan padi by the government mill at Bagan Serai in Perak. The corresponding figures for 1930 and 1931 could not be traced, but have been calculated on the assumption that the proportionate change in the average price from 1929 to 1930 and 1931 was roughly of the same order as changes in the unit value of padi in the trade returns; this was true for 1929, 1932 and 1933. The price paid by the government mill was almost certainly higher than the average price obtainable for Malayan padi in the interior, and to this extent the comparison is weighted in favour of padi.

The retail price of rice in Malacca has been taken from the official annual *Malaya Average Prices*; for inland centres like Kuala Lumpur, occasional figures only are available, and these do not differ greatly from the price in Malacca. The average yields of padi and rice have

[1] There are several reasons for the variations in the margin with the Singapore prices. Some of the charges (including the export tax—the up-country prices were quoted before payment of export taxes) were expressed as percentages of the price. Moreover, on a falling market supplies tended to contract and bidding for the reduced quantities was keener. Again, scrap rubber and other lower grades were not collected at times of very low prices, which also resulted in a falling-off of supplies for outlying districts. All these factors reduced the average spread between the Singapore and up-country quotations for such rubber as was still produced at times of low prices.

been calculated from the official estimates of output and acreage. For 1929 and 1930 the official estimates of total rice output have been raised by 10 per cent., as subsequent information revealed that the official figures under-estimated the yields in those years.

Costs of production are more difficult to estimate, especially as most items in the cost of rice production were paid for in kind, and often varied with the yield. The figure of 30 *gantangs* (240 lb.) of cleaned rice per acre as the rice equivalent of the cost of production is certain to be conservative. It is substantially below the estimate of the Malayan Rice Cultivation Committee of 1930. The figure has been adopted after correspondence with Sir Harold Tempany, formerly Agricultural Adviser to the Secretary of State for the Colonies, who was Director of Agriculture in Malaya throughout the depression. In comparing rubber and padi as cash crops, it was necessary to express in cash the costs of padi production. The figure of 30 *gantangs* was multiplied by the Malacca price of rice and one dollar deducted to allow for the absence of milling when the crop is sold as padi. The conversion of the expenses in kind into cash costs at a retail price necessarily inflates these figures ; on the other hand, 30 *gantangs* is undoubtedly a conservative estimate of the expenses in kind, while the estimated price of padi is also generous, so that the net figure (col. 5 of Table II) is unlikely to be seriously affected.

The expenses of rice production were appreciably higher than the cost of rubber growing on family-tapped smallholdings, as the rubber requires no plough, draught animal, manure or seeds. In June 1932 the Kuala Lumpur correspondent of the *Straits Times* estimated the cost of smallholders' rubber in Selangor at one-half cent per lb. excluding rent. The bulk of the smallholdings acreage under rubber in Malaya paid rent at approximately the same rates as did the estates. The cost of rent was about one cent per lb. in 1929–31 and about one-half cent in 1932 and 1933 following a general reduction in rents in 1932. Other items, notably the cost of coagulants and tools, have been assumed to average one cent per lb. in 1929–30 and one-half cent over 1931–33.

The figures differ slightly from those shown in 'Some Aspects of the Malayan Rubber Slump', *Economica*, November 1944, as they embody some minor revisions.

APPENDIX D

THE ECONOMICS OF PLANTING DENSITY[1]

IN the choice of planting density the rational course is not the same for estates and smallholders. The majority of the smallholders incur no cash wage costs and attempt to maximise the gross yield per surface unit. On their densely planted holdings the trees are of smaller girth and the yields per tree lower than on estates, but the yields per surface unit are higher. The estate employing paid tappers tries to maximise the cash profit per acre, and it is held that the higher profit per tree resulting from the higher yield per tapper on less densely planted areas more than offsets the reduction in gross receipts due to the lower stand. It has been claimed that very low stands, say 40 or 50 trees per acre, would give such high yields per tree that the profits per acre would be higher than on the more densely planted areas.[2] There is, however, not enough evidence to support this view, which would be valid only on extreme assumptions. The smallholder naturally also wishes to increase the output per tapper and obtain a higher reward for his own labour for a given expenditure of effort. A widely planted holding would, however, necessitate the collection and transport of latex from an area so extensive as to be beyond his reach, with his limited equipment and labour. In view of his small capital the smallholder must aim at obtaining a maximum output from a small area.

In deciding the optimum stand, the estates should, strictly speaking, consider not only the relative yield per tree at various planting densities, but should also estimate the ratio of the price of rubber f.o.r. estate and of direct costs per lb. over a period of years, as different assumptions about this ratio would call for different stands per acre.

This can be simply illustrated. Suppose that over a number of years a more densely planted area yields 1,000 lb. per acre, as against 800 lb. on a less densely planted area. Unless prime profits per lb. (the difference between the price f.o.r. estate and direct costs on the estate) on the second area exceed those on the first by at least 25 per cent. the more densely planted area will be the better proposition. Assume that tapping costs are 3 cents per lb. on the first and 2 cents per lb. on the second plantation. If the price exceeds other items in direct cost by 10 cents, the prime profit is 7 cents per lb. on the first and 8 cents on the second area ; the ratio in favour of the second is insufficient to offset the larger yield on the first plantation, which is thus the better proposition. If, however, the price exceeds direct cost

[1] Cf. pp. 68–69, above.

[2] A method which attempts to combine high yields per tree and per surface unit is discussed above, pp. 261–62.

other than tapping cost by 5 cents only, the ratio of prime profits per lb. between the two areas will be three to two, and the less densely planted area becomes the more profitable.

Thus in deciding on the optimum planting density, the choice should be influenced by assumptions about future costs and prices, as well as by such obvious considerations as yield per acre, quality of the soil, losses through disease and windfalls, and the possibilities and the economics of future thinning out on a selective basis. The thinner stand, with its lower tapping costs, would prove somewhat more profitable in a period of very low prices. It is also possible that planting density may influence the distribution of yields through time but on this subject there is no information. It would appear that these factors are not assessed very carefully in estate practice, partly no doubt because in view of the wide price fluctuations, assumptions about prices and costs for more than one year ahead are largely guesswork.

APPENDIX E

THE REDUCTION IN ESTATE COSTS, 1929–33[1]

THE fall in estate costs during the depression may best be illustrated by the figures returned by sterling companies to the Commercial Research Department of the R.G.A., which is by far the largest sample available compiled on a reasonably consistent basis.[2]

TABLE I

Average Cost of Production of Rubber Companies Furnishing Returns to the Rubber Growers' Association, 1929–33

(Pence per lb.)

Financial year ending in	*All-in cost*		*F.o.b. cost*		*Average London price of rubber for corresponding financial year*	
	Pence	Index [a]	*Pence*	Index [a]	*Pence*	Index [a]
1929						
1st quarter	6·58	*100*	5·71	*100*	9·54	*100*
2nd ,,	6·31	*100*	5·57	*100*	9·94	*100*
3rd ,,	5·88	*100*	5·26	*100*	10·29	*100*
4th ,,	5·93	*100*	5·29	*100*	10·26	*100*
1930						
1st quarter	6·32	*96*	5·45	*97*	9·37	*98*
2nd ,,	6·51	*103*	5·83	*105*	8·41	*84*
3rd ,,	5·70	*97*	5·12	*98*	6·97	*68*
4th ,,	5·35	*90*	4·72	*89*	5·91	*58*
1931						
1st quarter	5·05	*77*	4·40	*77*	4·97	*52*
2nd ,,	4·41	*69*	3·84	*69*	4·06	*41*
3rd ,,	3·93	*67*	3·38	*64*	3·48	*34*
4th ,,	3·48	*59*	3·02	*57*	3·17	*31*
1932						
1st quarter	3·09	*47*	2·71	*47*	2·69	*28*
2nd ,,	3·02	*48*	2·61	*47*	2·38	*24*
3rd ,,	3·13	*53*	2·63	*50*	2·31	*22*
4th ,,	2·78	*47*	2·34	*44*	2·34	*23*
1933						
1st quarter	2·34	*36*	Not available		2·22	*23*
2nd ,,	2·52	*40*	,,		2·50	*25*
3rd ,,	2·89	*49*	,,		2·84	*28*
4th ,,	2·95	*50*	,,		3·25	*32*

[a] The index figures are expressed as percentages of costs for the financial years ending in the corresponding quarter of 1929.

There is much miscellaneous information available to confirm these figures; company reports, statements by company chairmen, findings

[1] Cf. pp. 32–33, above.

[2] Their basis is summarised above, p. 12.

of *ad hoc* enquiries (such as that of the F.M.S. Rubber Taxation Committee of 1931), an interesting published memorandum by the Negri Sembilan Estate Owners' Association (1932), papers by well-known experts (Dr. Whitford, M. Yves Henri, and Mr. F. D. Ascoli); all these indicate a reduction of f.o.b. costs to, or below, 2*d*., and of all-in costs to around 2¼–2½*d*. by 1932.

The costs of 45 Malayan dollar companies have been extracted from a publication of a Singapore firm of stockbrokers. The costs are consistently compiled all-in cash costs delivered Singapore.

TABLE II

Average All-In Cash Costs of 45 Dollar Companies, 1929–33

(Straits cents per lb.)

	1929	1930	1931	1932	1933
Cash cost	22·76	17·82	10·99	7·60	8·05
Index	*100*	*78*	*48*	*33*	*35*
Singapore price of rubber	34·48	19·31	9·96	7·01	10·23
Index	*100*	*56*	*29*	*20*	*30*

The index figures in this table are expressed as percentages of the 1929 levels, while those in Table I show prices and costs as percentages of the financial years ending in the corresponding quarter of 1929. This must be borne in mind when comparing the fall in costs recorded in the two tables. For example, the index of the costs of locally-owned companies (Table II) is 33 for 1932; this should be compared with the fourth-quarter companies in Table I, the index of whose all-in costs stood at 47 in 1932, and that of their f.o.b. costs at 44. (It is the f.o.b. costs of sterling companies, rather than their all-in costs, which should be set against the cash costs of locally owned companies, which incur no, or only very small, freight charges.) For 1933 the index of the costs of locally-domiciled companies is 35 and that of the all-in costs of fourth-quarter sterling companies is 50 (the f.o.b. costs for that year are not available).

Thus by 1932 the average cost of these dollar companies was barely one-third of the 1929 level. The details show that the costs in 1929 of the cheapest producer among these dollar companies were 60 per cent. higher than those of the highest cost producer in 1933.

The locally registered enterprises were on the whole less strongly financed than the sterling companies, and were forced, and at the same time able, to cut salaries and wages more severely than the more prosperous enterprises. The Incorporated Society of Planters (the professional association of Malayan estate managers and assistants) was inclined to offer stronger resistance to reductions of salaries by companies with ample reserves; the Labour Department was also less prepared to consent to near-starvation wages on estates which still had cash reserves than where the alternative was closing down. Pressure by the authorities for prompt payment of rents was also greatest on companies with substantial cash reserves. It had been noticed early in the slump that the survival of many enterprises depended more on their financial resources than on their costs, and according to a Malayan wit the struggle was for the survival of the fattest, rather than for that of the fittest. The heavier cuts by the financially weakest enterprises offset to an arbitrary degree their poorer life expectations. It was by these means that there was a greater reduction in dollar company costs than that shown by sterling companies.[1]

The costs of 1932–33 refer to a period of abnormally low salaries and near-starvation wages; on the other hand, the output was derived entirely from unselected seedling trees and from areas which had frequently suffered from mistaken cultivation policies. It was argued at the time by a number of authorities, including Mr. (now Sir Eric) Macfadyen (past chairman of the R.G.A. and of the Planters' Association of Malaya), the late Sir Eric Geddes, (late chairman of Dunlop's), and by others, that in the long run these very low costs need rise only slightly, if at all, as the inevitable increase in salaries and wages would be offset by higher yields.

The relative fall in the various cost items emerges from the table on page 368, extracted from the R.G.A. cost returns.

The average costs of the last-quarter companies shown in Table III fell by 3·15*d.* (from 5·93*d.* to 2·78*d.*) between 1929 and 1932. The proportionate declines in the two most important items (collection, manufacture and dispatch, and general charges) were very similar, though, as will be suggested below, the fall in the former was due very largely to wage cuts, while increased efficiency played an important part in the reduction in general charges. The fall in the cost of the upkeep of the mature area to about one-sixth of the 1929 level by the end of 1932 is particularly striking; here, too, technical improvement was a factor besides postponement of expenditure and wage reductions. The comparatively small reduction in head-office expenses is in accordance with expectations.

It is tempting to estimate the relative shares of increased efficiency and of the wage and salary cuts in the remarkable reduction in costs. An accurate estimate—if it could be made at all—would be extremely lengthy, but an approximation is possible by comparing estate costs in 1937 with those in 1929. By 1937 Malayan estate wages were back at 1929 levels, while restriction, especially during the second half of the year, pressed very lightly on estate producers. F.o.b. costs in 1937 were about 75 per cent. of the 1929 levels, and all-in costs some 75–80

[1] The dollar companies whose costs were reviewed in Table II were among the largest and strongest of the locally-owned enterprises, and the fall in their costs slightly understates the average cost reduction which took place on locally-owned properties. Cf. Dr. Whitford's observation: 'The lowest cost estates are generally those without credit or without or only with very low cash reserves'. *Report on Plantation Rubber in 1932*, p. 8.

An extreme example was found in the action of the manager of a locally-registered company, the funds of which had vanished by 1932. He consented to stay on without any cash payment in return for a parcel of specially issued shares in the company. By 1934 the market value of the shares had risen sharply and the manager had made an excellent bargain.

TABLE III

Subdivision of Costs of Production of Rubber Companies Furnishing Returns to the R.G.A., 1929–32

(Pence per lb.)

Companies whose financial year ended in	*Upkeep of mature area* (1)	*Collection, manufacture and dispatch* (2)	*General charges* (3)	*Upkeep of buildings and machinery* (4)	*Depreciation of buildings and machinery* (5)	*Head office expenses* (6)	*Total* (7)
1929							
1st quarter	0·70	2·64	2·28	0·09	0·40	0·47	6·58
2nd ,,	0·70	2·58	2·18	0·11	0·29	0·45	6·31
3rd ,,	0·63	2·50	2·06	0·07	0·38	0·24	5·88
4th ,,	0·84	2·51	1·87	0·07	0·35	0·29	5·93
1930							
1st quarter	0·83	2·55	2·07	0·09	0·36	0·42	6·32
2nd ,,	0·94	2·57	2·22	0·10	0·26	0·42	6·51
3rd ,,	0·71	2·33	2·04	0·04	0·38	0·20	5·70
4th ,,	0·73	2·13	1·81	0·05	0·36	0·27	5·35
1931							
1st quarter	0·58	2·01	1·76	0·05	0·29	0·35	5·04
2nd ,,	0·39	1·82	1·60	0·03	0·23	0·34	4·41
3rd ,,	0·36	1·57	1·43	0·02	0·37	0·18	3·93
4th ,,	0·26	1·47	1·27	0·02	0·25	0·21	3·48
1932							
1st quarter	0·26	1·29	1·14	0·02	0·11	0·27	3·09
2nd ,,	0·20	1·20	1·19	0·02	0·14	0·27	3·02
3rd ,,	0·22	1·24	1·15	0·02	0·33	0·17	3·13
4th ,,	0·14	1·17	1·03	0·02	0·23	0·19	2·78

per cent. From the detailed cost figures of a number of Malayan enterprises it appears that direct f.o.b. costs were only some 5–10 per cent. below the 1929 figures, while indirect f.o.b. costs were some 30–35 per cent. lower. This bears out the conclusion [1] that a substantial proportion of the reduction in indirect f.o.b. costs reflected increased efficiency (including the abandonment of certain forms of expenditure, subsequently discovered to have been superfluous), while much the larger proportion of the fall in direct f.o.b. costs was the result of wage cuts.

[1] Cf. 'Rubber Production Costs During the Great Depression', *Economic Journal*, December 1943.

STATISTICAL APPENDIX I

RUBBER PRODUCTION, PRICES AND ACREAGES IN MALAYA AND THE N.E.I., 1929–33

TABLE I

Output and Price Statistics of the Malayan Rubber Industry, 1929–33

	Output in tons (to the nearest hundred tons)						Price per lb.			Percentage of mature estate rubber out of tapping (last month of quarter)
	Estates		Smallholdings		Total		London ribbed smoked sheet (pence)	Singapore ribbed smoked sheet (cents)	Singapore Chinese smoked sheet (cents)	
	Actual (1)	Seasonally corrected (2)	Actual (3)	Seasonally corrected (4)	Actual (5)	Seasonally corrected (6)	(7)	(8)	(9)	(10)
1929	246,000	—	200,000	—	446,000	—	10·3	34·5	33·9	
1930										
1st quarter	59,400	62,800	54,500	51,500	113,900	114,300	7·7	25·4	24·1	Not available
2nd " *	43,300	46,900	44,700	49,100	88,000	96,000	6·8	22·8	21·5	
3rd "	68,700	65,500	51,600	49,400	120,300	114,900	4·9	15·5	15·1	
4th "	65,500	61,700	46,500	47,300	112,000	109,000	4·4	13·5	12·9	
Total	236,900	236,900	197,300	197,300	434,200	434,200	5·9	19·3	18·4	
1931										(F.M.S. only)
1st quarter	58,400	61,400	53,300	50,300	111,700	111,700	3·9	12·4	11·5	16
2nd "	54,900	59,200	43,900	48,300	98,800	107,500	3·0	9·7	9·4	17
3rd "	62,700	59,500	47,400	45,300	110,100	104,800	2·7	8·4	8·2	18
4th "	63,800	59,700	52,400	53,100	116,200	112,800	3·0	9·2	8·9	17
Total	239,800	239,800	197,000	197,000	436,800	436,800	3·1	10·0	9·5	
1932										(Malaya)
1st quarter	60,700	63,700	44,500	42,000	105,200	105,700	2·6	8·0	7·7	20
2nd "	58,400	62,700	36,800	40,500	95,200	103,200	1·9	8·3	5·1	23
3rd "	59,700	56,400	45,500	43,500	105,200	99,900	2·4	7·1	6·8	23
4th "	61,300	57,300	50,200	51,000	111,500	108,300	2·5	7·6	7·3	22
Total	240,100	240,100	177,000	177,000	417,100	417,100	2·3	7·0	6·7	
1933										
1st quarter	55,600	58,500	43,300	40,700	98,900	99,200	2·2	6·4	6·3	22
2nd "	57,200	61,600	52,100	57,000	109,300	118,600	2·9	8·9	8·9	20
3rd "	62,700	59,500	60,900	58,000	123,600	117,500	3·8	12·4	11·7	19
4th "	65,300	61,200	63,500	64,100	128,800	125,300	4·1	13·2	12·3	17
Total	240,800	240,800	219,800	219,800	460,600	460,600	3·3	10·2	9·8	

* Production affected by tapping holiday in May.

TABLE II

Mature Area in Malaya and Yields per Acre, 1929–33

	Estates		Smallholdings		Malaya	
	Mature area (thousand acres) (1)	*Yield (lb. per acre)* (2)	*Mature area (thousand acres)* (3)	*Yield (lb. per acre)* (4)	*Mature area (thousand acres)* (5)	*Yield (lb. per acre)* (6)
1929	1,340	410	939	485	2,279	440
1930	1,387	380	960	460	2,347	415
1931	1,429	375	985	445	2,414	405
1932	1,464	365	1,023	385	2,487	375
1933	1,522	355	1,060	465	2,582	400

NOTES TO TABLES I AND II

Throughout 1929 prices were at levels at which there was no inducement to curtail output. Moreover, monthly output and export statistics for that year are in many ways deficient, as well as being affected in the early months by the aftermath of the Stevenson scheme, notably the shipment of stocks built up in anticipation of the withdrawal of restriction. For these reasons, annual totals only are given for 1929 against quarterly figures for subsequent years.

The unadjusted production figures are official. Seasonal variations have been eliminated on the basis of the data published by the U.S. Department of Commerce in *Trade Information Bulletin No. 804*. Smallholders' output was estimated by the Registrar-General of Statistics in the following way: smallholders' production = net exports + local consumption + changes in stocks − estate production. In practice this means: smallholders' production = total exports + end-monthly dealers' stocks + end-monthly port stocks + end-monthly estate stocks + local absorption − estate, port and dealers' stocks at the beginning of the month − estate production − foreign imports. The resulting figure actually shows sales of rubber by smallholders to dealers, which represents the output of a few weeks before. The figure is subject to a margin of error which may be considerable for any given month (particularly as a large proportion of the imports were wet rubber whose dry weight had to be estimated), but is very small over the year. After the introduction of regulation in 1934 with quarterly coupon issues, the monthly figures became erratic and unreliable, but the yearly total continued closely accurate. There are slight discrepancies (2,000–3,000 tons) between various estimates of the 1929 output, as the S.S. production for that year can be calculated only indirectly.

No regular series of Singapore prices of Chinese smoked sheet could be found in London. The figures quoted have been made available by the courtesy of the United Baltic Corporation; they are the prices paid by this firm for Chinese smoked sheet (generally grades no. 2 or 3).

The area out of tapping excludes areas rested under rotational tapping systems; another 3–10 per cent. of the mature area was untapped under this heading during the period under review.

Until June 1931 information about the estate area out of tapping was available for the S.S. and F.M.S. only, and as the former are definitely unrepresentative, F.M.S. figures only are given.

The acreage statistics of the various U.M.S. were still unsatisfactory in 1929–30, especially as regards the date of planting; they improved gradually, though the age distribution of smallholders' rubber is still somewhat conjectural.

Attention may be drawn to two points: the forward-rising trend of smallholders' output, and the remarkably high level of smallholders' production at the end of 1933, when it exceeded the rate of estate output (seasonally adjusted), though the mature smallholding area was about one-third less than the mature estate acreage. The mature acreage figures are based on the records of the I.R.R.C.; these differ somewhat from Dr. Whitford's estimates, though the discrepancy is very small when Dr. Whitford's revisions are allowed for. The figures have been rounded off to the nearest 1,000 acres and the yields to the nearest 5 lb.

TABLE III

Output and Price Statistics of the N.E.I. Rubber Estate Industry, 1929–33

	Output in long tons (to the nearest hundred tons)						*Batavia price of Java standard sheet*	*Percentage of mature acreage untapped (last month of quarter)*		
	Java		*Outer Provinces*		*Total estates*		*Guilder cents per half-kilo*	*Java*	*Outer Provinces*	*Total*
	Actual (1)	*Seasonally corrected* (2)	*Actual* (3)	*Seasonally corrected* (4)	*Actual* (5)	*Seasonally corrected* (6)	(7)	(8)	(9)	(10)
1929	65,400	—	85,800	—	151,200	—	50·4		See Notes	
1930										
1st quarter	16,400	15,400	22,800	24,100	39,200	39,500	Quarterly figures not available		See Notes	
2nd " *	12,800	11,800	18,200	19,100	31,000	30,900				
3rd "	18,400	26,700	22,900	21,900	41,300	42,600				
4th "	17,800	17,500	21,600	20,400	39,400	37,900				
Total	65,400	65,400	85,500	85,500	150,900	150,900	30·5			
1931										
1st "	17,300	16,400	23,000	24,300	40,300	40,700	11·3		See Notes	
2nd "	17,800	16,500	22,500	23,500	40,700	40,000	15·2			
3rd "	17,700	20,100	23,700	22,700	41,400	42,800	12·8			
4th "	17,400	17,200	24,200	22,900	41,600	40,100	10·8	11	8	9
Total	70,200	70,200	93,400	93,400	163,600	163,600	14·5			
1932										
1st quarter	16,700	15,900	24,600	25,900	41,300	41,800	9·0	14	11	12
2nd "	14,200	13,300	23,100	24,100	37,300	37,400	6·2	35	20	26
3rd "	12,800	14,600	21,100	20,100	33,900	34,700	7·8	38	21	28
4th "	15,000	14,900	21,100	19,800	36,100	34,700	7·8	22	21	21
Total	58,700	58,700	89,900	89,900	148,600	148,600	7·8			
1933										
1st quarter	16,100	15,200	23,800	25,100	39,900	40,300	6·7	17	20	19
2nd "	17,500	16,200	23,300	24,400	40,800	40,600	9·5	15	18	17
3rd "	19,600	22,100	24,000	23,000	43,600	45,100	12·8	14	17	16
4th "	20,300	20,000	24,900	23,500	45,200	43,500	13·0	11	16	14
Total	73,500	73,500	96,000	96,000	169,500	169,500	10·5			

* Output affected by tapping holiday in May.

TABLE IV

Mature Estate Area in the N.E.I. and Yields per Acre, 1929–33

	Java		*Outer Provinces*		*N.E.I.*	
	Area (thousand acres) (1)	*Yield (lb. per acre)* (2)	*Area (thousand acres)* (3)	*Yield (lb. per acre)* (4)	*Area (thousand acres)* (5)	*Yield (lb. per acre)* (6)
1929	374	390	503	375	877	380
1930	383	385	519	365	902	375
1931	393	400	536	390	929	395
1932	406	325	556	360	962	345
1933	430	380	596	360	1,026	365

NOTES TO TABLES III AND IV

The N.E.I. authorities used to publish preliminary monthly production figures of estate rubber, and these were followed by a revised estimate for the year. The preliminary figures were within 3–4 per cent. of the final estimates. In the calculations for the table, the difference in the preliminary and the final figures has been divided by four and added equally to the preliminary figures for each quarter. The official N.E.I. figures are in metric tons, and have been converted into long tons in order to maintain consistency throughout this study. For the same reason the yield figures of kilogrammes per hectare have been converted into lb. per acre.

As the estate acreage out of tapping was below 10 per cent. before 1932 it was not thought worth while to include these figures. The slight increase in the proportion of the acreage out of tapping in the summer of 1933 reflects the seasonal trend in Java where the coffee harvest affected the activities of the mixed rubber and coffee estates in July–August. Minor discrepancies arise from different treatment by the various authorities of the small quantity (300–800 tons annually) of native rubber bought up by estates, especially in Java, of *langs den weg* plantings (groups of trees planted along the roads and not in compact estates), and a few other small matters. In their aggregate these do not affect the figures by more than 1–1½ per cent.

TABLE V

Output and Price Statistics of the N.E.I. Native Rubber Industry, 1929–33

	Quarterly rubber exports, dry weight in long tons (to the nearest hundred tons)		*Capacity Estimates*		*Singapore price of medium blankets. Straits cents per lb.*	*Guilder cent equivalent (per half-kilo) of Singapore price of medium blankets*
	Actual	*Seasonally corrected*	*Division of Agric. Economics, N.E.I. Dept. of Agriculture (Metric tons)*	*Whitford (Long tons)*		
	(1)	(2)	(3)	(4)	(5)	(6)
1929	106,900	—	120,000	122,000	29·3	45·1
1930						
1st quarter	25,200	27,100			21·6	33·3
2nd ,,	26,600	27,300			20·4	31·5
3rd ,,	20,600	18,400			13·6	20·9
4th ,,	16,600	16,200			12·0	18·7
Year	89,000	89,000	150,000	162,000	16·9	26·1
1931						
1st quarter	23,200	25,000			10·9	16·9
2nd ,,	23,700	24,400			8·8	13·6
3rd ,,	21,100	18,900			8·0	12·3
4th ,,	20,400	20,100			8·8	10·1
Year	88,400	88,400	200,000	212,000	9·1	13·2
1932						
1st quarter	16,100	17,400			7·5	8·2
2nd ,,	10,700	11,100			4·9	5·7
3rd ,,	14,500	13,100			6·1	6·8
4th ,,	20,200	19,900			6·1	6·4
Year	61,500	61,500	250,000	264,000	6·1	6·8
1933						
1st quarter	13,500	14,900			4·8	5·3
2nd ,,	25,500	26,900			6·9	7·4
3rd ,,	36,300	33,400			9·4	9·9
4th ,,	38,700	38,800			8·8	8·8
Year	114,000	114,000	300,000	308,000	7·5	7·9

NOTES TO TABLE V

The monthly output figures of N.E.I. native rubber as given by the N.E.I. authorities (in metric tons) excluded the small exports from the Riouw Archipelago, a group of islands between Sumatra and Singapore, for which no export figures were available. Every year the authorities estimated the total of these shipments (around 1,000 tons annually in the early 1930's), and for the purposes of our calculation they have been divided by four and added in equal quantities to the official export figures of each quarter.

No monthly figures are available in London of the price of medium blankets before 1932. The figures for 1930–31 in the table are the prices paid for this, or very similar, grades by the Singapore office of the United Baltic Corporation ; they have been made available through the courtesy of that firm. The annual averages closely correspond to those of the market quotations which are available in London. The Singapore prices have been converted into guilder cents at the monthly rates of exchange supplied by the Chartered Bank of India, Australia and China.

TABLE VI

Total N.E.I. Rubber Production 1929–33; Estates and Native Producers

(Long tons, to the nearest hundred tons)

	Actual (1)	*Seasonally corrected* (2)
1929	258,100	—
1930		
1st quarter	64,400	66,600
2nd ,,	57,600	58,200
3rd ,,	61,900	61,000
4th ,,	56,000	54,100
Year	239,900	239,900
1931		
1st quarter	63,500	65,700
2nd ,,	64,000	64,400
3rd ,,	62,500	61,700
4th ,,	62,000	60,200
Year	252,000	252,000
1932		
1st quarter	57,400	59,200
2nd ,,	48,000	48,500
3rd ,,	48,400	47,800
4th ,,	56,300	54,600
Year	210,100	210,100
1933		
1st quarter	53,400	55,200
2nd ,,	66,300	67,500
3rd ,,	79,900	78,500
4th ,,	83,900	82,300
Year	283,500	283,500

STATISTICAL APPENDIX II

THE STATISTICS OF RUBBER REGULATION, 1934–41

TABLE I

Areas Planted with Rubber at 1st June 1934

(Thousand acres)

	Malaya	*N.E.I.*	*Ceylon*	*India*	*Burma*	*British North Borneo*	*Sarawak*	*Siam*	*French Indo-China*	*Total*
Mature Area :										
Estates	1,822	1,270	343	74	46	68	15	—	156	3,794
Smallholdings	1,229	1,458	231	45	30	49	177	200	9	3,428
Total	3,051	2,728	574	119	76	117	192	200	165	7,222
Immature Area :										
Estates	177	214	6	6	22	3	2	—	139	569
Smallholdings	81	263	24	5	11	7	34	166	10	601
Total	258	477	30	11	33	10	36	166	149	1,170
Total Area :										
Estates	1,999	1,484	349	80	68	71	17	—	295	4,363
Smallholdings	1,310	1,721	255	50	41	56	211	366	19	4,029
Grand Total	3,309	3,205	604	130	109	127	228	366	314	8,392

This table is based on the records of the I.R.R.C. The figure of the N.E.I. smallholding area is that of the 1934–36 tree census, together with the small area in Java, rounded off to the nearest thousand acres (see Notes to Table II). For Ceylon all properties under 100 acres each are included under smallholdings.

TABLE II

Areas Planted with Rubber at the End of 1940

(Thousand acres)

	Malaya	*N.E.I.*	*Ceylon*	*India*	*Burma*	*British North Borneo*	*Sarawak*	*Siam*	*French Indo-China*	*Total*
Mature Area:										
Estates	1,817	1,286	323	75	66	69	15	—	273	3,924
Smallholdings . .	1,295	1,706*a*	255	51	42	56	210	299	19	3,933
Total	3,112	2,992	578	126	108	125	225	299	292	7,857
Immature Area:										
Estates	290	281	36	8	2	5	3	—	38	663
Smallholdings . .	79	100*a*	25	3	1	3	12	120	1	344
Total	369	381	61	11	3	8	15	120	39	1,007
Total Area:										
Estates	2,107	1,567	359	83	68	74	18	—	311	4,587
Smallholdings . .	1,374	1,806 *a* 3,200 *b*	280	54	43	59	222	419	20	4,277 *a* 5,671 *b*
Grand Total . .	3,481	3,373 *a* 4,767 *b*	639	137	111	133	240	419	331	8,864 *a* 10,258 *b*

a, *b*, See Notes.

NOTES TO TABLES I AND II

Table II is based substantially on Table I of the Statistical Supplement to the *History of Rubber Regulation*. The two figures of the N.E.I. native acreage refer to two estimates, (*a*) the figure calculated from the tree count of 1934–36 which was used for regulation purposes in 1937–41, and (*b*) the estimate of a survey begun in 1939. No figures are available of the age distribution of the area on the basis of (*b*). The two estimates are discussed in the text, pp. 143–45 and 307.

It must be repeated that these acreage figures are only more or less close approximations, since the statistics were being constantly revised. The only figure which was never revised was the most inaccurate of all, the notorious estimate of 1,806,516 acres for the native area in the Outer Provinces of the N.E.I. This was only guesswork, but as the results of the 1939 survey (which suggested an area of about 3,200,000 acres) were not published until after the occupation of the N.E.I. by Japan, this somewhat grotesque figure was accepted and repeated year after year within and without the I.R.R.C. It is included in the Statistical Supplement to the *History of Rubber Regulation*.

Next to the N.E.I. native area, the Siamese acreage figure is the least reliable. Estimated by Dr. Whitford at 150,000 acres in the early thirties, it was officially claimed as 216,209 tappable acres in 1935, 277,650 acres at the end of 1937, 313,720 acres at the end of 1939, and 419,254 acres at the end of 1940. In the other territories the revisions generally did not, after 1934, exceed 5 per cent. of the planted area.

The age distribution of the planted area is even more conjectural, and various official reports in the different countries reveal considerable divergences in the (often variable) methods of estimating the year of planting, and in the different definitions of maturity adopted. In some administrations it used to be assumed that the age composition of smallholdings was the same as that of the estate area, in others more serious attempts were made to estimate or guess the figures from the scanty data available. The actual age of maturity varies in the different territories ; the trees are generally tappable in their sixth year, and this is the basis of maturity in the Malayan and N.E.I. statistics. Minor discrepancies arise through the overlapping of the planting season from one year to the next, and for budgrafts through the necessary passage of time between planting and budding.

The bulk of the planted area carried seedling trees. In 1934 some 9 to 10 per cent. of the Malayan estate area, 24 per cent. of the N.E.I. estate area and some 30 per cent. of all French Indo-China rubber was budgrafted (mostly immature rubber) ; in other territories, and on smallholdings everywhere, the proportion of budded rubber was negligible. In 1940 the figures were : Malayan estates 17 per cent., N.E.I. estates 35 per cent., French Indo-China 44 per cent.

TABLE III

A

Basic Quotas expressed (a) in lb. per acre, and (b) in lb. per mature acre

	Malaya		N.E.I.		Ceylon		India		Burma		B.N.B.		Sarawak		Siam
	(a)	(b)	(a)	(b)	(a)	(b)	(a)	(b)	(a)	(b)	(a)	(b)	(a)	(b)	
1934	340	370	245	290	285	300	215	230	165	225	210	230	235	280	245
1939	425	440	440	455	390	415	300	315	275	285	370	375	420	425	310

B

Quotas of Certain Classes of Producer (a) in lb. per acre, and (b) in lb. per mature acre

	Malayan estates		Malayan smallholdings		N.E.I. estates		N.E.I. natives		Ceylon						British North Borneo			
									Large Estates (over 100 acres)		Small Estates (10–100 acres)		Small-holdings		Estates		Small-holdings	
	(a)	(b)	(a)	(b)	(a)	(b)	(a)	(b)	(a)	(b)	(a)	(b)	(a)	(b)	(a)	(b)	(a)	(b)
1934	245	380	240	365	310	360	190	225	330	340	265	285	195	240	Not available			
1939	440	455	415	415	480	520	410	410	440	465	375	385	290	315	505	510	215	215

C

Percentage Shares (a) of Estates and (b) of Smallholdings in Certain Territorial Quotas

	Malaya		N.E.I.		Ceylon		British North Borneo	
	(a)	(b)	(a)	(b)	(a)	(b)	(a)	(b)
1934	61·1	38·9	58·3	41·7	85·2	14·8	Not available	
1939	61·2	38·8	50·3	49·7	83·8	16·2	74·8	25·2

NOTES TO TABLE III

The years 1934 and 1939 have been chosen for this table, as the first year of each of the two periods of regulation ; a year-to-year comparison would have been too unwieldy. For India, Burma and Siam the 1934 figures are based on the 1935 quotas, as these territories did not ratify the agreement until that year. The notable increase between 1934 and 1939 in the N.E.I. native quota per acre reflects the native quota revision of 1936, together with the substantial increase in the N.E.I. quota under the renewed agreement. The age distribution of Siamese rubber is so largely conjectural that an expression of the quota in terms of lb. per mature acre would be pointless. The same applies to a very large extent to the N.E.I. native area, but here the figures of the tree census have been used for what they are worth. As this census greatly underestimated the native area, the average over-all per acre assessment of the native producers was much less than appears from the table. It will be remembered that French Indo-China had no basic quota. The Malayan figures used for sections B and C are really the aggregate of standard assessments which exceeded the territorial quota proper by about $1\frac{1}{2}$–2 per cent. In 1939 the assessments of certain Chettiar-owned Malayan estates were included in the smallholding quota (cf. p. 96 above).

Except for experimental planting, there was no new planting between 1934 and 1939, and the difference in the per acre and per mature acre figures in 1939 reflect immature replantings in Malaya, the N.E.I. and British North Borneo, and the later maturity of young rubber in some territories (six to eight years from planting, instead of five years as in Malaya and in the N.E.I.).

It will be noted that the average assessment per acre or per mature acre of estates appreciably exceeded that of smallholdings in every instance, with a striking discrepancy in British North Borneo ; this in spite of the unquestionably superior yielding capacity of smallholders' rubber, with the possible exception of Ceylon. As a result, the shares of smallholdings in the territorial quotas were invariably below their shares in the planted or the mature areas, as can be readily seen by comparing section C of this table with Tables I and II.

TABLE IV

International Rates of Release, 1934–41

(Per cent.)

	1934	1935	1936	1937	1938	1939	1940	1941
1st quarter . .	—	75	60	75	70	50	80	100
2nd ,,	$87\frac{1}{7}$	70	60	80	60	50	80	100
3rd ,,	$87\frac{1}{7}$	65	65	90	45	60	85	100
4th ,,	$87\frac{1}{7}$	60	65	90	45	75	90	120

The basic quotas to which these releases applied are shown on pp. 85 and 152, above.

TABL

The Operation of the Special Export Tax on Native Rubbe

	Singapore price of medium blankets expressed in pence per lb. (1)	*Ordinary N.E.I. export duty on native rubber at 5 per cent* ad valorem *of f.o.b. values; pence per lb.* (2)	*Special N.E.I. export duty on native rubber average rate for month (dry); pence per lb.* (3)	*Approx. cost of shipping from N.E.I. port to Singapore processing and marketing; pence per lb.* (4)	*Approx. expenses from interior to N.E.I. port; pence per lb.* (5)	*Approx. average return to native producer; pence per lb.* (6)	*Singapore price ex export duties; pence per lb.* (7)	*Approx. price f.o.b. N.E.I. port; pence per lb.* (8)
1934								
June	4·8	0·1	—	0·9	0·2	3·6	4·7	3·9
July	5·2	0·2	0·7	1·0	0·2	3·1	4·3	4·2
August	5·4	0·2	1·9	1·0	0·2	2·1	3·3	4·4
September	5·4	0·2	2·7	1·0	0·2	1·3	2·5	4·4
October	5·1	0·2	3·0	1·1	0·1	0·7	1·9	4·0
November	4·8	0·2	3·0	1·0	0·1	0·5	1·6	3·8
December	4·9	0·2	2·7	1·1	0·1	0·8	2·0	3·8
Seven months	5·1	0·2	2·0	1·0	0·1	1·8	2·9	4·1
1935								
January	5·0	0·2	2·4	1·1	0·1	1·2	2·4	3·9
February	4·9	0·2	2·4	1·1	0·1	1·1	2·3	3·8
March	4·7	0·2	2·5	1·1	0·2	0·7	2·0	3·6
April	4·7	0·2	2·4	1·1	0·1	0·9	2·1	3·6
May	5·0	0·2	2·4	1·1	0·1	1·2	2·4	3·9
June	5·3	0·2	2·4	1·0	0·1	1·6	2·7	4·3
July	5·2	0·2	2·7	1·1	0·2	1·0	2·3	4·1
August	5·3	0·2	3·1	1·0	0·2	0·8	2·0	4·3
September	5·2	0·2	3·0	1·0	0·2	0·8	2·0	4·2
October	5·4	0·2	3·0	1·1	0·1	1·0	2·2	4·3
November	5·8	0·2	3·4	1·0	0·2	1·0	2·2	4·8
December	5·9	0·2	4·2	1·0	0·2	0·3	1·5	4·9
Year 1935	5·2	0·2	2·8	1·0	0·2	1·0	2·2	4·2
1936								
January	6·5	0·3	4·3	1·0	0·2	0·7	1·9	5·5
February	7·0	0·3	4·3	1·0	0·2	1·2	2·4	6·0
March	7·2	0·3	4·6	1·1	0·2	1·0	2·3	6·1
April	7·3	0·3	4·9	1·0	0·2	0·9	2·1	6·3
May	7·1	0·3	5·1	1·0	0·1	0·6	1·7	6·1
June	7·1	0·3	5·0	1·0	0·2	0·6	1·8	6·1
July	7·4	0·3	5·0	1·0	0·2	0·9	2·1	6·4
August	7·3	0·3	5·4	1·0	0·1	0·5	1·6	6·3
September	7·4	0·3	5·4	1·0	0·2	0·5	1·7	6·4
October	7·6	0·3	6·1	0·8	0·1	0·3	1·2	6·8
November	8·4	0·3	6·4	0·8	0·1	0·8	1·7	7·6
December	9·3	0·3	6·7	0·8	0·2	1·3	2·3	8·5
Year 1936	7·5	0·3	5·3	0·9	0·2	0·8	1·9	6·6

V

Exports in the N.E.I., June 1934–December 1936

Approx. f.o.b. price ex export duties N.E.I. port; pence per lb.	Ordinary N.E.I. export duty as percentage of		Special N.E.I. export duty as percentage of			Exports of native rubber; long tons, dry weight	Permissible exportable amount ex carry-over long tons
	(a) Price ex export duties (Col. 9)	(b) Average return to native producer (Col. 6)	(a) Singapore price (Col. 1)	(b) Price ex export duties (Col. 9)	(c) Average return to native producer (Col. 6)		
(9)	(10)		(11)			(12)	(13)
3·8	4	4	—	—	—	16,000	12,229
3·3	5	6	13	23	24	16,200	12,229
2·3	8	8	35	83	89	12,600	11,006
1·5	14	16	50	180	200	15,600	11,006
0·8	24	19	59	345	417	5,600	9,784
0·6	32	41	62	455	588	4,700	9,784
0·9	23	27	55	290	346	12,200	8,560
1·9	9	10	39	103	112	82,900	74,598
1·3	14	15	48	182	205	9,600	10,423
1·2	14	16	49	190	216	16,900	10,423
0·9	21	25	53	276	333	8,900	10,423
1·0	17	20	51	229	267	13,600	9,728
1·3	13	15	48	178	200	22,200	9,728
1·7	11	12	45	140	154	14,300	9,727
1·2	18	20	53	230	263	8,100	9,033
1·0	23	27	59	339	404	9,700	9,033
1·0	23	27	58	323	385	9,600	9,033
1·1	18	21	55	256	294	17,500	8,339
1·2	18	20	58	283	323	9,100	8,338
0·5	53	80	71	927	1,390	2,800	8,338
1·2	19	22	54	254	294	142,300	112,566
0·9	29	35	67	518	631	9,200	12,085
1·4	17	20	62	315	354	16,100	12,084
1·2	23	26	65	388	443	9,300	12,085
1·1	29	33	67	471	550	12,500	12,084
0·7	40	50	71	684	855	10,700	12,085
0·8	37	45	70	630	773	14,600	12,084
1·1	29	33	68	489	570	18,100	13,092
0·6	45	59	73	828	1,071	11,800	13,092
0·7	48	61	73	813	1,039	9,800	13,091
0·4	65	92	80	1,494	2,117	12,000	13,092
0·9	30	34	76	724	838	16,400	13,092
0·2	24	26	72	479	525	8,800	13,091
1·0	32	38	72	616	735	149,300	151,057

TABLE VI

The Operation of the Special Export Tax in the N.E.I., 1934–36

	Batavia price of smoked sheet (1)	*Rate of duty* (2)	'*Basic price*' (*column* (1) *less column* (2)) (3)	*Approximate expenses from interior to Singapore or Batavia plus* 5 *per cent.* ad valorem *duty* (4)	*Net return to producer* (5)	*Native exports; long tons, dry weight* (6)
	Guilder cents per half-kilo					
1934						
June . .	20·0	—	20·0	4·5	15·5	16,000
July . .	22·0	2·5	19·5	4·6	14·9	16,200
Aug. . .	23·0	6·5	16·5	4·6	11·9	12,600
Sept. . .	23·0	9·0	14·0	4·7	9·3	15,600
Oct. . .	20·5	10·0	10·5	4·7	5·8	5,600
Nov. . .	19·5	10·0	9·5	4·7	4·8	4,700
Dec. . .	19·0	9·0	10·0	4·7	5·3	12,200
Seven months .	21·0	6·7	14·3	4·6	9·7	82,900
1935						
Jan. . .	19·4	8·0	11·4	4·6	6·8	9,600
Feb. . .	19·0	8·0	11·0	4·6	6·4	16,900
Mar. . .	17·0	8·0	9·0	4·6	4·4	8,900
Apr. . .	17·0	8·0	9·0	4·6	4·4	13,600
May . .	17·8	8·0	9·8	4·6	5·2	22,200
June . .	18·7	8·0	10·7	4·6	6·1	14,300
July . .	17·9	9·2	8·7	4·7	4·0	8,100
Aug. . .	18·0	10·5	7·5	4·7	2·8	9,700
Sept. . .	17·4	10·0	7·4	4·7	2·7	9,600
Oct. . .	19·0	10·0	9·0	4·7	4·3	17,500
Nov. . .	19·9	11·3	8·6	4·7	3·9	9,100
Dec. . .	19·7	13·9	5·8	4·8	1·0	2,800
Year . .	18·4	9·4	9·0	4·7	4·3	142,300
1936						
Jan. . .	20·4	14·5	5·9	4·8	1·1	9,200
Feb. . .	22·1	14·5	7·6	4·8	2·8	16,100
Mar. . .	22·8	15·5	7·3	4·9	2·4	9,300
Apr. . .	23·4	16·5	6·9	5·0	1·9	12,500
May . .	22·9	17·1	5·8	5·0	0·8	10,700
June . .	23·3	17·0	6·3	5·0	1·3	14,600
July . .	24·2	17·1	7·1	5·0	2·1	18,100
Aug. . .	23·9	18·2	5·7	5·0	0·7	11,800
Sept. . .	24·1	18·7	5·4	5·1	0·3	9,800
Oct. . .	31·3	25·4	5·9	5·1	0·8	12,000
Nov. . .	34·0	26·8	7·2	5·1	2·1	16,400
Dec. . .	36·5	27·8	8·7	5·4	3·3	8,800
Year . .	25·8	19·1	6·7	5·0	1·7	149,300

NOTES TO TABLES V AND VI

Although some of the figures in these tables contain an element of estimate, they nevertheless illustrate the operation of the special export tax reasonably accurately. The figures in columns 10 and 11 in Table V for the last seven months of 1934 and for the years 1935 and 1936 are not the simple averages of the monthly percentage figures, but represent the averages of the monthly percentages weighted by the corresponding various prices. Conversion of various items from guilder cents to pence with inevitable rounding-off involves a few small inaccuracies in calculating the percentages.

Table V is more detailed and also much more relevant than Table VI, as the bulk of N.E.I. native rubber continued to be marketed via Singapore as medium blankets. Though Table V offers the more reliable guidance, Table VI is simpler, and the figures it summarises were more often discussed at the time. Column 3 of Table VI is the basic price, which was often referred to by the N.E.I. authorities as the pivotal price of the export tax machinery. There is a very large discrepancy in the annual average return to the natives as shown in column 6 of Table V, and column 5 of Table VI. This results from the comparatively small differences between the Singapore price of medium blankets and the Batavia price of ribbed smoke sheet, which were greatly magnified in the interior where the prices were quoted after deduction of the duty and of expenses.

There is a wide measure of agreement among competent authorities on the average cost of transport, processing and middlemen's charges from the most important native districts to the Singapore market. Dr. Whitford and the N.E.I. authorities estimated the figure at about 4 to 5 guilder cents per half-kilo of dry rubber in the mid-1930's. The largest remiller in Singapore recently, in private conversation, gave an independent estimate of 4½ guilder cents. A figure of 4 cents has been adopted in the tables to ensure that any error should be on the side of conservatism and should understate rather than overstate the burden of the tax. About one-half cent has been assumed as the cost of transport and middlemen's charges from the interior to the N.E.I. port of shipment, and the balance as the cost of shipping to Singapore and of processing and marketing there. These figures exclude the ordinary *ad valorem* export duty which has been calculated, as it was levied, on the basis of 5 per cent. of the export value of native rubber during the second preceding month.

The average rate of duty in the tables refers to the effective rate in force and not to the rates announced during the month ; hence the zero rate for June 1934.

The wide fluctuations in the net return to native producers (column 6 of Table V and column 5 of Table VI) indicate the disproportionate effect in the interior of changes in the market price or in the rate of duty. There is room here for an appreciable margin of error in any given month, but the yearly or even quarterly averages are unlikely to be seriously affected.

The export figures are accurate ; the wide month-to-month fluctuations reflect the reaction of shippers to the announcement of changes in the rate of the special tax, and to a lesser extent their views on the probable course of the market. There was a time-lag between the announcement of changes in the rate of the special tax and the date the new rate applied to dry rubber, and this led exporters to accelerate or withhold shipments in the interim period. These erratic fluctuations cancelled out over a period, and did not affect total shipments over say six months.

TABLE VII

Prices of Export Rights and of Coupons and Market Price of Rubber in the Second Month of each quarter, 1934–41

	Malaya			*N.E.I.*				*Ceylon*	
	Price of export rights	*Price of coupons*	*Singapore price of ribbed smoked sheet*	*Estate rights*	*Batavia price of ribbed smoked sheet*	*Native coupons*	*Singapore price of medium blankets (expressed in guilder cents per half-kilo)*	*Price of rights*	*Colombo price of ribbed smoked sheet*
	Straits cents per lb.			*Guilder cents per half-kilo*				*Rupee cents per lb.*	
	(1)	(2)	(3)	(4)	(5)	(6)	(7)	(8)	(9)
1934									
August		9	25		23			21	36
November		12	21		19			7	30
1935						No general			
February		12	21		19	individual		19	31
May	See	13	20	See	18	restriction;		19	29
August	Notes	11	19	Notes	18	Cf. Chapters		20	28
November		16	22		20	8–9		23	32
1936									
February		20	25		22			29	38
May		17	26		23			29	38
August		16	27		24			31	39
November	16	16	30		34			34	46
1937									
February	17	20	36	19	39	22	40	32	54
May	11	15	36	13	39	13	38	31	53
August	5	7	30	22	32	15	31	29	44
November	6	8	23	18	25	10	24	24	33
1938									
February	15	14	23	20	23	11	24	25	34
May	11	11	19	16	19	13	18	20	27
August	19	19	27	23	27	18	28	31	39
November	20	22	28	24	28	16	30	31	42
1939									
February	20	21	27	23	28	20	29	32	40
May	21	22	28	24	28	20	29	33	41
August	20	20	28	24	30	13	30	32	43
November	24	23	39	22	36	18	35	24	52
1940									
February	23	22	38	22	33	16	34	23	55
May	22	23	37	23	33	16	34	28	55
August	17	18	37	21	32	13	32	19	55
November	16	19	39	20	34	17	34	28	58
1941									
February	13	18	36	13	30	14	32	19	49
May	9	18	41	8	36	19	38	16	61
August	8 (July)	4	39	3	33	13	34	10	56
November	Not available			0	33	5 (Oct.)	34	1	56

NOTES TO TABLE VII

The second month of each quarter has been chosen to eliminate the often violent fluctuations in coupon prices at the beginning and end of the period of issue. Erratic variations still remain, e.g. Ceylon, November 1934, as the market was sometimes narrow, but the quotations faithfully reflect the general trend. The prices of rights and coupons are before payment of export duty and cess. This is of special importance for Malayan export right and coupon prices which were up-country quotations, and export duty, cess and transport costs of about 1½–2 cents should be added when these quotations are set against the Singapore price, which was the world price after payment of duty.

There are no regular quotations of the price of estate export rights before November 1936. Some sporadic figures are available from miscellaneous sources, and these suggest that in Malaya in 1934 the price of these rights was low, as many estates had difficulty in producing their full exportable amount in that year. In 1935 and 1936 the price of estate export rights was fairly high, both in Malaya and the N.E.I.; 12–16 Straits cents per lb. and 14–16 guilder cents per half-kilo indicate the order of magnitude. Transactions in these rights were, however, on a small scale until the period of high releases in 1937. The purchase in 1935 by the N.E.I. Government of 20,000 tons of rights for cancellation to reduce over-exports was an important exception. Some 29 cents per kilo was paid for these rights.

Medium blankets were, of course, quoted in Straits cents per lb., and the price has been converted at the average monthly rate of exchange between the Straits dollar and the N.E.I. guilder.

The Malayan quotations of estate export rights from 1937 to 1940 are from the *Annual Reports* of the Controller of Rubber, Malaya. No report was issued for 1941 and the figures represent the transactions of a few large companies to whose records the writer has had access. The prices of estate export rights in the N.E.I. have been taken from the *Economisch Weekblad*. The Ceylon quotations are from the *Administration Reports* of the Rubber Controller, Ceylon.

The coupon prices are somewhat approximate. For Malaya, the *Malayan Agricultural Journal* frequently published these, but occasionally this information had to be supplemented by reference to various other sources. Moreover, while export rights were transferable between administrations, coupons could only be transferred within each administration (S.S., F.M.S. and each U.M.S.), and there was thus one price for rights, but several prices for coupons, and there were often considerable local variations. The prices given here refer principally to Perak and Johore, and occasionally to Selangor; these States contain most of the smallholding area in Malaya.

The N.E.I. native coupon prices are the quotations in Palembang, and have been taken from the official *Reports on Native Rubber Cultivation* up to May 1940, and thereafter from the *Market Reports* of the Rubber Trade Association of the N.E.I.

It will be noted that at times of high releases (especially 1941) coupons were usually worth more than estate rights, while the reverse ratio held at times of low releases. The reason for the latter relation is given in the text, p. 123; the former reflects the relative under-assessment of smallholders. The high prices of rights and of coupons at times of allegedly unrestricted output (spring of 1937 and 1940–41) are of considerable interest.

TABLE VIII

Percentage of Mature Acreage out of Tapping at the end of June and the end of December, 1934–41

	Malaya		N.E.I. Estates		Ceylon		
	Estates (1)	Small-holdings (2)	Outer Provinces (3)	Java (4)	Large estates (100 acres and over) (5)	Medium estates (50–100 acres) (6)	Small estates (25–50 acres) (7)
1934 June	17	10	23	12			
Dec.	14	7	21	12			
1935 June	18	22	25	20			
Dec.	23	38	39	41			
1936 June	27	40	35	40			
Dec.	23	31	27	26			
1937 June	27	17	13	11			
Dec.	25	16	13	12	24	76	48
1938 June	20	33	35	34			
Dec.	29	36	41	35	45	60	62
1939 June	32	43	39	39			
Dec.	19	21	24	18	37	44	40
1940 June	16	20	18	13			
Dec.	10	16	14	10	27	37	38
1941 June	7	15	10	5			
Dec.	6 (Oct.)	—	—	—	4	5	8

Up to the end of 1937 the Malayan estate area out of tapping includes areas rested under rotational tapping systems, which are excluded from 1938 onwards. This seriously vitiates the comparability of the figures, as after 1934 some 10 to 20 per cent. of the mature estate area was usually untapped under this heading. The data are mostly from the *Rubber Statistics Handbook.*

Some of the percentages of the Malayan smallholding area untapped refer to the F.M.S., but the majority are for Malaya as a whole. The estimates of the mature smallholding area untapped are based on observations in various districts by field officers of the Department of Agriculture (published periodically in the *Malayan Agricultural Journal*), and are most hazardous. At best the figures indicate rough orders of magnitude.

The N.E.I. figures are from the *Economisch Weekblad.* There are no data of areas untapped in the native districts.

The Ceylon data are from the *Administration Reports* of the Rubber Controller. The figures are subject to a very large margin of error, especially for medium and small estates. There are no data before 1937, nor of the area out of tapping at the end of June for any year.

TABLE IX

Rubber Supplies, 1934–41

	Total exports	Exports under the scheme		Exports from other territories	
	Thousand tons (1)	Thousand tons (2)	Percentage of total (3)	Thousand tons (4)	Percentage of total (5)
1934 . . .	1,032	1,018	98·6	14	1·4
1935 . . .	830	809	97·5	21	2·5
1936 . . .	866	838	96·8	28	3·2
1937 . . .	1,166	1,132	97·0	34	3·0
1938 . . .	871	838	97·2	33	3·8
1939 . . .	990	953	96·3	37	3·7
1940 . . .	1,395	1,350	96·8	45	3·2
1941 . . .	1,520	1,475	97·0	45	3·0

The 1934 figure in column (1) was obtained by adding world net exports for January–May and 'net exports under the scheme' for June–December. Net exports from the various territories differed slightly from 'net exports under the scheme', chiefly because of the exclusion of exports from Singapore and Penang and the inclusion of rubber placed under customs control at the end of the year. The 1941 figures are approximate.

TABLE X

Net Exports of Rubber from Principal Producing Territories (net exports under the regulation scheme after 1934) as per cent. of World Exports, 1929–41

	Malaya	N.E.I.	Other quota countries	Siam	French Indo-China	Others
1929 . .	52·7	29·4	12·9	0·5	1·1	3·4
1929–34 .	52·1	32·1	11·4	0·8	1·6	2·0
1934 . .	45·9	37·3	11·8	1·7	1·9	1·4
1935 . .	44·7	34·6	11·4	3·5	3·4	2·4
1936 . .	41·6	35·9	10·8	4·0	4·7	3·0
1937 . .	42·3	37·3	10·8	3·1	3·7	2·8
1938 . .	39·7	34·5	10·5	4·8	6·8	3·7
1939 . .	36·6	37·4	11·5	4·2	6·6	3·7
1940 . .	38·8	38·5	11·8	3·1	4·6	3·2
1941 . .	37·8	41·8	11·1	3·0	3·3	3·0

Table XI

Absorption of Rubber, 1934–41

(Thousand long tons)

	U.S.A.	*U.K.*	*Other countries*	*Total*
1934	462	90	367	919
1935	492	95	349	936
1936	575	99	364	1,038
1937	543	115	437	1,095
1938	437	107	390	934
1939	592	123	382	1,097
1940	648	147	290	1,085
1941	780	156	292 (approx.)	1,230 (approx.)

Table XII

Principal World Stocks of Rubber outside the Regulated Area

	Year-end stocks (including stocks afloat); thousand tons	*Stocks in terms of months' absorption at average calendar yearly rate*	*Stocks in terms of months' absorption at December rate*
1934	726	9·5	9·9
1935	645	8·3	7·5
1936	464	5·4	4·9
1937	532	5·8	7·4
1938	465	5·8	4·9
1939	359	3·9	3·8
1940	668	7·3	7·7
1941	1,000 (approx.)	10·0 (approx.)	12·0 (approx.)

Tables IX–XII based on the *Statistical Bulletin* of I.R.R.C., and *History of Rubber Regulation*, Statistical Supplement.

Table XIII

Price of Rubber in London, 1934–41

		Ribbed smoked sheet in pence per lb.	
	Highest	*Lowest*	*Average*
1934	7·6	4·2	6·3
1935	6·8	5·2	6·0
1936	11·1	6·5	7·7
1937	13·8	6·8	9·5
1938	8·6	5·2	7·2
1939	12·0	7·6	9·0
1940	14·0	10·9	12·1
1941	14·6	12·0	13·6

STATISTICAL APPENDIX III

MALAYAN MIGRATION AND EMPLOYMENT STATISTICS, 1926–40

Table I

Arrivals in Malaya of South Indian Deck Passengers by B.I.S.N. Steamers, 1926–40

(Thousands)

	Assisted immigrants		*Unassisted immigrants*		*All deck passengers*		*Total*	*Official estimate of working class passengers among unassisted arrivals*
	Adults	*Minors*	*Adults*	*Minors*	*Adults*	*Minors*		
	(1)	(2)	(3)	(4)	(5)	(6)	(7)	(8)
1926	128	21	23	3	151	24	175	16
1927	104	20	29	3	133	23	156	21
1928	23	44	33	3	56	7	63	26
1929	70	12	30	2	100	14	114	23
1930	34	8	24	2	58	10	68	19
1931	Assisted		18	2	18	2	20	12
1932	immigration		16	2	16	2	18	7
1933	suspended		18	2	18	2	20	9
1934	33	12	40	4	73	16	89	27
1935	15	6	39	5	54	11	65	26
1936	3	1	35	4	38	5	43	24
1937	42	13	58	10	100	23	123	50
1938	4	1	36	4	40	5	45	14
1939	Emigration		21	2	21	2	23	2
1940	ban in force		14	1	14	1	15	1

TABLE II

Departures of South Indian Deck Passengers by B.I.S.N. Vessels, 1926–40

(Thousands)

	Adults	Minors	Total	Repatriated free of cost (included in cols. (1) & (2))		Official estimate of working class passengers and dependants among departures additional to repatriates
				Adults	Minors	
	(1)	(2)	(3)	(4)	(5)	(6)
1926	62	4	66	3	1	Not available
1927	82	7	89	8	2	
1928	82	9	91	14	4	
1929	71	6	77	5	1	
1930	122	30	152	56	22	
1931	81	20	101	41	15	
1932	67	17	84	42	15	
1933	28	5	33	7	2	
1934	25	3	28	1	1	
1935	34	4	38	5	1	15
1936	35	5	40	7	2	17
1937	39	5	44	5	2	23
1938	62	13	75	21	8	28
1939	37	6	43	8	3	12
1940	22	2	24	4	2	9

TABLE III

Migrational Surplus or Deficit, 1926–40

(Thousands)

	Adults (1)	Adults and minors (2)		Adults (1)	Adults and minors (2)
1926	+ 89	+ 109	1934	+ 48	+ 61
1927	+ 51	+ 67	1935	+ 20	+ 27
1928	− 26	− 28	1936	+ 3	+ 3
1929	+ 29	+ 37	1937	+ 61	+ 79
1930	− 64	− 84	1938	− 22	− 30
1931	− 63	− 81	1939	− 16	− 20
1932	− 51	− 66	1940	− 8	− 9
1933	− 10	− 13			

NOTES TO TABLES I—III

The figures cover all deck passengers, inclusive of those classed as non-emigrants under the Indian Emigration Act of 1922 (people with a residence of five years or over in Malaya). Minors (below 12 years of age) exclude infants (below three years) until 1930. The few hundred deck passengers arriving and departing by other than B.I.S.N. vessels are excluded.

Unassisted deck passengers were generally artisans, labourers, clerks or petty tradesmen. Although their numbers were always given to the last digit by the authorities, these were only approximate estimates ; they are, however, unlikely to be seriously inaccurate for these years.

The relatively high ratio, shown in Table III, of adults and minors together to adults in 1930–32, reflects the preponderance of family men among departing passengers.

The excess of departures in 1928 is explained by the reluctance of employers to engage additional labour, or even make good the wastage until the effects of the termination of the Stevenson scheme became clear.

The large number of working-class passengers paying their own fares up to 1938 (Table I) was indicative of comparative conditions in Malaya and Madras and of the restriction on the issue of assisted passages, which shifted the working-class traffic into the unassisted class. It is probable that in 1937 the official estimate of working-class arrivals among deck passengers (almost three-quarters of the unassisted arrivals) was on the high side, but even allowing for this factor the figure well reflects the anxiety to migrate to Malaya whenever conditions there were favourable.

It was not thought worth while to reproduce the migration statistics of Chinese deck passengers published in Malaya, as these were so inaccurate as barely to furnish even an idea of the order of magnitude involved. It is probable, however, that during the three years following mid-1930 Malaya lost by net emigration over 300,000 Chinese.

The quantitative significance of migration is seen when set against the census population. According to the 1931 census, the population of British Malaya totalled 4,385,000, including 1,709,000 Chinese and 624,000 Indians. Owing to the preponderance of adult males among migrants, the influence of migration on the labour situation was even greater than would appear at first sight.

Table IV

Numbers Employed at the End of Each Year on Estates, in Mines and Factories, 1929–40

(Thousands)

	1929	1930	1931	1932	1933	1934	1935	1936	1937	1938	1939	1940
South Indians	282	257	169	143	154	195	194	204	262	230	234	241
Chinese	110	115	115	101	105	127	123	146	172	133	157	153
Javanese	26	13	11	10	11	13	11	13	16	11	16	16
Others		18	16	16	22	26	21	23	30	24	36	48
	418	403	311	270	292	361	349	386	480	398	443	456

Table V

Numbers Employed at the End of Each Year by Government Departments, 1929–40

(Thousands)

	1929	1930	1931	1932	1933	1934	1935	1936	1937	1938	1939	1940
South Indians	35	54	45	36	34	34	38	42	45	47	49	46
Chinese	5	5	5	4	4	4	5	5	6	11	11	11
Javanese	8	2	2	2	2	2	2	3	3	2	3	3
Others		5	5	5	5	7	9	9	9	11	13	11
	48	66	57	47	45	47	54	59	63	71	76	71

The figures, which cover the whole of Malaya, refer to workers at places of employment with ten or more labourers. The Chinese employment figures were revised in 1930 and 1931 ; hence the rise in employment figures during the slump. Indian employment figures were by far the most reliable throughout.

NOTE ON TABLE I OF CHAPTER 15

Table I, p. 225, is based on the *Annual Reports* of the Controller of Labour, S.S. and F.M.S.; the figures in these refer to workers on 'places of employment' (employing ten or more wage earners) whose numbers had to be returned at the end of each quarter. After 1933 figures of rubber estate employment became available, and were published by the Registrar-General of Statistics in the annual *Rubber Statistics Handbook.* A comparison between these figures and those in the *Annual Reports* of the Labour Department (after all-Malaya figures were published) suggests that some 8,000–10,000 workers were on estates other than rubber plantations.

Until 1933, the first year for which the Labour Department issued all-Malaya figures, no consecutive series of estate employment is available for the U.M.S. For 1931 the figures are given in the 1931 *Annual Report* of the Planters' Association of Malaya. That report, the all-Malaya figures issued from 1933 onwards, and other subsidiary information suggest that the S.S. and F.M.S. accounted for about 70–75 per cent. of estate employment. In the U.M.S., estate employment was affected by much the same factors as in the S.S. and the F.M.S., and proportionate changes in the employment figures were of the same order in all the Malayan administrations. The importance of estate employment in the total Malayan labour market can be gauged from the continuous series of employment figures shown in Tables IV and V of this Appendix.

Figures of Indian employment are by far the most reliable. Chinese estate employment includes contractors' workers. There was a break in the Chinese figures in 1930, when owing to some revision the numbers in the F.M.S. were raised by about 6,000 thus registering a slight rise between the end of 1929 and the end of 1930 instead of an appreciable fall. Malays were included in the Javanese in some administrations and under Others in the rest, while Javanese were sometimes grouped under Others.

INDEX